Technology, Crime and Jus

As technology comes to characterise our world in ever more comprehensive ways there are increasing questions about how the "rights" and "wrongs" of technological use can be adequately understood. To date, the scope of such questions has been limited – focused upon specific technologies such as the internet, or genetic engineering, with little sense of any social or historical continuities in the way technology in general has been regulated.

In this book, for the first time, the "question of technology" and its relation to criminal justice is approached as a whole. *Technology, Crime and Justice* analyses a range of technologies (including information, communications, nuclear, biological, transport and weapons technologies, amongst many others) in order to pose three interrelated questions about their effects upon criminal justice and criminal opportunity:

- To what extent can they really be said to provide new criminal opportunities or to enhance existing ones?
- What are the key characteristics of the ways in which such technologies have been regulated?
- How does technology itself now serve as a regulatory force – not just in crime control but within social control more widely?

Technology, Crime and Justice considers the implications of contemporary technology for the practice of criminal justice and relates them to key historical precedents in the way technology has been interpreted and controlled. It outlines a "social" way of thinking about technology – in terms of its effects upon our bodies and what they can do, most obviously the various ways in which social life and our ability to causally interact with the world are "extended". It poses the question of whether anything like a "technomia" of technology could be identified – i.e. a system of norms and regulations where technology increasingly serves to regulate, as well as to be regulated. And if so, what would this mean for our traditional systems of law and the wider principles of justice these are meant to protect?

This book provides a key resource for students and scholars of criminology, law and technology studies.

M.R. McGuire is Senior Lecturer in Criminology and Criminal Justice at London Metropolitan University.

Technology, Crime and Justice

The question concerning technomia

M.R. McGuire

Routledge
Taylor & Francis Group

LONDON AND NEW YORK

First published 2012
by Routledge
2 Park Square, Milton Park, Abingdon, Oxon, OX14 4RN

Simultaneously published in the USA and Canada
by Routledge
711 Third Avenue, New York, NY 10017

Routledge is an imprint of the Taylor & Francis Group, an informa business

© 2012 M.R. McGuire

British Library Cataloguing in Publication Data
A catalogue record for this book is available from the British Library

Library of Congress Cataloging in Publication Data
A catalog record for this book has been requested

ISBN 13: 978-1-84392-857-7 (hbk)
ISBN 13: 978-1-84392-856-0 (pbk)
ISBN 13: 978-0-203-12768-1 (ebk)

Typeset in by Times New Roman
by Taylor and Francis Books

Contents

Illustrations

Figure

Tables

Introduction

The question concerning technomia

[We live in a time] ... when technology has ... cast doubt upon, while perhaps for the first time directly confronting, the very form of this question: what is the nature of the human?[1]

The bad parts of technology cannot be separated from the good parts.[2]

The sense that technology is "bad" has not been a sentiment unique to the notorious anti-technology manifesto of Theodore Kaczynski, the "Unabomber" who waged an idiosyncratic campaign of terror against the "industrial-technological system" (Kaczynski, 1995) in the 1990s. Rather, it reflects a recurring contradiction in our normative perceptions of technology, one where any benefits it offers are always compromised by the likelihood of their misuse. This arguably places criminology in a unique position within the social sciences for analysing technology. Not just because of the ever-present suggestion of criminality in our use of it, but also because criminology is armed with a range of concepts and resources uniquely suited to evaluating how its uses are judged to be licit, or illicit. It is significant then that, like just about everything else within the social world, crime and the criminal justice system have become increasingly mediated by technical thinking and technological forms. Many of the key processes of the justice system have become dependent upon technological mediation and technical concepts, just as the sense has grown that we are constantly confronted with new and innovative uses of technology by criminals. Indeed, for perhaps the first time in the history of criminal justice, a notion of "technology crime" has become an accepted criminological category, a threat (we are told) that can only be met by further investments in technology. This increased dependency upon technological solutions has begun to exert subtle shifts not just upon the various institutions of the justice system but upon the wider nature of regulation as a whole. In CCTV cameras or DNA profiles, in the more invisible constraints of a content filter or a car immobiliser, technology is now far more than a mere tool that we use to enhance our safety and security: it serves as a force that shapes behaviour in unprecedented ways.

Yet for all the potential utility of the criminological imagination in evaluating technology, or for all the obvious impacts upon the justice system, there cannot be said to have been anything like a coherent response on the part of criminologists or legal theorists to the challenges posed by these shifts. There have, of course, been numerous more limited discussions – evaluations of the potential of car alarms for crime control, descriptions of the misuse of the internet, accounts of biological and genetic profiling, questions about the validity of forensics and critiques of surveillance technology. But missing from all these varied discussions has been any sense of continuity – either in what makes an instance of offending or an application of control "technological", or what this entails for criminal justice itself. Not only has this left a far more comprehensive range of "technology crimes" and a more representative range of potential offenders badly underanalysed. It has also rendered our understanding of the wider implications of "technological justice" rather inadequate at present. One manifestation of this has been the uneven legislative responses to technology, where certain artefacts and practices are obsessively over-regulated and others scarcely acknowledged at all. But beyond its implications for criminal justice, the uneven management of technology has also had impacts on the relationship between technology and justice as a whole. Not just in the advantages it offers to the powerful, but in the way law often now seems to place the needs of technology above the rights of citizens. At its most extreme, technology has begun to acquire an increasing regulatory power of its own – operating as an autonomous force outside the realm of public scrutiny, accountability or even control.

In this book I want to try to consider how a more integrated approach to technology might contribute to a better, more just use of it within the criminal justice process (and beyond). By providing greater clarity in what we take technology "to be" I hope also to clarify what its increasing centrality within the operations of our justice systems might imply. But the problem is that almost as soon as one starts to think about what makes something "technological" a series of testing ambiguities begin to arise. Should technology be read in terms of a "high" or "low" sense – in terms of complex artefacts like a nuclear power station or simple ones like a pair of scissors? Is technology best conceived of in terms of "things" at all, or is it more a set of practices and processes? Are our technologies centred upon what we make, or the knowledge we require in order to make things in the first place? Most crucially of all, how, in terms of agency, does technology actually contribute to what we do? The standard, "instrumentalist" answer here (cf. Feenberg, 2002) – that technology functions as a form of "tool" – has threatened at least two intellectual cul-de-sacs. First, it has implied that technology is something that is socially neutral, with any positive or negative outcomes simply a matter of how it is "used". This assumption entails some undesirable outcomes. For if technology is no more than an inert tool – a mere instrument waiting to be invested with significance by its use – then it is not just agentically, but normatively neutral. In which case attempts to associate it with wrongdoing would appear to be seriously misplaced, since culpability – the basis for any legitimate attribution of criminality, is usually associated with the *mens rea* of an individual – their intention to offend, not the tool they happen to use. And if this is the case, technology would not seem to add anything of legal significance to behaviour, so rendering many of our more familiar categories of technological crime – from cyberbullying to bioterrorism – seemingly superfluous.

A second difficulty that arises from conceiving of technology as a mere tool is that there are very few objects or resources humans use that do not fit this description. And this creates an obvious danger that the trope of "technology crime" becomes nothing more than a synonym for crime in general, since here too there are very few forms of crime that do not involve at least some form of tool or assistance, however basic. The instrumentalist view also creates problems around the difficult question of agency and what this means for our notions of the technological offender and victim. The production and use of contemporary technology is often highly collective, especially when deployed by the kinds of social actors with the greatest access to the most complex technologies – i.e. state and corporate agents. Similarly, technological harms are not always restricted to individual victims, but are often experienced collectively. Without some viable sense of how collective agents misuse technology, or collective victims are damaged by this, definitive attributions of crime as "technological" are not always obvious. If, then – as seems desirable – we view technology as something more than a "mere tool", a force with its own distinctive causal and social power, the challenge is to say what precisely it adds to agency and how this might be legally construed.

Prima facie, matters have seemed to be slightly clearer when it comes to evaluating technology as a means for imposing or maintaining control. Here we seem more relaxed about directly attributing causal power to a technological intervention like CCTV or a water cannon. Does this then mean that technology is more "agentic" in crime control contexts than in the case of offending behaviours? Could technology really be a clearer determining factor in facilitating "successful" policing or "better" detection than in facilitating criminal activity? And if so, on what basis? Evaluating the success or failure of a technological intervention or demonstrating the basis for its legitimacy presents us with another set of difficulties. For if legitimacy is established on the basis of "science" or some quantitative metric, as has been common, a circularity threatens – since these too are infused with technical concepts. Underlying many of these difficulties is the way that it is now all but impossible to separate normative questions about technology (how effective, or how socially good or bad it is) from questions about the technologically normative (how technically well or badly a technology functions). Given this, Ellul's claim – that "capitalism did not create our world; the machine did" (Ellul, 1964, p. 5) – effectively becomes the claim that technical norms have outweighed socio-economic norms in shaping our world.

These and many other problems emphasise the danger in separating technology too far from what we are and do. In this book I aim to develop a framework that allows us to evade some of the impasses around what we should take to "be" technological, and the extent to which it is socially neutral, by viewing technology as part of our bodies and the capacities they offer us. If this approach is at all plausible, then it also becomes clearer why technology crime or control need not be seen as anything distinct from the scope or scale of human life – but as part of the same system of traditional law and regulation and the same concerns for justice that govern bodies. Of course any attempt, criminological or otherwise, to analyse technology faces the problem of its sheer variety and its constant evolution. In order to make this manageable this book will focus upon the technologies that appear to be of particular significance to criminal justice at present. And by seeing technology in terms of its bodily aspects three key classes of technology then emerge, classes originating from the kinds of spatio-temporal effects they enable us to engineer:

1   information and communication technologies (ICTs)
2   chemical, biological and nuclear technologies (CBNTs)[3]
3   "everyday" familiar technologies and artefacts, which include (seemingly innocuous) varieties like hairdryers or foodmixers, and potentially more harmful instances, in particular weapons. For reasons to be explained later this (ostensibly) less integrated class of technological objects will be referred to, for convenience, as "mid- or multi-range technologies" or MMRTs.

The centrality of ICTs in the context of criminal justice is obvious enough, given the radical new options for offending that they have seemed to present, the decisive shift in policing priorities – from the past to the future – they have caused, and the significant areas of new law they have generated. No less important, albeit less discussed, have been the impacts of CBNTs upon the justice process – whether in the form of enforcement tools like DNA profiles and biometric measures, or as enablers for emerging categories of criminality like "eco-crime". And whilst artefacts linked with the third class of "mid- or multi-range technologies" (MMRTs) have received ostensibly less criminological attention, major categories of technological offending like gun or knife crime can arguably be associated with them, along with new and important categories of consumer-based offences, liabilities and law. These three classes clearly do not exhaust every kind of technological artefact, nor do they represent mutually exclusive instances. For example, we might also include ICTs like mobile phones amongst our "everyday" technologies. Yet I will argue that this framework suffices to present us with a representative range of contemporary technologies for the purpose of criminological analysis. And in manifesting some of the key characteristics of technology it also offers us a representative range of technology as a whole.

A key question in what follows will centre upon how to manage the normative tensions in our perceptions of technology alluded to at the start, and how to strike a balance between regulating technology in ways that punish those who use it harmfully, whilst not undermining its benefits. This balance has not always been an obvious one but it provides a further indication why criminological thought occupies a potentially unique role in helping us to address the question of technology. For it is certainly not in a moral prescription or the operation of an ethics committee that the contours of our attitudes and regulatory practices around technology are seen most clearly. Rather, it is at the coalface of the justice system, where arguments are put forward, new rulings created and specific uses of technology judged legitimate or criminal.

In what follows I intend to highlight the significance of the criminological imagination in analysing technology by taking up Heidegger's famous "question concerning technology" in this more specific way. That is, rather than trying to make sense of technology in terms of its "essence" or any challenge that it poses to our metaphysics, I will ask an (ostensibly) more narrow question, one that centres upon the complex of formal and informal regulatory practices around its use. Pete Berger (1967) once referred to such orderings in terms of a "nomos" – the informal and formal codes governing a social practice – so that technology, like any other such practice, might also be thought of in terms of its nomos. These codes – which, for convenience, I will refer to as a "technomia" – are not unique to contemporary "hi-tech" societies. There seem always to have been certain standards or rules governing technology, not least the right reserved by many societies to punish those who misuse it. But no society has of course ever developed an explicit code of technological law or regulation – indeed even within our own society the regulatory practices around technology remain less than transparent. Yet the consequences of inadequate regulation for a high-technology society seem likely to be more serious than for a low-technology one. I hope, then, by posing a question concerning *technomia*, rather than technology, not only to make the "laws of technology" that constrain our world less obscure but to set out a more fundamental question: has "technological justice" now become something different from "social justice"?

Outline

The structure of this book will seek to draw these questions out as follows. In Chapter 1 some standard conceptions of technology are set out and evaluated in the light of the alternative view I advocate. In Chapter 2 I begin to address the question of technological crime and technological regulation by examining how the shift from pre-industrial, low-tech societies to our contemporary industrial order may have affected perceptions of technological misuse and methods of technological control. This provides a much-needed historical basis for the discussions in Chapters 3 to 6, which focus upon our key contemporary classes of technology – ICTs and CBNTs – and their impacts upon both criminal behaviours and the exercise of control. In Chapter 7 I widen the kinds of technology analysed to that familiar but as yet underdiscussed class of artefacts – the "everyday" mundane examples I refer to as "mid- and multi-range technologies". Finally, I turn in Chapter 8 to the wider question of technological justice itself, what this means in terms of the requirements of traditional justice systems and the extent to which it can be legitimated by science and the science–technology relationship.

1 Technology and its technomia

I am that which must always overcome itself.[1]

What connects the use of CCTV in monitoring public space to the use of malware in committing fraud or the resort to a taser gun in facilitating an arrest? Pointing to the role of technology in each case is a kind of answer, but doesn't tell us very much. Why, for example, would the use of software to effect the fraud mean that this was a "technological" crime, whilst a theft enabled by using a paperclip to pick a lock was not? In the absence of any robust sense of what technology is, defining crime or control as "technological" has often seemed rather premature, or lacking in clarity. In this chapter I intend to address such questions directly by considering some standard ways in which technology has been defined. I will evaluate these approaches in the light of an alternative, one that I argue both offers a greater flexibility in identifying things as technological and explains why they are social rather than merely inert devices. With this more robust understanding in place we can then better evaluate the role of technology within criminal justice and the extent to which it now enhances or undermines justice.

Technology as "crime": fire-theft, and subverting the divine order

It is not just the widespread prejudice that technology is "bad" that indicates a criminological imagination at work within our understanding of it. The mythological traditions of many premodern cultures often suggest that merely to acquire technology is for humanity to violate some (divine) order, with any benefits gained always subject to eventual retribution. These primordial fears have been most often seen in mythologies around fire (a regular metaphor for technology), something invariably obtained through trickery, fraud or outright theft.

Within Polynesian mythologies, for example, the ingenuity of the trickster hero Maui helped to secure technologies crucial to humanity, such as language or the art of fishing – though his greatest legacy was the gift of fire, stolen from the goddess Mahuike (cf. Luomala, 1961; Beckwith, 1970). Maui's primordial "tech-crime" brings inevitable sanctions, for it provokes Mahuike to punish humanity by setting all the land and ocean alight. A similar tale is told in the Hindu text the Rig Veda, this time involving the hero Mātariśvan (sometimes seen as a personification of Agni, the Vedic fire god), who recovers the fire which had been "hidden" from humans by the gods (cf. Marlow, 1954). Elsewhere, the Jewish Book of Enoch (one of the supposed lost books of the Bible) also implies a quasi-criminal origin for technology – this time originating in the actions of "fallen angels" like Azazel, who came to earth bringing fire, metallurgy and astronomical knowledge. An illicit association between angel and human results, producing a hybrid offspring called the Nephilim, who are destroyed when God covers earth with a great flood. Azazel is then bound in darkness until his eventual destruction on the day of judgement (cf. Nickelsburg, 1977). Similar associations between fire/technology and theft can be found almost everywhere – whether in the ancient Sumerian stories of the gifts of civilisation called "Me" and their illicit acquisition, Native American tales of the Coyote who stole fire or the ritual celebrations of fire theft by Ogo, a hero figure to the Dogon tribe of West Africa (Kramer, 1972; Azuonye, 1996; Judson, 1997, p. 40). But perhaps the best known of all such tales (to Western audiences at any rate) has been the Greek myth of the Titan Prometheus, one of the race of the pre-Olympian gods.

One variant of the Prometheus tale was related by Hesiod in his Theogeny (2006) where he told how Zeus, the leader of the Olympian gods, was angered at being tricked by Prometheus into accepting an inferior sacrifice from humans, and refuses to permit them the use of fire. But Prometheus – like Maui, Ogo and Mātariśvan – was noted for his resourcefulness and visits Zeus to plead humanity's case. During this visit, he lights a torch from the Sun's chariot, conceals it in a stick of fennel and then presents it as a gift to humanity. Zeus is outraged by the theft and orders Prometheus to be tethered to a rock, where his liver is devoured by an eagle – a punishment repeated every day, for all eternity. Humans are punished in equally draconian terms by way of a "gift" from Zeus – the fabled Pandora's box, which, when opened, spreads misery, disease and suffering in its wake.[2] Later versions of the myth place even greater stress upon Prometheus' role in bringing technology to humanity. For example, in his *Prometheus Bound* the playwright Aeschylus has Prometheus point out how

> [humanity's] every act was without knowledge till I came. I showed them the risings and settings of the stars … I invented for them also numbering … All technai [skills/arts] possessed by mortals came from Prometheus.
>
> (Cited in Humphrey *et al.*, 1997, p. 7)

Three fundamental themes within such tales characterise the way our relationship with technology has often been perceived. First, there is the recurring association with lawbreaking already noted – the sense that some basic "flaw" in human nature criminalises our acquisition of technology and is ultimately to blame for the "excesses of technological civilisation" (Winner, 1978, p. 108). A second, less discussed theme has been what makes our acquisition of technology unlawful – a violation of rules determined by a ruling elite (usually signified by the gods) who claim rights of ownership over it. A third theme, one that also parallels many contemporary dilemmas around technology, centres on how best to use what we have acquired. For, whilst Prometheus provided humans with "the wisdom of everyday life" i.e. the technical means for ensuring their survival – he omitted to provide them with the "civic wisdom" (*politike techne*) for using it properly. This may, in the end, have been Prometheus' greatest crime since,

> Without civic wisdom human beings are a menace to themselves, to other creatures, and to the earth itself [for] ... technological mastery, without civic wisdom, spells disaster.
>
> (Anderson, 1995)

The implicit criminality associated with our acquisition of technology seems therefore to originate first in a violation of the restrictions placed upon its use by the powerful and second from our failure to understand how best to use it. Both offences inevitably invite retribution – whether from a ruling elite or from nature itself.

These early myths explain a great deal about our frequently ambivalent feelings towards technology, or our readiness to defer to those who appear to "understand it better than we do". From Icarus' hubris in flying too close to the sun through to the taboos around artificial life presaged by Mary Shelley's modern "Prometheus unbound" – the Frankenstein monster, technological use has always come with implications of deviance.

Conceptualising and classifying technology

At first glance what technology "is" seems obvious enough. For most of us, technology is simply what Langdon Winner called "apparatus" (1978, p. 11), complex machine-built artefacts – be they small (like an iPhone), or big (like a jet aircraft). But such certainties begin to unravel almost as soon we press the question further. Since artefacts do not emerge in isolation, but from prior production processes, we might, for example, ask whether technology relates to the artefacts, the methods and materials used to construct them – or both? And if so, what is the connection? A deep ambiguity in our thinking is thereby suggested – technology as "something we do" (i.e. the processes and machinery involved in making artefacts), or technology as "the outcome of what we do" (i.e. the artefacts themselves). Nor is this the only ambiguity. As Mitcham (1994) has suggested, technology might equally be associated with how we know what to do – the skills, techniques and scientific understanding that guide our manipulations of nature and the production of artefacts. This focus upon technology as things (rather than knowledge) has, some have argued, been central to our failure to understand when its use is just, or unjust (cf. Grant, 1991).

It is of course true that theoretical questions around what technology is are of little importance to those – like carpenters or engineers – who make or develop technological things. Indeed the gap between theoretical and practical conceptions of technology has often seemed so profound that two differing traditions have been identified – a "humanities" approach represented by theorists like Heidegger (1949) or Ellul (1964) and an "engineering" approach of the kind seen in the work of Ernst Kapp (1877), or more recently of Norbert Wiener (1948). Each presents its own problems. Viewing technology in terms of its function and design certainly allows for conceptions that are more sensitive to real technical methods and solutions. On the other hand, knowing how to make or do something technological is not necessarily the same as seeing the continuities between distinct technological forms or being able to explain why there are continuities in the first place.

A more direct illustration of the ambiguities that arise in defining technology might be seen when we try to categorise new varieties. Take, for example, the proposed revisions to the International Patent Classification system (IPC) (Table 1.1). This is a legal tool for categorising new technologies, one which opts for typologisation over conceptualisation, and which organises type around technical function. The fact that these were further revisions to revisions already made in the face of new technologies indicates the danger in merely typologising rather than conceptualising technology. It is unclear, for example, whether the scheme defines technology in terms of artefacts or in knowledge-based terms (cf. category 26, "machine tools" in comparison to category 14, "organic fine chemistry") (Schmoch, 2008). And as a general approach it fails to dovetail very easily with other classification schemes – for example, typologies used in library and information referencing systems (see for example the Library of Congress scheme – LOC, 2009).

Criminologists have also tended to favour typologisation over conceptualisation by limiting their characterisations of technology to its functions within different stages of the justice process. For example, Byrne and Rebovich's (2007) distinction between "hard" and "soft" technologies may have been useful in linking certain artefacts with certain policing or judicial functions but offered no insights into the nature of technology itself. Bowling *et al.*'s (2008) more sophisticated framework was also dependent upon a functional typology, this time distinguishing between its "probative", "punitive", "surveillant" and "investigative" applications (similar typological approaches can be found in Grabosky, 1998 or Bean, 1999). Beyond these largely descriptive accounts, almost every other discussion of

Table 1.1 Proposed revisions to the international patent classification system for technology (cf. Schmoch, 2008)

	Field of technology
I: Electrical engineering	
1	Electrical machinery, apparatus, energy
2	Audio-visual technology
3	Telecommunications
4	Digital communication
5	Basic communication processes
6	Computer technology
7	IT methods for management
8	Semiconductors
II: Instruments	
9	Optics
10	Measurement
11	Analysis of biological materials
12	Control
13	Medical technology
III: Chemistry	
14	Organic fine chemistry
15	Biotechnology
16	Pharmaceuticals
17	Macromolecular chemistry, polymers
18	Food chemistry
19	Basic materials chemistry
20	Materials, metallurgy
21	Surface technology, coating
22	Micro-structural and nano technology
23	Chemical engineering
24	Environmental technology
IV: Mechanical engineering	
25	Handling
26	Machine tools
27	Engines, pumps, turbines
28	Textile and paper machines
29	Other special machines
30	Thermal processes and apparatus
31	Mechanical elements
32	Transport
V: Other fields	
33	Furniture, games
34	Other consumer goods
35	Civil engineering

Source: Schmoch (2008).

technology within the field has been limited to accounts of specific forms and their applications (CCTV, the internet and so on) (cf. Lazer, 2004; Pattavina, 2005). As a result there has been little real sense of any continuities between, say, biotechnology and information technology, or fingerprint technology and weapons technology. To develop a more robust sense of technology it is clear, then, that we need to look outside the discipline to some alternative traditions where this question has been posed.

Skill, making and revealing: the classical account of technology

The absence of anything like an industrial revolution in premodern societies ought not to be taken to imply that they lacked technology or eschewed technological thinking. As we will see in the following chapter, this preindustrial period was replete with artefacts and activities that we now think of as "technological" – such as metallurgy, cranes and pulley systems, waterwheels or the use of chariots. Equally importantly, it is here where we find the earliest attempts to conceptualise technical practices – particularly within the Greek world.

It has been common, then, to begin discussions of technology by invoking the etymological root of the term in the Greek word *techne*. But the fact that this can also translate as "art" is a warning that *techne* is an ambiguous term from the outset and cannot be taken as a straightforward synonym for technology in the contemporary sense (Roochnik, 1998). Plato associated *techne* with Socratic ideas of technical skill – a form of "practical" or "practitioner" knowledge which might be contrasted with *episteme* – theoretical, or perhaps scientific knowledge – the apprehension of nature and reality "as it really is" (cf. Plato, 1997, 477b).[3] This skill-based, expert knowledge conception meant that a carpenter was just as likely to possess *techne* as a doctor – albeit one based on woodworking rather than medicine. Indeed, the practical skills exhibited in *techne* extend to every kind of human activity – from horsemanship and sculpture to the governance of society. Plato specifically identifies statecraft as a *techne*, since the maintenance of social order is as much an outcome of good *techne* as is a woven basket (Plato, 1997, 342e).

Aristotle accepted a distinction between *techne* and *episteme* but also associated *techne* with *poiesis*, or the revealing of essences – in that "every craft is concerned with coming to be" (1999, 1140a 6ff). Aristotle also suggested that "constructed" things have important differences from "natural" ones, implying that whilst *techne* may imitate nature, it cannot produce anything natural. Aristotle seems to have anticipated a recurring taboo around technology here – that humans should never try to go "beyond" nature. Some commentators have seen an explicit link in this to the restrictions upon technological development during the medieval, scholastic period when Aristotle's views remained highly influential (see Blumenberg, 1957). But Aristotle may only have intended to clarify the necessity of observing a structural distinction between nature as a producer of things and humans as producers of things (cf. Schummer, 2001) and in this sense *techne* can serve to fulfil an inherent "aim" or *telos* of nature – by supplementing and completing it. Like Plato, Aristotle also held that for *techne* to contribute towards the development of a civilised society, additional forms of judgement were required to moderate it – specifically, intellectual virtues such as *phronesis* (practical judgement), *sophia* (wisdom) and *nous* (understanding) (cf. Tabachnik, 2009).[4]

The value placed on technical knowledge in the premodern world can be seen in the hugely diverse range of instruction manuals and guides to everything from engineering and architecture (as in Vitruvius) to pharmacology (as in the Chinese statesman Su Song's treatise *Ben Cao Tu Jing*). In many ways the idea of *techne* had greater flexibility than modern conceptions of technology – not just in the lack of absolute distinctions between theoretical and applied skills, but because *techne* could also serve as a kind of virtue – something that, applied wisely, could offer valuable guidance and support. The displacement of this more complex notion by ideas centred upon function, efficiency or artefact commodification will form one of the key themes of this book.

Transforming technology: industrialisation, progress and doubt

It was not until the nineteenth century that the term "technology" became commonplace – a fact clearly related to the rapid industrialisation of the period. But the transformation of *techne* into technology via industrial production and mass commodity forms had an inevitable impact upon our normative perceptions. The spectacle of industrial technology and its ambiguous effects upon both landscape and social life raised profoundly new questions about the nature of "progress" which have set the scene for many of the debates around technological change ever since. On the one hand there was the emergence of a kind of bullish optimism, where the new mastery over nature was seen as creating a world of ever-expanding opportunity and comfort. Events like the Great Exhibition of 1851 celebrated the seemingly limitless power of technology to liberate us from toil and starvation (Auerbach, 1999) and Bacon's vision of "a kingdom of man, founded on science [that] would be close to a kingdom of heaven" (1955, p. 24, note 21) appeared, for many, to be close at hand. Certainly, for nineteenth-century industrialists like Ure the "blessings which physio-mechanical science has bestowed on society, and the means it has still in store for ameliorating the lot of mankind" (Ure, 1835, p. 8; see also Bizup, 2003) could no longer be doubted.

At the same time, however, the sheer scale of social misery that industrialisation was unleashing inclined many, like the poet Robert Southey, to lament how "the immediate and whole effect of … manufacturing systems is to produce physical and moral evil, in proportion to the wealth it creates"

(1829, I, p. 197). This re-awakening of a "premodern mistrust of tech-nology" (Mitcham, 2003, p. 494), one which originated in *techne*'s violation of nature, meant that for others, abstinence from technology was the only counter to its evils. Commenting on the relationship between humans and technical artefacts, Ruskin wrote:

> Flowers, like everything else that is lovely in the visible world are only to be seen rightly with the eyes ... neither with microscopes nor spectacles. ... men should see with their own eyes, hear and speak without trumpets, walk on their feet, not on wheels, and work and war with their arms, not with engine-beams nor rifles warranted to kill twenty men at a shot.
>
> (2005, p. 200)

Thomas Carlyle nicely summarised these diametrically opposed perceptions of technology accepting that "man is a Tool-using animal ... without Tools he is nothing, with Tools he is all" (2000, I, p. 5) – whilst also complaining bitterly that his society was now one whose "true Deity is Mechanism ... [where] nothing follows its spontaneous course, nothing is left to be accom-plished by old, natural methods" (1858, III, p. 101). William Morris, no advocate of technological change himself, also offered a more nuanced view, accepting that

> if ... necessary reasonable work be of a mechanical kind, I must be helped to do it by a machine, not to cheapen my labour, but so that as little time as possible may be spent upon it, and that I maybe able to think of other things while I am tending the machine.
>
> (1896, I)

But, like other progressive thinkers, Morris was also aware that a far more developed system of regulation for this new technological age would be needed, insisting that "no-one (should) be allowed to ... darken the daylight with smoke, to befoul rivers, or to degrade any spot of earth with squalid litter and brutal wasteful disorder" (1884, p. 210).

Nowhere were these contrasting perceptions of technology more concisely set out than within the work of Marx. His fascination with technology is well recorded and he reportedly kept a notebook (now lost) where he care-fully noted every new technological development of interest.[5] But Marx was also a cogent critic of its exploitative potentials and set out, for the first time, a call for a "critical theory of technology" (cf. Feenberg, 1991). Though he never succeeded in developing this himself, recurring themes within his work suggest the kinds of thing he might have said, and these have been crucial influences upon the work of later critics of technology, in particular the Frankfurt School. For Marx, it was the transformation of technological artefacts into commodity forms that provided the key turning-point in our relationship with technology, one that was rooted in the extraction of surplus value from labour by industry. And the greater the level of technological enablement the greater the surplus value that could be exploited – for, "like every other increase in the productiveness of labour, machinery is intended to cheapen commodities ... in short, it is a means for producing surplus value" (Marx, K., 2007, p. 405). But in stressing how technology increases the level of surplus value that could be obtained from the newly technologised worker – often at terrible cost to their health and family life – Marx also highlighted how technology was a fundamentally social relation. Not just in the way it extended our capacity to work, but also as a means for obtaining and maintaining power. Our relationship with technology is therefore never neutral, for as a social relation it always reproduces and reinforces pre-existing inequalities within those relations.

Marx was therefore one of the first theorists to balance a critique of technology's progressive possibilities with its potential injustices. He readily acknowledged that, properly constrained, technology had significant eman-cipatory potential, though neither did he overestimate such benefits – posing Mill's question as to whether "all the mechanical inventions yet made have lightened the day's toil of any human beings" (Mill, 1909, p. 751 cited in Marx, K., 2007). For criminologists and legal theorists, Marx's critique of technology also offer some more specific lines of reflection. His analysis of the advantages of technology for control is familiar enough, but he was also aware of the often fertile relationship between technology and crime, noting how

> crime, by its ceaseless development of new means of attacking property calls into existence new measures of defence, and its productive effects are as great as strikes in stimulating the invention of machines.[6]

Marx thus anticipates Tarde's third law of criminal imitation (1903) – the law of insertion, where novel behaviour or new means (for example, the replacement of the knife by the gun) stimulates new offending (cf. Pfohl, 1994). But he also goes beyond the simplistic conception of an "arms race" between police and criminals, recognising how technological progress, when coupled with unorthodox thinking, can often generate more unpredictable forms of innovation.

The tensions we see in Marx and other nineteenth-century theorists between utopian and dystopian interpretations of technology have remained a common theme ever since. Weber, who developed his own very influential pessimistic position, predicted a relentless and detrimental technologisation of everyday life, one where the triumph of "instrumental" rationality – i.e. means–end, technically orientated ways of thinking – over substantive, value-oriented varieties was all but inevitable. Weber pointed to the "mechanical" thinking which technologisation fosters and was one of the first to highlight how many of the virtues associated with it – i.e.

calculability, predictability and efficiency – in fact created ideological conditions for new, technologically based forms of rule. At their most extreme these threaten to lead us into a "polar night of icy darkness" (1994) where a dehumanised, bureaucratic ruling order manages society through an iron cage of means–end rationalities (1992). Marcuse went further, identifying a more specific "technological" rationality. This replaces the individualistic thinking of the sixteenth century with a new compliance and passivity in the face of the "dictates of the apparatus" (1982, p. 145). Habermas' critique of science and technology (1970) further developed the idea of them as ideological forces which drive a "technisation of the lifeworld" (cf. Feenberg, 1996 for more on this point), though he also allowed that the shift towards an instrumental control over nature is not historically specific, but fundamental to human rationality as a whole. Foucault's analysis of technology's disciplinary role is no less critical of its distorting effect upon culture, though in relating this to a knowledge/power nexus, he offers a more nuanced perspective (cf. Gerrie, 2003). Elsewhere, the various critiques of post-industrial technologies set out by, amongst others, Daniel Bell (1976) and Marcell Castells (1996/2000) continue to highlight the negative interdependencies between economy, culture and technology (especially information technology).

The general pessimism of twentieth-century thinkers towards technology is probably not entirely surprising, given the impact of two technologically driven world wars, unease about the threats posed by industrial processes towards the environment and continued economic upheaval brought by new technologies. But it would also be wrong to claim that the kind of optimism seen in the nineteenth century completely vanished (see for example Weinberg, 1980). The 1951 Festival of Britain, or the New York World's Fair of 1939 maintained an ongoing faith in technological progress – with lavish stands from Dupont portraying "the wonderful world of chemistry", or the General Motors Futurama exhibit, which celebrated the continuities between "democracity and superhighways" (*sic*) (cf. Zukin, 1991). But, unlike the nationalistic idealisations of the nineteenth century, this was now a highly corporatised view of technological progress – one familiar to contemporary audiences in glossy advertorials about "vorsprung durch technik" or the "science" in hair conditioners. The robust technological optimism exhibited by early twentieth-century optimists like the Futurists, Le Corbusier or the Bauhaus may have certain parallels with cyberspace evangelists who believe that blogging or tweeting will "change politics" (Morozov, 2011), but questions about the ownership and corporate control of technology are now never far away. For every advance in medicine, transport and so on there must always be consideration of whether this will ultimately translate into a social or a commercial benefit.

Throughout all these debates about the good or the evil in technology, a crucial conceptual stand-off can be traced. On one side are those who hold the "instrumental" view of technology – viewing it as a "neutral" tool where use or misuse is determined only by the social actors in question. On the other are those who hold that it is a substantive social force, one located within a network of human relations and interests that requires distinctive varieties of regulatory intervention (cf. Feenberg, 1991, p. 5; Tiles and Oberdiek, 1995). A seminal version of this "substantive" position on technology was first set out by Heidegger.

Contemporary views of technology (I): Heidegger and phenomenological conceptions

Heidegger's much-cited paper "The question concerning technology" (1949/ 1977) can be described as a "substantive" rather than an instrumental position because, for him, technology can never be a neutral tool, or mere means to an end. Rather it has become "an environment and a way of life" (Feenberg, 1991, p. 8). Heidegger doesn't offer us any very clear or novel conception of what technology "is" – he is far more concerned with its "essence", how this has changed and what the effects of this are upon our being. His starting-point was the Greek notion of *techne*, and this led him to advocate a return to the more harmonious, nurturing relationship with artefacts which (hc claims) *techne* facilitates, and a rejection of the wholesale technological reordering of natural resources that has turned nature into a "standing reserve" ripe for exploitation. For Heidegger, this shift signifies a new kind of age, one where the understanding of traditional craftsmen who worked with nature has been supplanted by a technical order that transforms everything into possible subjects of technological processes: processes ultimately destructive to both nature and social life. The sense that "everything man encounters exists only insofar as it is his construct" (Heidegger, 1977, p. 27), has led us to forget that *techne* can help us to enact *poiesis* – a realising of the potential of nature that Aristotle once highlighted. Instead, technology has become something that "occupies" us, transforming our being and everything else it touches into a form of "raw material" – mere inputs and outputs of production processes (1977, p. 17). Thus, his famous claim that the "essence of technology is nothing technological" (1977, p. 4) is not meant to be a definition, but a reminder that we need to "go beyond technology" if we are to resituate our being towards it. It is only in so doing, Heidegger argues, that we can enjoy its benefits rather than being enslaved by it.

Since Heidegger never provides any clear conceptual conditions for what makes something technological it is not surprising that he offers no practical guidance on how technology might be better regulated to avoid these negative outcomes. But his legacy in thinking about technology is clear enough – especially for those who view it phenomenologically, i.e. in terms of its meanings and how these might be "rehumanised". Thus, Borgmann's later solution to Heidegger's question required a shift away from the increasing role of technological things as "device paradigms" towards what he calls "focal" things or practices (see Borgmann, 1984). As device paradigms, technological artefacts largely function as means–end solutions for the efficient delivery of commodities. This distances us from the world – in contrast to focal things, which "require a practice to prosper within" (ibid., p. 196). Thus, listening to music on a device paradigm like a digital music player requires less involvement than listening to it in a concert hall, or even on a vinyl disk – both of which have their own distinctive customs and practices. Unlike consuming fast food, or staring at computer screens, taking part in focal activities like gardening, running or eating family meals together, serves to "engage ... and occupy ... us fully" (ibid., p. 205). In this way focal practices serve to resituate us with regard to technology, for they "guard in its undiminished depth and identity the thing that is central to the practice and shield it against the technological diremption into means and end" (ibid., p. 209).

In his 1964 text *The Technological Society*, Jacques Ellul set out an even more extensive phenomenological critique of technology. Following Lewis Mumford, Ellul defines the more encompassing concept of "technique" – a notion of the technological that goes beyond artefacts and comprises a "totality of methods rationally arrived at and having absolute efficiency (for a given stage of development) in every field of human activity" (1964, p. xxv). Taking his cue from Marcuse, Ellul was wary of the technological life, arguing that "technique has taken over the whole of civilization. Death, procreation, birth, all must submit to technical efficiency and systematization" (ibid., p. 128). Ellul was particularly sceptical about the likely impacts of this shift upon justice – arguing that "technique cannot be otherwise than totalitarian. Everything is its concern" (ibid., p. 125). Given that technology shapes our responses into ones of "reflex" rather than reflection (1992), an amoral regulatory order is generated, one where "everything which is technique is necessarily used as soon as it is available without distinction of good or evil. This is the principal law of our age, the primary law" (1964, p. 99).

Contemporary views of technology (II): networks, posthumanity and control

By advocating a more intersubjective, social understanding of technology, phenomenological approaches offer an obvious challenge to the instrumentalist view that it is socially neutral, or rooted in subject–object distinctions between us and "it". More recent views of technology have been still more explicit about its social character – invoking ideas of socio-technic connectivity and physical fusion – ways in which the body begins to become indistinguishable from technology in virtue of being networked or even "hybridised" with it. Latour's "actor network" theory has been an influential position of this kind, emphasising human-technic continuity by seeing it as a collective subject – or what he calls an "actant" (cf. Latour, 1994; Brown, 2006). The entanglements between technologies and subjects induce reciprocally transformative effects which entail that "you are another subject because you hold the gun, [and] the gun is another object because it has entered into a relationship with you" (Latour, 1999, p. 179). In this way,

> It is by mistake or unfairness, that our headlines read, "Man flies," "Woman goes into space". Flying is a property of the whole association of entities that includes airports and planes, launch pads and ticket counters. B-52s do not fly, the U.S. Air Force flies. Action is simply not a property of humans but of an association of actants.
>
> (1994, p. 35)

Donna Haraway located these "techno-social" fusions in more overtly body-centric terms – arguing that we are all "theorized and fabricated hybrids of machine and organism; in short, we are cyborgs" (1991, p. 150; see also Clark, 2003). And though her original concern here was with resituating gender identities, an obvious implication of Haraway's claim is to make cyborgs new kinds of subjects, ones that do not just supersede our traditional ontologies but that "give us our politics" (ibid; see also Hayles, 1999).

These so-called "post-humanist" accounts of technology, where "technology is 'co-mergent' with the social and natural worlds" (Feenberg, 2002, p. 28) are not quite as novel as they first sound. Their philosophical roots lie in Nietzschean conceptions of a new "post-human" stage of humanity, or in narratives of the human-technic such as Mary Shelley's distinctive account (cf. Weiner, 1966). In their modern formulation such views have clear implications for criminal justice. For if an actant or a human-technic can be a collective subject, then it can also be agentic – with obvious consequences for regulating familiar collective subjects like corporations.

Deleuze and Guattari (1983) offered their own distinctive take on the idea of the "post-human" – one which has had a more direct impact upon criminological thought – most obviously in Deleuze's construct of the technologically driven "society of control" (1992). Ideas of the machine, the assemblage and the network play a crucial role within their work, though it should be stressed that Deleuzean machines only serve as technological objects in a rather abstract sense. Like its physical counterpart, the Deleuzean machine serves to denote collective centres of activity and doing, which may encompass highly varied flows such as wealth, information or desire. Their claim that "there is a human technology which exists before a material technology" (1988, p. 39) also stresses the social roots of technology and reminds us how certain technologies have been central to the evolution of power and justice. For as Deleuze suggests,

> The old societies of sovereignty made use of simple machines – levers, pulleys, clocks; [and] the recent disciplinary societies equipped

themselves with machines involving energy, with the passive danger of entropy and the active danger of sabotage; the societies of control operate with machines of a third type, computers.

(1992)

It is clear that Deleuze follows Castells, Poster (2001) and other commentators in making digital technology the "language" of a control society (1992, p. 2), so underplaying the role of other equally influential technologies – not least the bio-chemical varieties. Nonetheless his association between specific forms of technologisation and modulations in control has been a highly plausible one to many.

The technological norm: engineering, efficiency and disaster

The previous accounts say a lot about social norms and technology, but are less clear on the regulatory impacts of technical function. In this context "engineering" centred approaches of the kind advocated by Mitcham (1994) offer a useful critical balance by conceptualising technology in terms of how it works – or ought to work. The crucial idea of a technological norm emerges here and can be conceptualised in at least two ways. One is simply correct function – just as it is a technological norm for a hairdryer to dry hair, so it is a violation of technological norms for a jet airplane to crash (cf. Vaesen, 2006). For our purposes, technological norms also entail certain regulative aspects. This is partly because such norms often require regulation or legal control – for example, where an artefact fails to meet its norms then it is often the case that criminal or civil/tort actions may result. But regulative, behavioural impacts are also seen in the standardisations of production and behaviour that technological norms entail – what Canguilhem called "the characteristics necessary for consistent manufacture" (1989, p. 246). This more active, shaping aspect of technological norms is reflected in the contrast between what has been termed the "constitutive" norms of a technology and its "regulative" norms. For example, a constitutive technological norm of car driving is having a car (no-one can drive without one), but the norm becomes regulative when it also makes us modify our behaviour – like reducing speed or wearing a seat belt (cf. Hildebrandt, 2008a, p. 177). Thus, where a technological norm is regulative, certain behaviours are required or selected for – and often in ways upon which other forms of regulation, not least the law, have little bearing. The implications of this for due process or for justice are a theme that we will return to frequently in what follows.

Violating a technological norm can produce extreme consequences when it results in the kinds of accident or catastrophe highlighted in Paul Virilio's important reflections upon technology. Virilio pointed out how with every new technological artefact or process comes a necessary possibility of malfunction, failure or human error – what Virilio calls "the technological accident" (see his 2007). Thus, with the car came (necessarily) the car crash, just as the advent of the computer brought an inevitable possibility of the computer crash. Most disturbingly of all perhaps – especially in the technologically dependent, globally interconnected world we now inhabit – is the prospect of what Virilio has called "generalised accident". As Virilio points out,

> nobody has seen this generalized accident yet. But then watch out as you hear talk about the "financial bubble" in the economy: a very significant metaphor is used here, and it conjures up visions of some kind of cloud, reminding us of other clouds just as frightening as those of Chernobyl …
>
> (1995)

In the wake of the banking collapse of 2008/9, the oil spills of 2010 and the Japanese nuclear incidents of 2011 we have an increasingly vivid sense of the kinds of global havoc the failure to meet technological norms can now produce. It is not surprising, then, that a key influence upon the shift towards risk management-style philosophies has been the desirability of ensuring that technological norms are satisfied. But in the context of justice, foregrounding technical norms over social ones is questionable indeed Virilio, like Ellul and Deleuze, appears convinced that this is rarely positive, in that "totalitarianism is latent in technology" (1996; see also Kellner, 1999). This sense that technological normativity carries a hegemonic force which threatens our legal order has become increasingly influential of late. However, we should never forget the ancient prejudice in this – that technology is, by its very nature, a human violation that threatens to destroy the natural order.

Technological extension

Though the previous approaches to technology offer useful critical insights, the question of what it "is" remains rather unclear. For this reason I want now to turn to another, less discussed approach – one that incorporates aspects of the post-human stance but which (I argue) provides a more general conceptualisation and therefore a more effective basis for understanding how technology functions within criminal justice contexts.

One source for this position can be found in the views of Ernst Kapp, perhaps the first theorist to think of himself specifically as a "philosopher of technology". Kapp argued that technologies can be thought of as "kinds of [human] organ projections" (1877), so that "in the tool, the human continually produces itself" (ibid., pp. 44–45).[7] For example, bent fingers find their technic parallel in hooks, just as the function of a cupped hand in gathering water can be more completely realised by the technology of a wooden or a ceramic bowl. Elements of Kapp's position go back at least as far as the seventeenth century, for example in Robert Hooke's claim that scientific instruments like the microscope or telescope remedy the "infirmities" of the senses "with Instruments, and, as it were, adding of artificial organs to the natural" (cited in Shapin and Schaffer, 1989, p. 36).

Freud was more explicit about the nature of these technological organs, viewing them as "prosthetics" which have come to offer humanity various evolutionary advantages.

> With every tool [man] is perfecting his own organs, whether motor or sensory, or is removing the limits to their functioning. Motor power places gigantic forces at his disposal, which, like his muscles, he can employ in any direction; ... by means of spectacles he corrects defects in the lens of his own eyes; by means of the telescope he sees into the far distance; by means of the microscope he overcomes the limits of visibility set by the structure of his retina ... With the help of the telephone he can hear at distances which would be respected as unattainable even in a fairy tale. Writing was in its origin the voice of an absent person; and the dwelling-house was a substitute for the mother's womb, the first lodging.
>
> (1962, pp. 90–91)

Similar views can be found in more recent work by the anthropologist Arnold Gehlen (1965) or, more familiarly, in McLuhan's (1964), which argued that "all technologies are extensions of our physical and nervous systems" (p. 90).[8] Like Kapp, McLuhan closely relates technological extensions to our limbs – to use one of his famous examples, the wheel "extends" the foot, just as the hammer extends the arm. But McLuhan's view also allows technology to provide for more complex (and thus less overtly body-centric) varieties of extension. Even language – one of our original and most important of extensions – transcends this organ analogy in that it "does for intelligence what the wheel does for the foot" (ibid., p. 79). And as Freud also acknowledged, language goes beyond a merely prosthetic layer of our being by setting the conditions for a technology that has shaped our very nature – that of writing – "the technology that has been the means of creating civilised man" (1962, p. 84).

McLuhan was very clear that extension is not an instrumentalist "tool" based process but something profoundly social. Indeed instrumentalist views simply do not "stand scrutiny", since technology can "never ... do anything except add itself on to what we already are" (1964, p. 11). As such, every extension brings with it all the vested power, self-interest or injustice implicit within our existing social order. The charge that McLuhan is a technological determinist (see for example Williams, 1967) is also unfair. He was certainly willing to grant technology a great deal of determining power, arguing (for example) that forms of media work us over completely. They are so persuasive in their personal, political, economic, aesthetic, psychological, moral, ethical, and social consequences that they leave no part of us untouched, unaffected, unaltered.

(1967, p. 26)

But this is no "one way" determining, rather it is a more subtle reciprocal relationship, one where "we shape our tools, and thereafter our tools shape us" (as put by Lewis Lapham in his introduction to McLuhan's 1964/1994, pp. xi–xii). McLuhan makes technology as dependent upon us as we are upon it, in that we serve as "[the] sex organ of the machine world, as the bee of the plant world, enabling it to fecundate and to evolve ever new forms" (ibid., p. 56).

McLuhan's permutation of the organ extension, "prosthetic" stance on technology has often been interpreted as utopian, but he is more than aware of technology's negative potentials. As Freud recognised, there is a price we must pay for becoming a " kind of prosthetic God" (1962, p. 37). For in putting on "auxiliary organs" "[man] is truly magnificent ... [but] these organs have not grown onto him and they still give him much trouble at times" (ibid., pp. 37–38). Similarly for McLuhan, with every extension comes a unique range of possible harms what he calls technological "amputations" (1964). For example, whilst the wheel extends our mobility, it also robs the foot of the need to walk – thereby creating the risk of a sedentary society. In turn, the emergence of information technology has presented us with an more potentially destructive amputation – on the one hand extending our communication potentials but also "numbing" our senses, and creating a new "age of anxiety" (ibid.). And for McLuhan, any evaluation of technology requires that we pay as much attention to its form as to what it seems to do – a point not always appreciated when his famous dictum that the "medium is the message" is cited.

Technology as enablement: extension and range

Viewing technology in terms of extension does not just help to underline why it has a social character, it also resolves some of the key ambiguities in defining it. For example, the seeming gulf between notions of "high" and "low" categories of technology becomes less wide when artefacts like a flint scraper, or a sharpened stick, can also, like a satellite or a microscope, be seen in terms of extensions to what we can do. Differences between technological forms then lie primarily in the *kinds* of extension they provide and the complexity of social organisation required to produce them. But the view is not yet quite satisfactory. For while extension places the body (and therefore the social) firmly at the centre of our understanding of technology, a further modification is required to clarify what is really entailed by this. In the end any technological extension comes down to helping us perform better or to do and experience things that were previously hard, perhaps impossible. In other words, the defining contribution of the hammer that helps me to drive in nails more powerfully than before, or the audio DVD that lets me experience music more intensely and more accessibly than before is a causal one.

However, since this additional causal reach might be latent – i.e. might never be used – the causal criterion is not yet quite general enough. In my (2007) I dealt with the problem of latency in technological extension by relating it to the philosophical conception of a "power" or capacity (cf. Mumford, 2003; Cartwright, 2007). Capacities are by their very nature latent, since they need never be actualised – for example, salt may have the capacity to dissolve in water, but will never display this unless actually placed in water. Similarly, the percussive capacity of a hammer or the softness of a mattress may never be used, but this need have no bearing upon the fact that in the right circumstances they may be. Thus it is more accurate to say that it is the potential forms of enablement offered that count in making an artefact "technological". It is this notion of a capacity, or potential enablement, that will serve to define the main classes of technology to be analysed in what follows. To make the distinctions between these classes more robust I will also use a second variable – one relating to the distance or range from our bodies at which any technological form enables us to act.

The first and obvious of these ranges is within the immediate "reach" of the body itself – the distance at which our arms extend, or the scale at which we are able to pick things up, to see or to hear things. Many of our most familiar and traditional technologies operate within this range – the cooking-pot, which extends our capacity to heat food, the blanket, which enhances our capacity to retain heat and so on. So too do many of our more complex contemporary technologies, such as the food mixer, which extends our capacity to chop, cut or mix foodstuffs. Beyond the immediate causal range of the body our capacity to interact with objects now extends towards two spatio-temporal "vanishing points" – the "very far" and the "very near" – that is, the microscopic scale normally beyond our capacity to see or to touch. Technology now provides us with various artefacts that enhance our reach across these extended spatio-temporal ranges – the telephone, which offers us the capacity to talk to someone beyond the point at which our voice can normally be heard, or the microscope, which offers us the capacity to see things beyond the vanishing point determined by the light-processing powers of our retinas. In what follows I will associate these capacities and their respective ranges with three classes of technology:

(I)   *Chemical, biological or nuclear technologies* (CBNTs)
       We can think of these technologies precisely in terms of the way
       they enable us to interact and manipulate objects at "very close up"

or micro-distances. Familiar examples here might include genetic technologies, chemical processing technologies or subatomic and nano technologies.

(II) *Information communication technologies* (ICTs)

Conversely, these technologies operate by extending our capacity to interact with objects or individuals at spatio-temporal ranges beyond our normal bodily reach in a process of "distanciation", or "doing things at a distance" (Giddens, 1990). These extensions have been associated with telecommunications technologies like the radio or the telephone, or information technologies like digital computing networks, which serve to "compress" time and space (Harvey, 1989).

(III) *Mid- and multi-range technologies* (MMRTs)

At the spatio-temporal "mid-point" between (I) and (II) are what will be referred to here, for convenience, as "mid-range" technologies – those which enhance our capacities for more effective interaction within the scale and range determined by our physical bodies. Examples here might include everything from a nutcracker, to a pen, a kettle or a scarf. But since certain artefacts within this class may also extend interaction beyond this range – for example, weapons – I will also refer to them as "multi-range" technologies.

There are some obvious qualifications to be made about this method of classifying technology. It is clear first that there is not any absolute separation between these classes – indeed, there are often major interdependencies between them. For example, the functioning of ICTs has been hugely dependent upon our success in manipulating micro-phenomena such as electro-magnetic forces and particles, just as our successful manipulation of genetic material is often highly dependent upon our access to enhanced information storage and processing capacities. Moreover, as we will see in Chapter 7, the way we access and interface with any technology must always be "body-centric" at some point, so that any artefact could therefore be argued to depend ultimately upon (III).

Such qualifications aside, I will argue that the scheme offers more than a convenient way of organising technology. For it is not just that we think of the powers offered by technology in terms of distinctive spatio-temporal ranges. It is also plausible that it identifies precisely those technologies that are having the greatest impact upon contemporary criminal justice.

Technology, crime and justice (I): crime, regulation and technological control

We are now in a better position to consider the issues that will occupy the rest of this book – the relationship between these classes of technology and our justice systems and the extent to which this relationship is a satisfactory one. It has already been suggested that something of significance is now afoot here – a situation where, in addition to merely assisting or facilitating the process of justice, technology seems to be acquiring an increasing role in determining it. As indicated, the growing influence of technological norms upon social norms provides one kind of metric for this trend. Another can be seen in the deference to formal rationality stressed by Weber, where we see how "technical norms. ... have to do with efficiency of means" (Feenberg, 2002, p. 65) – a goal that now exerts as much influence upon justice policy as it does elsewhere. But the role of technology in shaping justice is also discernible in a still more fundamental development, its increasingly "autonomic" power to regulate us (cf. Hildebrandt and Rouvroy, 2011) – often outside the constraints of due process or public accountability.

In his (1999) Lawrence Lessig offered one characterisation of a regulation by technology in terms of "code" – specifically the code that drives information technology. Code, he argued, sits alongside other traditional regulatory forces (like social norms, the market and the law) but plays its own part in shaping what we can do by "constrain[ing] some behaviour [and] making other behaviour possible, or impossible" (Lessig, 1999, p. 89). We are all familiar with the basic idea here – the internet filter that blocks certain searches or the password that enables access – constraints that operate largely autonomously and according to technical rather than legal or normative imperatives. But Lessig also implied that code is – in effect – an instance of wider "architectures" – i.e. more general forms of technological shaping that operate outside of computer environments. It does not take much reflection to see how this might be plausible. Take, for example, Latour's notion of technological regulation – one illustrated in his widely discussed example of the "Berlin key" (see his 2000). Its particular design – a two-headed key that forces the user to open and lock the door in a particular way – "demonstrates how a technological device regulates and constitutes the interactions of a resident, the key, her door and others who wish to enter the house" (Hildebrandt, 2008a). In this way the technological norms of the key – its shape and mode of locking – "constrains human actions, inviting or enforcing, inhibiting or prohibiting types of behaviour" (ibid.). And crucially, it does this without reflection or debate nor any normative assessment of the desirability of our behaviour's being so constrained.

Once we look more closely it becomes apparent just how far our world is now permeated by examples of "technological regulation" (cf. Reidenberg, 1998; Hildebrandt and Rouvroy, 2011). These might be as simple as the road hump, which makes us slow down, or the gastric belt, which regulates our food intake (cf. Yeung, 2008). Or it might take a more dynamic form – like an electric fence or "obey or pay" form of control such as automated speeding fines (Brownsword, 2008, p. 38). As technological controls increase in sophistication so, seemingly, do their regulatory scope – even now extending into the body itself, as, for example, in the role of bodily screening as a determinant of employment chances, access to insurance or the right to cross international borders. The seemingly relentless expansion of technological regulation has begun to pose some interesting questions for our justice systems. For however much the regulatory power of a DNA sample or an internet filter is made to ape more publicly transparent controls, the "technological justice" that results is one that often operates with few of the safeguards, balances and accountabilities we have previously taken for granted.

Technology, crime and justice (II): technomia

The idea that technology constitutes a dominant or hegemonic force in society is not, of course, a new one. In his idea of a technics – the total cultural system that characterise our relationship with technology – Lewis Mumford distinguished between its "democratic" and "authoritarian" forms. The former involved "small scale method[s] of production, resting mainly on human skill and animal energy" whilst the latter required centralised political control where "herculean feats of mechanical organization rested on ruthless physical coercion, forced labour and slavery" (1934, pp. 2–3). Ellul's similarly broad reading of technology in terms of "technique" was less inclined to see a democratic side, arguing that technique "cannot be otherwise than totalitarian" (1964, p. 125). Elsewhere, this idea that technology now constitutes a form of rule in and of itself has been reflected in other familiar conceptions such as a "technocracy" (cf. Fischer, 1989), a "technopoly" (Postman, 1993) or the advent of a "technopolis" (Winner, 1978).

We do not need, however, to see such a relentless, totalitarian subjection of humanity by technology to understand how it might play a central role in shaping society. We might, for example, follow Langdon Winner in thinking of technologies as "institutional structures within an evolving constitution", structures which "give rise to a new polity" (1978, p. 32). But it is clear enough that it is not a polity which has been arrived at through any kind of open debate, for in the technopolis "somnambulism characterises technological policies" (ibid.). It is in such policies – or the lack of them – that I will argue that an analysis of the regulatory power of technology is best situated. This, in turn, further illustrates why a focus upon technology within the criminal justice system offers a particularly fruitful entry-point to an understanding of its wider control power. For it is at the regulatory "coal face" of the criminal justice system – perhaps more than anywhere – that we can discern the true contours and extent of technical power, most obviously in the kinds of limits we choose to place upon it. In what follows, then, I intend to suggest that a better starting-point for understanding the extent of any technocracy is to focus upon its "nomos" – Pete Berger's (1967) term for the body of rules, codes and formal or informal regulations that governs a social practice. And the task of outlining the contemporary nomos of technology – what, for convenience,

I will refer to as its "technomia" – will be organised around three basic questions:

1   How is technology regulated? That is, what kinds of regulatory structures, legal or otherwise, are judged to best constrain technology uses?
2   Under what conditions are such regulatory structures considered to be violated and at what point does a violation become criminal? In particular, how well integrated are uses of technology defined as criminal with breaches of other less obvious or transparent rules – such as violations of professional codes, or safety standards?
3   What are the kinds of ways in which technology itself acts as a regulator, and to what extent does our contemporary technomia license a blurring between technical and legal control?

In one sense, then – as questions 1 and 2 indicate – a technomia can be seen to emerge from the rules and accompanying violations directed at technology. Such rules are of course indicative of who has power to make them, and how far they are prepared to subject wider social considerations to technological imperatives. When interpreted as an extension to an existing social order, technology simply embodies this pre-given power. But in a context where technology often seems to impose its own de facto forms of justice, question 3 becomes an equally essential part of any such inquiry. For if it turns out that there is a disjunct between our technomia – the system of technological regulation that we currently have – and justice – the system of regulation (technological or otherwise) that we think best protects our interests – such a question can hardly be ignored.

Of course it might be argued that appealing to the construct of a technomia is no more than an exercise in regulatory heuristics rather than the identification of any genuine legal reality. Not only is it clear that no society has ever had an explicit nomos around technology, but the very idea that there could be any such formal system is questionable. Technological change is now so constant and so rapid that it seems likely to always outpace "top-down" attempts to control or regulate it – whether by legal means or otherwise. Yet it is also undeniable that we are surrounded by rules and regulations around technology, some legal and formal, but many more that are informal and that lack any clear legal status. And beyond these are a range of attitudes and beliefs about technology – the technological a priori suggested by Marcuse – that seem to underscore and reinforce such attitudes. If the concept of a technomia helps unravel any of this invisible order, it will be one worth pursuing.

Technomia and justice

Being able to identify some kind of regulatory order around technology – a technomia – is one thing. Being able to say that this is a just or "unjust" order is another, more far-reaching normative question. Answers to such a question will of course depend significantly upon the kind of theory of justice one prefers, or the kind of justice imagined to be at stake (cf. MacIntyre, 1988). For example, if the issue is taken to relate to social justice, then considerations around the equitable distribution of technology are likely to figure centrally. Here it is obvious enough that certain social groups have far superior access to technology than others (i.e. a better internet connection, superior medical care and so on), and as our world becomes more technology dependent such divides are only likely to worsen (cf. Warshauer, 2003; Rooksby and Weckert, 2006). Our concerns will be largely focused upon justice within legal or criminal justice contexts – though it should be clear enough that the issues of social justice and criminal justice are closely intertwined. In particular, if one concurs with one traditional view of justice – that it is about "fairness" – social injustice might well be seen as a form of criminal injustice – even if the law does not so define it. Conversely, a system of technological regulation that is unjust seems likely to result in a social order that is also unjust (indeed this is, arguably, the way to interpret the claims of Marcuse, Ellul and other critics of technology). Quite how fairness is determined, or indeed whether it really is the most useful sense of justice, has been a subject of vigorous debate (cf. Rawls, 1971 and Nozick, 1974; Sen, 2009), but a minimum requirement has been something like a symmetry condition – one captured in Aristotle's formulation that "equals should be treated equally and unequals unequally" (1999, V.3. 1131a10–b15). That is, who you are should not make any difference to the course of justice, unless there is some relevant variation that needs to be taken into account. For example, if someone is singled out for CCTV surveillance purely because of their clothing, or is denied internet access because of a previous drug conviction, then obvious questions about whether technology is being used in a just way seem to arise. The related notion of proportion also seems relevant in deciding fairness – technological or otherwise. The idea that somebody should be punished more severely for a knife offence because of their ethnicity, or should have their limbs amputated because they sent an offensive e-mail seems intuitively "unfair". And even those who advocate retributive notions of justice would usually judge an erroneous punishment to be unfair, since the whole logic of the position is for the guilty party to be punished.

Since the way technology use or misuse is regulated is often a matter of criminal law, other notions of justice – for example, those based around rights (cf. Dworkin, 1977; Nickel, 2006) – will also be relevant in what follows. As we shall see, however, it is not always obvious how the language of rights can be made to apply to the extended social life that technology creates. Formal statements like the US Declaration of Independence, the UN Declaration of Human Rights (1948) or the European Convention (1954) have all represented attempts to codify Locke's (1988) claim that everyone possesses basic rights independent of anything granted by the state. But since these are largely concerned with certain more obvious rights such as life, freedom or property it remains, as yet, unclear how these can be made to apply to a world saturated in technology for in this extended world, the prosthetics of the post-human may become as important to us as our more delimited bodies once were.

2 Foundations

From eotechnic justice to industrial control

> Give me a lever long enough and a fulcrum on which to place it, and I shall move the world.[1]

Defining history in terms of a "stone age", an "iron age", an "industrial age" or our more recent "information age" reflect just how readily a determining influence of technology upon culture has been accepted. The history of technology itself is a rich field to which I cannot do any justice here (see Singer *et al.*, 1954 and Pacey, 1991 for some sense of this) but there have been certain attempts to offer more precise periodisations – for example, Mumford's (1934) characterisation of three key technological "eras" – the Eotechnic (1000–1750 – handicrafts, low technologies), the Paleotechnic (1750–1900 – industrialisation) and the Neotechnic (1900–2000). In general, however, the distinction between "pre-industrial" and "industrial" societies remains the most familiar historical model of socio-technological development – however simplistic – and it is one that I will retain in what follows. There is, however, a potentially misleading conclusion that the distinction implies – that technology crime and control is largely a feature of industrial (i.e. technologised) societies. In this chapter I want to suggest a far longer and livelier engagement with technology by lawmakers and lawbreakers than this. Not only will this give us a sense of the nomos around technology in the premodern or "eotechnic" era – our primordial technomia, if you like. It will also provide a firmer basis for understanding the dramatic technological shifts of the eighteenth and nineteenth centuries, when so many of the familiar components of our contemporary criminal justice systems emerged – from professional police forces to prisons and forensic science methods.

Pre-industrial technological crime: patterns and portents

Finding definitive examples of technological crime, technological regulation or technological misuse in the pre-industrial era appears to be confronted by several problems. One variety emerges from the distinction between

industrial and pre-industrial societies – a distinction that has been challenged on various historical grounds (cf. Hartwell, 1990). An obvious
implication here is that if technology remained largely stable and similar in
the pre-industrial era, so too must have any crime or control involving
technology. But the idea that this remained completely unchanged over such
a long period seems as implausible as the idea that prehistoric technologies
like an antler pick or a flint axe are technically contiguous with later artefacts like a suit of armour or a flintlock. There are also important cultural
questions. For example, could the kind of technology crime and control that
might be witnessed in Han dynasty China, or in ancient Rome, really be
compared to that experienced in medieval Paris, or in sixteenth-century
London? Defining the misuse of premodern technologies as criminal is
further complicated by the huge variations in what constituted offences. For
example, the role of axes in enabling the widespread deforestation of the
landscape that occurred throughout the pre-industrial period was not
obviously "eco-crime", since forestry clearance was a socially acceptable
activity at this time (cf. Winner, 1978, p. 17). Similarly, given that slavery
was also socially accepted, to what extent could the technologies used
to sustain it – such as slave-ships or manacles – really be associated with
premodern technology crime?

Locating an adequate range of historical sources for meaningful analysis
of these early trends might also seem to pose problems. In fact, there is a
range of documentary evidence around technology available from the
ancient and classical periods – for example, the technical records kept by
Chinese imperial court bureaucrats (cf. Needham, 1954); legal codes such as
the Roman book of Twelve Tables or the Babylonian code of Hammurabi
(cf. Watson *et al.*, 2001); and travellers' tales and historical accounts
of technology such as those provided by Herodotus and Thucydides. More
technical sources can be found in texts like Vitruvius' *Architecture*, Front-
inus' work on aqueducts (cf. Humphrey *et al.*, 1997; Cuomo, 2008), early
Indian mathematical texts (Yadav and Mohan, 2010) or Islamic works on
astronomy and medicine (cf. Hassan and Hill, 1986). Detailed sources from
the early medieval period are more lacking at first – though court and legal
documents, together with personal narratives and other more technology-
specific texts begin to become more widely available from the late fifteenth
century onwards (cf. Singer *et al.*, 1954; White, 1962; Gimpel, 1976). From
this point, as the scientific revolution began to gather pace, an increasingly
rich range of documentation provides a richer overview of licit and illicit
technological practice. Clearly, much work remains to be done in tracing
and analysing source material over this long period, but even with the
limited research tools that are available a surprising amount can be said
about technology crime and control in the pre-industrial world.

Some of the richest available evidence centres on the role of technology
within our two most familiar categories of criminality – violence and
property crime. Then, as now, weapons provided the most obviously

"technological" way of enabling violence, given the greater likelihood that most individuals would carry some form of stabbing, smashing or choking device (whether specifically designed for violence or, like a pike, for other tasks). Less common, but still available, were weapons enabling violence at a distance, such as spears, slings, the bow and arrow or sophisticated military devices like the ballista, or siege catapult, which served armies for nearly 2,000 years during this period (cf. van Creveld, 1989; O'Connell, 1989). By the sixteenth century Chinese inventions like the cross-bow and, of course, gunpowder had further increased the potential range, accuracy and destructive power of the technologies of violence (cf. Kelly, 2004).

Whilst there can be no question that such technologies enabled significant levels of harm throughout the premodern period, is it possible to say anything about "how much", or to correlate this more specifically with violent crime? It seems clear enough that technological superiority in military terms was often a factor in promoting actions now prohibited by international law – in particular, genocide. The ingenuity of the Assyrians, for example, which led to new technologies of war like the siege engine, was highly respected, just as their proclivity for using it as a tool for slaughter was widely feared. Inscriptions left by their seventh-century BCE ruler Assurbanipal that celebrate how "I destroyed, I devastated, I burned with fire, I impaled their men with stakes over against their cities" indicate typical Assyrian technologies of subjugation (cf. Luckenbill, 1926, pp. 176–180). The use of technological power in supporting genocide was common, whether this was the dissection of Israel by the Roman military machine (up to 2,000,000 Jews killed [Josephus, 1987, ix 3]) or the Mongol hordes' use of disciplined cavalry to devastate central Asia – which even on conservative estimates left around 28 million dead (Rummel, 1998, lines 441–535). Sophisticated technological devices also facilitated extensive violence in state-sponsored entertainment. Suggestions that up to a million individuals may have died in the gladiatorial spectacles that took place between the advent of Imperial Rome (around 20 BCE) and the outlawing of combat as entertainment by the Emperor Constantine in around 325 CE indicate how effective this could be (Grant, 1967).

Violent crime seems to have been higher in the ancient world overall – a trend that continued into the late medieval period, when most historians and criminologists concur that a gradual decline began (see, amongst many here, Johnson and Monkkonen, 1996; Emsley, 1987). By the twelfth to the thirteenth centuries, the proportion of those who fell victim to violence in England may have been as high as 23 per 100,000 population (cf. Sharpe, 1996; Eisner, 2003) – a figure that fell to just under 7 per 100,000 by the 1600s, and still further to around 2 per 100,000 by the beginning of the nineteenth century (see also Beattie, 1986, chapters 3–4; Eisner, 2003). Such estimates are, of course, highly provisional at best, so that any conclusions about the kinds of tools or weapons that enabled this must also be treated with caution. Certain inferences seem plausible enough, however. Given that access to sword technologies would have been expensive, casualties resulting from this more "advanced" weapon were more likely to be associated with war or ritualised forms of combat like duelling than with opportunistic crime or crimes of passion. Duelling was not uncommon, even after it was criminalised – and could often be bloody. One estimate suggests that in France alone around 4,000 deaths between 1589 and 1607 could be attributed to duelling (Baldick, 1970), whilst around a third of the 172 duels recorded during the reign of George III of England (1760–1820) produced fatalities and two-thirds (96) serious woundings (cf. Norris, 2009). Legal restrictions upon who was permitted to carry swords (see below) also meant that "technologically enabled" violent crime was more likely to involve other, more improvised devices. For example, one study of violence in East Anglia during the period 1422–42 has suggested that over a quarter of murder cases were facilitated by everyday tools such as turf shovels or hedge stakes (Maddern, 1992). This pattern seems to be supported by an analysis of 364 killings investigated at assize courts in Hertfordshire and Sussex during the 1590s, which indicates that "the vast majority were not the result of calculated violence, rather they occurred during acts of sudden, unpremeditated aggression [involving] … a variety of knives and blunt instruments" (Cockburn, 1977, p. 57).

Not surprisingly, weapons technology also played a key role in assisting property-related crime. Robbery and theft comprised around three-quarters of offences tried before assize courts in the early 1300s – a proportion that seems to have remained fairly constant until the eighteenth century, when, like violent crime, it too began to fall (Sharpe, 1996, pp. 23ff). The use of clubs, garottes or stabbing instruments to effect such offences seems likely, though the advent of firearms from the sixteenth century began to dramatically widen the technological options. Around 7 per cent of robbery cases investigated in assizes during the 1540s involved the use of "pocket dags" or firearms – a trend that caused the Privy Council to lament that it was now "a common thing for … thieves to carry pistols" (cited in Cockburn, 1977, p. 57).

By the sixteenth century, Elizabethan tinkers had become notorious for concealing specialised burglars' tools in amongst their wares – one source relates how a knight who spotted a set of skeleton keys amongst a tinker's goods tricked him into carrying a letter to the next gaol, where he was promptly detained (Salgado, 1992). Specially designed tools like hooked staves were used to steal linen or clothes through windows and records of a dedicated profession associated with this – the "hooker" or hooksman – exist from at least the 1500s (cf. Harman, 1566; Taylor, 2010). Elsewhere, the gangs of "cutpurses" who plagued cities in the seventeenth and eighteenth centuries enhanced their already ingenious techniques for theft by using the simple but effective technology of close organisation. There is even evidence of technical skills like these being passed on in special underworld "schools" (Salgado, 1992). Enhancements to a thief's capacity might also be achieved through relatively "low-tech" options like animal, or even human, extensions to the body. There is evidence, for example, of a dog who was trained to pick pockets by one Tom Gerrard, a housebreaker executed at Newgate in 1711 (Rayner and Crook, 1926), and the use of young boys or "divers" who could climb through windows too small or high for adult thieves was a common technique (Hallsworth, 2005). But more sophisticated technologies were also used for theft. For example, George Clerk and John Ramsay, thieves executed at Newgate in 1675, were found to have administered various concoctions to their victims, including potions containing opium poppies, in order to put them to sleep whilst they were robbed (Rayner and Crook, 1926).

Much like today, property crime seems to have been a more fertile area for technological innovation than violent crime. One useful illustration of the ongoing technological struggle between crime and its prevention can be seen in various subversions of the "the purest example of the tool" (Simmel, 1978, p. 210) – money itself (cf. McGuire, 2007). The shift in monetary systems from simple barter towards coinage (Davies, 2002) required a number of supporting technologies such as metallurgy and coin-making devices, or more precise measurement tools like scales to ensure parity of exchange. But, as technology became central to sustaining monetary systems, so, in turn, were greater opportunities for technological innovation in stealing created, with the emergence of counterfeiting techniques from around 700 BCE – very soon after the first coins – being an early example (Davies, 2002). In Rome, forgery became one of the seven main categories of crime during Sulla's pre-Imperial reorganisation of the courts (Dillon and Garland, 2005, p. 529). Execution was the normal penalty for counterfeiting in China – especially after the introduction of paper money during the thirteenth-century Yuan dynasty, when warnings about fraud were printed on the notes. Like contemporary forms of hi-tech theft, the tactic of stealing money simply by copying it was the province of the criminal specialist, who had access to the necessary resources. "Insiders" – in particular those responsible for producing coinage – were especially likely to exploit their access privileges. The Emperor Nero perfected this form of state theft by continually debasing the Roman coinage – replacing up to 14 per cent of the silver in the denarius coin and 11 per cent of the gold in the aureus coin with base metals (cf. Butcher and Ponting, 2005). The fact that there was up to 60 per cent devaluation of the denarius (and its effective termination as a trading item) in early Imperial Rome indicates how widespread the practice was (ibid.). Even by the medieval period it remained a kind of economic policy for monarchs to raise capital in this way (Spufford, 1989, pp. 289ff). Status helped to determine the severity of punishment for counterfeiting – in Rome the penalty for forgery by slaves was death, compared to exile for freemen (Bauman, 1996), and there are numerous records of executions for this offence within other early societies. Later Visigoth law required serfs to have their right hand amputated, whilst high-status offenders were merely arrested (Cave and Coulson, 1965, pp. 128ff).

The lucrative possibilities raised by counterfeiting continued to stimulate technological innovations in copying into the medieval period. Venetian records indicate a rash of fake coins during the thirteenth and fourteenth centuries, and one renowned coin forger in Venice even set up a mini-mint in his own home. Here he was able to beat out copper ingots and then cut and stamp them using dies stolen from the mint (Stahl, 2008) – manufacturing over 13,000 fake coins even with these fairly limited technical resources (ibid.). Equally crucial to the success of premodern counterfeiting were the inadequate technologies for detecting it – in particular the lack of effective systems for checking the authenticity of coinage (cf. Singman, 2000).

Pre-industrial "hi-tech" crime?

As well as the use of simple technologies in enabling property or violent crime in the premodern period, there is also some evidence worth considering for the misuse of more complex tools, especially those involving communications technologies. Significantly, these saw a number of fundamental shifts over this period – from the invention of paper in China to the later advent of postal networks (Poe, 2011). If, as some theorists of communication have suggested, language itself can be viewed as a technology (McLuhan, 1964), then it might be argued that the earliest "communication" crimes involved its misuse (by lies or deceptions, for example). The severity of sanctions directed against deceit indicates the extent to which it violated norms in predominantly oral cultures. The Babylonian Code of Hammurabi was insistent that the offence of lying was so serious that the "hand of God" was the only power deemed to have the moral authority to punish it (King, 2004), though Roman law provided for more pragmatic penalties – in the Twelve Tables it was specified that liars should be hurled from the Tarpeian Rock in the centre of Rome (VII, 23, see IAS, 2011). The "bearing of false oaths" was still a serious offence by the time Anglo-Saxon law had become the predominant judicial system in northern Europe, though it now carried the lesser sentence of confinement for between 40 and 120 days (cf. Loyn, 1984; Magennis, 1995). However, "lie detection" technologies of the time were even more suspect than their contemporary equivalents. In Egypt, innocence was established only if a hot poker held to the tongue did not stick, whilst ancient Chinese law required suspected liars to talk with a mouth full of dry rice, with guilt proven should any fall out (cf. Kleinmuntz and Szucko, 1984).

Enacting harm from a distance – one of the key characteristics of contemporary communications crime – could be found within the prototype postal networks that began to enable interaction over wider ranges. Though the method of dispensation was less instantaneous, early long-distance messaging technology could facilitate assassinations, conspiracies or frauds. The arrival of the magnetic compass from China by the thirteenth century was another technology that extended social interaction ranges and the general increase in pillage and piracy from the fifteenth century on – especially following the discovery of the gold-rich Americas (cf. Lewis, 1937; Garner, 2002) – might be associated with this. But one of the *loci classici* for an association between communications technology and crime in the pre-modern era came with the advent of printing in Europe during the fifteenth century. The surge in intellectual property theft involving unauthorised reproductions of original texts and pamphlets that followed was complemented by a rise in the reproduction of fake official documents such as letters of authentication, court orders and so on (cf. Hiatt, 2004 for some examples). And with this technological shift came a new kind of nomos around property and technology that is still of central importance – the development of legal structures protecting the "right" to copy (Deazley *et al.*, 2010).

Offences involving the second class of "high" technologies discussed in this book – those centred upon chemical or biological phenomena – are less obvious in the pre-industrial period, though still identifiable. The period was not entirely divorced from the use of such phenomena, though this was of course based more upon practical, folk knowledge than on genuine scientific understanding. The result was that superstition was as likely to shape the uses of these technologies as was informed knowledge – Ellul (1992), for example, discusses prohibitions against the use of iron tools to till the soil in case this offended against the natural order. Perhaps one of the most obvious tools of this kind was chemical, involving the use of poisons that could be extracted from a variety of sources, including plants such as aconite, minerals such as arsenic and, of course, snake venom. The ancient Egyptians displayed a sophisticated understanding of chemistry in their embalming techniques and were more than ready to use this knowledge punitively. For those suspected of passing on priestly secrets execution "under the penalty of the peach" (Blyth and Blyth, 1906, §II) – involving the use of pnissic acid extracted from peaches – was the sentence. The scale of poisoning in the ancient world is evidenced in the fact that the world's first law specifically prohibiting it – the Lex Cornelia – was passed by the Roman lawmaker Sulla in around 82 BCE (Wax, 2006). In turn, the penchant for using poison as an assassination tool meant that the "food taster" became an essential technology of security in royal courts from China to Persia and beyond (cf. Emsley, 2006). By the middle ages, the proclivity of the Borgias and other leaders for engaging in spectacular "dinner-party" executions of their rivals (Collard, 2008) had created a need for further security technologies of this kind. Silversmiths began to construct cups made from materials like agate, rock-crystal or ostrich shells – substances believed to indicate the presence of poisons in liquids (ibid.). Seventeenth-century Venice and Rome were even reputed to host "schools of poisoning" where students were instructed in differing poison types and methods of administering them, along with the chance to study specialist texts such as Porta's *Natural Magic* with its detailed "how to" sections (Emsley, 2006).

The use of biological knowledge and technology in assisting deviance was less obvious, though something like this might be seen in practices like infant exposure. For, in a sense, these were crude attempts to manage the gene pool – by disposing of unwanted genetic variants like females, or disabled infants (Patterson, 1985; Boswell, 1988). The practice was especially tolerated in both Greece and Rome, and Roman commentators of the time were puzzled by the failure of other ancient civilisations to engage in it – Strabo, for example, thought the Egyptians most odd because they "raised every child that was born" (Strabo, 1932, 17.2.5). However, the fact that children were often abandoned in temples where they could be collected by childless couples indicates that the custom was probably not intentional biological malpractice.

Not surprisingly, some of the more sophisticated uses of bio-chemical technology to enact harm are to be found within the theatre of war. From China and Iran to India or Europe there were ingenious ways in which biological or chemical substances were used to enhance military capacity. One popular tactic was to dispatch chemicals into enemy ranks as a way of sowing confusion and/or death – most often in the form of noxious smoke. So-called "Greek fire" (an incendiary weapon made from a chemical formula now lost) was used as a form of defence by the Byzantine Empire against the Turks for over 500 years and the suggestion by Sun Tzu, the Chinese general, that what he called "fire weapons" were useful devices on the battlefield (2009) appears to have been heeded, given records of Chinese armies using incendiary bombs (Roland, 1992; Mayor, 2003). Aggressive uses of pathogens and toxins can also be seen in the deployment of so-called "scorpion bombs", which were sometimes catapulted into enemy cities and troop formations (Mayor, 2003). Awareness that infections could be spread aggressively seem to have been widespread, so that early forms of biological warfare, usually involving attempts to spread diseases, complemented the use of incendiary chemicals on the battlefield. Ancient swordsmen were reputed to smear human faeces on their swords in order to create infections and there are also stories of arrows dipped into putrefied human blood for the same end (Mayor, 2003). Prototypical bio-warfare was most dramatically extended in the notorious Siege of Caffa in 1346, when the Tartar armies catapulted the corpses of plague victims into the city (Wheelis, 2002); but attempts to contaminate water sources by the use of diseased animal carcasses were more common. It was not until the Strasbourg Agreement of 1675 (between France and Holy Roman Empire) that the use of "odious toxic devices" was first made the subject of explicit legal prohibitions (cf. Zanders, 2003).

Regulating technology in the pre-industrial era

This attempt to control the use of toxins in war appears to be a rare instance of technological regulation in the pre-industrial era, but such efforts were not entirely absent. One more obvious example centred upon the rules of access to technology, and the role of class and status in determining this has already been noted. Thus, slaves were forbidden to carry any kind of weaponry in most ancient societies – unless in the strict service of their masters (Mendelsohn, 1932; Westermann, 1984). There were similar restrictions in the medieval period, when only lords, knights and privileged commoners were entitled to bear arms (cf. Kacuper, 1988). But control of weapons might also be determined by where they were carried – such as in the prohibitions governing sacred or high-security zones. In Rome, no one was permitted to carry weapons into the inner city of Rome proper – the *pomoerium* – and even the Praetorian guards, the military elite responsible for protecting the emperor, were compelled to wear civilian dress when entering this part of the city (Beard *et al.*, 1998).

As today, the control of communications technology was subject to the interests of power, though public morality also exerted a certain influence. Indeed the very term "censor" originates from the original Roman office where the main duty of counting the public in a "census" was augmented by the task of overseeing texts considered to offend against public morality (Suolahti, 1963). In early China, Emperor Qin Shi Huang's assertion that the kingdom needed protection from the "dangers" of poetry, history and philosophy resulted in ruthless controls over communication, including the burning of every book except those dealing with agriculture, medicine or prophecy (Bacz, 2008). With the advent of printing, issues around censorship and freedom of expression were brought into a new focus, and blasphemy and sedition quickly figured as the most common offences. The flood of new texts led to Pope Paul IV issuing the first "Index of Prohibited Books" in 1559 (a list which continued until 1948), whilst monarchs such as France's Charles IX attempted to prevent the publication of any printed document without express royal permission (cf. Polastron, 2007). In England, an explosion of seditious pamphlets around the Civil War period highlighted the political problems posed by the new printing technologies. Just five printers had existed in London in 1500, but a surge in new "start-up" businesses followed the advent of cheaper type-face technologies, significantly extending possibilities for public information and expression. Cromwell's Printing Act of 1649 attempted to stem this tide, restricting the printing of pamphlets to London and imposing a requirement for licences (Seibert, 1952). But arrests and imprisonment for "seditious pamphleting" continued into the eighteenth century – even the author Daniel Defoe became a high-profile victim in 1702 (cf. Thomas, 1969).

A crucial factor in shaping modern technology regulation was of course the development of modern science from the fourteenth and fifteenth centuries onward. The various attempts to impose control over the practice of alchemy – the predecessor of modern chemistry – highlight some of the fascinating contradictions of this emerging technical nomos. For alchemy was both sponsored and suppressed, depending upon the interests at work. The received view – that alchemy was forbidden because it involved "consorting with demons" – is certainly not false; the figure of Dr Faustus reflects wide public unease about the alchemists' aim of transmuting base metals into gold, or finding an "elixir of life" (Haynes, 2006). But other, less metaphysical rationales were also involved in attempts to suppress it. One set of concerns centred upon whether the creation of alchemical gold would result a currency that was "legal" (a so-called "specie") for exchange (Nummedal, 2007, p. 110). There were also suspicions of fraud, with texts like Maier's *Examen Fucurom Pseudo-Chymicorum* detailing common tricks used to simulate the "transmutation" of gold. Pope John XXII's ruling of 1317 charged alchemists that they "spondent quas non exhibent" (promise what they do not produce) and specified punishments such as branding or immolation, whilst Charles V of France banned the use of alchemical equipment altogether in 1380. Other monarchs were more pragmatic – Edward III of England, for example, employed two alchemists in the hope that they might be able to produce gold at will, and subsequent monarchs followed this line (cf. Nummedal, ibid.). But fears of devil-worship meant that public attitudes were less tolerant. The private home of the celebrated alchemist Dr Dee – Elizabeth I's private astrologer – was ransacked by a mob whilst he was away and John Lambe, a confidant of the Duke of Buckingham, was stoned to death by an angry mob in London after being exposed by the Royal Society in 1627 (Salgado, 1992). The new scientific method was also subject to suppression – for example, Galileo's development of the telescope led to one of the more notorious attempts by the state to regulate science. When he published details of what he had observed through this new, distance-compressing technology as evidence of the "heretic" Copernican heliocentric model of the solar system, Galileo was tried and convicted by the papacy and placed under house arrest until his death (Reston, 1994).

More mundane forms of technological regulation can be seen in controls around public health and industrial technology. In his third satire, Juvenal complained of the "smoke pouring out of buildings" in Rome (1992), whilst the foul smells generated by the use of urine in the fulleries meant that the dyeing of clothes was restricted to specially designated areas of the city (Wacke, 2002). There were also Roman by-laws controlling drains and the production of effluent (Wacke, ibid.; see also Bauman, 1996; Harries, 2007). The prototypical industrial technologies of the medieval world generated similar complaints about public nuisance and threats to health. Amongst the earliest known attempts at emission controls were those enacted against the burning of sea coal in the city of London in 1306, with certain offenders even being executed for breaching these rules (Isaac, 1953).

City officials appear to have been equally preoccupied by noise pollution – a 1397 edict, highlighting blacksmiths' culpability for the "great nuisance, noise, and alarm experienced in divers ways by neighbours around their dwellings" (Geddes, 1990, p. 174–75) required them to relocate away from settled areas. Regulation was also aimed at protecting professional standards and conduct within industry. Spurriers (or spur-makers) – a specialised variety of blacksmiths – seem to have acquired a particular reputation for drunkenness, and the fires used in their production processes often burned "to the great peril of themselves and the whole neighbourhood" (ibid.). As in Rome, exasperated residents sometimes took up civil cases against anti-social industrial producers. In 1377 a London armourer named Stephen atte Fryth had formal complaints taken out against him on the grounds that "the blows of the sledge-hammer when the great pieces of iron ... are being wrought into ... armor, shake the stone and earthen party walls of the plaintiffs' house ... and disturb the rest of the plaintiffs and their servants, day and night" (ibid.). Such controls seem to have done little to stem the growth of industrial pollution in the capital. By the 1600s the essayist John Evelyn was complaining about the "hellish smoke of (London) town ... [which] ... impairs the health of its inhabitants" (Evelyn, 1995). Following the Great Fire of 1666, Evelyn suggested that the king impose a variety of early "zoning controls" over industry during the rebuilding of London, expressing the hope that

> the necessary evils of brewhouses, bakehouses, dyers, salt, soap and sugar boilers will now [be dispersed] to some other parts about the river towards Bow and Wandsworth.
>
> (1995/1998, p. 154)

Some of the most demanding controls we know of were directed at the technologies of agriculture and food production. There are of course well-recorded religious codes governing food hygiene and consumption in the Middle East, India and elsewhere, but wherever food production became more industrialised, formal state controls seem also to have been imposed. Ensuring adequate supplies of food and water to large population centres was an obvious technological necessity from the very earliest times and is evidenced by the detailed regulations imposed upon this. In sixth-century BCE Athens, the laws of Solon set out concise prescriptions on where and how to extract water (Plutarch, 1914, Vol. I), and effective management of the complex systems of pumps, water-wheels and aqueducts that later supplied Rome required a specialised cadre of technocrats – the *curatores aquarum* (cf. Berger, 1953). In Egypt, meat inspectors were employed to check quality, whilst in Republican Rome baking was a heavily supervised activity, under the auspices of special officials (the *aediles*) (Erdkamp, 2005). In medieval York, laws were imposed prohibiting the sale of meat kept for more than 24 hours and there are numerous records of innkeepers and shopkeepers who were prosecuted for selling pies containing undercooked or tainted meat. (cf. Carlin, 1998). But of all the varieties of technological regulation in the pre-industrial world, amongst the most developed involved rules around health and medicine. We know of rich medical traditions stretching back as far as ancient Egypt, where Herodotus noted how "there are plenty of physicians everywhere. Some are eye-doctors, some deal with the head, others with the teeth or the belly" (2004, II). The Babylonian Code of Hammurabi contained at least ten laws specifically directed at medical practice – some stipulating extremely harsh sanctions for failure, for example:

> If a doctor has treated a man with a metal knife for a severe wound, and has caused the man to die, or has opened a man's tumor with a metal knife and destroyed the man's eye, his hands shall be cut off.
> (King, 2004, p. 218)

This "lex talionis" approach towards medical regulation was certainly a strong incentive for doctors to avoid error (cf. Magner, 1992), but more informal regulation also played a part in shaping medical practice – especially in controlling those permitted to practise. In Egypt, only certain classes or castes could practise medicine, and similar restrictions seem to have operated in Babylon and India (Carrick, 1991).

The reputation of Egyptian medicine was eventually paralleled by Greek practitioners – most famously the surgeon Hippocrates, who advocated a more recognisably scientific approach to the body, commending observation over superstition. Though he authored a number of other texts with technological themes (Cuomo, 2008), Hippocrates remains best known for his ethical prescriptions around medical practice, with the "Hippocratic oath" still recited as a symbolic rite of passage by doctors in many jurisdictions (cf. Temkin, 2002). Standards of medical practice were especially fastidious within the Islamic world, where texts such as Ali Ruhawi's tenth-century *Adab al-Tabib* (Ethics of a Physician) or Abu al-Hasan Al-Tabari's ninth-century work *Firdous al-Hikmat* (The Paradise of Wisdom) echoed Hippocrates' commitment to developing rules for "good practice". Some suggestions – such as the advice that doctors should "wear clean clothes, be dignified, and have well-groomed hair and beard" (cited in Al-Ghazal, 2004) were more about hygiene and presentation than technical proficiency, but there were also restrictions on certain medical practices. In the *al-Tabib*, for example, doctors were recommended not to "give drugs to a pregnant woman for an abortion unless necessary for the mother's health" (Al-Ghazal, ibid.).[2] The preference for professional codes and self-determining standards in the Greek and Arabic worlds indicates a desire to keep central government out of medical regulation – a philosophy maintained in the modern era by bodies such as the General Medical Council (GMC) in the UK, or the American Medical Association (AMA).

Inevitably, religious authority also played its part in regulating early medical practice with various moral directives, such as restrictions on anatomical dissection. However, the belief that damage to the physical body might undermine chances of resurrection was not limited to Christian contexts – pre-Christian Rome also held dissection to be sacrilegious, and there are records of prohibitions enforced by the Emperor Antonius Pius (cf. Toynbee, 1996). Such restrictions significantly impacted upon the work of physicians like Galen, who was forced to work in Pergamum, where a nearby gladiators' school provided him with legitimate opportunities to further his anatomical knowledge by examining their wounds (cf. Hankinson, 2008).

The "self-regulatory" brakes upon medical practice imposed by professional codes of conduct were gradually supplemented by more formal legal controls. The fourth-century CE Codex Theodosianus indicates the existence of a highly formalised hierarchical system of medical control in late Rome, overseen by the *Comes Archiatorum* – a kind of "chief surgeon" who presided over a group of around 14 medical officials known as *archiater* (cf. Matthews, 2000). Some were directly assigned to the emperor, others to the public, and their main role was to supervise local doctors (*medici*) in the districts they presided over or to arbitrate in medical disputes. In what seems to have been a kind of prototypical state medical system they were also paid by the state to provide free care for the poor. Elsewhere, the Justinian code of 529 CE was one of the earliest legal systems requiring education and proof of competence for doctors, with penalties for malpractice and limitations upon the numbers of practitioners. In Europe as a whole, the hiatus in centralised control of medical practice and technology that came with the fall of Rome did not last for too long. By 1140 Roger II of Sicily had passed edicts that required properly organised medical teaching with "set courses, examinations and qualifications", a precedent followed soon afterwards, in 1224, by the Holy Roman Emperor Frederick II (Gradwohl, 1976).

Pre-industrial technology control and regulation by technology

Evidence within the premodern era that technology was not only regulated but also served *to* regulate is most obviously seen in its use as an enhancer of power. Superior access to military technologies – iron swords over bronze swords, for example – is a clear example of its direct contribution to control, though control by technology could also be manifested in more unusual ways. In ancient India, for example, the secret services used an ingenious form of early bio-control in the form of female agents (*visakanyas* or "poison damsels") who saturated their bodies with poisons in order to execute enemies of the state by tempting them with sex (Penzer, 1980).[3] More predictable, however, was the use of early communication technologies to strengthen control.

Control and early ICTs

The use of written records as a technology for bolstering sovereign power has been widely noted (cf. Innis, 1950/2007). Successful management of the new agriculturally based empires like Egypt or Sumer depended heavily upon a capacity to maintain records – such as of the annual flood levels of the Nile, or the amount of grain kept in the royal storehouses. With this technology came a new social class – the scribes – a prototypical information elite that wielded significant power. In Sumer their role in overseeing legal contracts and processes gave them a unique access to the workings of the state (Sjöberg, 1975). Scribes were even more powerful in Egypt, since they were also often members of the priesthood.

The development of state messaging networks complemented writing and record keeping with the creation of distinctive "communication" based forms of power. Early optical or sonic messaging technologies (like fire beacons or drums) may have been rudimentary, but, organised properly, could still be highly effective ways of extending political reach. King Darius of Persia, for example, reputedly created a system where messengers stood on hilltops and shouted to each other – thereby delivering messages over distances that might take up to 30 days to cover on foot (Diodorus Siculus, 1947, 19.17 5–6). Networks based upon couriers working on foot or by horse could be even more effective. For example, the power of the Inca emperors had much to do with their postal system, which was operated by relay runners called "chasqui", stationed every 1.4 kilometres on the mail trail. The system reputedly provided a one-day delivery for every 150 miles of road and permitted emperors to enforce their dictates quickly and efficiently (cf. Hyslop, 1984).

In England, the first integrated postal system was created by Henry VIII – and was immediately associated with extensions to surveillance power (Brayshay *et al.*, 1998), serving as it did as "the government's mouthpiece, eyes, and ears" (Ellis, 1958). A "secret office" that existed alongside the official service was authorised (by royal warrant) to open and intercept any mail and pass on material of interest to the Secretary of State (Desai, 2007). By the late 1700s warrants had also been issued requiring that the mail of the political opposition or foreign diplomats could be opened as a matter of course (ibid.). The reputation of the British Post Office for surveillance became so bad that citizens in the American colonies were determined to establish a parallel "constitutional post" – first set up by Goddard during 1774, and adopted as the model for the American system as a whole in the Second Continental Congress of 1775. Goddard's messaging system aspired to new, more ethical principles of communication which required that "mails shall be under lock and key, and liable to the inspection of no person but the respective Postmasters to whom directed" (cited in ibid., p. 50).

The widespread disrespect for privacy rights in the United Kingdom and the philosophy that "secrecy made legality unimportant" (ibid., p. 25) was manifested within every succeeding shift in communications technology. For example, the surge in public communication that followed the introduction of the uniform penny post in the 1840s significantly extended surveillance practices. This pattern – enhanced communication technology, followed by enhanced scrutiny – has some obvious parallels with later technologies like the internet, especially in the lack of accountability or transparency. Following a letter-opening scandal in 1844, a House of Commons committee defined the direction in which communications control was heading, remarking that "to leave it a mystery whether or not [the] power is ever exercised, is the way best calculated to deter the evil-minded from applying the post to improper use" (cited in Pedersen, 2006).

Premodern bio-control: disciplining the body

Early forms of chemical control in the premodern world can be seen in the use of poison, which was as useful for technological regulation as it was for crime. Other technologies of bio-chemical control were centred more upon the macro-level and the use of the body as a disciplinary subject. Amongst the milder examples here were restraint technologies like the stocks, or the cangue (or wooden collar) used in China. But premodern bio-control also developed a sophisticated variety of technologies that turned the body into a site of pain delivery. These technologies of pain dispensation were sometimes used for primitive judgments of guilt – as in the practice of the "ordeal". Here, rudimentary technologies of fire and water were used to decide culpability (Lea, 1973; Leeson, 2010) – for example, suspects were required to retrieve a ring from a cauldron of boiling water or to carry a piece of red-hot metal a predetermined distance. Innocence or guilt was then established by the extent to which the body could subsequently "regenerate" itself within a predetermined period of time.

Pain dispensation within premodern justice systems reached an apogee of technical sophistication in the practice of torture. Chinese authorities displayed a particular ingenuity in this regard – for example, in the use of the "Pao-Luo" (human grill), seen during the Zhou dynasty, where suspects were forced to walk across heated metal beams, or the later "death by a thousand cuts", where considerable bio-medical expertise was deployed in inflicting the maximum possible pain upon victims (van Gulick, 2008). The classical world was no less accomplished in the creation of sophisticated torture devices – for example, the "brazen bull" involved placing victims inside a hollow bronze-cast bull which was slowly heated over an open fire. A complex technology of tubes and airstops then turned the dying screams of the victim(s) into a sound resembling the braying of a bull – providing additional amusement for spectators (Dubois, 1991). By the medieval period an impressive array of torture technology attested to the ongoing development of a "science" of pain delivery. One the best-known artefacts, the rack, may have been a fairly simple piece of engineering, but in the hands of a skilled operator could attain very precise correlations between the turning of the handles and targeted pain delivery (not too much or too little). And of course the rack was often merely an "entrée" into a far wider field of pain-delivery technologies. There was, for example, the "Judas Cradle", which required a victim to be seated on a triangular-shaped seat where he or she was slowly impaled. Or the "Chair of Torture" – a formidable piece of engineering incorporating anything between 500 to 1,500 spikes that covered the back, arm-rests, seat, leg-rests and foot-rests. As the victim's wrists were tied to the chair any struggles made the spikes penetrate the flesh even further. More highly engineered versions also provided for holes under the chair's seat where hot coals could be placed in order to "enhance" the agonies of a victim's puncture wounds with severe burns. Similarly fiendish ingenuity was at work in the (largely self-explanatory) function of devices such as the "pear of anguish", the "breast ripper", the "thumbscrew" or the "knee splitter" (see Innes, 1998 and Kellaway, 2002 for these and other examples). Executions too could be fairly developed technological spectacles – even the gallows could be a precision instrument, providing instant death through a broken neck, or the long, lingering and painful variety associated with the infamous "hangman's dance".

But the premodern world was not completely lacking in more evidentially based forms of crime control – and there were even precedents for the use of chemical or biological tools in shaping this. Almost every history of forensic science begins with tales of the Chinese judge Song Ci, who worked around the thirteenth century (cf. McKnight, 1981). In his memoirs, *Collected Cases of Injustice Rectified*, Song Ci discusses a number of cases over which he presided where "forensic" style techniques were used. One famous example involved a man who had been murdered with what appeared to be a sickle. In order to detect the murderer, the investigator instructed everyone in the village to bring their sickle to a pre-arranged location where flies, attracted by the lingering smell of blood, eventually gathered on a particular one – so forcing the owner to confess to his crime. Elsewhere, the Caroline Code of 1533 (proclaimed by the Holy Roman Emperor, Charles V) was one of the first regulatory systems to suggest that expert medical testimony might be required in order to guide judges in cases of "murder, wounding, poisoning, hanging, drowning, infanticide, and abortion and in other circumstances involving injury to the person" (Polsky and Beresford, 1943).

Though science had clearly not yet developed sufficiently for the contemporary "gold standard" in establishing guilt – genetic information – to be available, the body could be used to provide other physical indicators. For example, heart and pulse rates, or the extent to which a suspect blushed during questioning, were advanced as methods for "reading" evidence of deviant actions or intentions at various points. In his 1730 Essay "An Effectual Scheme for the Immediate Preventing of Street Robberies and Suppressing all Other Disorders of the Night", the writer Daniel Defoe suggested how an investigator might apply such techniques, arguing: "take hold of [an offender's] wrist and feel his pulse, there you shall find his guilt", for it is impossible for "the most firm resolution of even the most harden'd offender [to] conceal and cover it" (cited in Matté, 1996, p. 11). But Defoe was also concerned about the kind of justice involved in "making a man ... evidenced against himself" (ibid.) – a concern that has become no less pressing for subsequent generations.

Industrialisation, Luddism and the new technomia

Defoe's comments reflect a world in transition – not just in terms of industrialisation, but in terms of the justice process and the "scientific", technology-centric system that was about to emerge. There are obvious dangers in being too definitive about when the merging of science and industrial technology into the "complex" (cf. Mumford, 1934) of an "industrial revolution" took place. For example, developments between 1870 and 1914 – which included new forms of power (especially electricity), communications (telegraph and telephone), transportation (aeroplanes and the internal combustion engine – the car), production (most obviously Fordist mass production) and mass media (such as film and photography) have sometimes been identified as a far more significant phase of technological change than the late eighteenth and early nineteenth centuries (cf. Landes, 2003). Given that this later period also saw the birth of the modern corporation – one of the key influences upon an equally significant shift, the mass commodification of technical artefacts – the idea of a "single-phase" industrial revolution clearly requires caution. But, however one periodises industrialisation, there is no doubting the huge shift in productive power generated within its earlier phases. New technologies like Hargreaves' Spinning Jenny meant that, by 1790 alone, something like ten times more yarn was being made than in 1770, and by 1800 spinning had become the main industry in the UK. Elsewhere, coking and blast furnaces improved annual iron production from around 50,000 tonnes at the beginning of the nineteenth century to over 10 million tonnes by its end (Jackson, 1996).

But with production growth came a range of harmful impacts upon social mobility, income, communication and leisure. An increasing concentration of the population into factory production centres, the disruption of families through long working hours and child labour, or the creation of widespread poverty in the midst of plenty (cf. Hobsbawn, 1969) all fuelled the emerging pessimism about technology that was discussed in Chapter 1. Nor were such doubts restricted to intellectuals like Morris, Ruskin or Carlyle. For those upon whom technological change most immediately impacted – the workforces within the new mills and factories – more concrete resistance quickly became evident, provoking what has since become an emblematic instance of "anti-technologism". The spark was a series of disturbances that took place in stocking manufactories in Nottingham-shire between 1811–12 – provoked by the introduction of a new kind of spinning/weaving machine for making stockings more cheaply, though at a lower quality. A series of letters began to be sent to factory owners signed by one "General Ned Ludd and his Army of Redressers", which demanded justice for sacked workers. Within a few weeks a wave of factory break-ins had begun that resulted in the destruction of more than 200 of the new machines. Elsewhere, mills were besieged or torched and unrest began to spread to other parts of the countryside in what was soon dubbed the "Luddite" uprising (even though "Ned Ludd" was almost certainly a fictitious figure and it was never an "uprising").

The response of the governing elite set another precedent for this new order – a readiness to favour the interests of new technology over the rights and livelihoods of working people. Over 12,000 troops were quickly dispatched to Nottingham – a larger force even than Wellington had used during the Peninsular War (Thomis, 1970) – and by June of 1812 an inti-midating army of 30,000 soldiers were camped out on the moors above Manchester, ready to crush any further signs of protest. The use of military force was quickly complemented by draconian new legislative controls, like the Frame-Breaking Act of 1812, which stipulated the death penalty for anyone daring to damage this new device.

The reality of these "Luddite" disturbances and their subsequent portrayal as the paradigmatic example of resistance to new technology is, however, questionable. In fact the Luddites were only one part of a tradition of opposition to industrialisation seen in working-class England. From the Plaisterers' Insurrection of 1586, the Felt-Makers' Riot of 1591, the Southwark Candle-Makers' Riot of 1592, and the tearing down of fences by the "Levellers" in their protest against land enclosure, there had been a long history of technological change generating resistance in England (Stevenson, 1979; Brenner 1995; see also Randall, 1995 and 2004, p. xiii). And anti-machine rioting continued for some time after the events of 1812, with the Lancashire power-loom riots of 1826 proving especially violent (Randall, 1995). It also seems clear that Luddite animosity was directed more at those manufacturers who had acquired huge wealth very quickly (usually by treating their workforces with extreme harshness) than at the technology per se. Nor was there any general attack upon stocking-making machines by protestors – only the "wide frame" versions held to be respon-sible for "deceitfully wrought" garments were targeted (Randall, 1995; cf. Jones, 2006 for similar qualifications). Thus, though the charge of "Luddism" has been a common way of delegitimating challenges to tech-nology, there were more important legacies from the protest than a stubborn refusal to embrace technological change. Not only did the protests help to inspire the mass social movements that sought to provide better conditions for those disadvantaged by technologisation. They also issued a new kind of challenge – to create a coherent body of law, regulation and control around our technological enhancements. It is one that remains, as yet, unanswered.

Urbanisation, crime and control: the new spaces of crime

One of the most significant of the new technological forms that emerged with industrialisation was the modern city – though this is not something that has always been seen as technological per se. Of course, as technological "complexes", cities have always enhanced our species' capacity to live in closer proximity, in greater numbers and in greater comfort – offering as they do more effective sewage and waste disposal technologies, enhanced provision of shelter and better access to food. But the power of the industrial city is witnessed in the sheer scale of the demographic reorganisations they facilitated. It took over 200 years between 1500–1750 for the population of England to double (from 3 million to 6 million) but less than a hundred (between 1780 to 1860) for the figure to double again, a doubling process then repeated in less than 40 years, between 1860 and 1900 (Jeffries, 2005). The exponential growth in population facilitated by the shift towards urban centres meant that, by 1900, most of the UK's population was living in towns and cities such as London (where the population trebled from around 750,000 to around 3 million by 1900), Liverpool (where it rose from 22,000 to 450,000) or Manchester (up from 18,000 to 376,000) (ibid.).

The shifts in the nature of crime and control that followed can be closely associated with the development of densely populated urban centres. A first, and obvious, set of consequences was related to a seeming increase in the volume and variety of criminal opportunities. On the one hand, higher levels of wealth – particularly amongst the newly affluent middle classes – created larger numbers of potential victims. In turn, this new wealth also accelerated social division, with the proximity of the very poor to the very rich evidenced in Booth's poverty maps of London (Booth, 2010) producing obvious temptations for illicit acquisition. And the densely packed structures and streets of the modern city provided for greater anonymity for would-be criminals, and more places to "disappear" (cf. Emsley, 1987).

Rapid urbanisation created widespread perceptions of a rise in crime – especially in relation to property offences. Engels, for example, reported that crime was "higher in Britain than any other country in the world" (see Philips, 1993, p. 158) and figures for crime, published for the first time in 1810 by the UK government, suggested that the 4,000 or so individuals indicted for trial in 1805 had risen to over 31,000 by 1842 (Philips, ibid.). Later commentators have also interpreted such figures to imply a "vast increase in crime" (Perkin, 1969, p. 162) during the early industrial period – whether in terms of volume or of organisation – i.e. the emergence of new street gangs (Hobbs, 1994, pp. 444–45). But some caution is also necessary, especially as it has become clearer how readily technological change is associated with a perception of new crime waves. A common counter-argument – that any rises in crime can be attributed to rises in the population (rather than any increase in offending itself) – is slightly undermined by the fact that the rise in the recorded crime rate was nearly double the percentage increase in population (Taylor, 2010). However, the number of new offences created over this period may have inflated figures somewhat – in 1833 alone, for example, the list of serious crimes was increased from 50 to 73 (Taylor, ibid.). How best to interpret crime data over this period has been the subject of complex debates (see for example Tobias, 1972; Sindall, 1990; Hudson, 1992; Taylor, 2010).

Any argument that technological processes like industrialisation or urbanisation caused a rise in crime must also be considered in the light of the new technologies designed to control it – most obviously what Ellul called the "technical apparatus of the police" (1992). For, given the new capacities for detection and arrest that this brought, any "rise in crime" may simply have been a rise in prosecutions (see Emsley, 1987 for one version of this argument). Officials at the time were well aware of this possibility, an 1827 Cabinet report indicating that:

> only a portion of cases committed for trial … is to be deemed indicative of a proportionate increase in crime and that even of that proportion, much may be accounted for in the more ready detection and trial of culprits.
>
> (Cited in Philips, 1993, p. 159)

Certain qualifications therefore seem to be required before the conclusion that crime "rose" over the period of industrialisation can be accepted, still less that it was technology that was responsible. For example, the fact that indictable offences fell by over a third between 1850 and 1900 – when a plethora of new technologies, from electricity to the automobile, emerged (Taylor, 2010, p. 18) might suggest a different conclusion.

Whatever the verdict on levels of crime, the contribution of industrialisation to contemporary technological justice seems clear enough. For with it came a variety of tools now central to any modern criminal justice system. In addition to the police themselves, these might also include:

1   A new class of specialised, technology-driven crime experts – the "detectives".
2   Prototypical crime science methods that these agencies could draw upon – such as blood analysis, fingerprinting or the use of statistical mapping.
3   A shift in the technology of penality and punishment, away from "premodern" spectacles and towards new, more "humane" forms of control centred on the prison.

4   A rise in other technologies of scientised social control, such as asy-
     lums or hospitals and the creation of the disciplined body.
5   The emergence of new theories of criminality, in particular, a new
     discipline directed at the scientific understanding of crime, regulation
     and control – criminology itself.

Hi-tech crime and control in the nineteenth century

What conclusions might be drawn about the uses of more advanced technologies in the nineteenth century – particularly the ICTs and CBNTs that
will be the focus of the rest of this book? In terms of offending, there are
clear lessons to be drawn from the way new technologies of communications
and transport, like the telegraph or the railways, were perceived at the time.
Certainly, no one ever spoke of "telegraph crime" or "railway crime", and
any new offending patterns that emerged cannot be separated from the new
class of offences designed to manage them. For example, in the ten years
after 1895 there was a 50 per cent rise in the number of cyclists prosecuted,
along with a sharp rise in motoring offences – though this was clearly connected more to the new laws around transportation than to any specific
upsurge in technology crime (Taylor, 2010, p. 21). As seems typical with new
technology, there were also less rational concerns. In 1862, for example, the
Railway Traveller's Handy Book warned passengers that: "In going through
a tunnel it is always as well to have the hands and arms disposed for defence
so that in the event of an attack the assailant may be immediately beaten
back or restrained." Such advice followed upon a series of scares about an
influx of thieves and con-men onto the new train system (Kalla-Bishop,
1977), just as the advent of the telephone provoked worries that it might
help to extend the power of organised crime (Pool, 1983; McGuire, 2007).
Such concerns seem minor compared to contemporary hyperbole – even
though the impression made upon the public by these new communication,
information and transport technologies was equal to anything we have
seen with the internet. Huge crowds flocked to demonstrations of the new
telegraphic technology and the *Illustrated London News* reported how
"public jubilees" and "systematic displays of popular joy" took place in
the USA following the laying of the Atlantic cable in 1858 (Illustrated
London News, 1858).

The rapid exploitation of communications technology for control
purposes has stronger resonances with contemporary experience. The pre-
cursor to the electronic telegraph – the optical signalling system developed
by Claude Chappe – was under French state control from the outset
and the very first message it carried (on 15 August 1794) was a military
communiqué reporting French success in retaking the city of Le Quesnoy
from the Austrians and the Prussians (Coe, 1993, p. 6). It was not long
before the new criminal justice agencies also took advantage of it – even
by the late 1840s UK police had used the telegraph to apprehend two

high-profile suspects (Standage, 1998; McGuire, 2007). By 1856, police forces in Boston, Philadelphia and New York had created telegraph networks linking chiefs' headquarters to precinct offices, with others quickly following suit (Tarr, 1992, p. 10). Riots and outbreaks of urban unrest in the emerging US cities between the 1830s and the 1860s provided further motivations for enhanced police communication. Municipal authorities established large reserve forces ready to intervene at the first signs of disorder, and telegraphic alarm systems connected to precinct headquarters were sited along the beats of police officers. As the Mayor of Philadelphia commented in 1855, "Now the police force has but one soul, and that soul is the telegraph" (cited in Tarr, 1992, pp. 10–11). Citizens were not slow to recognise the function of this "soul" in enabling the suppression of their protests. During the draft riots of the 1860s in New York, rioters attacked telegraph poles and pulled down lines to impede police responses (Tarr, ibid.)

The advent of the telephone enhanced the power of police communications still further. The technology was quickly used to link police stations in Albany, New York State (Thomas, 1974), and by the early 1880s experiments were being conducted in Chicago on the use of the telephone as an operational device (ibid.). Combined telegraph/telephone signalling points emerged, with patrol wagons situated at each precinct office ready to respond to calls for assistance. "Success" was both immediate and dramatic – in the USA arrests facilitated by these new call boxes rose from 6 to 44 per cent of the total between 1881 and 1885 (Tarr, 1992, p. 12; Stewart, 1994). As the *Scientific American* presciently observed, civic organisation would now become

> sensitive at every point, and the transmission of intelligence from there to the brain and subordinate nervous ganglia – that is the central and district police stations – will be practically instantaneous.
>
> (Cited in Tarr, 1992, p. 12)

In addition to enhanced operational interconnectivity, these new networks inevitably offered the authorities a chance to build upon their already considerable capacity for surveillance. A telegraph network could often be "tapped" very simply – either by attaching a feeder wire to the main cable and then reading off the signals as they were fed through (Petersen and Zamir, 2001) or, more simply, by influencing the telegraph operators upon whom the system depended. If an operator couldn't be bribed or coerced into handing over messages, there was always the option of acquiring the paper tapes upon which the dot-dash messages were printed out – by fair means or foul. The ease in intercepting telegraphic communications worked both ways – creating some rich opportunities for financial and other frauds. Wheatstone, who helped to develop the UK telegraph network, designed a "pocket cryptograph" machine or cipher machine to keep messages secret – particularly from intrusive postal officials, who caused complaints from the public to rise from 1 in 2,000 to 1 in 600 following the General Post Office's takeover of the system (Roberts, 2011).

The industrialisation of chemical and biological science from the seventeenth century onward generated other new contexts for "hi-tech" styles of offending. The discovery of new techniques for soda-ash production in 1773, or the patenting of the Deacon process a few years later (which enabled the separation of chlorine from chlorine gas) (Jackson, 1996) were just some of the many milestones that had shifted chemistry away from laboratory curiosity to industrial tool. But the industrialisation of chemical knowledge brought in its wake harms that no one had properly anticipated – not least a surge in pollution emanating from the new factories, and disease and death for huge numbers of individuals living and working around them. Rapid and large-scale damage to local environments provided one of the more obvious indicators of this – by 1877, for example, a Royal Commission survey of the River Tawe in South Wales found that a river that had been all but pristine less than 60 years before was now a toxic brew of copper alkali, sulphuric acids, iron sulphates, slag, cinders and coal (Markham, 1994, p. 162). But industrial pollution was not just an aesthetic or environmental challenge. It also brought major health problems, with sharp rises in respiratory and intestinal diseases, along with a succession of epidemics of diseases such as cholera and typhoid (Haley, 1978).

The limited controls upon pollution imposed by earlier regulators were quickly made redundant by this upsurge of toxicity in the environment, and even by 1819 the first Parliamentary Select Committee on the effects of Steam Engines was aware that something more needed to be done about industrial emissions (Parliamentary Papers, 1819). The idea that the public had a "right" to live in clean environments, or to be protected by government against sickness and illness, was a profoundly new concept in technological regulation. But the fact that there was little understanding of how air and other pollutions might be injurious to health meant that little pressure was placed upon manufacturers to do very much about it (cf. Beck, 1959, p. 479). Thus, seminal research like Chadwick's *Report on the Sanitary Condition of the Labouring Population of Great Britain* (1842) noted "atmospheric impurities", but paid little attention to the responsibility of industry for this. Aside from a few obvious observations (for example, that flowers in gardens were now often covered in soot), government largely deferred to business in the regulation of industrialised science. Whilst further Parliamentary Select Committee reports of 1843 and 1845 addressed the issue of industrial control more keenly and set out ways in which legislation might help to reduce "smoke nuisance" (Parliamentary Papers, 1843 and 1845), six bills on clean air were thrown out between 1844 and 1850 (Ashby and Anderson, 1981).

The arguments against emission controls made by factory owners and industrialists sound eerily familiar. They were, reported various committee members, "only concerned with the immediate outlay ... [so that] ... the advantages [of controls] were too remote to be taken into consideration" (Beck, 1959, p. 482). Claims that there was "no proof" that devices for reducing emissions would work, or that the pressures of foreign competition meant British manufacturers could not "afford" the expense of emission controls might almost have been advanced yesterday. In the end, however, the manifest effects of industrialisation made it impossible to completely defer to the demands of commerce. Thus the 1847 Improvement Clauses Act (which focused on factory smoke) was further complemented by the 1866 Sanitary Act and the 1875 Public Health Act, which created new regulatory authorities, directed to take action against smoke nuisances and to set new standards for housing, sewage and drainage, water supply and contagious diseases (ibid.). But new laws were one thing; enforcement of them was quite another. Though factory inspectors had been appointed under the Nuisance Removal Act of 1856, their powers were very limited – for example they could only enter factory premises under limited circumstances between 9 am and 6 pm. The Alkali Act of 1863 created an "Alkali Inspector" with four assistants, who were appointed to stop hydrochloric gas being dispatched into the atmosphere from "alkali works". These emissions included hydrogen chloride, which became hydrochloric acid when exposed to the atmosphere and severely damaged vegetation. The Act required that 95 per cent of emissions should be stopped and was successful at first – resulting in a drop from 45,000 tonnes of annual emissions to less than 45 tonnes (Russell, 2000). But in a sign of what was to come, the Inspector soon became responsible for setting standards as well as enforcing them – a move that inevitably led to an overly cosy relationship with the industry and a resulting lack of accountability and transparency in decision making. And whilst the second Alkali Act of 1874 required industry always to use the best available technologies for reducing pollution problems, enforcement and penalties for offenders remained grossly inadequate. Only around three prosecutions occurred between the early 1900s and 1970s (Russell, 2000).

The harmful impacts of the emerging chemical industries were also seen in a range of commercial by-products – in particular food and pharmaceutical items. The increasing tendency of food manufacturers to add chemical substances like phosphorus to medicines, tonics or even breakfast cereals from the mid to late 1800s was at the centre of new issues of criminality (Crellin, 2004, p. 76). In 1861, *Reynolds Weekly* pointed to new public scandals, like the "Bath-bun poisoning and the Bradford poisoning cases [which] brought the issue of food adulteration to the attention of various public bodies" (7 April 1861). Similarly, there were few regulations at this point on what could be placed in medicines, and the significant rise in chemically induced deaths that resulted brought the activities of new pharmaceutical corporations like Burroughs Wellcome in the UK or Parker Davis in the USA into a new focus (Crellin, ibid.). Such deaths could only be partly attributed to public misuse of the more widely available, commercially produced chemicals. For example, whilst the 1851 Arsenic Act was a response to a surge in poisoning (Bartrip, 1992), over 500 deaths between 1837 and 1838 were a direct result of the widespread commercial use of arsenic in soap, wallpaper – or even as an aphrodisiac (Whorton, 2010).

Biological science offered fewer opportunities for harmful exploitation, since it was not yet as advanced or as commercially developed as chemistry. As a result, what we might think of as "biological" crimes were still largely restricted to military or medical contexts. For example, in the 1760s British forces engaged in colonial Indian wars in North America were reported to have advanced the possibilities of biological warfare by distributing blankets contaminated with smallpox to the local population – though evidence for this has been disputed (Fenn, 2000). Instead, some of our best examples of wrongdoing involving biological technology and knowledge come with the development of modern medicine, which was often assisted by practices that did not just violate ethical and moral considerations, but that were (in terms of contemporary law) unquestionably criminal. The lurid crimes of those who answered medical science's need for bodies for anatomical dissection by murdering to order (like Burke and Hare) has often deflected scrutiny away from the organised and widely tolerated trade in corpses between criminal gangs and the medical elite (Frank, 1976). And whilst the Anatomy Act of 1832 helped to increase the supply of cadavers for medical research, it did so at the expense of any justice for the poor whose bodies could now be routinely transferred from the workhouse direct to the dissection chamber (Richardson, 1987).

Supplementing the grey legal areas around dissection were a range of questionable medical practices involving the use of untried drugs, deliberate infection, experimentation and other forms of exploitation. The Apothecaries Act of 1815 had attempted to introduce some degree of professionalism into the dispensing of drugs, but conflicts of professional interest between the Society of Apothecaries and the Royal College of Surgeons created regulatory inconsistencies between those working in the medical profession and those selling remedies (Coley, 2000). The steep rise in numbers of doctors practising in the UK (from 14,415 in 1861 to 35,650 in 1900 – Robinson, 2011) forced the medical establishment to take the question of medical regulation more seriously – though the formation of the British Medical Association in 1856 and the General Medical Council in 1858 ensured that, as elsewhere with technology, self-regulation was the preferred model (Bynum, 1994).

The weakness of the self-regulatory approach was quickly witnessed by the failure of these new professional bodies to do anything about the growing exploitation of marginalised or vulnerable members of society in research. One notorious example of this can be seen in a well-documented series of shocking biological research programmes carried out in the USA on plantation slaves and working-class black citizens during the nineteenth century (see Schiebinger, 2004). Respected surgeons like Dr J. Marion Sims of Carolina were subsequently found to have conducted numerous experiments on black female slaves, usually without any anaesthesia (Axelsen, 1985). Slaves were placed in boiling hot ovens to study the effects of heat stroke, had parts of their bodies amputated to test analgesics and underwent many other distressing experiments (cf. Washington, 2007). What qualms were raised about this tended to have more to do with whether results from black or other "subhuman" classes could be extended to the whole (i.e. white) population. Like many other medical researchers of this time, Sims was widely honoured (even today the Medical University of South Carolina maintains a J. Marion Sims Chair in Obstetrics-Gynecology).

A technomia for the industrial age

The emergence of the new technologies of the industrial age brought with it new perceptions of harm and criminality, and with this, new kinds of rules and regulations that determined the practices around them. Since there was no real sense of "technology crime" there was less motivation for new legislation than today – even though there were certainly technologies of equal power and social significance. But for the first time in history, a more coherent programme of technological regulation began to be developed – though this also involved a growth in self-regulatory codes and professional standards for science- and technology-related occupations. In turn, more informal social norms also began to solidify – not least new social pressures to use technology responsibly and with consideration for others and for the environment. But, however obvious the need for controlling industrial technology and its commodities may have been, other factors continued to undermine these new regulatory frameworks. Arguments for business tended to win out over arguments for public health and safety – a fact aided by the concern of states to attain commercial and technical supremacy. The shift from pre-industrial to industrial society thus laid the foundations for our contemporary technomia, whilst also indicating its future inadequacies.

3 Tele-crime?

Misusing information and communication technologies

All right internet – what do you want from us?![1]

From the earliest lie to the latest internet scam, the exploitation of communications and information for illicit gain has been a long and ongoing story of technological adaption and extension. But, as with the other technologies considered in this book, this process of extension seems to have accelerated over the past 250 years. The telegraph, the telephone and, more recently, computing and the internet have dramatically transformed the reach of human interaction and the ways in which information can be manipulated. For many, this has resulted in a distinctively new technological era, one where "the fundamental sources of productivity and power" are now rooted in "information generation, processing, and transmission" (Castells, 2000, p. 21). With this, it is argued, has come a new kind of society, one mediated by "the network" which "constitute[s] the new social morphology of our society ... [and] ... substantially modifies ... processes of production, experience, power, and culture" (Castells, 1996/2000, p. 500). But for many, this new information/network age is already tainted, bringing not just an "explosion" in crime (Ruiz, 2007) but paradigmatically new forms of criminal behaviour altogether. In this chapter I want to consider some of the typical misuses of information communication technology and to evaluate whether these really constitute the new ground zero of crime that is claimed, or whether the way such behaviour is modelled – most obviously by the construct of "cybercrime" – has hindered our understanding of the problem.

Communication & information: putting the IT in ICT

Why is a connection between the technologies of information and communication presumed to hold? One kind of answer to this question is to remind ourselves that communication simply is the (successful) exchange of information. For example, suppose one asks, "What is the weather like in London today?" and the reply "blyzrghhh" is given. Unless "blyzrghhh" is a word in an unknown language such a reply would seem meaningless. More accurately, it would fail to communicate anything because it contained no information. Without information, communication cannot usually take place, just as a requirement of information is its (in principle) communicability (cf. Dretske, 1981; Floridi 2003).

A more "technological" response to this question might begin with what are sometimes referred to as "analogue" and "digital" forms of representation (Goodman, 1976). The use of analogue methods distinguished earlier communication technologies, where information transmission was coded in terms of the physical properties of objects like smoke, sound or ink. The advent of alphabets and, later, formal languages composed of discrete (i.e. digital) symbols allowed information transmission to become independent of the properties of the medium (cf. Goodman, 1976). This has culminated in a convergence of communication with computation, and a "technology constituted by the merging of data-processing and tele-communications by way of computers and cybernetics" (Mitcham, 2004, p. 328). The network is crucial to this mode of communications and information, but whilst the internet may be the most familiar example of an ICT in this sense, it is just one amongst many others – from Wi-Fi and GPS networks to SMS and the mobile phone. Fundamental to the power of ICTs is the flexibility of digital representation and the way this now allows almost any form of information (spreadsheets, sound files, banking data or holiday photographs) to be exchanged between any location on the network. With such flexibility, it is no surprise that temptations for misuse have arisen. The bigger surprise, perhaps, is the failure of so many of our institutions to adequately plan or prepare for it.

ICT-enabled crime: some initial assumptions

Early discussions around ICT-enabled crime were fixated upon what it "was" and the extent to which it was "new". Terms like "e-crime", "computer crime" or "network crime" never quite captured the sense of novelty as much as the concept of "cybercrime", which quickly became the most influential of these characterisations (cf. Thomas and Loader, 2000; Wall, 2001). I have argued elsewhere (2007) that, with the adoption of this term, a language game was initiated that has generated a number of problems for policy and practice – problems deriving from its tacit acceptance as a model as well as a definition of offending. But before being drawn into this debate too quickly, it will be useful first to restate some of the more obvious knowns and unknowns about crime involving ICTs.

That there "really are" criminal uses of ICTs or that, given certain qualifications, the internet has played a significant role in assisting many of them is clearly not in dispute. But just as the advent of gelignite as a method of safe cracking was simply a more powerful variation upon crowbars in the age-old use of force in theft, so too has the impact of ICTs upon crime, for all the neologisms and technical variations, been more of a case of scale than of novelty (cf. Yar, 2005; McGuire, 2007; Wall, 2007). Arguably, just as significant as the technological background to this have been social factors – especially the enhanced role of the network (cf. Wellman and Hay-thornthwaite, 2002). Networks themselves are hardly new, or distinctively "technological" phenomena – a neolithic trading system might also count as an example (Castells, 2009, p. 21; see also McNeil and McNeil, 2003). Rather, the crucial criminological tipping-point seems to be the increased volume and range of interactions that digital communication networks provide. Networks that facilitate greater complexity of interaction, over wider distances, automatically imply greater numbers and varieties of potential victims. It may be true that the extended interaction this promotes is usually more "anonymous" than face-to-face varieties and so produces "disinhibition" or "deindividuation" effects (Suler, 2004; Williams, 2005) – but whether these can be definitively correlated with criminal behaviour remains unclear. Just as significant as networked communication (though far less discussed) are the effects of digital representation itself. For this has done more than extend the range or character of social interaction: it has also effected fundamental shifts in the nature of social exchange – in particular, exchanges involving property. In hindsight, our failure to manage or to understand this shift may have been of greater criminological significance than the advent of digital networks themselves.

The range of crimes ICTs now facilitate covers almost every area of harm, though their particular associations with fraud and property crime will be reflected in the following discussion. Whilst some offending activities – especially related to anti-social behaviour – have received far less attention than they ought, others – in particular the extent to which ICTs can be associated with enabling physical harms – have, by contrast, often been the subject of near-hysterical coverage. It is with the controversial issue of physical harm that I will begin.

Digital crimes against the person: primary physical harm

It is plausible to claim that ICTs play an indirect role in facilitating the physical harm of an individual, but can they ever be said to constitute a "primary" – i.e. direct causal factor in this, as is often implied? Though some of the earlier, more lurid panics about "murder by internet" (cf. Kirsner, 1998) seem now to have subsided, suspicions remain that this technology constitutes a source of extreme physical risk. In late 2008, for example, in the most recent permutation of the "violent psychopath online" trope, a series of headlines highlighting the danger of the "Facebook Killer" emerged that linked the social networking site to a series of assaults and murders (see for example Allen, N., 2008; Coles, 2009; Daily Mail, 2010).[2] Very similar claims were of course made in the wake of earlier communications technologies, like television, cinema or even comic books

(Wertham, 1954), but the real degree of influence such technologies exert upon offending behaviours remains as unclear now as it was then. Pointing to an "influence" is not the same as pointing to a direct cause, nor does it rule out the role of other "influences" – from the weather on the day to the mood of an offender.

The readiness to ascribe agency to ICTs without clarifying its modalities or degree has not just resulted in the creation of unnecessary fears. It has diverted attention away from the few instances where we do have evidence for a more direct link with physical harm – as in the minimal coverage of injuries that arise from using ICTs. Some are not that credible, for example so-called "Wii-itis" – named after the rise in numbers of individuals reporting muscle injuries when using the Nintendo Wii interface (cf. Bonis, 2007). But others remain seriously under-researched – for example the health implications of newer interfaces like touchscreens. Other varieties of physical harm are not in doubt – in particular the rise in repetitive strain injuries (RSI) arising from the use of ICTs. Typists were prone to this condition long before the advent of computers, but with the spread of texting and keyboard use the problem has increased significantly. In the UK alone injuries attributed to RSI rose by around 25 per cent between 2001–5 at an estimated cost to industry of up to £20 billion (RSI, 2010) – though fewer than 12.5 per cent of employers have offered any kind of support for such injuries, in spite of the all but universal compulsion to use ICTs in many workplaces (TUC, 2010).

Another area of potential physical harm arises from the electronic fields generated by ICTs, though evidence for this has been hotly disputed. One recent, very detailed study rejected any link (Cardis *et al.*, 2010), though critics of the research argued that it concealed an increase in glioma – the most deadly of brain tumours – amongst heavy users of mobile phones (Cookson, 2010a). They also pointed to the significant role of the telecoms industry in funding the research (contributing over $6 million to its total $24 million cost). And in spite of continued warnings from government and experts such as the National Radiological Protection Board (NRPB) that children aged between 8–14 should restrict mobile phone use and children under 8 years should avoid it altogether, the research failed to clarify the risks posed to children (cf. Adam, 2005). A more recent evaluation by the International Agency for Research on Cancer (IARC) classified mobile phones as a grade 2B risk – i.e. "possibly carcinogenic" and therefore to be handled with caution (IARC, 2011). Here, as elsewhere, science has proved to be a useful tool for employers or manufacturers in obscuring their potential liabilities around technology.

A third possibility of physical harm arises from claims that ICTs "damage the brain". This charge has surfaced in various claims – for example, that (excessive) game playing restricts frontal lobe development (Matthews, 2001) or that internet use reduces the capacity to concentrate (cf. Carr, 2010). The belief that information technology can alter brain function arguably dates back at least to Socrates' claim in the *Phaedrus* that books "create forgetfulness", and similar scares about communications technology have been recycled ever since (see, amongst many others, Murray, 2000; Lehrer, 2010) But the "internet makes you stupid" claim is not decisive, given a number of studies that appear to demonstrate the exact opposite. For example, recent research has suggested that even moderate use of search engines can help to reduce memory loss or stimulate key areas of the brain associated with cognitive function (Than, 2009). The charge of psychological harm is, by contrast, a more plausible one that I will return to shortly.

Digital crimes against the person: secondary or indirect physical harm

Evidence that ICTs constitute a direct cause of physical harm therefore seems, at best, mixed. However, indirect harm – i.e. what happens as a side effect of an online interaction (such as a subsequent sexual assault) – appears to present a more tangible threat. But attributing indirect responsibility to an ICT here still faces an obvious ambiguity – how long there must be between an initial encounter and any subsequent abuse for the link to be genuinely causal. Must it be the next day, the next month, or would even the next year also count (see my 2007 for a discussion of this dilemma)? The readiness to create new offences around online interaction has led to the inevitable sense that this, like similar problems, is "growing" (cf. Sapienza, 2009 as a recent example). But here too, a lack of good data and difficult questions around valid comparators and sample sizes have made it difficult to properly quantify the real risks.

Threats posed to children by the way they use ICTs – for example, excessive or addictive behaviour patterns (cf. Hough, A., 2010) – have been especially difficult to evaluate. Amongst the most sensitive of these concerns has been the problem of "grooming" – where children are manipulated by sexual predators into damaging on- or offline encounters – and the fear that this has been "massively underestimated" (Barnardo's, 2011). However, as a recent report for the UK Council for Child Internet Safety (Spielhofer *et al.*, 2009) pointed out, given that there is very little definitive or clear research available on grooming or sexual harassment, what metric might best serve to definitively establish levels of risk here? One option has been to refer to the number of calls made to child helplines about sexual enticement or grooming. The US National Center for Missing and Exploited Children (NCMEC) recently reported around 6,384 cases of "online enticement of children for sexual acts" in the USA, based on its phone logs (Choo, 2009). But since it was not clear whether each call corresponded to a distinct case this figure may already be misleading, and in any case, online enticement figures recorded by the NCMEC fell substantially between 2007 and 2008, from 11,422 incidents to 8,787 incidents (ibid.). CEOP (the UK Child Exploitation and Online Protection Centre) reported that it had "safeguarded" 630 children over the four years since 2006 (CEOP, 2010) – though of course the concept of safeguarding is itself ambiguous and might mean offering advice as much as responding to an imminent threat.[3] If we compare this figure to the 75+ per cent of UK children who used the internet between 2004 and 2005 – over 3 million individuals (Livingstone and Bober, 2004) – then it amounts to fewer than 0.02 per cent of users at risk. This is still unacceptable, but nowhere near as serious as many other technology hazards, for example the child killed or injured every ten minutes on British roads (Childalert, 2011).

Further problems arise where attempts are made to quantify how often an online encounter leads to harms in an offline one. The recent claim that "one in 12 of the eight million British children with internet access have gone on to meet someone in reality" (Kidshield, 2010) sounds alarming, but of course gives no indication of the extent to which online encounters become offline assault. Yet without this further data the figure is all but meaningless in demonstrating any concrete risk. Whilst no one will dispute that protecting children against predators who misuse this technology is an enforcement priority, the majority of online interactions remain perfectly safe and probably pose less risk than following up on encounters with strangers in other kinds of social milieux (like parties). Perhaps a more obvious area for concern is the fact that, in 2009, around 45 per cent of parents in the UK were still using no filtering controls (Spielhofer *et al.*, 2009).

There is also a risk that the readiness to see danger in the use of ICTs by young people may itself be a source of harm – by limiting the way they use them, for example (Simpson, 2005), or by legitimating interventions into their lives that are just as disruptive. Take the recent scares over "sexting" – the exchange of intimate images or poses between teenagers (Reed, 2009). This quickly became a "child abuse" issue – largely because experts said that this was how we ought to interpret it. The result was a series of young people arrested and criminalised for doing what young people have always sought to do – exploring their sexual identities by looking at each other naked (cf. Ferguson, 2010). It is certainly important to prevent such images being used later for bullying or humiliation, but the fact that sexting has resulted in the USA in children as young as 13 being arrested and placed on "sexual offenders" registers for the rest of their lives hardly seems an appropriate response (see Ahmed, 2009; Pawloski, 2010).

One more objective sense of the extent to which ICTs have caused rises in sexual or other assaults would seem to come from the actual figures for rape and assault and any correlations with actual perpetrators. If strangers online pose the level of danger we are told they do, we should presumably see evidence of significant rises in assaults perpetrated by strangers over the 20 or so years since internet use has expanded. But in almost every jurisdiction where such data is available a similar pattern emerges – the majority of rape victims still do not meet their assailants online but are previously acquainted with them. In the UK, for example, 85 per cent of rapes in 2004 were carried out by perpetrators known to the victim (often husbands or partners), not strangers (Kelly *et al.*, 2005, p. 15). And between 1986 and 2000 there was around a 6 per cent decline in sexual assaults upon females below the age of 20 years – precisely the group usually imagined to be targeted by the online groomer (ibid.). Between 2006 and 2007 rapes and sexual assaults on females fell by anything up to 11 per cent (Kershaw *et al.*, 2008, p. 67) and of the 9 per cent or so of sexual assaults that did occur at the hands of strangers over this period there is no indication of the extent to which this originated in a prior online contact. We see a similar pattern in the USA – where incidents of rape seem to have declined from 2.8 per 1,000 to around 0.4 since the late 1980s – again roughly from around the time of the inception of the internet (Fahrenthold, 2006). And, as in the UK, most rapes were committed by somebody known to victim – usually an intimate partner. Thus, in 2007, 64 per cent of female homicide cases involved a perpetrator who was a family member or intimate partner – with less than 10 per cent carried out by strangers. And between 1993 and 2008 (again a key period in the growth of the internet, when we might expect a significant rise) fatal assaults on US females by strangers declined by nearly 75 per cent – from a rate of around 15 per 1,000 to around 5 per 1,000 (Catalano *et al.*, 2009).

It is not so much, then, that there are not examples of secondary harms involving ICTs; more that, at present, the way we evaluate them needs far greater rigour – especially in relation to other equally serious, but less publicity-worthy, harms. Suppose, for example, a question was posed as to whether the use of ICTs to guide missiles or drones into populated areas constituted any less of a technology risk to the public than their use by online groomers or sexual deviants. It is by no means clear what the answer should be, but the fact that no one has even posed this question indicates how uneven analysis has been to date.

Digital crimes against the person: ICTs and psychological harm

ICTs seem to pose more immediate physical risks in terms of the psychological damage that using them may cause. There are least two modulations of this risk: harm arising purely within an online interaction (such as addiction, or hurt caused by hate speech); and harm arising as part of a more continuous form of contact between on- and offline worlds – as, for example, in variations upon traditional bullying or stalking behaviours. The spatial extension of agency that ICTs enable is crucial here, since, unlike physical harm, almost anything that can be done to damage an individual's psychological well-being at close proximities can also be enacted at a distance. As a result, setting out a definitive list of psychological harms ICTs may enable is probably impossible, especially given the controversies around whether some activities (e.g. watching pornography online) really are harmful or not. Table 3.1 lists some of the more familiar categories.

Table 3.1 ICTs and psychological harm

Action/harm	Typical examples	Legal status
Stalking	Repeated phone-calls which cause distress Use of tracking software to monitor or observe someone without permission	USA: Around 47 states possess anti-stalking laws. Amendments to the Violence Against Women Act (47 U.S.C. 223) have increased protection at the federal level. Europe/UK: Only 8 of 26 European nations have specific anti-stalking laws. In the UK the Protection from Harassment Act (1997) is most often used.
Bullying	Hurtful text messages Insulting phone calls	USA: Now a proliferation of "cyberbullying" laws at state level. A new federal law (HR1966) was proposed, but not passed. Europe/UK: No specific "cyberbullying" law in UK. Other legislation such as the Telecoms Act (1984) or the Communications Act (2003) used to prosecute abusive callers.
Hate speech/threats	Abusive remarks posted on blogs Racist websites	USA: Limited hate-speech regulation because the First Amendment protects free speech. Europe/UK: The UK Public Order Act (1994) regulates threatening speech. The Racial and Religious Hatred Act (2006) was amended to make it more specific to the internet.
Defamation	Libellous articles posted online	USA: No federal law and limited state protections. Onus usually on the victim to indicate malice or damage to their reputation. Some prosecutions for speech in chat rooms have used existing law. Europe/UK: Increased use of libel law against statements in online sources, in particular Twitter. New UK defamation law may weaken options for prosecution.
Moral degradation	Exposure to pornography Violent imagery	In USA and Europe laws preventing offensive publication exist, but "psychological damage" remains medically controversial and uncriminalised.
Addiction	Compulsive use of sex sites Inability to divert attention from mobile phones Computer gaming	Not criminalised in USA or Europe.

Though there is nothing in this catalogue of potential psychological harms that could not be effected without the use of contemporary ICTs, the habit of attaching the prefix "cyber" (as in cyberstalking, cyberbullying and so on) to such behaviours often serves to impose a pseudo-conceptual unity upon very different varieties of behaviour. In the case of bullying, for example, it also implies the following, highly questionable assertions:

1   That there is something different about abuse facilitated by the internet from traditional bullying or stalking conducted at closer spatial ranges.
2   That there is something different about abuse facilitated by the internet to that enabled by traditional ICTs such as the telephone or the telegraph.
3   That it is ICTs themselves that are the source of the harms, rather than particular continuities between "on-" and "offline" behaviours.

A poison-pen letter may clearly cause just as much psychological anguish as a hurtful text message (see for example Campbell, 2005) but no one ever felt the need to turn writing a rude note on a blackboard into a criminal offence. Why, then, does a different sense of justice operate where bullying occurs electronically? The argument that this makes it more "public" carries some weight (cf. Kowalski *et al.*, 2008), though whether it is enough to justify the extensive sanctions being created around it is less clear.

Whilst legislatures in the UK or Australia have been content to use older laws to manage this problem – such as those aimed at harassment or stalking (cf. Childnet, 2007) – the US justice system has been highly active in creating new legal structures around the issue. Even by 2003, 45 US state legislatures had extended existing provisions against stalking or harassment to electronic communications (Conn, 2004). And by the end of 2008, 19 states had enacted further legislation more specifically directed against the perceived new problem of "cyberbullying" (NCSL, 2008). As if this were not enough, a proposed Cyberbullying Prevention (or "Megan Meier"[4]) Act was also proposed at federal level in 2009. However, the Act also threatened to criminalise behaviours with little obvious connection to bullying – an indication of how poorly the implications of this rush to legislate had been thought through. For according to the Bill's provisions, any individual who dared to criticise politicians or companies, or to use strong language and opinions in blogs and e-mails could, in theory, be charged with "coercing, intimidating, or causing substantial emotional distress" (cf. Volokh, 2009; Kravets 2009).

Perhaps the real question for criminologists and legal theorists is not whether ICTs are used for bullying or other abuses – it would be odd if they were not, given the extensions to social life that they enable. The real issue is, once again, whether technological extension is being regulated in a balanced or just way. We might, for example, point to the failures to effectively control the use of ICTs in disseminating hate speech, or the way threats of hate-inspired violence made online have often been translated into definitive instances of offline violence (see for example Dixon, 2011). And questions about culpability might equally be directed at the media or politicians in fanning the flames of online hate – for example, the notorious "cross-hairs" shooting targets used on Sarah Palin's campaign website, which many linked to the subsequent massacre of Arizona citizens by a right-wing fanatic (Hulse and Zernike, 2011). Proper scrutiny of the full spectrum of physical harms that ICTs may enable appears to be a distant prospect at present – but without this our understanding of how best to regulate them will remain limited.

ICTs, theft and fraud

The role of ICTs in facilitating property crime seems to have had more significant criminal impacts than physical harm, though again, recurring misperceptions and overreactions have tended to undermine proper understanding and effective policy responses. McIntosh's influential analysis (1971) of how theft is "reorganised" by technical and social change has often been cited in this context (see Mann and Sutton, 1998) but rather overlooked as an explanation. For, conspicuous by its absence in the often very technically oriented discussions of online fraud, piracy or identification theft, has been any effective discussion of an equally important influence – the socio-economic shifts in the nature of property with which ICTs have been associated. At least two aspects here – shifts in the nature of value and access – are worth special notice:

1   Value: A crucial change in the relation between property, ICTs and theft has been the transmutation in the kinds of things which can be stolen. To say that money (or indeed property in general) has now become "more abstract" (cf. Aglietta, 2001) is not false, but nor does it tell us quite enough. If greater abstraction is about less fixed physical locations, it is clear enough that electronic funds, or intellectual property (such as a film, or a digital music file), are more "abstract" forms of property than cattle or a gold bar. But abstraction is a long-term trend in property (McGuire, 2007), one stretching back to the origins of trading itself and the emergence of what we now think of as money (Simmel, 1978; Davies, 2002). So a more productive way of thinking of the new interfaces between ICTs and property is to focus less upon the abstraction process and more upon what really underlies property – the fact that it is not just about what is "ours" but about what we take to be valuable. For classical economists like Smith or Ricardo (or Marx), value primarily resided in labour – a view rejected by neoclassicists like Jevons and Marshall, who associated it more with what is desired and the extent to which the forms of this are

exchangeable within a market (cf. Dobb, 1973). In both cases, value is affected by the impact of mediating technologies – in particular the proximities at which these enable exchange to take place. For example, exchanges of property at spatially close proximities seem to be associated with values that inhere within objects themselves – such as grain, or iron – values which require little technological mediation. But as societies began to trade over wider distances it became essential for value to be more easily transferrable – transporting cattle to the market is, after all, a complex logistical task. Thus the wider and more extensive trading networks seen in mercantile empires like Rome, China or Persia required more flexible technologies to mediate value exchange – which usually meant coin-based monetary systems. A similar pattern can be discerned in the gradual adoption of paper money, shares or trading bonds, which were also technological shifts responding to the emerging needs of capitalism for the kind of globally distributed trading networks that are now the norm. As we arrive at the most recent stage of integrated global economies, where social and financial interactions now occur instantaneously, and "indifferently" to distance (Cairncross, 1997; Agnew, 2001), this long-term migration of value into its more extended liquid forms (Bauman, 2000) has also (and inevitably) been further accelerated. In this most recent stage, value has mutated into something like the pure information seen in high-frequency trading, where wealth is a "flow" permeating through the information economy – sometimes at speeds of less than 3 milliseconds per value exchange (Castells, 2000; Bowley, 2011). But retained throughout is a crucial desideratum of value – that it be a commodity convertible into other value-forms (be these physical objects like cars or food, or services like healthcare or travel). And as digital information has assumed the traditional role of money – i.e. acting as a representation of the value one is said to possess (for example, in the form of one's credit rating) – it increasingly possesses a value of its own. In turn, this has created new functional relationships with other forms of information – in particular the authentication information necessary to secure access to digital property. This then directs our attention towards a second key aspect of contemporary property and the opportunities for illicit acquisition that it offers – the means and modes of access to it, and the role information plays in "unlocking" this value.

2 Access: ICTs offer an obvious convenience in managing our property – the capacity to access and interact with it from anywhere at any time (by ATM, online banking accounts and so on). But it is one that comes at a price. For there is now a powerful sense in which almost every "new" technique for theft now reduces to how easy it is to obtain access to the electronic networks that mediate value. The relationship between value and the modes of access to it has been a long-standing one and criminologists have made particular study of the way access

to a target influences patterns of theft (cf. Felson, 1994). In societies where value primarily resided in objects, protection of access was also "objectlike", centring upon defensive structures like walls and doors, or even strong-boxes. In such contexts, force (i.e. breaking open the strong-box) was a more usual tactic for theft than guile. But as technology has made value (and therefore the modes of access to it) more liquid, more sophisticated strategies for obtaining access become necessary. The role of guile and know-how in technological theft (for example, counterfeiting) was noted earlier, so it is no surprise that, with the growth of an information economy, the importance of these strategies has also grown. The crucial aspect here – a gradual blurring between obtaining access and effecting theft – has meant that, for anyone with sufficient guile to acquire access to a node within a value-network (like a personal account within a banking system), access to other values within the network (i.e. other accounts) also then opens up. And therein lie three of the key problems and difficulties for the control of ICT-enabled property crime. First, as value becomes homogenised and "informatised" within and across multiple networks, access to one network can often permit access to others – making theft both more straightforward and lucrative than in previous times. Second, just as with traditional banks, the tendency to place value in centralised repositories like data stores makes theft far easier. Third, the failure to manage the obvious response to these transitions – making access to networks more difficult – has been poorly handled. Partly, the fault is our own – an inevitable result of our difficulties in understanding these complex transitions in the nature of wealth. But equally if not more culpable here have been those whom we defer to as "experts" – the banks, credit card companies, commercial organisations and governments responsible for regulating these most recent impacts of technologisation upon property. The often catastrophic failure on the part of these agencies to manage this shift responsibly and to anticipate the new forms of security it requires has been one of the more significant but less discussed aspects of contemporary ICT crime.

Theft as access to value networks: four contemporary options

A useful metaphor for elucidating the importance of access within contemporary ICT-mediated theft is the notion of the key (see my 2007). Traditional keys operated in analogue terms – that is, by requiring the physical properties of the key to match the physical properties of the lock. By contrast, contemporary "keys" permit access to property by numeric (i.e. digital) codings, or by codings in terms of the self. These two methods are often now interrelated – for example, as increasingly complex mathematical "signatures", like PIN codes or passwords, become the electronic keys to our property, more authoritative ways of guaranteeing that the person using this mathematical key "really is" who they say they are become required. Aspects or features of the self, like personal details, or bodily features, have thus also become crucial to accessing our property.

It is no accident, then, that identity – or better, identification – has become so central to discussions around theft online. But acquiring identification has, ironically, been made far easier by the range of indicators now used to define it. In what might be called its "second order" form, identification is bureaucratically determined – by documents like birth certificates, utility bills or passports. Increasingly, the shift towards the use of "first order" identification – where the body itself becomes the guarantor – involves the so-called "biometric" method of identification (voice, fingerprint, iris and so on) that will be discussed in more detail in Chapter 5. But in whatever form identification comes, the fact that it is now a primary key to digital property has made it an inevitable target for thieves. More importantly, once attained, it can provide far more reliable and lucrative modes of accessing property than a crowbar ever did. But what this is not is a theft of anyone's identity – it is simply the theft of a key, albeit in its contemporary form as a mode of identification. The uneven way in which relations between identification in its first- and second-order forms have been managed has left significant spaces open for exploitation – especially in the use of one to reinforce the credibility of the other. Obtaining "seed" identification documents, such as birth/death certificates, can often be sufficient to create identities, which, as we will see, has been just as common a strategy for theft as stealing someone's identification.

As we can see in Table 3.2, these shifts now present four basic options for contemporary theft – some more familiar than others. These options are playing out in very different ways. For example, one unforeseen consequence of the use of personal details, or the body itself, as a key has been to offer criminals new permutations for the use of physical violence. Though the data on this is limited at present, there seems to have been a clear rise in cases of individuals who have been assaulted or tortured in order to force them to hand over PIN codes or passwords – a scenario only like to increase (for some examples see Morris, 2006; Edwards, 2009; Sutcliffe, 2010). Another has been the increased importance of disguise – whether this be the more straightforward subterfuge of a phishing e-mail or sophisticated subversions of encryption (itself, of course, a way of "disguising" sensitive information) seen in the spoofing of trusted secure site-encrypted SSL addresses (denoted by the "https" prefix) (cf. Krebs, 2006). In turn, as McIntosh (1971) correctly forecasted, these developments in thieving have created new criminal cultures and skills. The increased value of identification has turned it into an especially desirable criminal commodity – with everything from licence plates, passports or other identification documents being traded in online carding forums, or less visible marketplaces. Similarly, a market for computing skills and tools has inevitably grown (Espiner, 2010) and has led, in some cases, to a further professionalisation of theft. But a

Table 3.2 Digital property: four modes of illicit access

Access type	Methods	Associated techniques and terminologies
By force	1 *Against individuals*. For example, physical violence or blackmail used to force an individual to hand over a PIN code or other kinds of access details. *Psychological* force may involve extortion or blackmail. 2 *Against systems*. For example, the use of distributed denial-of-service attacks (DDoS) to overwhelm a system's capacity to respond.	Extortion Blackmail DoS (denial of service) or DDoS (distributed denial-of-service) attacks
By deception	1 Deceiving or persuading victims to hand over access details or money. Traditional advance fee frauds like the notorious 419 'Nigerian letter' e-mail frauds have now been complemented by multiple variations (see for example Goldberg, 2010). 2 Mobile users persuaded to call back numbers at a premium rate. 3 Persuading users that they need to buy or to install special software to protect their computer against threats. This may also allow installation of malware that records personal information.	Phishing Pharming Spear-phishing (attacks targeted on specific individuals) Spoofing Scareware Premium call scams
By theft	1 Stealing/copying access details at the point of use. For example 'skimming' a victim's card details. 2 Stealing/copying access details remotely or using automation. For example, 'malware' or keystroke trojans, software placed secretly on an individual's ICT which then passes on access details like passwords and PIN codes (cf. Paget, 2007). 3 A special version of this form of theft is where value is acquired by its *exact replication* or 'cloning'. Counterfeiting money has been augmented by the copying of objects with value in their own right, e.g. a piece of music, or an image. Downloading or digital piracy of original content has been the most widely discussed contemporary example of this.	Cloning Skimming Trojans Account takeover (commonly used term for illicit acquisition of personal banking details to facilitate subsequent fraud) Pirating File sharing
By open door (incompetence)	The leaving open of a "door" to electronic property – usually as a result of the incompetence of a guardian. E.g. • loss of files or passwords • leaving access details in the open where they can be easily seen.	Data breaches Shoulder surfing Loss of data files

reverse trend has also been discernible, one where sophisticated tools like the "bot-net" – banks of computers harnessed by malware for the purposes of synchronised attacks – can be bought in kit form for very little. This and the sale of other digital crimeware has begun to open up ICT-enabled theft to individuals with little or no computing ability and even less organisation (Ormerod *et al.*, 2010). The received view has been that the organisation of digital theft is quite unlike that of traditional organised crime, operating in a networked, flat management form – more like Atkinson's "flexible firm" model – consisting of a core of IT experts and a periphery of low-skilled temporary employees (cf. Hobbs, 2001). However, the real picture seems likely to be much more complex than this, and organised digital crime may now incorporate everything from "geeks gone bad" engaged in one-off heists to well co-ordinated hub formations and even more traditional organised groups (cf. McGuire, 2011).

Access by "open door": incompetence in the financial and security sectors

One of the least discussed yet most common ways in which illicit access to digital property has been obtained is through what I have previously dubbed the "open door" mode of access (2007), which, as the name suggests, arises from an electronic equivalent of leaving the safe door wide open. One of the early assumptions about ICT-enabled theft is that the public were often culpable in furthering it – an inevitable outcome of our naivety online and our habit of leaving access details unsecured or disposing of them carelessly. But, as internet activity has become more centrally managed, guarding access has increasingly less to do with public responsibility and far more to do with decisions taken by the institutions that govern and manage this new economy. The global banking crisis of 2007–9 may have finally brought the competence of financial institutions into a more critical light, but we should not forget that it was also a sign of a wider failure to manage security within the new ICT-mediated global economies. This is not just about the warp-speed computing that facilitates "high frequency trading" (cf. Kirilenko *et al.*, 2011), but two rather more basic failures of management:

1   The repeated and ongoing loss of personal data held by companies, which exposes customers to theft (cf. PRC, 2011). In a context where almost any purchase now requires us to leave extensive personal details in the care of vendors, a reciprocal respect for the duty of care might be expected. Yet, in 2010 financial institutions alone were responsible for 60 per cent of all data breaches/losses where personal details were lost or exposed to unauthorised scrutiny – a doubling from the previous year (Symantec, 2010).

2   Slow provision of (or outright refusal to provide) effective methods of protecting our digital property by financial institutions. Take as just

one example the ongoing failure by US financial and political institutions to adopt simple chip and PIN forms of security for cards – a failing that has now made the USA a major centre for card fraud, resulting in 80 per cent of non-EU fraud against EU payment cards being committed in the USA (OCTA, 2011, p. 21). Though the EMV magnetic card strip system still used there can be easily skimmed or cloned, US financial and commercial institutions have consistently refused to introduce more secure systems, on the grounds that the $6 million or so that it would cost to introduce is "too much" (Kitten, 2010).

ICT-enabled theft has also been significantly amplified by the poor governance of network infrastructures – in particular the internet. Take, for example, the ongoing delays in introducing the new DNSSEC protocol – meant to address the major security holes in the DNS (domain names system) that is the backbone of the web (Murphy, 2010). Or what of the ease with which the .co.uk domain name has been allowed to be used fraudulently? Unlike many other jurisdictions, the UK did not prohibit the purchase of its domain name (it could be obtained for as little as £5) and this inevitably allowed criminals to exploit public trust in it. UK police made much of their success in closing down around 1,000 sites such as these in 2009 (Thompson, 2009), but the underlying problem – the need to make the use of the UK domain names far more secure – was not dealt with. Thus the advent of new domain names in 2011, some using Arabic and Chinese lettering, seems likely to pose major new security problems, with no obvious systems in place to deal with them (Talbot, 2011). Demands by the UK policing agency SOCA (Serious Organised Crime Agency) that the domain name management company Nominet allow it to close down any website hosting suspected criminal activity (Williams, 2010b) seem like an overly draconian response, but are typical of the unaccountability in ICT regulation that will be explored in the next chapter.

Similarly cavalier attitudes to security can be seen in the actions of those who build the hardware. The problem of mobile phone theft presents a familiar example. In spite of dramatic rises in handset theft (cf. Mailley *et al.*, 2008), it took many years to implement more effective security measures like the Central Equipment Identification Register (CEIR) – an international database designed to enable blocking of stolen handsets within 48 hours. But major holes remain – the CEIR can be easily evaded by using networks that haven't yet signed up to the register, or that exist outside this regulatory system (Ray, 2007). And, like the banks, mobile phone companies rarely display much sympathy when their own systems leave customers with huge bills for calls made where a phone is stolen. For example, even where credit limits have been placed on an account prior to a theft, payments have still been demanded (cf. Schneier, 2005; Brignall, 2008). The eagerness on the part of providers to punish the public for their own failings has been spectacularly demonstrated in the disproportionate responses to digital downloading. Mass criminalisation, extensive centralised filtering and individuals fined up to $1.5 million for downloading have been just some of the responses to piracy (cf. Lavoie, 2009; Wall and Yar, 2009). But many problems have, arguably, been self-inflicted. For example, if effective anti-copying measures had been developed early on, or the new ways of distributing and accessing content had been better anticipated and facilitated, downloading might have been significantly curbed. And the film and music industry have been more than happy to downplay the benefits they have enjoyed from the digitalisation of the entertainment industry – indeed some have even argued that piracy has offered certain advantages, such as increased product exposure (Croxson, 2007).

So, whilst we all know that ICTs have created new methods and opportunities for theft, we should not forget that they have also come with a culture of incompetence that has vastly facilitated it. Emblematic of this has been a new kind of tolerance to crime – where banks write off small losses or conceal larger ones and police rarely bother to investigate minor cases of card fraud (BBC, 21/06/2007). Thus, just as essential to our understanding of the rise in ICT-enabled theft as knowledge of its methods is an appreciation of the regulatory failings of the institutions and systems for managing digital property.

Crimes against the extended community: terrorism and anti-social behaviours online

Harms centred upon property or against the person have inevitably generated most of the headlines about ICTs and crime. But we should not overlook other problems arising from the extension of social interaction – especially harms to this extended social world and its communities. Whilst it is the more dramatic threats, such as terrorism, that have dominated the headlines, other varieties of anti-social behaviour, such as vandalism, offensive speech, intrusion or abuses of trading also acquire their own kind of character in this extended social context, posing threats to the extended community life in much the same way as they do to within more traditional, spatially immediate communities (see Williams, 2006; McGuire, 2007 for some examples).

In the public imaginary, the more serious examples of these kinds of offence probably still centre on technical disruptions such as hacking, or the dissemination of viruses and malware. The role of malware or illicit access has of course been most often associated with financial crime, but has also been deployed for more political ends. A feeling that hacking was in decline has had to be re-evaluated in the light of increased activity by groups such as "Anonymous" and "Lulzsec" or the challenge posed by websites such as Wikileaks – though the debate about the extent to which this is disruptive, or serves as a vital critical ingredient of online life is, of course, a highly politicised one (Sengupta, 2011). Other political threats, particularly terrorism (or the inevitable "cyber" terrorism) – have usually been judged in even more catastrophic terms. There is little doubt that attempts to destabilise information and communications capacity have been on the increase, but determining responsibility for attacks upon networks (or their rationale) has been far less obvious. The "received" view – that responsibility for hacking or cyberterrorism primarily lies with states like China and Russia or groups like Anonymous or even Al Qaeda – does not appear to be entirely supported by available evidence. Computers based in the USA accounted for 34 per cent of web-based attacks against users in 2009 – nearly five times as many as China, at 7 per cent of the total (Symantec, 2010, p. 25). Similarly, the "Stuxnet" virus of 2010 – one of the most sophisticated instances of "targeted" malware to date – appears now to have been a well-organised operation largely driven by Western and Israeli agencies. Stuxnet's target – the Siemens S7–417 and 315 programmable logic controller – was highly specific and just happened to be central to the operation of the Iranian nuclear power plant at Bushir. On most intelligence evaluations, Stuxnet helped to postpone full Iranian nuclear weapons capacity by several years, though it also emerged that it had damaged systems in other jurisdictions – not least the Indian space programme (Bhattacharyya, 2010) – whilst Russian experts warned that it had raised the threat of serious nuclear accidents worldwide (Coughlin, 2011).

State involvement in online disruptions cannot therefore be overestimated, though is probably to be expected, given the strategic importance now allocated to "securing cyberspace" and the huge investments in cybersecurity (cf. CSIS, 2008). Whether what results is "cyberwar", "cyberterrorism" or merely the "advanced persistent threats" (APTs) that now preoccupy cybersecurity experts, the current picture is mired in claim and counterclaim. On the one hand we might see Google's (apparent) withdrawal from the Chinese market in 2010[5] as confirmation of the widespread belief that China has been using ICTs as part of a strategy for global cyber-hegemony for some time, a strategy also seen in the regular probing of Western data systems to acquire valuable commercial information (cf. Borland, 2008). On the other hand, there has been a lack of evidence for any consistent programme of cyberterrorism. The plain fact is that no one is quite sure of the real situation (cf. Morozov, 2009) and many incidents turn out to be far less dramatic than originally portrayed. For example, the supposed "cyber/war/terror" compromise of Estonian netspace in 2007, interpreted by experts as a "massive series of attacks" by Russia in response to nationalist tensions there (Traynor, 2007), seems to have been the work of a 20-year-old student seemingly operating alone from his bedroom, though this too has been disputed (Arthur, 2008). Overall, we should not be too surprised that the extension of social life by ICTs into a "globalspace" has resulted in a recalibration of struggles between both states and non-state groups within this wider arena.

More mundane forms of anti-social behaviour and disruption seen here also fail to fit many standard preconceptions. In 2009, for example, the country producing the most malicious activity was the USA (a repeat of 2008) at 19 per cent of the total – double the level of malicious activity of the next-ranked country, China at 8 per cent (Symantec, 2010). And though Russia, like China, is often viewed as one of the major sources of infections, it contributed only 3 per cent of the total in 2009 – the same amount as the UK and 2 per cent less than Germany (ibid.). State involvement in net censorship provides a further challenge to our preconceptions around online anti-social behaviours. Censorship of electronic communication has been strongly associated with undemocratic regimes such as China or Iran, though there is no lack of content filtering and net control in other jurisdictions (cf. RSF, 2011 for examples). Sometimes this is based on moral concerns – India, for example, has now forced Yahoo!, Flikr and Microsoft to block any citizens searching for sexual context (Chamberlain, 2009). Sometimes it is pure moral paternalism of the kind exercised by the self-appointed Internet Watch Foundation (IWF) in the UK, which censors sites with little transparency or proportion – as its recent denial of access to pages from Wikipedia on the grounds they were "offensive" to UK users demonstrated (cf. Davies, 2009). The UK Home Office regularly blocks freedom of information requests about the IWF's activities, whilst placing pressure upon ISPs to filter other varieties of content it deems "offensive" or undesirable (ibid.). Democratic states also filter content on political grounds. The much-vaunted US advocacy of net freedom appears rather hypocritical in the light of its own manoeuvres to deny airspace to any content that it regards as politically inconvenient. The attempt to restrict access to the embarrassing revelations about US foreign policy contained on the Wikileaks site counts as an obvious example here (cf. MacAskill, 2010). The US has also sponsored the controversial Children's Online Protection Act, which set up lists of "blacklisted" websites and compelled libraries and schools to place draconian limitations of access upon students and children (Zhang, 2010). Many far less transparent forms of political filtering emanate from within the private sector, which regularly wages campaigns of disinformation or destabilisation against any online content it deems inconvenient to its commercial interests.

The commercial world has been implicated in a variety of other anti-social behaviours that damage extended social interaction and its community life. The use of cold calling, intrusive advertising or the installing of tracking software all count as examples of disruptions to our use of ICTs, or a placing of commercial interests above those of the "netizen". Having to continually navigate pop-up ads, cookies and tracking software results in inconvenience and damage to browser functionality, just as the subtly misleading provisions around opt-in or opt-out boxes, or unreadably long terms-of-service conditions arguably constitute manipulation and "disrespect" towards users. One of the few legal responses to such tactics – the criminalisation of unsolicited or "spam" e-mails in the US – appears to have had limited success, in spite of a few high-profile prosecutions (Arora, 2006). High rates of unsolicited e-mail continue to flow – with over 75 per cent of spam traffic in 2009 coming from ostensibly "legitimate" sources linked to the medical, financial or retail sectors (ibid.). There is often tacit collusion between commerce and the state in all of this. For example, the 2003 Privacy and Electronic Communications Regulations – the only spam-specific laws in the UK – still permitted companies to send unsolicited e-mail on an opt-out basis. Even the Information Commissioner accepted that enforcement was so weak here that there were no successful prosecutions in the two to three years following the UK's implementation of this EC directive (MacCleod, 2005). And though there have been many estimates of the cost of spam e-mail to UK businesses (one recent suggestion was around £1 billion in lost productivity – Thomas, 2005), estimates of the cost and bother to private citizens from unsolicited e-mails or from corporate intrusion and bullying have been conspicuously lacking. As I have argued elsewhere (McGuire, 2010), there is an interesting case to be explored around compensating "owners" for the extensive buying and selling of their personal information obtained without transparency. Not only does this trade arguably disrespect consumer rights, it represents a serious failure equitably to distribute profits from the new "information" property.

Elsewhere, deep concerns have been expressed about the divisive impacts on the internet being created by the operations of major organisations like Google, Facebook, Apple or data management businesses like LexisNexis. For many, the extended community is being fragmented by the way access to the web is being mediated by commercial apps, or personalised search filters (Pariser, 2011). As a result, "captive islands" – enclosed or personalised dataspaces that undermine the open platform aspect of online interaction that was its initial strength – are being created (Menn and Nuttall, 2010). There is also an increasing threat to "net neutrality" – equal access to the internet for all users – from providers who seek to charge more for certain services (Gustin, 2010). In prospect is a corporate takeover of a public space that is not just unprecedented but that no one has ever voted for.

Modelling ICT-enabled crime: "cybercrime"?

The advent of internet-enabled crime in the late 1980s and early 1990s persuaded many that this was such a new and distinctive form of offending that it needed a distinctive criminological classification. But it is one thing to call a crime enabled by an ICT a "cybercrime", quite another to suggest that this characterisation offers us any kind of explanatory enlightenment. In my (2007) I posed the following problem: in using the term "cybercrime", do we also run the risk of entering into a certain kind of language game, one that comes with an a priori theoretical model that imposes its own self-fulfilling prophecies? Even if it is accepted that the terminological horse has bolted from the stable and we are stuck with the term (Wall, 2007), this ought not to prevent us from pressing critical questions about the tacit assumptions that come with it.

Perhaps the single most misleading assumption that has ridden on the back of the term "cybercrime" has been the idea that it happens "in cyberspace". At one point, the cyberspace idea was an all but universal ingredient of discussions of crime on the internet – even turning up in influential commentaries such as Lessig's (1999). Within the context for which it was originally intended – the cyberpunk science fiction of the 1980s – the concept was harmless enough. But when transformed into an explanatory grounding for the "how" or "where" of ICT misuse it has offered support for two far more questionable assumptions. First, that there is a viable ontological distinction between "real space" and "cyber" (or virtual) space, and second, that part of what makes cybercrime different is that cyberspace is an inherently anomalous or unregulatable space. Such assumptions have had highly negative effects on policy and policing since, if the space is "anomalous", then it is subtly transformed into a digital equivalent of Agamben's "state of exception" (2005), where only special powers are sufficient to regulate it. For without them, it is argued, we risk "losing control" of cyberspace. It is no accident, then, that perceptions of cybercrime as an endlessly growing, exponential spiral of criminality have been central to the way it has been reported over the last ten years or so. Even as far back as 1997, cyber attacks were significantly "on the rise" (Wired, 1997) and by 1998 they had become the new "crime wave on the web" (Nelson, 1997). Not much had changed by 1999, with a "growing threat" of internet fraud (BBC, 19/11/1999), which by 2000 had turned into a "surge" in cybercrime (Communications News, 2000). In 2001 a "rising tide of cybercrime" was being observed (Ward, 2001) – a tide that was still "rising" in 2002 (CNN, 2002). By 2003, the tide had risen so far that it had become a "computer crime wave" (Godwin, 2003) – one which "risked the future of the Net" (Boyd, 2003). The internet survived until 2006, though cybercrime had now become "more widespread, skilful, and dangerous than ever" (Naraine, 2006), with the result that, by 2007, "police were struggling to cope with the rise" (Bennetto, 2007). Police seem to have been able to cope, for by 2008 cybercrime was back to being only "a growing threat" (New Scientist, 2008) – a brief respite from a new "crisis" in 2009, which again saw "the cybercrime threat rising sharply" (Weber, 2009) – just in time for the apocalypse of 2010/11, by when it had again become "out of control" (Liebowitz, 2010).

The trope of an eternally rising graph of offending is questionable on methodological grounds, but then discussions of "cybercrime" have often been riddled with rarely challenged exaggerations or plain misrepresentations of data. What is sometimes called (with typical hyperbole) the "financial crime of the 21st century" (Lemos, 2007) – the "phenomenon" of (so-called) identity theft is one of the many examples of this that might be discussed. As already suggested, identity theft has been a misleading concept from the outset and has obscured the real issue here – how identification, the use of first- or second-order authentication as a (digital) key to property – is being misused. But blurring the technical details around identification into the metaphysical miasma of identity has been a useful strategy for software security firms or insurance companies in creating lucrative business opportunities around the need to "protect" identity. The "80% per annum rises" in identity theft that have sometimes been claimed (cf. Gartner, 2003) have certainly not hindered the marketing of products designed to "protect users from identity fraud thefts". But the value of such schemes was criticised by the UK consumer watchdog Which as little more than "inspired marketing which cashes in on public concern", resulting in products that are "almost worthless" (Greek, 2006).

More research on the way statistics around cybercrime are generated and then recycled as received truths within the public domain would clearly be useful. For example, claims that the FBI had identified 10 million Americans as "victims of ID fraud" in 2004 became commonplace throughout the US and world media in the mid 2000s. Less well reported was the fact that the statistic was actually based on private sector data that had nothing to do with the FBI, that significantly overestimated this total and that included frauds that related to new credit cards rather than the theft of anybody's identity (cf. Cate, 2008). Similarly, claims by the UK Home Office that the cost of the offence to the UK economy had risen from £1.3 billion to £1.7 billion between 2002 and 2006 (Home Office, 2006) were also widely recycled – even though the methodology used to arrive at this figure was also widely questioned[6] (cf. Gilligan, 2005). Amongst the many statistical sleights of hand deployed was the trick of inflating the total by incorporating figures for other varieties of fraud only barely related to identity,[7] or including the estimated costs of enforcement measures. More damningly, the claimed rise flew in the face of a fall in all frauds in 2005. Only "card not present fraud" (where cards are used to buy things over the internet) rose, whilst most categories – in particular "account takeover fraud (often used as a kind of synonym for "identity theft") – dropped by as much as 24 per cent (APACS, 2006).

Overall, there seems in fact to have been a stabilisation in this variety of digital offending – in spite of continued warnings from the financial industry. In its 2007 report the UK Fraud Prevention Service, CIFAS, lamented that "the most surprising statistic during this period is that identity fraud overall has stabilised when compared with the same period in 2006" (CIFAS, 2007) – a fall repeated in 2008, when identity fraud fell by 3.7 per cent (CIFAS, 2008). CIFAS's response to this inconvenient statistic was to then move the goalposts. Suddenly included now were the use of fake identities (which did show a rise) – though inventing an identity is clearly not the same as stealing one. Evidence for a stabilisation in identification fraud in the UK also seems to be supported by similar trends elsewhere. In the USA, for example – where card security is notoriously weaker than in the UK – identity theft/fraud also seems to have stabilised or to have declined since 2003 (PRC, 2007). US data also suggests that, far from this being a "problem of technology", many frauds of this kind arise at intimate, rather than remote proximities – often involving family members or friends (BBB, 2005). More recent data has also indicated that up to 60 per cent of data losses in 2009 relating to personal information or identification were caused by the financial sector itself – up from 29 per cent in 2008 (Symantec, 2010). Indeed one of the highest-ranking IT security concerns has been criminal behaviour arising from employees or insiders within these firms (Computer Economics, 2007).

Though there has been a general shift away from some of the cyber-utopianism that characterised early internet use and the emergence of a more realistic overview of what ICTs can, or cannot enable (cf. Lehmann, 2011), the contributions of the cybercrime construct in lending support to many contemporary control mechanisms and associated erosions of liberty and rights remain seriously under-discussed. The construct has enabled politicians to legitimise coercive programmes of new legislation or extra-judicial control by continually referring to the "otherworldly" anomalousness and the transjurisdictional lawlessness of the "vacuum of a lawless space" that is cyberspace (Espiner, 2008). Yet claims that "threats to cyberspace are on a par with 9/11", (Shiels, 2008) or that "large scale cybercrime" is one of the "tier one" threats that now confront the UK (Shah, 2010) obscure the increasingly accepted reality that the internet may be one of the most regulated technologies there has ever been (Goldsmith and Wu, 2006).

At the heart of many of the misrepresentations is the recurring failure to properly address one of the key questions around technology crime – namely how and to what extent the technology is agentic. In the case of cybercrime the failure to clarify the causal role of ICTs has been especially debilitating, given that these are invariably identified as primary enablers over any other factor. Even in 1999, the writer Douglas Adams was pointing out how:

> Newsreaders still feel it is worth a special and rather worrying mention if, for instance, a crime was planned by people "over the Internet." They don't bother to mention when criminals use the telephone or the M4, or discuss their dastardly plans "over a cup of tea," though each of these was new and controversial in their day.
>
> (Adams, 1999)

Not much has changed since. Of course there seems a compelling sense in which things are so different with computers that it is more useful to talk of "cybercrime" than "road-assisted crime" or "cup-of-tea-enabled crime".

For surely, it might be said, computers make a far more distinctive contribution to the criminal act than other technologies that might assist along
the way? But the question, again, is how. Given that remote theft can be
effected by postal communication or by telegraph, remote bullying or sexual
stalking by telephone, or even by smoke signals, then there seems nothing
in what this technology does that is ultimately unique. All we are left with
is the notions of scale and range – and whilst technology clearly enhances
these, they are not themselves "technological" facts. It is ironic, then,
to see how technology has been also underestimated within the cybercrime model. A disproportionate focus upon the internet, for example, has
continually diverted attention from the growing threats posed by other
ICTs – especially in relation to telephone-enabled crime, whether this is the
(now classical) subversions of phone phreaking or the rapidly emerging
criminal opportunities that 3G and smartphone technologies are creating
(cf. BBC, 02/11/2011).

Hyperspatialisation, hypercrime and other models

Shifting towards more neutral characterisations such as "e-crime", "netcrime", "computer crime" or even the "tele-crime" of this chapter might be
one option for evading some of the theoretical baggage that seems to come
with the concept of cybercrime. But not only would this mean a loss of
terminological convenience; it would also obscure some of the distinctive
characteristics of ICTs in furthering crime of this kind. And greater clarity
around this certainly seems desirable if better operational and policy
responses are to be formulated. As suggested here, one defining set of characteristics centres upon the causal role played by extensions to the speed
and distance of social interaction and the instantaneous transfer and
processing of information that ICTs enable. Though, as we have seen,
the possibilities of "time-space compression" (Harvey, 1989) and instantaneous interaction between anyone, anywhere at any time go back at least
to telegraph and telephonic technologies, contemporary ICTs have clearly
taken these possibilities to a new level. Instant connectability is now complemented by a second distinctive characteristic – the enhanced connectivity
enabled by enhanced networking. The interactive potentials of earlier,
isolated networks like postal systems have now been absorbed into a proliferation of wider networks of various sizes and socio-technic kinds,
into a highly multi-layered system – a "networking of networks", as I have
called this (2007). The networking of networks has been only partly
acknowledged in the "network" society concept (cf. Castells, 1996–2000; van
Dijk, 2006), for this goes far beyond the remit of the world wide web or
global trading systems, forming a complex that encompasses everything
from data networks or private "intranet" systems to digital power-grids.
These new dimensions of interaction serve to extend individuals outward
from mere nodes of a network into extended, multidimensional "always on"

zones of interaction – generating forms of being far beyond the "multiple identities" once associated with online presence (Turkle, 1995).

A third, crucial contribution of ICTs is the enhanced capacity they provide to interact with information as well as other individuals – information that rapid computing power now allows to be represented in many ways, from spreadsheets or dating sites to computer models of distant planets. Our capacity to interact with these representations has tended to be seen in terms of the "virtual" – where virtuality is associated with fictional objects and worlds. In fact digital representations offer far more than just vivid, immersive versions of what our imaginations have always provided. For interactions with information in its digital form usually have far more to do with reality than with fiction. Indeed, so finely tuned have digital representations become to what they represent that precise causal effects can now be calibrated with them – effects also indifferent to the distance between these and the represented object. The development of what has been called "tele-action" (Minsky, 1980) means that our capacity to access our online bank is of the same order as our capacity to move stones around or conduct soil tests on planets many millions of miles away. This use of information to mediate causal interaction represents a sea-change in social life and social order.

The sheer power of these shifts suggests that, in extending social inter-action, ICTs also do far more – they profoundly reorder our experience of space and its traditional constraints. So profoundly that, as I suggested in my (2007 and 2008), we might now think of this in terms of the creation of a new social space altogether – a kind of "hyperspace" where every point is, in principle, seamlessly connectible to every other. In other words, the development of ICTs might also be seen in terms of a process of "hyper-spatialisation" – a process that began with the origins of communication and information technology and has reached a new phase of development. And if there is a shifting of social life into a "hyperspatial" form, then the criminological consequences of this might in turn be thought of as "hypercrime" – new criminal behaviours centred upon exploiting the characteristics of this extended spatial medium. But, in the end, however we choose to conceptualise ICT-enabled offending, it is hard to see how more effective responses can be developed without properly identifying its key causal characteristics.

Trends in ICT-enabled crime: organisation, automation and agents

As already acknowledged, a major problem in analysing any technology-enabled crime is how quickly that analysis risks becoming redundant in the face of technological change. The dramatic and ongoing developments in ICTs have especially underlined this caveat. This serves as a reminder that it is only by focusing upon the social aspects behind such shifts that we can hope to get beyond descriptions of technical innovations, to a more general analysis of what may be emerging with them. As we shall see in following chapters, there are many other technologies that, arguably, pose far greater risks of harm and destruction to our world than do ICTs. At the same time, the very real changes that ICTs are exerting upon social life mean that they cannot be lightly ignored.

An increased blurring between extended "virtual" social spaces and everyday life is likely to represent one of the important trends, one that will widen the spaces for abuse, and increase security risks. The idea of "virtual property", and the possibilities of its theft, illustrate one of many possible issues here (Castronova, 2007; Lim, 2010). But we should remember that, if such property is exchangeable (which it increasingly is), then virtual property forms a continuum with more traditional varieties that will open up new ways in which criminals can exploit on- and offline continuities. This means that a "theft" in an online social world like Second Life is likely to have effects that go far beyond this. More possibilities for physical harm may also begin to open up from this increasing seamlessness between our extended selves and our normal physical bodies. Whilst the concept of "virtual" rape or assault may have been somewhat of a red herring (McGuire, 2007, pp. 122ff), and psychological harm likely to remain the more likely outcome here for the time being, there is no question that our post-human future will begin to reorder what our sense of pain or physical impairment might be – and the options for inflicting it.

As the internet becomes submerged within wider networks, criminal behaviour will inevitably follow the digital representations and structures it can use best. The failures of the cybercrime model have, as we have seen, been instrumental in leading policy makers to overlook the latest example of this opportunism – the increasing role of smartphones and their "apps" as crime tools. In 2010 alone, a single wallpaper app for the Android system compromised up to 4 million users' personal data, which was transferred to China (Leyden, 2010). And of course, smartphones are one part of an increased merging between ICTs and objects within the wider environment that is creating an "internet of things" (Moskvitch, 2011), an environment of "ubiquitous computing" and "ambient intelligence" where everything merges into the "brand-new world of allatonceness" (McLuhan, 1967, p. 63) that characterises a hyperspace. The scope of this is limited by our interfaces at present – keyboards and even touchscreens create an inevitable distance between the user and their interactions. But our interfaces are becoming more invisible and seamless and the inevitable criminal consequences of everything from clothing to lamp-posts, becoming interconnected, online-addressable resources is a technological accident just waiting to happen.

Little thought has also been given to the implications of intelligent surfing or automated behaviours. The impending arrival of Web 3.0 – the "semantic" web, like the shift to cloud computing, will require huge new centralised databases which will increase, not decrease, vulnerabilities and create new challenges to privacy. The world of "personalised" access this promises threatens not just increasingly personalised attacks by targeted malware (cf. Kunert, 2011), but an ideologically skewed environment where the information available to us is determined on the basis of what a corporate algorithm decides is "most personal" to us (cf. Pariser, 2011). In turn, the kind of automated offending made possible by "bot-nets" is only the beginning of a range of new legal and policing challenges of this kind. Other automatons that occupy digital space – such as hot-word search programmes or spiders, are a mere shadow of the intelligent behaviours presaged by "genetic algorithms" able to learn and adapt their behaviours (Fogel, 2006). At present such systems are not of course self-determining, but as the viability of machine intelligence grows, so too do the possibilities that automated agents might, on occasions, begin to act independently. At present there is no viable sense of what the relevant culpabilities would be in such a scenario.

Nor, in conclusion, should we forget how this extension of physical space will also produce shifts in the nature (and power) of certain agents to effect harms – together with new capacities for evading any sanctions. The hyper-space created by ICTs has, as already suggested, permitted significant new varieties of offending by state and corporate agents. A major challenge for law enforcement will lie in how it reconciles its duties to its political (and commercial) masters with those to the public at large. If technological justice is not merely to be justice for the few, then regulating the misuse of ICTs will need to incorporate a far wider sense of what misuse entails than has been the case to date.

4   Tele-control

From police whistles to the surveillance society

Tell me about yourself – your struggles, your dreams, your telephone number.[1]

Though information and communications technologies have proved useful to criminals, the capacity they offer for control "at a distance" means that their impacts upon regulation have, in many ways, been more striking. In the contemporary context a sense that ICTs enable a widening panoptic gaze has fuelled the idea that this is now a "surveillance society", or a "society of control" (see amongst many examples Deleuze, 1992; Lyon, 2001 and 2007; Garland, 2001; Bogard, 2006; Kerr *et al.*, 2009; Coleman and MacCahill, 2010). In this chapter I intend to consider whether these notions are reasonable evaluations of the impacts of ICTs upon the justice system and whether the capacities they offer for observation and knowledge gathering are being as equitably – that is as justly – distributed as we might hope.

Towards modern ICTs: the emergence of surveillance and instant response

In his influential *Empire and Communications* (1950) Harold Innis posited a recurring historical link between the control of communications systems and the exercise of power, one that can be traced back as far the prototypical communications technologies of ancient empires. The decentralised forms of power that operated in ancient Sumer might, for example, be directly associated with the weight of the clay tablets that were the main communication medium – since this made the issuing of commands over any distances extremely difficult (cf. Innis, 1950, p. 6). In Rome, by contrast, access to the light and easily transportable papyrus secured from its Egyptian provinces, together with the advent of the brush pen, enabled far wider communications. And given the bureaucratic structures necessary for managing the highly distributed economy of Rome's extensive empire (ibid.), this also allowed for more effective centralised control.

The way ICTs have been used to manage the contemporary criminal justice system and other institutions of control emphasises the continuing relevance of Innis's argument. One obvious and recurring example of this has been the almost immediate deployment of any of the new communications technology for surveillance purposes. It is no surprise, then, that the telephonic technologies of the early twentieth century were adopted by police as quickly as the telegraph network of the nineteenth century had been. The mayor of New York had agreed to sanction tapping the telephone lines of suspected criminals as early as the 1890s (cf. New Yorker, 1938; Fitzgerald and Leopold, 1986) and this practice spread quickly in the USA, boosted by the predictable security concerns raised by the First World War. In 1916 a huge telephone surveillance network was revealed during investigations by the New York State legislature, encompassing thousands of tapped lines connected to the Custom House by a centralised switchboard. As the *New Yorker* later reported, "every time a suspected alien lifted his receiver a light showed on this board and a stenographer, with headset clamped on, took a record of the conversation" (New Yorker, 1938; Diffie and Landau, 2007). Evidence also suggests that more informal, "private" or commercial investigators quickly adapted to the telephone as a control device. We know, for example, of an extensive surveillance operation conducted by private investigators during the First World War against an employee of J.P. Morgan who was suspected of passing on details of Allied munition orders (New Yorker, ibid.; cf. Fronc, 2009 for other examples of early private surveillance in the USA). The rapid and unregulated spread of telephone tapping in the USA was eventually placed on a sounder legal footing by *Olmstead* v. *United States* in 1928 – in spite of the prescient observations of the Supreme Court Judge Brandeis, who warned of the unprecedented opportunities for "tyranny and oppression" that it might offer (Brandeis, 1928).

The extent of early phone tapping conducted in the UK is, by contrast, rather harder to gauge, given the notorious "culture of secrecy" (Vincent, 1999) that tended to characterise the operations of government there. But it too seems to have been substantial. Thus, the creation of a national telephone service in 1912, managed by the General Post Office, seems to have come with an almost automatic assumption that intercepts could occur without the need for any proper authorisation. This policy continued until 1937, when the requirement for official approval from a Secretary of State was created (Spencer, 2009). But open discussion about the monitoring of communications had to wait until the late 1950s. Following a series of revelations about phone-tapping, a *Times* leader questioned whether something "so repugnant to every idea of what constitutes freedom within a society … [that] it has attached to it the aura of the police state" should ultimately be permitted at all (cited in Vincent, 1999, p. 188). The Birkett Report of 1957, which followed these newspaper revelations, was the first and open parliamentary debate in the UK about communications interception since a series of "letter opening" scandals in 1844 had raised similar public concerns (ibid., p. 189; Spencer, 2009). One of the judges noted how "the origin of the power to intercept communications can only be surmised" (Vincent, ibid.), but there was no real mystery here – the technology itself created a de facto "right" to listen that was simply assumed by the powerful. In 1900, about the best technology on offer to protect against this changing technomia of public surveillance was the "whispering device" developed by the S&M Co., a small amplifier that could be fitted into telephone mouthpieces in order to allow users to "whisper and avoid eavesdropping" (Murray Associates, 2011). In terms of effective protections, not much has improved since then.

The imminent advent of instantaneous one-to-one "wireless" communi-cation was about to shift the balance of communications power even further – in spite of Hertz's rather downbeat conclusion that his discovery of radio waves in 1887 had been of "no use" (Susskind, 1995). Even by the late 1920s, police in Detroit had begun to adopt radio technology and commu-nication as a new operational tool (Poli, 1942), and though contact with patrol cars was one way at this stage, a fundamental shift in the nature of policing interventions – from post hoc to real-time responses – had been signalled. Within ten years or so, the advent of the modern communications era in policing was presaged when forces in the USA began using the earliest kind of personal handset – the "walkie-talkie". Though the shift towards radio communication took a little longer within UK policing, another new technology had also begun to enhance the capacity of control to "see" at a distance – the radar, which proved so crucial to eventual Allied victory in the Second World War. For the first time in history, an invisible sensory field had become available to the state that allowed it to monitor space as a whole (Buderi, 1996).

By the 1970s these new communications capacities had begun to manifest the hyperconnected global reach to which we are now accustomed. The instantaneous imaging and messaging capacity provided by the new satellite communications systems was complemented by rapid developments in computing and information, to provide the basis for the modern ICT and its imminent spread from the specialist to the personal market. In the late 1960s James Q. Wilson had commented that the main difficulty for law enforcement centred upon a "lack of adequate information" (1968, pp. 57–64). Fewer than 2 per cent of US police departments with under 100 employees used computers before 1987 (Heaton and Garicano, 2007), yet by 1993, 95 per cent of all officers worked in departments with computers (NIJ, 1998). In an age when the largest database in the world is now reputed to be the National Security Agency's database of US citizens' phone call records (Cauley, 2006) and police now call upon a formidable array of computers, databases, smartphones, satellites and other ICTs to perform their role, "information poverty" is one of the lesser problems they face. The question of what to do with all the information that such technologies are providing has now become at least as important an issue as acquiring it in the first place.

In order to make sense of the complex relationship between ICTs, control and criminal justice that we now see emerging I will consider three functions that these technologies now enhance:

- communication and coordination
- the acquisition and storage of information
- the interpretations of such information.

Assumptions that, in each case, these technologies have created significant improvements in operational efficiency are one question that this chapter aims to subject to critical scrutiny. The wider question – whether they have also improved justice – follows directly from this.

Communication and coordination

A key part of Innis's argument about control and empire is that effective communication between its operatives invariably enhances the capacity to coordinate responses to threats. It is a relationship we see again and again – whether in the extensive post and transport system which bound together the two million square miles of the Chinese Empire (Chang, 2007), the 100,000+ miles of roads in the Roman Empire (Wiseman, 1970) or the "global telecommunications hegemony" of the USA (Hugill, 1999, p. 236). Contemporary ICTs are not only central to coordinating law enforcement but have helped to create an integrated system of control that enables unprecedented connections between security, policing and even military agencies. This shift has been acknowledged within the criminological litera-ture in terms of the idea that policing has become "networked", "nodal" or "pluralised" (Johnston and Shearing, 2002; Crawford, 2006; Jones and Newburn, 2006). Whilst this sounds impressive, what it actually means is less clear – and there have been increasing concerns that the uncritical acceptance of the network model has obscured some underlying functional failures (cf. Yar, 2011).

Coordination and communication capacities appear to be significantly enhanced by "seamlessness" – i.e. where one communication medium does not interfere with another. Hence the drive within most advanced police agencies to shift from analogue to digital communications systems (see for example NPIA, 2010a). Digital communication does not just offer better-quality signals, but two other aspects of seamlessness – first, easier ways of interfacing with digital information resources and second, communica-tions harmonisation or "interoperability" between state security and emergency services. There are some obvious practical reasons for greater interoperability – not least the problems created by analogue radio systems for effective co-ordination between agencies during disasters or crises.

The 9/11 Commission made special note of the catastrophic communication failures between policing, security and emergency services during the attacks upon the World Trade Center (Benjamin, 2005), concluding that "the technical failure of … radios [was] a contributory factor … in the many firefighter fatalities in the North Tower" (9/11 Commission, 2004, p. 323). The 7/7 bombings in London in 2005 saw similar failures of interoperability between radio systems used by police, ambulance and fire services, a situation worsened by the fact that analogue signals would not function underground (GLA, 2006; Smith, R., 2007). And a contributory factor in the deaths during 7/7 was delays in implementing recommendations about interoperability following the Kings Cross underground fire 12 years previously (BBC, 05/06/2006). The role of institutional inertia in compromising the goal of interoperability was also seen in failures of communication occurring during the 2005 Hurricane Katrina disaster, when technology that could have secured this was available, but never used (Faulhaber, 2006).

The ideal of "interoperability" has now been realised in the UK by an investment of over £2.9 billion in the new TETRA (TErrestrial Trunked RAdio) digital radio network operated in conjunction with O2 under the brand name "Airwave". The system comprises a single high-speed encrypted voice and data communications system which, in theory, is secure from interception by criminals scanning police radio frequencies (PT, 2009a). But the transition was not without its problems – the length of time taken to implement Airwave was criticised in a National Audit Office report (NAO, 2002) and it has been plagued with a number of technical problems. Figures released under a Freedom of Information request, for example, indicated that it had failed on up to 93 occasions between 2005 and 2008 (BBC, 16/03/2009) and most spectacularly during the UK riots of 2011. Questions and controversies have also arisen around the speed of data transfer and, perhaps even more seriously, around the health and safety of both handsets and broadcasting masts (Philips, 2002; Tetrawatch, 2010). Similar technical "glitches" and repeated failures hampered the introduction of a $2 billion emergency radio network designed to link emergency agencies and local police and fire departments in New York State (Buettner, 2008).

"Information seamlessness" is now as essential to the coordination of control as communications interoperability. The calls for intelligence led models of policing have had important impacts upon the way that information technology is now used to coordinate security operations (cf. Ratcliffe, 2008). By late 2009, around 50 per cent of police officers in the UK were using "smartphones", which enable immediate access to various information resources – i.e. databases like the Police National Computer (PNC), the National Fingerprint Identification Service (IDENT), the National Automatic Number Plate Recognition (ANPR) or the Driver and Vehicle Licensing Agency (DVLA) databases – together with intelligence briefings and other types of information (PT, 2009b). The Coalition Government's report on "reducing bureaucracy" in policing (i.e. making budget cuts) specifically highlighted "the potential of mobile technology to reduce bureaucracy [and] increase efficiency" (Berry, 2010, p. 30) as part of the philosophy that "joined up technology with access to reliable information is the lifeblood of modern policing" (ibid.). Hence, even in a climate of financial restraint, funding for smartphone technology was scheduled to increase by nearly £80 million, with an additional 15,000 handheld computers in use by early 2010 (Lomas, 2008).

A second, less transparent desideratum for control in the use of communication and coordination networks is "exclusivity". We saw how postal systems operated for the sole benefit of rulers in earlier empires, and this tradition has been maintained wherever possible – for example, in the hot lines set up between Churchill and Eisenhower during the Second World War, or the US Government Emergency Telecommunications Service (GETS) and Wireless Priority Service (WPS), which provide special communications priority for federal and security employees (NCS, 2011). The analogue radios used by police, which depended upon VHF or UHF frequencies, made it easy for eavesdroppers to "tune in" using commercially available radio scanners and, though this was largely a hobby pursued by radio enthusiasts, "listening in" to police and emergency broadcasts was made technically illegal in the UK under the 2006 Wireless Telegraphy Act. The switch to digital communication should, in theory, prevent all eavesdropping, given that communications are encrypted, though discussions of ways in which TETRA might be hacked can be found on various specialist blogs and forums (see for example POP, 2011). But, as with interoperability, exclusivity has not always been pursued in ways consistent with the law. For example, the Greater London Authority's (GLA) report on the 7/7 bombings found that the City of London Police had "acted outside" an agreed framework by forcing the suspension of public cellular access for up to four hours after the incident, causing distress and uncertainty to the public – especially those with relatives involved in the incident (GLA, 2006, p. 152). Proposals by the New York Police Department to jam mobile phone networks in the event of "serious incidents" were also criticised as a step too far, given that such powers might be used during other perfectly legitimate activities such as public demonstrations (Shachtman, 2009; see also Hsu, 2009a). An ultimate expression of exclusivity (and an unprecedented seizure by politicians of power over communications) would be the kind of "kill switch" advocated by certain security experts that could totally close down the internet in the event of "national cyber-emergencies" (Sandoval, 2011).

The need for investment in ICTs in order to deliver well-coordinated security and policing responses seems obvious enough, though the question of what the often significant investments have actually delivered has not always been very effectively addressed. The usual justification – that "reductions to crime rates" result – is one that we will return to in subsequent contexts, but a specific legitimation strategy here has been the argument that enhanced communication provides "more information" to citizens. There are now a plethora of websites set up by police, government and private agencies that aim to "serve" the public by allowing them to report crime, examine local crime hotspots, scrutinise images of offenders and even – following the US lead – access details of where sex offenders live (cf. Almandras, 2010; Leppard, 2011). But the limited research done in this area makes it hard to say how informative or useful such websites really are – the fact that up to 75 per cent were scheduled to be closed down by the Coalition Government (Bentley, 2010) hardly seems a ringing endorsement of their public utility. There have also been concerns about negative consequences – such as vigilantism, causing an increase in fear of crime, or damage to local property prices (Fay, 2011).

Concerns with cost efficiencies have, in many cases, led to a gradual handover of these communications technologies to the private sector, though it is far from clear that cost savings or increased efficiency have been the result. In the UK, for example, it has emerged that some public bodies may be charged to use the new privately managed Airwave system – even though this was originally taxpayer funded (Tetrawatch, 2010). There are also questions around national communications autonomy – for example, a sizeable chunk of the $20.81 billion-worth of goods that Israel exported to the USA between 2003–7 consisted of telecommunications products (USA Today, 2003; ForeignTradex, 2010). More troubling are concerns about civil liberties that the collusion between private sector-sponsored technology and security and policing agencies raises. Legitimate demonstrations are often now used as strategic exercises for testing police communications or in coordinating quasi-legal control tactics like "kettling" (Dodd and Lewis, 2011). Similarly, the use of extensive radio coordination between private security operatives, police and local authorities in managing citizens engaged in the legitimate pursuit of a night out with friends raises new questions about the limits of control (Edwards, 2010). In turn, the increase in numbers of gated spaces controlled by radio-coordinated security guards reinforces the image of a privatised security state where ICTs serve less to protect the public than to dictate their movements (Kohn, 2004).

Listening, watching, sensing and tracking

ICTs have also been a central influence in extending a second traditional desideratum of control – the capacity to watch, listen or even "sense" behaviour within selected environments. So profound have their effects been here that a new kind of social order – the surveillance society – is claimed to have emerged as a result (Lyon, 2007). Digitisation now offers full spectrum surveillance – i.e. a capacity to collect and observe not just aural communications but a rich range of (often real-time) visual and behavioural data. But, as with enhanced coordination, more can sometimes mean less. For in addition to questions about the methods and legitimacies of gathering such data, wider issues are emerging around how better to make sense of it. And very often, decisions about interpretation may be more significant than the data-gathering process itself.

Take, for example, message interception, where the available data has been multiplied not just by the advanced forms of eavesdropping ICTs now provide but by the greater volume and variety of what there is to listen to. Whether it is cookies and keystroke-sensing software or mobile intercepts and satellite monitoring (cf. Bennett, 2001; McGuire, 2010; Angwin, 2010), ICTs have become the most "listened in to" environments in history. A typical "extension-amputation" effect of technology can be discerned here – on the one hand, ICTs enable us to express ourselves more widely; on the other, the digital traces we leave in doing this (on text messages, blogs, tweets or social-networking sites) provide evidence that might then be used to constrain this freedom of expression.

Message interception has been legitimised through a significant new body of legislation granting state and corporate eavesdroppers a "right" to eavesdrop. One of the landmarks in this new order of technological regulation was the notorious Communications Assistance for Law Enforcement Act (CALEA) in the USA, passed in the mid-1990s, which – for the first time in communications history – imposed a legal compulsion upon companies to design communications technologies in such a way as to enable policing and security agencies to monitor them (EFF, 2006).[2] This set the scene for a flood of subsequent legislation – such as the UK Regulation of Investigatory Powers Act of 2000 (RIPA), which required every internet service provider (ISP) to install "black box" software to intercept and record internet communications; the 2001 UK Anti-Terrorism Crime and Security Act (ATCS), which permitted the retention of net data for longer periods, and the US PATRIOT Act, which granted unprecedented listening powers to the US executive (see Bloss, 2007). And in spite of their promise to roll back surveillance powers, the Strategic Defence and Security Review (2010) set out by the UK Coalition Government maintained and even extended proposals by the previous administration to retain data on all internet activity for possible later use by security services (cf. Williams, C., 2008a; Arthur, 2010; Slack, 2010).

In addition to interceptions conducted by public authorities, a formidable array of (commercially available) listening devices, like tracking cookies and keystroke software, have also opened up surveillance possibilities to many parties beyond the state. Consumer surveillance is probably now one of the most common of all surveillance practices, though we should not overlook the huge growth in corporate espionage that parallels this (cf. Lace, 2005; Turow, 2006). Corporate snooping capacity often more than matches state listening powers, even though it is often conducted at the very boundary of legality (Nasheri, 2005). In the UK, the illegal surveillance operations conducted by Rupert Murdoch's News International (van Natta *et al.*, 2010;

Doward and Stevens, 2011) or the use of the monitoring software Webwise to gather illicit marketing data by the company Phorm have typified the general disdain with which communications and privacy law is often regarded by the powerful. And though News International's hacking of the phones of private individuals was both extensive and damaging to the victims concerned, police showed little interest in pursuing the company in comparison to other, similar offenders – for example those involved in the Wikileaks affair, where several arrests were made almost immediately (Halliday, 2011). Similarly, Phorm's method of scrutinising individuals' personal data and of redirecting users (without their consent) to its website resulted in a number of legal challenges under the RIPA legislation (BBC, 05/06/2008) and requests to the City of London Police to investigate. However, the police took the decision not to prosecute on the (rather peculiar) grounds that the case would be "too complex" and that there was "no criminal intent" on the part of Phorm (Hanff, 2008).[3] The European Commission subsequently alleged that the UK government's failure to respond to Phorm's secret trials of its behavioural advertising technology meant it had not met its obligations under EU Data Protection Directives, and as a result decided to sue it (Williams, C., 2010a).

Complementing these enhanced listening technologies have been developments in photographic and film technologies that enable a variety of control agents to "watch" without having to depend upon the direct witness of someone in the field. The gradual transformation of the camera from an art or entertainment technology into a control device has been most obvious in the development of a CCTV scanscape – with Britain, notoriously, amongst the world leaders here (Norris and Armstrong, 1999; Goold, 2004). CCTV has been one of the most heavily funded security technologies in the UK, and by the late 1990s represented over three-quarters of total spending on crime prevention (Welsh and Farrington, 2008). Recent Freedom of Information requests have indicated that nearly £315 million was spent by a selection of local authorities between 2007–10 – with £10 million spent by Birmingham alone (Deane and Hamilton, 2010). As elsewhere, this technology is being gradually digitised and though this enhances image quality and connectability to other media it has also opened up the possibility of hacking. Most computers now come standardly equipped with web-cams and there are well-known ways in which these can be "taken over" and diverted to spy on users (cf. Beam, 2009).

But for all the investment in this technology, the returns have been at best ambiguous – as the UK government's own research has suggested (cf. Gill and Spriggs, 2005). A comprehensive review of 44 separate studies of CCTV throughout the UK (Welsh and Farrington, 2008) found that there were only limited contexts where CCTV appeared to enhance crime control (in relation to opportunistic crime around car parks, for example), and its overall worth was judged to be far less clear. Even the Metropolitan Police noted in an internal report that only around one crime is solved for every 1,000 cameras installed (Hope, 2009). The suspicion that CCTV, like other technical control measures, simply displaces crime to other areas – and may even help to inflate offending (by inducing a false sense of security on the part of the public – cf. Schneier, 2008) has often been challenged, though never very convincingly (cf. Waples *et al.*, 2009). And even in the area where CCTV is meant to excel – delivering images that provide evidence of criminal acts – there have been problems. In its recent National CCTV Strategy report the Association of Chief Police Officers (ACPO) complained that around 80 per cent of CCTV images were of such poor quality as to be unusable (Gerrard *et al.*, 2007) – and of course it is not hard to render an expensive investment in cameras all but useless by the simple expedient of wearing a baseball cap or scarf to obscure the face. Police have conceded that there is now little fear of CCTV on the part of street criminals (Hope, 2009), so that, without legislation compelling us to be visible for monitoring purposes, the electronic eye seems likely to always be subject to some form of evasion. The prospect of such legislation is not entirely absurd – controls on "hoodies" in many shopping centres, proposals to "ban balaclavas" during demonstrations (Higginson, 2011) or the criminalisation of wearing the burqa (Bryan, 2010) indicate an emerging variety of regulatory requirements seeking to enforce citizen visibility.

Advocates of CCTV continue to insist that its advantages outweigh its disadvantages and that if CCTV doesn't work well enough "yet" this is because its technology is not sufficiently powerful enough "yet". One proposal has been for a unified CCTV system, where both public and private cameras are centrally registered and networked together to permit more continuous and intensive scrutiny (cf. Page, 2007). Yet CCTV already looks to be a rather dated visual control technology in the face of the power of global satellite systems. Advanced optical magnification used by spy satellites like the Ikon/Keyhole-12 means that objects as small as ten centimetres can be recognised, with the interconnections between satellites now offering almost total global coverage (PI, 2007). But in spite of this power, the legalities around satellite imaging are even less developed than for CCTV and seem likely to prove emblematic in the struggle to create effective regulation of visual monitoring (cf. Best and Elea, 2011). In the USA, proposals by the Bush administration to allow police to view spy satellite data (in particular data from high-resolution military satellites capable of seeing through clouds or penetrating buildings) were eventually blocked by the Obama administration in 2009 (Hsu, 2009b). Such controls, however, have been a rarity. Many employers already use satellite positioning to track employees (PI, 2007), and recent claims by UK police that the use of aerial spy drones was necessary to assist in "reducing cash machine fraud", "tractor theft" or the "prevention of fly-posting" (Lewis, 2010) indicate how unconcerned control agents have been with providing plausible legitimisations of their enhanced visual power.

Digital and mobile cameras, or software such as Google Earth or Street View, have further augmented surveillance possibilities, with consequences as yet unclear. Digital cameras provide useful "eyes on the street" – both for law enforcement and for exposing injustice, whether this is the killing of protestors or the abuse of prisoners at establishments like Abu Ghraib (Jordan, 2006), though the capacity to use these visual technologies is not yet very equally distributed. Certain locations are blocked because of security fears, whilst powerful private individuals (the saga of Dick Cheney's "missing" house comes to mind) can demand invisibility – (cf. for example Weinberger, 2008). Nor, as we shall see later, are law enforcement agencies very comfortable about having their own activities recorded. Technologies like Street View have highlighted increasingly sensitive questions about visibility rights and issues of intrusion. Images of naked children, politicians' houses or deceased relatives captured on Street View's cameras may offer a new way of experiencing public (and private) space, but for many such transparency goes too far (Matyszczyk, 2008; McKeegan, 2010; Shiels, 2010). The result, at present, is a technomia of visual monitoring that is at best legally ambiguous, at worst overtly unjust.

A less discussed but equally significant extension to the audio/visual monitoring powers now provided by ICTs is the capacity to "sense" or "track" objects within a control space. Capturing digital traces of ICT use is one thing, but certain technologies have provided the kinds of tracking capacities previously restricted to "low-tech" extensions like the hunting dog. Thus, the extended spatial awareness offered by GPS is being augmented by devices providing enhanced sensory awareness – like heat-sensing technologies, which reveal objects in the infra-red spectrum, or odour-sensing technologies, which extend the power of the nose (see for example Wilson and Baietto, 2009). One of the most pervasive and powerful of contemporary tracking systems is seen in the RFID (Radio Frequency Identification) tag, which combines computing and radio technologies to create digital markers capable of uniquely identifying almost any object it is attached to (cf. Garfinkel and Holtzman, 2005). Initially deployed for tracking retail products across the supply chain (partly for efficiency in stock taking, but also for theft prevention), the use of RFID tags has now been extended to everything from animal husbandry to monitoring hospital patients (ibid.). It is hardly surprising, then, that RFID has become both a panacea of control and a new nightmare for privacy (cf. Albrecht and McIntyre, 2005). Whether one is passing through an airport or browsing in a shopping mall, RFID tags are increasingly likely to be embedded in all kind of objects in the environment – from passports to consumer products like shaving razors and even children's clothing (Crace, 2007). There is also evidence that RFID has been used by stores to identify and track individuals without their permission (Albrecht and McIntyre, 2005; Paget, 2010). In spite of claims by manufacturers and retailers that the range at which RFID can be read is limited, it has been demonstrated that, even with fairly basic technology, information can be retrieved at distances of between 500 feet and 1 mile. (cf. Paget, 2010). Given that RFID tags are often linked to databases with significant personal information, obvious scenarios of criminals using scanners to obtain such data, or stalkers using scanners to track individuals, then open up. At present, however, the regulation of RFID and the extent to which it infringes rights remains very unclear (EPIC, 2010).

Just as communications technology initially shifted policing from post hoc to real-time interventions, sensing and tracking technologies have begun to extend temporal responses into the future, feeding directly into the risk-management philosophies that now shape criminal justice. Enabling practitioners to anticipate offending has been most effective in contexts where routine or repetitive watching tasks are involved and "offences" are relatively easy to define – for example, ANPR, or speed cameras (cf. Pughe, 2006; Wells and Wills, 2009). More sophisticated pattern-recognition technologies directed at complex identification tasks, in particular facial recognition, represent a further stage (cf. Brey, 2004; Introna and Nissenbaum, 2009). The hope is that such technologies will offer capacities for "recognising" offending behaviour patterns – for example, "how suspicious" an individual's stance or movements might be, or how far their appearance (clothing, hairstyle, ethnicity, etc.) matches certain prefigured risk profiles. New software such as the ineptly named CRUSH (Crime Reduction Utilizing Statistical History), imported from the USA by several UK police forces, promises to enable "predictive analytics" which "anticipates" offending (Thompson, 2010). The worryingly subjective aspects involved in programming algorithms to recognise risk profiles is a point we will return to later.

It is clear, then, that digitisation has created a convergence between visual, aural and tracking technologies capable of generating highly information-rich environments. On the plus side, a world of "augmented reality" has begun to emerge where digital information of all kinds can be imposed on the external environment (Beaumont, 2009) and tagged objects can be linked to various databases. The result – being able to point our smartphones or other digital devices at objects in this environment to buy tickets, find local restaurants, read information about what we are seeing or even identify potential sexual partners in the vicinity – clearly has some obvious advantages (cf. Geers, 2011). Whether these will outweigh the obvious potentials for abuse is another matter. For, of course, such capacities can also be deployed in other directions, not least for the creation of "ambiently intelligent" (Hildebrandt, 2008) spaces – an internet of "things" where every object within a field serves as a node for recording and transmitting information, so enabling our augmented presences to be observed in increasingly finer-grained detail (Wright *et al.* 2010).

Storing and processing knowledge: the database state?

ICTs do not just extend the capacity of our senses to gather or anticipate information, they have also played a central role in enhancing the way we store, retrieve and collate information. Storing information for control purposes has its origins in official (or unofficial) record keeping – such as historical, tax, legal, census and other data – but the advent of the digital database has so far expanded storage techniques that "database forms of monitoring" have been argued to be the result (Ayres, 2007). But, if it is true that "control over personal information is the database era analogue of control over labour power in the industrial revolution" (Andrejevic, 2009), then it is also true that we are still awaiting the data equivalent of the labour rights that (eventually) came with industrial development. Certain limited protections, such as the 1998 Data Protection Act in the UK, the European Directive on Data Protection or the Australian Amendments to the Privacy Act (2000), have been created, along with new bureaucracies to police them, like the Office of the Information Commissioner in the UK. But there are at present significant variations within differing jurisdictions around such protections – with the USA, especially, lacking in any robust national data protection legislation, or, indeed, any right to privacy in its constitution (PI, 2010). Such gaps have allowed the private sector there to conduct one of the most aggressive programmes of acquiring and trading in personal information anywhere in the world. This has also led to legal clashes with other jurisdictions, especially Europe, where a range of US companies like Google and Facebook are under investigation for possible breaches of privacy rules over their use of personal data (Bodoni, 2011).

One more obvious impact of large databases upon the criminal justice process has been their effects upon policing, where "Information richness" has been central to the ongoing transformation of policing towards proactive "joined-up" approaches. As a result, policing has become highly dependent upon database resources like the Police National Computer (PNC) in the UK or the US National Crime Information Center managed by the FBI (FBI, 2009). The ever-extending scope of the PNC offers its own insights into this transformation of policing. Introduced in 1974, the PNC is now accessible from over 30,000 terminals nationwide and has moved far beyond its original remit as a record of stolen vehicles, serving instead as an all-purpose intelligence resource. Officers can use it to retrieve information about individuals who have been arrested, cautioned or convicted – for example, their addresses or distinguishing marks; information about certain categories of stolen property, in particular firearms; information about registered owners of vehicles and details of engine or chassis numbers (cf. Williams, 2009). Elsewhere, the role of data storage in enhancing identification capacity can be seen in its impacts upon the use of fingerprint data. Accessing this was originally a very cumbersome process requiring police to forward fingerprints gathered from scenes of crime to expert centres such as Scotland Yard for matching. This process has now been considerably streamlined by the creation of a universally accessible fingerprint database, IDENT1 – the latest title for the National Automated Fingerprint Identification System (NAFIS). The significant increase in speed of matching this has provided means that, by 2004, increases of over 220 per cent in monthly fingerprint identifications were being claimed (MHB, 2004). However, control of IDENT1 was outsourced to a private contractor called Northrop Grumman Information Technology, which stood to gain at least £122 million from UK taxpayers for its eight-year contract. The difficulties arising from a major software bug that caused the near shutdown of the service for over a week in 2004 raised various concerns about the efficiencies gained by this outsourcing. But these delays were nothing in comparison to Northrop Grumman's role in the six-day shutdown of the US State of Virginia's governmental IT network, for which it was fined (Dignan, 2010). Northrop Grumman's repeated attempts to suppress Freedom of Information requests about the details of its contract for running IDENT1 are a reminder that claims of technological efficiency are rarely based on very transparent evidence (ICO, 2010).

The readiness to defer to technological norms in determining justice when using criminal justice databases has been especially highlighted by the controversies around the National DNA database (NDNAD). The NDNAD is now claimed to hold the DNA profiles of over 5 million individuals – around 8 per cent of the population, by far the highest proportion of the national population as compared to other countries at present; and UK police have congratulated themselves on being a "world leader" in using it, claiming an average of 3,000 matches a month (Williams and Johnson, 2008; NPIA, 2010b). Central to the legitimisation of the NDNAD has been the argument that it offers a more efficient and effective form of crime control. Prima facie, this has seemed hard to doubt, with over 41,000 crimes matched against records on the database in 2006–7 (amongst them, over 500 rapes) (NPIA, 2007). At this time the claimed overall detection rate was around 26 per cent, rising to 43 per cent where DNA evidence was available (ibid.). But matters become less clear when set against other measures. In 2000/2001, for example, when the database contained records of around 1.2 million people, it was claimed to have "helped solve" 0.29 per cent of recorded crimes (ibid.). What "helping solve" means is of course already vague, but by 2008, when a further half a million individuals had been added to the database, it "helped solve" just 0.36 per cent of crimes, a decline from the 0.37 per cent of the previous year and, at a less than 1 per cent rise over ten years, hardly evidence of a dramatic rise in the conviction rate (Oates, 2008a). By 2010 the number of crimes the database had "helped solve" was still below 1 per cent (Travis, 2010) and the overall rate had declined by around 11 per cent over the previous year – raising obvious doubts about whether this is the best return on an investment, especially given that running costs had nearly doubled over this period (Kablenet, 2008).

Collisions between the use of the NDNAD and human rights law have raised different kinds of concerns. One variety has involved the disproportionate representation of certain ethnic groups on the database – up to 77 per cent of black males had details stored, compared to just 22 per cent of their white equivalents (Leapman, 2006). Another concern has related to the legitimacy of storing details at all. In 2008, following an appeal to the European Court of Human Rights by two men whose DNA had been retained on the NDNAD (with no charges having been made against them), the Court ruled that it was illegal for the government to retain DNA profiles and fingerprints of those not convicted of any crime (Staley, 2005, Williams, 2008b). Yet, by late 2009 fewer than 30 per cent of requests from innocent parties to have their DNA records removed had been granted by police and there was little sign of the government's exerting any pressure on police to comply with the ruling (Whitehead, 2009). Moreover, the government still proposes to retain DNA data indefinitely if an arrest is for what is termed a "qualifying offence" (usually serious violent, sexual and terrorism offences) or if the individual has a criminal record – even where no further conviction is secured or charge made (cf. Liberty, 2011).

The extensive linking together of databases has been central to the way that the traditional notions of the person (offender or otherwise) have shifted. For example, the potential links that could be made between an individual's records on the PNC and other databases, such as the Motor Insurance Bureau, suggests the emergence of what has been called the "data-vidual" (Aas, 2006) – where the self becomes both shaped and constituted by its data presence. Such interconnectability offers security advantages, but also of course poses major issues of rights and accountability. For, once entered onto a database, it becomes all but inevitable that an individual will appear on others – whether these operate within the state sectors, such as healthcare, social services or education, or within the still more numerous private sector contexts. For access to databases such as the Criminal Records Bureau (CRB) database is no longer restricted to policing or security operatives. Records are also open to many social actors with no connection to the criminal justice system – in particular, employers – and though the CRB can, in theory, only be consulted with an individual's consent, the "right" is clearly rather a limited one, given that consent is often all but compulsory to secure employment. With up to 14 million Britons now requiring such checks, major impacts on citizens' life and prospects can result. At the international level, data sharing is now conducted in even more comprehensive and invisible ways. For example, the UK's inclusion in the European Prüm treaty database permits any European police force reciprocal access to databases with DNA or fingerprint records, along with car registration and other personal information (Blau, 2007). Similar data sharing and potential violation of rights can be seen in continued expansions of transjurisdictional databases like the Passenger Name Record (PNR) register or the Terrorist Finance Tracking programme (TFTP), which has allowed the US government to scrutinise the flight details or the private banking transactions of European citizens (Waterfield, 2010; BBC, 02/02/2011).

The profitability of data sharing has been astutely exploited by web giants like Google and Facebook, along with a range of new companies that have built their business on storing and selling huge amounts of data – often in quasi-legal ways (cf. Leyden, 2011). Profit may accrue from the selling of data, or from more indirect uses – for example, in developing market awareness of consumer behaviours. Consumer databases such as the Crucible system, used by the retailer Tesco, are said to process over five billion pieces of data per week in order to cluster customers into "spending types" who can be targeted more effectively (Welstead, 2007). In turn, Crucible is linked to numerous other key private sector databases – in particular, those run by credit reference agencies like Experian or Creditas. But, like many other companies that trade in data, Tesco has been highly secretive about Crucible and has repeatedly refused requests from journalists under the Data Protection Act to access their personal details stored on the system (cf. Tomlinson and Evans, 2005). In the new "black economy" of personal information and relentless profiling such reticence quickly vanishes when it comes to selling access to this data (Elmer, 2004). The relentless transformation of individuals into commercially targeted data hubs brings harms that go beyond privacy issues – all too often it has resulted in addictive consumption that leads to debt, mental health issues and even suicide. (cf. Fitch *et al.*, 2010). Yet the influence of the socio-technical logics driving commercial databases has penetrated so far into the criminal justice system that it has even begun to shift relations between police and the public. For example, the MOSAIC relational database, operated by Experian (which correlates consumer types with postcodes) has now been widely adopted by the police as a method of profiling local communities. How far the use of spurious sociological categories like "Global Connectors" or "Rural Isolationists" will improve police–community relations is questionable (Asthana, 2004).

A major, but as yet under-researched, fall-out from our presence within multiple databases is the possibility of "error amplification" – where an error on one database leads to errors on every other. By 2008, around 12,000 or so individuals had been shown to have been erroneously listed in the CRB, and similar errors can be found in almost every context where databases shape policy (Oates, 2008b). Take, for example, the highly coercive E-verify database run by US Homeland Security, which US employers are required to use when taking on any new workers. Data entered on E-verify is linked and cross-referenced with immigration databases, but problems have arisen with legitimate job applicants or new employees being repeatedly identified as "illegal". The firm Intel, for example, had 12 per cent of the workers it hired in early 2008 rejected on this basis, though almost every one of them turned out to be a legitimate US citizen. Such misidentifications eventually prompted both the US Chamber of Commerce and sections of the business community to sue Homeland Security in order to prevent the forcible imposition of E-verify upon employers (Frank, 2009). Error amplifications become especially fraught where there is data sharing between state and private databases, as the experience of the British citizen John Irving indicates. Irving suddenly found himself being repeatedly refused loans and bank cards for no ostensible reason and, to compound these irritations, he was then detained at an airport by foreign immigration officials who had decided that Irving was involved with the Saddam Hussein regime. It eventually emerged he had been mistaken for another John Irving – a chain of mistakes that had originated in errors made by the credit card company American Express, errors further compounded when other financial institutions accepted the mistaken association and passed on this misinformation to the authorities (Daily Mail, 2007).

The challenges to justice created by data sharing come into stark focus in the light of the claim that at least a quarter of UK databases are in breach of data protection or human rights laws (Anderson *et al.*, 2009). And these are just the ones we know about – for there are also many more covert databases where sensitive information about citizens may be used against them. In 2008/9, for example, the Information Commissioner's Office mounted an investigation into a database shared by large construction companies such as Taylor Woodrow, Laing O'Rourke and Balfour Beatty, which kept covert information on over 3,000 workers relating to their trade union affiliation and activity, employment details and even personal relationships. Employers paid a £3,000 annual fee to use the resource – effectively denying individuals employment in advance of any job application (ICO, 2009). Elsewhere, the UK National Public Order Intelligence Unit (NPOIU) was also found to be holding a covert searchable database with details of activists, climate protestors and journalists – most of whom had committed no criminal offence (Lewis and Valle, 2009). Though the database potentially violated section 8 of the Human Rights Act, police have so far evaded any legal sanctions. In an age where public-spirited citizens who report a crime may find themselves (unknowingly) recorded on a database and may even find this information used in subsequent police action against them (Whitehead, 2011), we have to ask whom the advent of database monitoring has really benefitted.

Communications and knowledge: evidence, pattern and interpretation

On one estimate, around 150 exabytes (1 billion gigabytes) of data were created in 2005, a figure that had increased nearly tenfold – to 1,200 exabytes – by 2010 (Economist, 2010). This has created not just data-storage issues but also new kinds of problems around what to do with all this data. There are particular issues for the justice system, in the face of this data deluge, given that detecting crime or establishing innocence may depend not just upon the correct piece of data being located, but upon it being interpreted correctly. Police complain that they are literally "drowning" in the amount of data they have to process (see for example Espiner, 2006) and in both the 9/11 and 7/7 incidents there was enough information left by the bombers for the incidents to have been prevented if it had been properly collated and interpreted. Similar oversights occurred prior to the apprehension of the 2009 "Christmas bomber", Umar Farouk Abdulmutallab, where there were again ample indicators that pointed to a potential attack (Scherer, 2010). The use of ICTs to "read data" has therefore become just as important as using them to collect, or store data.

The US Institute of Justice's recent technology wish-list highlights this goal, declaring the Institute's pressing need for "tools that identify and extract relationships hidden in large, complex law enforcement agency data sets, or spatial and temporal data analysis tools that examine data in new and unique ways" (Holder *et al.*, 2009). The use of so-called "data mining" tools to scan across as well as within databases is now a common crime-control technique, permitting collation of various intelligence sources such as phone logs, transport tickets, card-spending patterns and so on (cf. Adderley, 2003; McCue, 2007). Data-mining software attempts to categorise relationships of this kind by defining classes, clusters, associations and sequential patterns, though fitting these together meaningfully remains a far from an exact science (cf. Han and Kamber, 2006). The inevitable "solution" to this – more technology in the form of automated interpretation algorithms – is hardly reassuring and raises obvious questions about reliability. As we have just seen, nothing can rule out the possibility of false matches or a gradual accretion of almost baseless "information" about an individual that highlights them as a risk. Precisely these concerns have emerged around the FBI's National Security Branch Analysis Center (NSAC), a data-mining project involving links and searches across up to 1.5 billion public and private records about US citizens or foreigners – in effect a back-door attempt to revive the (supposedly defunct) "Total Information Awareness" (TIA) initiative by the Bush government (Singel, 2009a). There have been major questions about its method of finding associations and the many false positives that the NSAC software potentially creates, since these often have little to do with any offending behaviour on the part of an innocent citizen (NRC, 2008).

A second series of concerns have focused on the ways in which data is acquired in the first place. In the NSAC project there is evidence that companies have often been compelled to release information under subpoenas issued by the FBI – though there are also many others which, without consulting customers, have been eager to grant access to their data. For example, the airline company Jetblue was forced to apologise after it emerged that it had secretly passed on details of over 5 million passenger itineraries to the FBI (Singel, 2009a). But maybe the most serious concern is the false sense of security that data mining creates and the belief that whatever patterns are detected must be more "trustworthy" because they have avoided human interpretation or bias. The fact is that no matter how slick the algorithm, or how many associations it finds, at some point human actors must interpret these associations and decide whether they are worth pursuing or not. And, as an apposite saying amongst statisticians goes, "torture data long enough and it will confess to anything", so that at some point interpretation always risks becoming a matter of wish fulfilment (cf. Gandy, 2006). Interpretive issues even enter into the initial programming of an algorithm – for example, a decision to code data according to one conceptual taxonomy rather than another – a point well known to anyone who has ever had to code a questionnaire. Where the objectivity of automated analysis fails, we are left with the personal expectations and biases of the analysts. There have been a number of useful studies that have highlighted the potential problems of human prejudice here. For example, in one study of CCTV operators (Smith, G., 2007) it emerged that they often developed their own "cultures", which strongly influenced what they selected to look at – and how. Another study found that over 90 per cent of surveillance targets were males and that 85 per cent of these were in their teens or twenties, wearing hoods or what were judged to be similarly "high-risk profile" forms of clothing (Norris and Armstrong, 1999, cited in Smith, G., 2007).

Dispensing justice

Beyond their impacts upon policing and detection, ICTs also now play a significant part in shaping every other stage of the criminal justice process – sometimes even the outcome itself. At the most basic level, this may relate to tasks such as digitising court records or, more substantively, assisting in the provision of evidence or the management of offenders. In the UK, many key administrative tasks such as scheduling hearings, generating court orders and managing fines are now handled by the Libra Case Management System, whilst databases like the UK's National Offender Management Service (NOMS) have become central to the tracking of offenders through the system (Anderson *et al.*, 2009).

Digitising legal documents would appear, at first sight, to be a largely uncontroversial project with benefits like faster transfers of data between police and solicitors, easier uploading of court information from handhelds for police officers, and more convenient record keeping for lawyers (cf. ISIS, 2009, p. 10). But upon closer inspection these benefits also entail some less desirable outcomes. In the USA, digitisation has provided new revenue streams for the private sector, though at what benefit to the public has not always been clear. Evidence suggests that costs of around $4 million were incurred by the US Department of Justice in 2009 – merely to access its own documents on PACER, the electronic filing system provided by the Administrative Office of the United States Courts (Singel, 2009b). PACER generated profits well in excess of $50 million in 2006 as a result of charging everyone from journalists to private citizens and even the Attorney General a fee to examine court documents (ibid.). The advent of digital court data in the US has also made it easy for private data brokers such as Lexis-Nexis to repackage it and then resell it to public bodies like libraries or government agencies (ibid.). Digital data has also benefited certain agencies in the UK – for example ACPO, which has sold on data from the PNC (Lewis, J., 2009). Western law firms are also now actively exploiting the distance-enhancing capacities of ICTs by "outsourcing" technical support, or document management, to India and other markets (Lloyd, 2007).

A more significant impact of ICTs upon the court-room can be seen in the spatial extensions or hyperspatialisations of justice they have begun to facilitate. The UK's so-called "virtual" court initiative made much of this, though there was nothing "virtual" about this other than a video link between a defendant at a remote location and the court-room. Nor was the use of video evidence (live or taped) very new – the 1999 UK Youth Justice and Criminal Evidence Act created provisions for "vulnerable witnesses" (defined as children under 18, witnesses with mental disorders or "intimidated" witnesses) to give evidence by pre-recorded or video link (cf. CPS, 2011). In the US there is an even longer tradition of what is called "video conferencing", which stretches back to its first use in 1993 – in committing a defendant to a psychiatric facility (Price and Sapci, 2007; see also Toksen, 2007). Subsequent evaluations of the virtual court project found no great improvements in efficiency, and overall costs turned out to be higher than for traditional court processes (PA, 2010). And such initiatives have also been strongly criticised by the chief executive of the Law Society, who argued that, irrespective of improved efficiency or any other technological norm virtual courts are claimed to advance, they also help to "create an imbalance between the power of the state and the rights of the individual, which is beginning to undermine the rule of law" (Baksi, 2009). There seems to be an obvious danger that conducting justice remotely might create a separation between lawyers and their clients. Moreover, since defendants are often interviewed from within the confines of police cells, rather than the neutral space of the court-room, there will always be suspicions that pressures can be exerted upon the defendant (consciously or unconsciously). It is telling then that, within the US system, video evidence has been most frequently used in immigration cases, where defendants are usually locked away in detention camps far from the court-room. This has produced repeated criticisms that the practice "dehumanises" defendants and (because of the lack of visual or other cues available to judges) raises the likelihood of conviction (Appleseed, 2009).

The gradual introduction of "digital evidence" such as e-mails, browser histories or digital audio and visual files into the court-room is also raising its own kinds of concerns. An obvious issue is the dependence upon technical experts that it creates, given that evidence may be in a form – such as a computer data log – that is too complex for judges or jurors to understand. Technical issues also arise around how best to establish that such evidence has not been tampered with – an obvious danger, given the flexibility and inherent copyability of digital files (cf. guidelines set out by ACPO, 2006, and other problems discussed by Kerr, 2005). And, as we have seen, with any offence conceived of as "technologically enabled", establishing a definitive link between a digital trace or file and an act of wrongdoing is far from straightforward. In turn, admissibility poses its own set of problems – for example, though CCTV footage is usually now accepted in most UK courts, up to 80 per cent of it has been judged to be potentially inadmissible because of poor quality (Gerrard *et al.*, 2007). And if a CCTV data file or tape has not been kept secure and confidential, or the system has not been properly registered, questions also arise about whether it might breach the Data Protection Act. In both US and UK courts, permission to use evidence gathered using hidden video cameras will usually be admissible in a court of law only if a crime has been committed – irrespective of whether permission was granted to film or not. This creates the slightly odd situation of its being against the law to install cameras in places like in-store dressing rooms, but perfectly legal to use footage from them if it happens to show shoplifters in these areas. Evidence that police have vacillated or failed to hand over vital evidence of this kind to the courts raises other concerns (see for example Hattenstone and Taylor, 2010).

Amongst the most significant impacts of ICTs upon legal and court processes have been the potential compromises of the justice process posed by jurors' accessing the internet for various purposes. A conviction of a rapist in 2005 was declared "unsafe" after internet print-outs were found in the court-room, and the decision to jail a juror in the UK for communicating with a defendant by Facebook indicates the fundamental challenges to legal process that this technology is now creating (Hill, 2010). In spite of calls from judges for juries to avoid "researching" facts about defendants online, many in the legal profession have accepted that it is now an "unmanageable task" (ibid.) and may even signal the end of the jury system as we know it (Johnson, 2010). Similarly, the role of other social networking sites, like Twitter, in helping to circumvent injunctions has been argued to be undermining the very basis of libel law (Binham and Croft, 2011).

At the post-judicial stage, the spatially compressing powers of ICTs are also evident in extensions to the traditional prison. The result – a kind of "hyperspatialisation" of the panopticon – has begun to extend the process of punishment far beyond physical prison walls, into a wider punitive landscape. But far more prosaic concerns than Bentham's original rehabilitative ideals around the panopticon are at work here. Claims about cost and efficiency gains in dealing with the punishment of convicted offenders obscure what seems to be the real aim behind these extended forms of confinement – managing the continuing rise in prison populations. The practice of electronic tagging, whereby prisoners can be released early from prison environments, provided they wear an electronic marker, suggests one of the more literal manifestations of the extended prison. The advent of GPS technologies (cf. Elzinga and Nijboer, 2006) has significantly improved the tracking and identification of tagged prisoners, but a great deal of scepticism remains around the practice. For some, the effects have been positive – prisoners convicted of minor offences can complete their sentences outside of prison, so avoiding more dangerous inmates or morally degrading environments. Others reject this, insisting that tagging prisoners is not far removed from treating them like animals (see Nellis, 2006; Nellis *et al.*, 2010). Advocates of more populist punitive stances, by contrast, have complained that tagging is not "sufficiently retributive" in that it does not punish individuals as effectively as does confinement (Lee, 2002). There has certainly been a danger that tags can be easily removed or disabled (by sitting in the bath, for example), so allowing offenders to ignore the curfew orders that tags are meant to enforce (Delgado, 2007). A more serious charge has been that tagging prisoners directly endangers the public. In 2006, for example, over 1,000 violent offences were reported to have been committed by tagged prisoners in the UK, including at least one attempted murder (Morris, 2006). A predictable response – attempting to fix technical problems by way of a technology fix, has not been entirely reassuring. Inserting RFID chips or other tags below the skin would certainly make their removal far more difficult (Brady, 2008), but whether it is a good idea to import techniques used for the management of cattle into the justice system is controversial, to say the least. In another sense, however, this simply mirrors uses of RFID for spatial control elsewhere – for example, the increase in RFID tagging and GPS tracking of children by parents (cf. Johnson, 2009a).

Beyond surveillance? ICTs, justice and the order of invisibility

The wholesale penetration of ICTs into the operations of the criminal justice system has taken place with almost no debate and even less reflection upon its worth. The all but universal presumption has been that ICTs are a technology that benefits every aspect of the justice process – whether this means better, more "intelligence led" policing, improved information about crime for the public or more effective court processes. Similar presumptions have driven the perception of ICTs in wider regulatory contexts, whether in the recurring fantasy of a data-driven, "joined up government", or the idea that consumer profiles result in "better service" for us all. Technological norms such as efficiency drive many of these presumptions – as they do elsewhere – but this does nothing to answer deeper questions about their real impact. Do they really enable more and better communication – or is it less and of lower quality? Have they produced more effective policing, or simply distanced officers from the communities they police? More crucially still, has this increased role for ICTs produced better and wider justice, or has it in fact changed the nature of justice forever?

That there have been benefits does not seem in doubt. ICTs have made obvious improvements in identifying the guilty or overturning false convictions – for example, through the greater availability of surveillance footage or internet browser logs. The evidence that they help to provide has also helped in exposing wider injustice – whether this be digital images of unacceptable working conditions or evidence of bullying and violence. Access to the internet has helped to inform the public about repressive state behaviours and corporate malfeasance, together with improved access to information and resources that may assist in the legal process. ICTs have also helped to make the actions of criminal justice practitioners more accountable. Being able to record police brutality on a mobile phone, or using a digital network to expose racism or corruption, has made a clear contribution to greater transparency in the justice system. And the communicative power of ICTs in helping to coordinate protest or galvanise resistance has even been argued to have created whole new forms of popular politics (cf. Brants and Voltmer, 2011). Thus, whilst some of the naive optimism about the emancipatory potential of ICTs that characterised the 1990s may now have passed (Morozov, 2011), this need not blind us to the very real and concrete potentials that remain.

But neither should such gains obscure the wider questions around justice that these technologies also raise. One issue above all has stood out within the digitisation of social relations and the technomia around this – namely, the extent to which it is now possible to stand *outside* the reach of digital networks. In this sense, the thesis of the surveillance society or questions around privacy rights are all, arguably, sub-issues within a far wider question – the visibility that the hyperspatialising powers of ICTs often seem to enforce, whether we like it or not. This wider "visibility" – which may be observational or informational – offers a paradigmatic instance of the extent to which technological norms now shape social norms. In this context, visibility goes far beyond the world of spectacle once postulated by Debord (1994) – for whilst ICTs are of course central to the ongoing commodification of the image, they also decisively underpin the newly regulatory power of the visible.

At the centre of this shift has been the age-old tension between the *oikos* and the *polis* – between private and public space (cf. Habermas, 1991). What was once a seemingly unbridgeable gulf has been gradually eroded by the capacity of ICTs to redistribute presence in new ways. In this context, the much-vaunted question of whether there is a "right" to privacy (cf. Thomson, 1975; Inness, 1992) can now be seen in the light of a more fundamental question – whether there is a "right to be invisible".

A common perception here – that privacy is something that we once had "more of" but upon which we must now accept limitations (Etzioni, 2000) – has been instrumental in legitimising the regulatory power of visibility. But claims that "privacy is no longer a social norm"[4] can be argued to contradict the historical evidence here. For it makes just as much sense to claim that we were once far less private than we are now – many traditional societies possessed no word for "privacy", and even in the West the first extended discussion of this as a "right" does not appear until the late nineteenth century (cf. Warren and Brandeis, 1890). So, far from being the relic of a bygone era, concerns with privacy could also be seen as a very modern concern, one directly manifested in behaviours like the introspective gaze of the mobile phone owner or the increased rate of people living alone. We might also see this shift in regulatory terms – most obviously in the way states and their policing agencies now use ICTs to demand citizen visibility – whether in identification documentation or the all but obligatory presence on a database. Beyond this are a myriad small ways in which the demand for visibility has been incorporated into our everyday social norms. As we all know, even the most straightforward transactions – from buying a theatre ticket to reading a newspaper – now require registration and extensive surrender of personal details. Similarly, the failure to own devices that make one visible – like a mobile phone – often constitutes a new, low-intensity social offence, not only violating our new expectations that friends or family should be visible to us, but making it impossible to access many important services.

In this context it is not just members of the new "invisibility elite", such as state or corporate actors, that act to enforce the visibility of the less powerful: in a sense, we are all complicit in policing of this kind. In a world where at least 44 per cent of people confess to monitoring their partner's activities online, where up to 70 per cent of parents covertly observe their children's use of the internet and 53 per cent admit to using search engines to find out about friends, colleagues or prospective dates, regulating visibility has clearly become a new kind of techno-social norm (Madden *et al.*, 2007; OII, 2008). Our own willingness to become objects of scrutiny is a particularly telling indicator of this shift – over 47 per cent of us confessed to "Googling" ourselves on a regular basis in 2007 – twice as many as who admitted to this in 2002 (Madden *et al.*, 2007). Such attitudes form an obvious continuum with the general willingness to publish details about ourselves online or simply to hand them over when requested – attitudes equally contiguous with the now seemingly universal desire for our 15 minutes of "fame" or the contemporary cult of celebrity.

Of course, if visibility were a property that was distributed equally, it might be accepted that this new order was, by and large, a just one. One obvious sense of an "equitable distribution" in this context might be the requirement that "if you can watch or acquire information about me, then I should be able to do the same with you". Or, alternatively, "if you have the right to profit from information about me, I should I have the right to profit from it too". The fact that, on both counts, there are major asymmetries and forms of exploitation by the powerful suggests that, if justice is about fairness, this new order of visibility cannot be an entirely just one. As we already know, it is not just that there are few technical limits upon the state's capacity to listen, to watch or to record the behaviour of its citizens. There are also limited legal constraints – especially given the widening of rights to record citizens' movements on CCTV, satellite or other imaging technologies that states and business have granted themselves. The German politician who sued Deutsche Telecom to access his phone logs and found that it had retained data from his mobile phone that could be used to track all his movements over a long period (Die Zeit, 2011) is just one amongst many such stories. Location data, like other varieties of data, is something providers now simply acquire as a matter of course, without feeling any duty to consult the public.

Citizens do not just lack the reciprocal technical capacity to match these asymmetries in visibility – they also have significantly inferior legal rights in this regard. Filming representatives of the state is now illegal in the UK under Section 58(a) of the 2006 Terrorism Act – with the result that even where police officers are in the act of filming the public, it is illegal to film them doing so. Such powers have resulted in a number of controversial incidents where citizens have been threatened or arrested by police – often for little more than taking tourist photographs of buildings (see for example Lewis, 2009a and 2009b). In the USA, where there has traditionally been greater respect for the balance between state and citizen power, the urge to accommodate such asymmetric visibility rights has begun to visibly distort the law. There have been several arrests for filming police officers, justified on the flimsy grounds that it was the sound recording, not the pictures, that contravened US law – specifically state laws preventing the "wiretapping" of conversations without consent (Watson, 2007). The zealousness of the US criminal justice system in pursuing these kinds of eavesdroppers hardly compares very well with its limited responses in the face of the unprecedented (and probably) illegal increase in the wiretapping of US citizens under the Bush presidency. Especially when – as the Wikileaks scandal showed – those who use ICTs to make state malpractice visible are treated with unprecedented severity – including even the threat of execution (Pilkington, 2011).

Technology increasingly both feeds and reinforces such inequities. On the one hand, developments like the new HTML5 programming language now come with built-in features that facilitate the gathering of private details (Vega, 2010). On the other hand, technology is easily adapted by the powerful to evade visibility – for example, the many invisible databases that offer vital public information but that can be shielded from net searches to evade public access (CDT, 2007). Elsewhere, the tendency for business to provide only automated phone access or nothing more than an e-mail address to customers is not just about cost cutting, or a reduction in direct contact. It is part of the same order of invisibility as that which enables private equity companies to acquire vast parts of the economy without anyone even knowing who they are.

Of course, visibility is just one aspect of the regulatory impacts of ICTs and the hyperconnectivity they bring to social life. We might also look, as McLuhan did, to the return to "oral cultures" that global connectivity brings – one where we are not just immediately aware of every rumour but, as in an oral culture, share a readiness to believe them. With a capacity to rapidly spread information through networks, a new age of panics is ushered in, one where "terror is the normal state" (McLuhan, 1962, p. 32) and where politicians actively pander to public fears, using technologically driven forms of justice to manage crises that barely exist. A fusion of technomia with populism results, one that has barely begun to be analysed.

5 Micro-crimes

Misusing chemical, biological and nuclear technologies

On prussic acid we break our fast, We brunch on morphine stew
We dine with match-head consommé, Drink carbolic acid brew
Corrosive sublimate tones us up, Like laudanum ketchup rare
While tyro toxicon condiments, Are wholesome as mountain air.[1]

In comparison to the furore around ICTs, the relative silence about the impacts of chemical, biological and nuclear technologies (CBNTs) upon offending has been rather odd – especially given the considerably higher (i.e. potentially catastrophic) risks posed by their misuse. Insofar as criminologists have considered these technologies, their focus has tended to be upon selective macro consequences rather than the technology itself – for example in "green" issues such as GMOs, or workplace harms such as toxic fumes (see Edwards *et al.*, 1996; Pearce and Tombs, 1998; Bierne and South, 2007; Walters, 2007 and 2010; White, 2011). In this chapter I want to consider why a more unified focus upon CBNTs and the extraordinary capacities they offer us to manipulate matter at the micro-level is important in clarifying the distinctive varieties of technological harm they can generate.

The emergence of "micro-crime" in modernity

The discussions within this and the following chapter will relate to technologies centred upon the three broad disciplines that emerged from the scientific revolutions of the 1600s – specifically: chemistry, the study of the composition and properties of matter; biology, roughly, the study of organic matter and life; and physics/nuclear physics, the study of physical laws and processes, in particular those relating to atomic and subatomic particles. As industrialisation has transformed this knowledge into material artefacts and commodities, CBNTs have come to play an increasingly central, albeit invisible, role in shaping many of the most crucial ingredients of our contemporary world, from the food we eat to the medicines we take and even the air we breathe.

The transformation of these abstract sciences into material goods and professional expertise has certainly not been a uniform process. For example, though industrialised chemical engineering and production was under way from at least the early nineteenth century (Furter, 1982), it was to be a further 100 years before breakthroughs in genetic science enabled the industrialisation of biological knowledge, or the first commercial exploitations of atomic power (Krimsky, 1991).[2] Given their embryonic state at the start of the twentieth century, then, it is not surprising that the nomos around CBNTs was also relatively undeveloped. The new awareness within Victorian society that industrial emissions needed some form of control was discussed in Chapter 2, but legislation and enforcement remained minimal throughout most of the nineteenth century. As a result, in the industrial town of Bradford alone there were around a thousand annual deaths from respiratory diseases in the early 1900s (Richardson, 1986), and it was not until new controls like the UK's 1926 Smoke Abatement Act that any very effective regulation of industrialised chemistry began. As in the USA, with its hotchpotch of state and city ordinances, the scope of such legislation remained uneven, excluding the considerable pollution caused by domestic fires or the growing risks posed by automobile exhaust fumes (Reitze, 1999). It was not until the 1950s that a need for more comprehensive controls was acknowledged, in new laws such as the UK's Clean Air Act (1956) or the US's Pollution Control Act (1955).

Deference to the demands of industry was as powerful a factor in obstructing regulation as it is today. The complaint by the Sheffield Iron-masters in 1845 that allowing government officials to check emissions was "worse than one of the plagues of Egypt" (cited in Ashby and Anderson, 1981) presaged how virulent industry's resistance has often been. In the US, the court system displayed a "pronounced tilt in favor of protecting polluters" (Reitze, 1999, p. 4), one that the emerging commercial–technological complex was happy to exploit. One more obvious result was a steady rise in the production of refined lead – especially the tetraethyl lead used to create high-octane petrol (EPA, 2010). The presence of lead in consumer goods, in particular in toys, resulted in the hospitalisation of many US children with (often fatal) conditions such as paralysis, blindness and convulsions (Rabin, 2006), but the Lead Industries Association (LIA) aggressively lobbied against any controls. The LIA even threatened to sue researchers who found evidence of harm, and actively undermined campaigns by the US Children's Bureau to provide information on lead-free paint to concerned parents (Rabin, ibid.). It also succeeded in blocking proposals by the Massachusetts Department of Labor and Industries to ban lead paint in 1933 and, in an internal industry circular, later exulted:

> It was particularly important to obtain a hearing and settlement in Massachusetts ... otherwise we might have been plagued with [similar regulations] in other States, affecting the use of white lead.[3]

The emerging food and drugs industry presented another context for new biologically or chemically based criminalities. Sales of proprietary medicines in the UK more than trebled between 1850 and 1900 (Corley, 2003) in the wake of advertising campaigns that made extravagant claims of success. But for every "wonder" product like Beechams Pills – which quickly doubled annual production levels to over 300 million pills (Corley, ibid.) – other, more deadly concoctions, were for sale. Popular tonics such as "Mrs. Winslow's Soothing Syrup for Teething and Colicky Babies" often had high morphine content, which resulted in a number of infant deaths (cf. Swann, 2004). Only after sustained pressure from campaigners did new legislation such as the US Biologics Control Act of 1902 require companies to ensure that all medicines had requisite levels of purity and safety.

Public safety was also threatened by the role of CBNTs in food production – especially the practice of adulterating food with chemicals like coal tar or phosphate to enhance its preservation or appearance (Crellin, 2004). Widespread protests against such irresponsible behaviour influenced the passing of the US Pure Food and Drug Act in 1906, which created a new testing regime for consumer products, together with the threat of prosecution where food or drugs were found to have been adulterated (Young, 1989). However, the law was quickly challenged by the pharmaceutical industry[4] and the Supreme Court ruled in its favour, accepting that the law did not prohibit therapeutic claims – merely "false and misleading statements" about the identity of a drug or what it contained (Sobel, 2002; FDA, 2010). Some of the Act's more obvious loopholes were tightened up in the later (1938) Federal Food, Drug, and Cosmetic (FDC) Act, which defined new quality standards for foods and the requirement that any new drug be "shown safe" before it could be marketed (Sobel, 2002).

The excesses of the late nineteenth-century British food and drugs industry were addressed by legislation such as the 1875 Sale of Food and Drugs Act and the 1890 Public Health Act – but a much looser regulatory environment overall operated than in the USA (cf. French and Phillips, 2009). Indeed it was just as likely that those who campaigned for healthy food, like Thomas Allinson (struck off the General Medical Council in 1892), might be prosecuted as offending food companies (Pepper, 1992). Allison's characterisation of doctors as "professional poisoners" did not help his cause – but, though the *Lancet* railed at his "wholesale disparagement of ... fellow practitioners" (Pepper, ibid.), BMA pamphlets such as *Secret Remedies* (1909) and *More Secret Remedies* (1912) indicated that doctors were aware of the dangers posed by patent medicines. As the 1914 Parliamentary Select Committee Report on the problem concluded,

> secret remedies making grossly exaggerated claims of efficacy ... are put upon the market in many cases by cunning swindlers who exploit for their own profit the apparently invincible credulity of the public.
>
> (HC, 1914)

The increasing power of the pharmaceutical industry meant that such concerns were not transformed into effective controls – indeed no further parliamentary investigation of the industry took place until nearly a hundred years later (HC, 2005a). Thus, early legislation such as the Dangerous Drugs Act of 1920, or the Therapeutics Substances Act of 1925 had far too general a focus and a statutory distinction between medicines, drugs and poisons was not made until the Medicines Act of 1968 (Applebe, 2005).

Other risks were posed by a sudden rise in sales of disinfectants and other chemical cleaners during this period. Articles in popular magazines highlighting the dangers of germs and praising the "sanitary value of bleach" (cf. Literary Digest, 1924) created new fears around hygiene. This accelerated a commercialisation of CBNT-related products that sometimes led a gullible public to engage in high-risk purchases – as, for example, in the surreal "radium craze" of the 1920s. Radium-infused products such as face creams and tonic waters were widely marketed as "liquid sunshine" – catch-all cures for ailments as diverse as impotence or insanity (cf. Clark, 1997; Rentezi, 2008 and 2009). Corporations like U.S. Radium lobbied heavily against investigations into mounting fatalities amongst workers in their factories and made a series of out-of-court settlements with litigants, until they were eventually forced to close in 1927 (Clark, 1997).

Growing questions about the misuse of CBNTs were not just manifested within the commercial domain. The medical establishment was also implicated in often shocking applications of these technologies for experimental research. One notorious example involved a study of the effects of syphilis on 600 black men in Macon County, Alabama conducted by the US Public Health Service in 1932. Though vaccines were available, these were withheld for the purpose of "more accurate testing" – so exposing many of the experimental subjects to the inevitable, yet perfectly avoidable, consequences of infection (Jones, 1993). Details of this experiment were kept secret for over 50 years, until a class action suit forced the US government to offer an apology and a settlement of $10 million to the surviving victims and their families (ibid.). Evidence of an even more cynical US medical experiment of the 1940s to test penicillin, which involved deliberately infecting mentally ill Guatemalan citizens with syphilis, emerged only in late 2010 (Fox, 2010).

New techniques such as lobotomy – surgical removal of parts of the prefrontal brain lobe in order to "cure" mentally disturbed patients – raise further questions about the inadequate regulation of medical practice at this time (cf. Shutts, 1982). US surgeons like William Freeman (who conducted the first lobotomy on US patients in 1936) developed savage versions of the technique – for example, his "ten minute" lobotomies involved driving an ice-pick up into the brain through the eye sockets (ibid.). Even Stalinist Russia had banned the practice by the 1950s, but lobotomies were conducted in the USA until the late 1960s, with an estimated 40,000 individuals being damaged as a result (including high-profile patients such as Rosemary Kennedy, JFK's sister) (El Hai, 2005). Justifications for lobotomies were often highly dubious – women were far more likely to undergo the procedure than males, often for trivialities like masturbation or "being quarrelsome as a wife" (cf. Braslow, 1997, pp. 152ff). Yet no one was ever prosecuted or compensated for the cognitive damage that resulted – indeed the pioneer of prefrontal lobotomy, Antonio Egaz Moniz of the Lisbon Medical School, received a Nobel Prize (in 1949) for his work.

The popular "eugenics" movement of this period also raised no particular legal concerns, though it involved medical practices and philosophies eventually regarded as criminal when conducted by Nazi scientists (cf. Carlson, 2001; Bashford and Levine, 2010). The philosophy enjoyed widespread support amongst the scientific and political elite, not least Presidents Theodore Roosevelt and Woodrow Wilson (cf. Gould, 1981), and had influential supporters in democratic nations as varied as Australia, Sweden, Japan, France, Ireland and Switzerland. It also had direct impacts upon legislation, with new laws permitting forced sterilisation and the criminalisation of "miscegenation" or interracial marriage (cf. Pascoe, 2009). Around 20,000 individuals deemed "unfit to breed" were sterilised in the USA alone, amongst them African Americans, criminals and prostitutes (Pernick, 1996). Sweden's 1934 Sterilization Act, which permitted sterilisation of the mentally ill, was repealed only in 1970 – with the result that only Nazi Germany forcibly sterilised more individuals than Sweden (Pred, 2000; details of Australian eugenics policies can be found in Garton, 2010).

It is easier, with hindsight, to see how the emergence of industrialised, commodified bio-chemistry and its related professions in the early twentieth century created a new order of technological risk. From medical science to food production, or from industrial chemistry to household cleansing products, a distinctive range of potential harms began to emerge, though these were rarely defined as criminal. The unprecedented expansion in the misuse of these technologies that was to occur in the First and Second World Wars brought the dangers of CBNTs into a much clearer focus, but we should not forget that the basis for what were later to be defined as "crimes against humanity" had originated in the technological innovations of advanced, democratic states.

Industrialised war (I): chemistry, biology and physics on the battlefield

The total wars of the twentieth century marked a decisive turning-point in our perception of CBNTs as a source of harm. There were precedents for their use within earlier conflicts – the use of gas on the battlefield had, for example, been considered in the earlier US Civil War and the Crimean War (Coleman, 2005). But the First World War saw the most extensive and sophisticated deployment of CBNTs for military ends to date, in particular the use of three distinct chemical agents:

1   Tearing agents/tear gases (such as xyxl bromide), which attacked membranes in the eyes, nose and mouth causing crying, coughing or temporary blindness.
2   Poison gases or asphyxiants (such as chlorine or phosgene), which destroyed the respiratory system of the victim, usually leading to a slow and painful death from asphyxiation.
3   Blistering agents, especially the "mustard gases" that attacked exposed skin, producing blisters equivalent to third-degree burns.

The use of gas on the battlefield may have marked a new stage in the unfolding of chemical harm, but its overall military effectiveness has been questioned (cf. Meselson, 1991). The French had deployed tear gas as early as 1914, but this was scarcely noticed by the enemy, and whilst the Germans' use of chlorine at the second Battle of Ypres in 1915 was more successful, they encountered what was to prove a central difficulty in deploying chemical agents for lethal ends – how best to deliver them. Their initial technique – letting the wind direct the gas – somewhat backfired when changes in wind direction simply blew it back into the faces of German troops. In the end only around 3 per cent of all (military) casualties were related to gas and, of these, just 6 per cent were fatal (Harris and Paxman, 1982). More serious was its effect upon less well-trained and protected civilians – a prelude to the kinds of damage CBNTs were to inflict later in the twentieth century. The German mustard gas bombardment of Armetières in 1917 alone saw close on a thousand civilians injured, around 10 per cent of them fatally (Cullen, 2008, p. 234). Both France and Germany also explored the weaponising of biological agents like botulism and brucellosis (cf. Wheelis, 1999), and the German military purportedly used them in Finland, even outlining a proposed bio-warfare programme on the US mainland during the latter part of the First World War (Koenig, 2007). Fortunately, such weapons were never used on the battlefield.

   Given that the Hague Treaty of 1899 had prohibited the military use of toxic chemical agents, their deployment in the conflict should have been a clear offence (Taylor and Taylor, 1992). But the heavy reparations paid by Germany following its defeat had far more to do with the (political) goal of curbing its imperialist ambitions than with its use of chemical weaponry – after all, both sides were culpable in this. The new post-war convention restricting the use of chemical and bacteriological weapons, the Geneva Protocol of 1925, was soon exposed as equally toothless. Mustard gas continued to be used during various colonial engagements of the 1920s and 1930s – for example, by Italian fascists in their invasions of Libya and Ethiopia (Kali-Nyah, 2000).

Industrialised war (II): the Second World War – the new laboratory of micro-crime

When Rudolph Hess, deputy Führer of the German Reich, remarked that "National Socialism is nothing but applied biology" (see Kühl, 2002, p. 31), it was not just a statement of Nazi philosophy, but an indication of a new kind of relationship between the state and science – especially biological science. Hess's comments merely highlighted what many industrialised nations like the US and the UK were also exploring – the use of biological technology as a resource for social control. Evidence of the Nazis' readiness to misuse such technologies was seen as early as 1933, when the new "Law for the Prevention of Progeny with Hereditary Diseases" established a mass-sterilisation programme, to be administered by "Genetic Health Courts" (Proctor, 1988). These courts (usually held in secret and without appeal) enforced the sterilisation of individuals with obvious deformities, along with other "undesirable" conditions such as schizophrenia, hereditary epilepsy, blindness and even alcoholism. From the mid-1930s onwards, German doctors were also being trained in "race hygiene" – selective breeding of those deemed to have appropriately Aryan characteristics – and the sterilisation of "genetically inferior" individuals (ibid.). Under the Aktion T-4 programme of 1939, doctors were also licensed to "euthanise" individuals not felt to conform to Nazi racial stereotypes, and over 5,000 congenitally deformed children were "mercy-killed" – usually by lethal injection or starvation (Burleigh, 1995).

Military uses of chemical or biological agents were, by contrast, surprisingly limited – though this was a tactical rather than an ethical decision. Both sides had built up huge chemical stockpiles and there were research programmes into new varieties of chemical and biological weapon. Highly toxic nerve gases such as Sarin (developed by the Germans) were one outcome (cf. Tucker, 2006), whilst files released to The National Archives indicate that the British had also experimented with various bio-agents – for example, anthrax "cakes" designed to infect German cattle (Bowcott and Evans, 2010). Where there was no fear of retaliation there was little hesitation in using such agents, and the Japanese invasion of China in 1937 saw an extensive deployment of chemical and biological agents, usually against the civilian population. Fleas infected with bubonic plague were released, and cholera and typhoid cultures were deposited into water sources – resulting in the deaths of an estimated 200,000 Chinese citizens (Barenblatt, 2005). Most notorious of all was Japan's Unit 731 laboratory complex, where some of the most serious war crimes of the Second World War took place. As well as engaging in biological and chemical weapons research, 731 was also the site of medical atrocities equal to anything carried out in the Nazi death camps. Human guinea-pigs were deliberately infected with diseases like anthrax and syphilis, and pregnant women and children were subjected to horrific operations without any anaesthetics (Williams and

Wallace, 1989). But pursuit of the national self-interest meant that most staff at 731 not only escaped prosecution but went on to have extremely successful post-war careers. General McArthur, the Supreme Commander of American forces in the South Pacific, was keen to maintain a US monopoly on bio-warfare secrets and, in return for data and cooperation, granted scientists at 731 immunity from prosecution (Harris, 1994) – just as the Russians kept their own counsel about these events (Maga, 2001). Shiro Ishii, the camp commandant, was reputedly granted residency in the USA, where he continued to engage in bio-chemical weapons research (Williams and Wallace, 1989).

The political self-interest in obscuring Japan's bio-chemical crimes has meant that it was the experiments conducted by the Nazis in their prison camps that became the most familiar example of how medical and biological science can be perverted. The subsequent Nuremburg trials set out a range of war crimes of this kind, including:

1   High-Altitude Experiments. Victims placed in low-pressure chambers and exposed to high-altitude conditions.
2   Freezing Experiments. Victims frozen, forced to remain in a tanks of ice water for long periods and subsequently rewarmed in various ways.
3   Infection Experiments. Victims deliberately exposed to diseases such as typhus, yellow fever, jaundice, tetanus and gangrene to test the effectiveness of potential remedies such as sulfanilamide.
4   Bone, Muscle and Nerve Regeneration and Bone Transplantation Experiments. Bone sections, muscles and nerves were removed from victims, often without anaesthetic.
5   Experiments with Poison. Adulterating a victim's food with poisons to test potencies and antidotes. Survivors were often killed to enable autopsies.

(US GPO, 1949, p. 8)

Research into genetic manipulation was also pursued, with experiments conducted on over 3,000 identical twins by Josef Mengele at Auschwitz amongst the most infamous. Mengele's interest in comparing the differing effects of blood transfusions, amputations or infections upon identical gene bases resulted in untold suffering for the genetic guinea-pigs he selected – though it also produced reams of new scientific data (cf. Posner and Ware, 1986). Major ethical questions have subsequently arisen about the use of such data – in particular, whether technical knowledge gained in criminal ways can ever be used legitimately. The fact that over 45 research articles published between 1945 and 1991 directly cited evidence based on Nazi experiments indicate that many scientists have been perfectly comfortable with the idea (Post, 1991).

In 1934, Leon Whitney of the American Eugenics Society had celebrated the "far sighted men and women in the USA and England [who] have long been working towards something very like what Hitler has now made compulsory" (cited in Kühl, 2002, p. 36) – a signal that complicity in the misuse of CBNTs was not restricted to Nazi scientists. Such moral ambiguities were also seen in the intensive atomic weapons programmes of the period. For example, the case for the defence in the killing and injury of over 200,000 civilians at Hiroshima and Nagasaki (AtomicArchive, 2010) rests upon a utilitarian calculus that sets the lives lost at these sites against the many more which "might" have been lost if a land invasion of Japan had been attempted. Others have been more inclined to see the bombing as unambiguously criminal – a calculated decision by President Truman and the US military to ignore the imminent Japanese capitulation in order to test the potency of their new weapon – whilst also delivering a political message of intent to the Soviet Union (cf. Alperovitz, 1995). But, whilst many scientists were prepared to offer their expertise, many were not. Leo Szilard and over 60 US scientists engaged in atomic weapons research at the Manhattan Project sent a petition to President Truman warning that dropping an atomic bomb on Japan without offering any warning or chance to surrender would "weaken our moral position … in the eyes of the world" (Szilard, 1945). Not only was their petition ignored, but the FBI began an intensive scrutiny of Szilard and Einstein, judging that their "Emergency Committee of Atomic Scientists" implied that they were being used by "various Communist front organizations" (Jerome, 2002). The charge of mass murder is one that has never quite gone away, in spite of the indignations of the American political establishment.

The post-war period, emerging criminalities and problems of control

The extraordinary range of harms directly attributable to CBNTs during the Second World War produced a collective political consensus that more effective regulation of these technologies was now essential. The war crimes trials in Nuremberg were the most immediate and obvious legal response, though these were of course largely directed at the German military and political high command, rather than specific uses of these technologies. Instead it was with the Nuremberg Code of 1948, which set out a new framework for regulating medical practice, that the post-war regulation of CBNTs began to develop in earnest. Not surprisingly, many of the subsequent agreements were primarily directed at the control of weaponry – especially nuclear capacity. National self-interest in promoting the commercial potential of these technologies, together with the long-term political stand-off between East and West, therefore meant that it was not until the 1980s that anything like a coherent global approach towards CBNT-enabled harm began to emerge. For example, the Chemical Weapons Convention was signed only in 1993 – nearly 70 years after the Geneva Protocol – and this still excluded defoliants like the notorious Agent Orange or explosives like napalm. And as conventions or treaties, such agreements are not, of course, legally binding, and as a result have been extremely difficult if not impossible to enforce (see Table 5.1 for a timeline detailing a few of the major agreements).

A further weakness of such conventions is that they tend to operate at state level – and so fail to address the often significant culpabilities of commerce in the use of CBNTs. Not surprisingly, the Second World War saw German companies involved in some of the worst atrocities of this kind. Familiar names like Bauer, Siemens, Telefunken, Krupp and Deutsche Bank were all found to have been involved in war crimes (AJC, 2000) and Bauer (under its previous name of IG Farben) helped to fund the Nazi Party. IG Farben was an enthusiastic participant in medical experimentation, often requesting particular tests or providing drugs for ongoing ones, and helped to develop a range of bio-chemical substances used by the Nazis, most notoriously Zyklon B, the gas used in the concentration camps (Borkin, 1978). More surprising was the involvement in war crimes of many corporations within Allied countries – for example US companies such as DuPont, Ford, GM, Kodak or Standard Oil (Dobbs, 1998). The US Ambassador to Germany, William Dodd, noted the "clique of US industrialists … [who] … extended aid to Fascism … and who are helping keep it there" (cited in Seldes, 1943); and the role of Wall Street in helping to finance the Nazi war effort is well recorded (see for example Higham, 1984). Especially shocking was the involvement of the computer giant IBM, which assisted in developing technologies used in the death camps. The CEO of IBM, Thomas Watson, was an enthusiastic Nazi supporter and was awarded an Order of Merit medal by Hitler himself. Trading under its German subsidiary Dehomag, IBM developed products such as the Hollerith punch-card machine, initially used to code German census data but later adapted for a variety of more sinister bureaucratic tasks, including identification of prisoners, organising mass transportation to the camps or generating lists of the murdered (Black, 2001).

Few of these or the many other respected US and European companies that were complicit in furthering such harms (see Corporate Watch, 2010 for more examples) have ever faced any form of sanctions. Indeed, even the 24 directors of IG Farben tried at Nuremberg had mostly been released by 1951. The subsequent catalogue of environmental damage, industrial injury, mass poisonings or the as yet uncertain effects of biological manipulation on the gene pool in which the private sector has been implicated during the post-war period suggests that the failure to hold to account companies complicit in war crimes may have been a lost opportunity for more effective regulation later on.

Analysing contemporary micro-crime

A key difficulty in making sense of the huge range of CBNT-enabled harms that now confronts us is finding a framework that might

Table 5.1 Major treaties, conventions and protocols on CBNTs since the Second
World War – a selection

Title	Purpose
1948: The Nuremberg Code	Set out principles governing permissible medical experiments; for example, requirements for volunteers to freely consent to participation.
1964: Declaration of Helsinki	Set out ethical principles around medical research involving human subjects.
1968: Nuclear Non-Proliferation Treaty (NNPT)	Aimed at preventing proliferation of nuclear weapons; 189 signatories – important exceptions include India, Israel, North Korea and Pakistan.
1972: Biological Weapons Convention	Aimed at prohibiting development, production, stockpiling and use of biological weapons, together with destruction of existing stocks by 2012; 162 signatories.
1970s–1990s: SALT, START talks	US and Soviet initiatives aimed at consensual limitations upon nuclear warheads.
1980: Convention on the Physical Protection of Nuclear Material	Aimed at enhancing cooperation in protecting nuclear materials against theft or misuse during transportation, at plants or elsewhere. Signatories directed to make such attempts criminal offences.
1989: Basel Convention on the Transboundary Movement of Hazardous Waste	Attempts to control the movement of hazardous waste and to limit transfer from advanced industrial economies to less advanced ones. As yet unratified by the USA.
1989: Montreal Protocol	Accompanied Vienna Convention for the Protection of the Ozone Layer to set out legally binding reductions in the use of CFCs (chlorofluorocarbons).
1993: Convention on Biological Diversity (CBD)	Aimed at conserving biological diversity through sustainable policies and fair distribution of benefits arising from genetic resources.
1993: Chemical Weapons Convention (CWC)	Prohibits development, production, stockpiling and use of chemical weapons, together with destruction of existing stocks by 2012; 188 signatories.
1994: International Atomic Energy Agency (IAEA) Convention on Nuclear Safety	Aimed at securing global nuclear safety by protecting nuclear installations from radiological hazards or accidents; 11 countries have signed but not ratified the Convention, e.g. Israel, Syria and Egypt.
1996: Comprehensive Test Ban Treaty	Prevents testing of nuclear weapons across all environments; ratified by 148 states; the USA is only a signatory.
1998: Convention for the Application of Prior Informed Consent (PIC) Procedure for Certain Hazardous Chemicals and Pesticides in International Trade	If ratified, would ensure that countries have the opportunity to make informed decisions on whether to allow hazardous chemicals to enter their territories (not yet in force).

Continued

Table 5.1 Cont'd

Title	Purpose
2001: Stockholm Convention	Restricts use of a range of chemical pollutants that persist in the ecosystem, for example, DDT.
2001: International Treaty on Plant Genetic Resources for Food and Agriculture	Aims to guarantee food security by conserving and sustaining global genetic plant resources. Farmers to be granted "rights" to access genetic resources – i.e. the sale or exchange of seeds. Also known as the International Seed Treaty.
2003: Cartagena Protocol on Biosafety	Subsidiary agreement to the UN Convention on Biological Diversity (CBD). Aims to regulate international trading and use of genetically engineered organisms to preserve biological diversity and human health.
2005: International Convention for the Suppression of Acts of Nuclear Terrorism	Designed to make any act of nuclear terrorism criminal and to secure states' cooperation in the policing and prevention of such acts.
2005: Kyoto Protocol	Protocol to the 1994 United Nations Framework Convention on Climate Change. Sets binding targets for 37 industrialised countries (excluding the US and China) for reducing greenhouse gas emissions by an average of 5 per cent up to 2012. In 2011 Canada became the first country to withdraw from the protocol.

accommodate them. One option pursued by criminologists has been to focus upon specific harms like pollution, or waste disposal. Unfortunately this has tended to obscure the technological basis of these harms as well as the continuities between them. An alternative framework which makes the origins of these harms within industrialised technology more apparent is therefore desirable. One option might be to concentrate on three key stages of the industrial process and the harms, risks and criminalities that can arise at each.

1 Stage 1 RESEARCH and DEVELOPMENT – i.e. unethical forms of experimentation or irresponsible management of hazardous research materials.
2 Stage 2 PRODUCTION – i.e. harmful outputs of the industrial process such as toxic waste or pollution.
3 Stage 3 OUTPUTS – i.e. threats to health from CNBT-related consumer commodities like cleansing products.

This framework by no means accommodates every kind of harm that it is possible to associate with contemporary CBNTs, and excludes less obviously industrialised misuses such as medical malpractice. It is also obvious that criminal behaviours may straddle these neat stages – as where inadequate research is linked to harmful consumer products. But since we need to start somewhere, it at least provides some kind of device for making sense of the negative impacts of CBNTs in a more connected way.

Research and development (R&D)

R&D is now essential for many of the commodities and artefacts associated with these technologies, but criminal interventions have been rare at this stage. As the safety implications of CBNTs have become more obvious to the wider public this appears to be changing. Especially disturbing has been how easily the research process can be distorted to serve vested interests – as the success of the tobacco industry in funding research that "disproved" links between smoking and cancer (long after medical consensus had accepted it as a fact) illustrates (see Landman and Glatz, 2008). Though up to 650 million people may have already died as an indirect result of this campaign of misinformation (WHO, 2010a), tobacco companies have been highly accomplished in using "research" to evade legal liabilities.

Mismanagement of research resources provides another kind of context for misconduct. In 1999 Genewatch identified over 500 research sites in the UK that were experimenting with genetically modified organisms (many of them universities), 34 of which were involved in large, possibly industrial-scale uses (Genewatch, 1999). The inadequacy of crucial safeguards – in particular, independent monitoring of safety in the containment of modified organisms – was criticised and a number of actions taken by the Health and Safety Executive at universities or institutes where proper safeguards were not in place were highlighted. But of seven "serious" breaches of contained use regulations between 1993 and 1999 only one – against Edinburgh University – resulted in a prosecution (ibid.). Similar concerns have been flagged up around the 130 or so civilian nuclear research centres worldwide that are still using weapons-grade uranium in their work (Bunn, 2010), many of which have poor security – few if any guards, and a lack of adequate fencing and other barriers.

The increasing readiness on the part of regulators to intervene into chemical, biological or nuclear research on moral reasons provides other possible instances of wrongdoing at this stage. For example, the power of veto was used for the first time during the Bush presidency to overturn a bill in Congress that had lifted a ban on stem-cell research, arguing that a "moral boundary" would otherwise be crossed (BBC, 19/07/2006). Though the veto was swiftly lifted by the subsequent Obama government, this was then challenged by a federal judge – threatening to suspend over 60 research projects dependent on state funding (Stolberg and Harris, 2010). The complex (and ongoing) legal battles around stem-cell research in the USA are paralleled by the inconsistent controls seen within other jurisdictions worldwide. In Europe, countries such as Italy, Germany, Holland, Portugal and Ireland have opted for limiting or prohibiting such research altogether, whilst attitudes in the UK and Sweden have been more favourable (cf. ESC, 2007).

Research into cell cloning has proved equally controversial, though the controversy here is not so much about the cloning of individual cells but about attempts to clone entire living organisms. Ethical concerns have been supplemented by practical ones centring upon the health and longevity of clones – especially given evidence suggesting that cloned animals may have shorter lifespans and greater likelihood of illness (cf. Tooley, 1998). By 1997 UNESCO's Universal Declaration on the Human Genome and Human Rights had concluded that "practices which are contrary to human dignity, such as reproductive cloning, shall not be permitted" (cf. Plomer, 2005, p. 74), and most governments have largely concurred with this ruling. But the legal framework around research into cloning technologies remains far from clear. For example, whilst the UK Human Reproductive Cloning Act of 2001 prohibits reproductive cloning of humans, the Human Fertilization and Embryology Act (2008) permits "therapeutic cloning", which can be used to "grow" cells suitable for use in treating degenerative illnesses like heart disease. Article 3 of the European Charter of Fundamental Rights also prohibits reproductive cloning, though this is not legally binding and there are few signatories to date (cf. Hayes, 2008). In the USA, though funding has been denied for research into human cloning, the act is not itself banned – with variations across the 15 states that have laws specific to cloning (see NCSL, 2008 for details).

Further evidence of the interest courts are taking in regulating research was seen in the recent actions taken against climate change researchers that forced them to hand over details of their work (Pearce, 2010), or injunctions attempting to stop work on the Large Hadron Collider (LHC) at CERN, the European laboratory for particle research. The idea that the LHC might create a series of mini-black holes that would "swallow" the earth from within (Overbye, 2008) provoked a law suit in Hawaii that was thrown out, along with a separate attempted injunction in the European Court. The muddle-headed understanding of science at work in both these cases indicates how the use of the justice system to regulate research may often prove unwieldy. As we saw in Chapter 2, the state has rarely displayed a very informed understanding of how science and technology work (cf. Bailes, 1986). Nonetheless, new precedents for intervention into research are beginning to be set out, a trend that scientists will not be able to ignore.

Risk, CBNTs and the production process

Still greater risks emerge where research is transformed into industrial production. Workplace hazards are obvious enough – for example, there was a 29 per cent rise in transportation accidents and workplace fatalities in the UK chemical industry alone between 2006 and 2007 (CBA, 2008), an indication of the dangers now posed by "toxic" capitalism to workers (cf. Pearce and Tombs, 1998). UK Health and Safety Executive (HSE) statistics for 2007/8 indicated that even within the service sector there were around 3,000 "major" industry-related injuries, including chemical burns to the eye, unconsciousness or individuals unable to work for in excess of three consecutive days (HSE, 2008). And as a UK report from 1998 suggested, merely living near a site where CBNTs are in operation can pose deadly risks, with mothers in homes within 3 km of toxic waste landfills 33 per cent more likely to produce offspring with birth defects than those living further away (Dolk *et al.*, 1998). Similarly, transporting materials vital to industrial production has been increasingly associated with harm (cf. NRC, 2006; NOAA, 2009). Particular problems are posed by the growing cost of disposing of hazardous waste within OECD jurisdictions – estimated to be around US$100–2,000 per tonne in the early 1990s, compared to between $2.50 and $50 in Africa (Brack and Hayman, 2002). Inevitable motivations for criminal dumping have resulted, with evidence that companies have sometimes "outsourced" this to organised crime (cf. Ruggiero, 1996). A €1 million fine was imposed on the company Trafigura in 2010 for dumping toxic oil waste in the Ivory Coast that injured thousands of local residents and a further out-of-court settlement of around $50 million was made with those who had been harmed (Milmo, 2010). But such prosecutions remain rare, and the failure of countries like the USA, Australia and New Zealand to sign up to 1989 Basel Convention on Hazardous Waste Disposal suggests that controls are unlikely to be enforced any more strongly in the immediate future.

Deferring to industry to set its own safety agendas has resulted in a variety of accidents and disasters in the chemical, nuclear and (increasingly) biological sectors over the last 50 years. In the UK the explosions at Flixborough in 1974, or in India the disaster at the Union Carbide plant in Bhopal that killed up to 25,000 individuals (cf. Eckerman, 2004; Vickers, 2004) ought perhaps to have sounded more urgent warning notes about the regulation of the chemical industry. But serious incidents have continued to occur. In 2000 cyanide and heavy metals were released from a gold ore processing plant at Baia Mare, Romania into river systems from Romania through to Bulgaria (Greenpeace, 2002; Cunningham, 2005) and only a year later 300 tonnes of ammonium nitrate exploded at the Grande Paroisse chemical factory in Toulouse, France, wrecking buildings 3 km away in the city centre and leaving 29 dead (Aria, 2007). Similar trends are to be found in the nuclear industry. In spite of major incidents at the Three Mile Island Nuclear Generating Station in Pennsylvania (Walker, 2004), or the 1986 reactor meltdown at Chernobyl, which caused 60 immediate deaths, up to 10,000 subsequent thyroid cancer deaths and spread radioactive contamination as far afield as Japan and the USA (WHO, 2002), further incidents continue to emerge. In 2008, around 30 cubic metres of liquid containing unenriched uranium from the Tricastin nuclear plant near Avignon were released into local water sources, with over 100 staff exposed to low-level radiation (BBC, 24/07/2008), and the failures of the Fukushima plant in Japan following the 2011 tsunami seem to have been directly attributable to inept planning and regulation (IAEA, 2011). The development of the biotechnology industry has begun to contribute to this catalogue of disasters. There have been more than 100 accidents and missing shipments in American laboratories handling the world's deadliest germs and toxins since 2003 (AP, 2007), whilst a mix-up between laboratories in 2007 resulted in the deadly H5N1 bird flu being administered to ferrets in the Czech Republic before it was noticed – risking the creation of a new hybrid that could unleash a pandemic (Siddique, 2007).

Any new technology comes with the risk of what Virilio called the "technological accident" (2007), but there is also a danger that too great a focus upon major incidents may lead us to underestimate other CBNT-enabled harms. All too often they can be perceived as "inevitable outcomes" of industrial processes – undesirable yes, but risks we "have to take", given our dependence upon such industries for vital goods and commodities. But an insidious slow drip of smaller problems may, in cumulative terms, pose risks as great as any major disaster. For example, there has been little effective evaluation (and even less media coverage) of the 1,750 leaks, breakdowns or other incidents in UK nuclear facilities between 2002 and 2009 (Macalister and Edwards, 2009).

There have also been repeated failures to punish those responsible for the misuse of CBNTs or to adequately compensate victims. For example, Dow Chemicals, who bought the Union Carbide company responsible for Bhopal, paid compensation of only around $470 million, claiming that this absolved it of any further financial liability – in spite of continuing birth deformities and local water contamination (Vickers, 2004; Eckerman, 2004). The US Supreme Court has refused victims permission to pursue compensation claims in US courts and, despite an international arrest warrant for manslaughter outstanding against Warren Anderson, the CEO of Union Carbide, the US government has resisted his extradition (even though an extradition pact exists between the US and India).

Why controls have been so poor is often a mystery. For example, given that 80 per cent of chemical products and outputs in the 1990s came from just 16 countries (OECD, 2001), the regulation of the chemical industry should, in theory, be fairly straightforward – especially given the existence of complex legal tools like the 2006 REACH legislation (Registration, Evaluation, Authorization and Restriction of Chemicals), which aims to protect "human health and the environment through the better and earlier identification of the intrinsic properties of chemical substances" (EC, 2006) or regulatory agencies such as ECHA (European Chemicals Agency) (cf. Doria, 2007). But lobbying by the UK Chemical Industry Association (CIA), the American Chemistry Council and similar organisations continues to elevate the interests of industry over public safety (cf. Hickman, 2010). Evidence has also begun to emerge of covert tactics used by chemical companies to actively undermine controls – in particular US environmental protections around global warming. One strategy has been the creation of intermediatory lobbying groups, posing as neutral voices, which have challenged the US Environmental Protection Agency. For example, the mysterious "Coalition for Responsible Regulation Inc" was subsequently found to have strong links to the chemical company Solvay (Goldenburg, 2010).

Outputs: the problem of toxicity

In 2008 the number of products withdrawn from the market in the EU rose by 16 per cent over the previous year, with many of the problems arising from fumes, or potentially toxic chemicals contained in the products (Rapex, 2009). A focus upon toxicity provides one useful approach towards identifying some of the dangers posed by many commercial outputs of CBNTs. One example can be seen in "food crimes" (cf. Walters, 2007), such as the increasing presence of toxic bio-chemicals like pesticides in what we eat. But in spite of long-standing evidence that the pesticide DDT was deadly to wildlife and could be instrumental in causing cancer, diabetes, premature births and low sperm counts in humans, it was not until the ratification of the Stockholm Convention in 1971/72 that its use was banned. Widespread pesticide use continues, and the Convention has also failed to curb toxicities arising from other chemical substances such as antibiotics or bactericides. Nor has it prevented an increasing use of hormones or hormone-like chemicals in livestock to enhance meat or milk production – even though this has been associated with a rise in cancer rates (cf. Turnidge, 2004).

Another context where toxicity within food production creates risk is in the use of food additives – now a multi-million-dollar industry worth over $5 billion in the USA alone in 2001, with year-on-year predicted rises of around 3 per cent (BCC, 2002). Artificial colourings and food preservatives such as sodium benzoate (widely used in fizzy drinks, cakes or sweets) have been linked with hyperactivity or attention deficit hyperactivity disorder (ADHD) in children (Smithers, 2007), and the UK FSA (Food Standards Agency) has now revised its guidance lines, warning parents to avoid giving children foods containing such substances. Similarly, additives like sodium nitrite, used as a colour fixative and preservative in meats; aspartame, a widely used sweetener; and butylated hydroxyanisole (BHA) and butylated hydrozyttoluene (BHT), used in cereals, vegetable oils and chewing gum to prevent oxidising of fat, have been associated with cancer, nerve damage and nausea. But, as elsewhere, prosecutions and more effective regulation have been difficult in the face of intense pressure from the food industry. The US Grocery Manufacturers Association alone spent nearly $1 million in the first quarter of 2010 lobbying against stricter food regulations and other issues – up by over 10 per cent from the previous year (AP, 2010).

Potentially harmful chemicals are now found even within food packaging. Take, for example, bisphenol A (BPA), commonly used in plastics, liners for drink cans or babies' milk bottles – a substance that has been linked with heart disease, breast and prostate cancers, diabetes and neurobehavioural abnormalities. BPA remains legal in the UK, even though the US Food and Drug Administration (FDA) has now reversed previous scepticism and advised its removal from baby products (BBC, 16/09/2008; Hickman, 2010). European controls around BPA, like (EC) No. 1935/2004, merely require that any packaging or coating containing it "does not make food harmful" – hardly a model of legal clarity. Similarly, phthalates, a group of chemical "plasticisers" used in food packaging and other consumer products (in particular, children's toys), have been associated with risks to reproduction and liver damage and linked to problems in the wider environment such as a rise in "feminised" fish, or animals with genital deformities and reproductive problems (cf. WWF, 2000). Industry bodies like the British Plastics Federation or the American Chemistry Council have rejected any notion that these chemicals are harmful, pointing to studies (often funded by them) that claim to prove that BPA is one of the "most thoroughly tested of all chemicals" (Hickman, 2010). Whilst the European Union and other countries, such as Japan, Mexico and Argentina, have banned the use of phthalates, the US 2008 Consumer Product Safety Improvement Act (CPSIA) has only restricted their use in children's toys (Szabo, 2008).

CBNTs and individual offenders: mad gassers, poisoners and dirty bombs

In the 1930s and 1940s a series of mysterious attacks were reported in the US states of Virginia and Illinois. A man dressed in black from head to toe began a bizarre criminal campaign that involved randomly spraying gas into the homes of local residents, resulting in nausea and headaches. Reports of attacks by the "Mad Gasser of Mattoon", as he became known (aka the "mad anaesthetist"), caused panic throughout the region but no culprit was ever apprehended and law enforcement officials eventually concluded that the incidents probably had more to do with mass hysteria than genuine crime (Bartholemew and Victor, 2005). The tale anticipates a key set of themes in the way CBNT-enabled threats have been constructed in the public imaginary: uncertain or hysterical perceptions of danger, the use of invisible substances and a "lone fanatic" ready to use deadly micro-substances to inflict indiscriminate mass harm. It also sets the scene for one of the most difficult issues in the analysis of contemporary CBNT-enabled crime – evaluating what kind of offender poses the greatest risk: the individual, or the collective (e.g. corporate or state) agent? The obvious contemporary parallel of the mad gasser, the contemporary bio-chemical or nuclear criminal par excellence – the terrorist – offers us one set of reflections around these themes.

The threats posed by terrorist uses of CBNTs might be considered in terms of the research, production and output stages outlined earlier. At the research stage, one widely discussed scenario has been the possible recruitment of "rogue" scientists into a terrorist or criminal cause. Precisely how scientists might be recruited to (for example) genetically modify diseases to make them more lethal, or prepare radioactive materials for a bomb has, however, been less clear (see for example Gunaratna and Steven, 2004, p. 61; Jenkins, 2008, pp. 140ff). Even where there has been evidence of recruitment this has not tended to come from the fabled "rogue" states, but from strategic allies – for example, the scientist Abdul Qadeer Khan, who helped to create the Pakistani nuclear capability (cf. Kremmer, 2008). And where threats are posed by scientists within hostile states (such as Iran) there has been little hesitancy (and few apparent problems) in using the simple expedient of assassination as a mode of "regulation" (cf. Erdbrink, 2010).

At the second stage, where threats are posed against production facilities, or the transportation of hazardous materials, risks have seemed greater, though again, there are important limitations here. For example, causing a leak at a nuclear power plant would require a direct attack upon the reactor core, either using explosives or by crashing objects (most obviously a plane) into it. There have been claims that this was a possible plan during the 9/11 attacks (cf. Holt and Andrews, 2007), but even assuming that the high levels of security around a nuclear plant could be breached in the first place, reactor cores are usually extensively protected by thick concrete shields, so the likelihood of causing sufficient damage to create a leak remains low (POST, 2004a). As a result, security analysts have judged chemical plants to be an easier target, though there are wildly differing estimates of the volume of casualties that might result from any such attack. One assessment by the US Army Surgeon General in 2001 suggested that as many as 2.4 million people could die if terrorists secured a chemical release in a densely populated area, but a more detailed recent study indicates a maximum of 10,000 casualties (Schierow, 2006, pp. 10–11). Overall, the criminal risks of chemical terrorism seem not to have been very substantive so far – at most, two attempts in the USA had been identified by 2006 (ibid., p. 4)

A prerequisite for any attempted biological, chemical or nuclear terrorist attack is acquiring the relevant materials – by no means a straightforward task (cf. Shea and Gotton, 2004; Smith, 2005). The full extent of any viable criminal market trading in CBNT-related substances like nerve gas, plague variants or enriched uranium remains unclear – though there have been well-documented attempts to acquire deadly materials of this kind. The International Atomic Energy Agency (IAEA) recorded around 550 unsuccessful attempts to trade in radioactive or nuclear material, including low-grade radioactive waste, between 1993 and 2001 (IAEA, 2001) and 2008 saw 20 reported incidents within the old Eastern Bloc area where depleted uranium and similar materials were intercepted (NTI, 2009; Borger, 2010). Biosecurity is more pressing, given that trade in viruses or deadly chemical substances seems an easier option. Again, however, good evidence for any major market of this kind remains limited at present.

Whilst a terrorist-initiated nuclear explosion is highly unlikely, the "dirty bomb" threat, where radioactive or chemical materials are spread over a wide area by explosives, is now a well-established risk scenario (Acton *et al.*, 2007; Dingle, 2005). Since most experts agree that not enough material could be spread in a deadly enough way to constitute a truly catastrophic risk (cf. Zimmerman and Loeb, 2004), attention seems better directed at less exotic bomb-making materials – in particular chemical fertilisers (NaCTSO, 2011). Such materials have been far more successfully deployed by "home-grown" groups comprising right-wing terrorists than by Islamic groups – for example, the conservative fanatic Timothy McVeigh, who used a fertiliser bomb to kill 168 people in Oklahoma in 1995 (Hoffman, 1998). Chemical bombs have been widely used in Iraq, Eastern Europe and in the 7/7 attacks in London (NaCTSO, 2011). State-sponsored attacks or assassinations have also involved more successful uses of CBNTs than terrorists have yet achieved. The killing of the former Russian agent Alexander Litvinenko in London in 2006 was probably carried out by Russian intelligence, which, in the first recorded use of the radioactive substance polonium as a weapon, poisoned Litvinenko by placing it into his tea (Sadovnikova *et al.*, 2006).

The newest set of concerns around terrorist access to CBNTs centres on the use of biological agents. Not only might these prove to be more deadly than chemical or nuclear agents, but also "virtually impossible to anticipate and defend against" (CIA, 2003; Cordesman, 2005). Three factors must be in place for a bio-attack to be successful: an effective biological agent, an effective method of delivery and a viable target – and significant difficulties arise with each. Most security evaluations have concluded not only that development of effective bio-agents such as smallpox, botulism or anthrax micro-organisms would be very difficult, but also that the means for their delivery (whether by aerosol spray, the postal system or even a "bio-suicide terrorist") would be highly unreliable (cf. Söderblom, 2004; Sharan, 2007; NAS, 2008). The most extensive recorded biological attack occurred between September and October 2001, when five people were killed as a result of weapons-grade anthrax spores being sent through the US postal system. The attack succeeded in crippling the US Postal Service and in closing the centre of government on Capitol Hill but, in the end, no global terrorist conspiracy was involved – rather, the culprit was a US army scientist suffering from mental health problems (Warrick, 2010). Most other attempts so far at biological attacks have been motivated on similarly trivial or internecine grounds – for example, the salmonella poisoning by members of the Rajneesh movement in Oregon in 1984, or the Sarin nerve gas attack on the Tokyo subway in 1995 (Ostfield, 2004).

Recent reports of "biohackers" – individuals assembling new (and potentially harmful) organisms with rudimentary facilities – suggest that there are other kinds of individual misuses of biotechnology that may merit more serious attention (Harmon, 2009).

In a recent report, the influential RAND Corporation concluded that terrorism was a far higher threat in the 1970s and that of the 3 million Muslims in the USA fewer than 300 have been associated with any terrorist cause (Jenkins, 2010). The obvious conclusion here seems to be that, whilst terrorist organisations or cells (Islamic or otherwise) cannot be ignored as a source of risk, "lone-wolf" offenders such as the right-wing fanatic Anders Breivik, who slaughtered over 90 people in Norway in 2011 (Cooper and Sanchez, 2011), may pose just as much of a threat. Similarly, when risk-managing the threat from misuse of CBNTs, nor should the threats posed by older, "more traditional" bio-chemical substances be forgotten. Poison, for example, arguably retains its age-old role as the "chemical weapon" par excellence, with figures from the US suggesting an increase of about 18 per cent in this form of murder between the 1980s and 1990s (Westveer *et al.*, 2004). The wider availability of toxic consumer products, or the increase in new (commercially available) pharmaceutical tools – in particular, legal medical drugs like fentanyl, insulin or muscle relaxants such as succinylcholine – offer new opportunities that may be one factor in this increase. The case of Shirley Allen, who had the novel idea of using anti-freeze to murder her husband for insurance purposes (Flowers and Flowers, 2004, p. 109), indicates the scope for innovation that the availability of such products now provides.

More extensive analysis in this area might also consider less conventional forms of offending. For example, a relatively new and controversial variety of criminalisation relating to biological processes is where individuals are judged to have used their own body as an offensive "weapon" – specifically, where the HIV virus is judged to have been "deliberately" transmitted (cf. Bernard, 2007). Many jurisdictions have introduced legislation specific to HIV transmission, though most countries use existing laws – in the UK, for example, prosecutions have generally used the charge of "recklessly inflicting grievous bodily harm" set out in the 1861 Offences Against the Person Act (GNP, 2005; Carter, 2006). The number of countries convicting at high rates for the offence has increased – research conducted in 2005 indicated Austria, Sweden and Switzerland as the European countries with the highest number of attempted prosecutions (over 30), with the UK at between 1 and 4 (Carter, 2006). Yet the way law has been applied here does not seem very consistent with any notion of "bio-chemical justice" – with prosecutions tending to disproportionately target ethnic minorities, migrants or homosexuals (GNP, 2005; see also UNAIDS, 2008). We might also wonder about the justifications for this particular form of bio-control. Given the many kinds of deadly infectious diseases, singling out HIV transmission raises inevitable suspicions that these new laws are more about fear and prejudice towards HIV than about any attempt to develop a coherent technomia of biological infection.

CBNTs and collective offenders: big (bad) pharma

The organisational complexity of technical production – what Latour described as its "technogram" (1987, p. 138) is equally rooted in its "sociogram" – the configuration of socio-technic elements required for it to function. The inherently collective aspects of technical production should remind us that collective offenders may be equally as common as their individual counterparts. Examples of this can be found in almost every area where technology has been industrialised, but one candidate that has attracted particular attention has been the global pharmaceutical industry and its often dubious practices. Pharmaceuticals now represent one of the most profitable area of industrialised bio-chemistry – and pharmaceutical companies are amongst the most successful US and European corporations (Fortune, 2008). Consumers in the USA alone spend around $200 billion a year on prescription drugs – with annual increases of up to 12 per cent (Angell, 2004). But profits from this spending bonanza are heavily skewed toward around 15 or so developed countries that together receive over 70 per cent of these financial benefits (ibid.).

Braithwaite's classic analysis of "big pharma" (Braithwaite, 1984) showed how it was riddled with traditional varieties of corporate crime – more than in almost any other contemporary business sector. Bribery and lobbying are amongst the more common practices, and these occur at every level, from government health officials to doctors themselves. In 2001, for example, TAP Pharmaceuticals was required to pay $875 million to settle civil and criminal charges of fraud whilst marketing Lupron, a prostate cancer drug (Dembner, 2001). And in 2009 Pfizer – one the largest US pharmaceutical companies – was found to be involved in an even more elaborate healthcare fraud involving attempts to induce doctors to prescribe its drugs, some of which had not been federally approved. "Entertainment" was provided to targeted doctors (including paid trips to exotic locations) as a way of influencing what drugs they ordered or recommended (AP, 2009). As a result of its actions, Pfizer was ordered to pay a $2.3bn criminal and civil penalty. In more recent revelations it emerged that Pfizer was also implicated in the use of dirty-tricks campaigns designed to influence the outcome of clinical trials in the third world (Bosely, 2010).

Given this background of casual corporate criminality, the involvement of the pharmaceutical industries in some of the most serious and prolific misuses of CBNTs is not surprising – though these are almost always conducted within the remit (if not the spirit) of current law or international agreements. One example has been the practice of deliberately withholding certain drugs from markets, or interventions to prevent access to cheaper (so-called "generic") alternatives. Such manipulations have (arguably) resulted in far greater mass casualties than any bio-chemical terrorist has ever been able to achieve. For example, up to 14 million or so people die each year from diseases like acute respiratory infections, malaria and tuberculosis – diseases that can be entirely preventable if generic drugs are available (Reiss and Kitcher, 2008). Yet not only is it perfectly legal for pharmaceutical companies to fix the market in this way, but such behaviour is actively sanctioned by World Trade Organization rules – in particular the so-called TRIPS (Agreement on Trade Related Aspects of Intellectual Property Rights) agreement, designed to protect intellectual property (cf. Tyfield, 2008). Following allegations of counterfeiting instigated by pharmaceutical companies, TRIPS has also been used as a basis for seizures of perfectly legitimate low-cost generic drugs by customs officials in Europe (Khor, 2009). The ease with which pharmaceutical companies have been able to use the law to protect their commercial interests – no matter what the cost in human life – was brought into sharp focus in 2001 when more than 40 of the world's leading pharmaceutical companies decided to sue the South African government over its decision to relax laws around the importation of generic HIV drugs – even though up to 25 million of the 40 million people infected worldwide are resident in Africa, over 4 million of them in South Africa (CNN, 2001). After an international outcry, the companies reluctantly yielded to pressure and permitted cheaper alternatives – with the result that the price of the retroviral drugs then fell by up to 54 per cent over the following year (Poku *et al.*, 2007). Such concessions have been an exception – in spite of recent pledges to "share data" with governments and others to help drug development (Lister, 2010).

But withholding drugs is just one area of questionable conduct amongst the many other examples within the industry; we might include:

- Uneven and inequitable development of drugs – in particular those most likely to provide more active revenue streams. For example, research into treatments for relatively minor (but more profitable) conditions like baldness or impotence has far outweighed that conducted into malaria (Silverstein, 1999). Thus, between 1975 and 1996, for example, around 1,223 new chemical entities were developed – but only 11 of these were intended for the treatment of tropical diseases (WHO, 2001). Companies have also been accused of promoting fear in order to create new markets – in particular for vaccines. During the H1N1 "swine flu" scare of 2009, GSK alone stood to make around $1.7 billion from vaccines and companies were accused of pressuring the World Health Organisation into buying far more than were needed – in spite of evidence suggesting they were not likely to be very effective (Capell, 2009). Industry specialists have made particular note of the "upside potential" for profit that the vaccine market presents – with sales projected to rise by 13 per cent for 2012, compared to 5 per cent for the pharmaceutical market in general (ibid.). Future "health scares" requiring new vaccines seem likely to be a recurring scenario.

- Bodyhunting. Controls on the conduct of clinical drug trials that now exist in developed countries have resulted in a rise in drug testing in third world countries. Local governments often actively collaborate in what is, effectively, the use of the bodies of the poor as medical guinea-pigs – though this is usually spun in benevolent terms, as a way of "helping them gain affordable medicine" or healthcare. However, given that many of the drugs tested have little relevance to the needs of local populations, such investments are not entirely altruistic. There are also obvious concerns around whether the effects of treatments upon individuals in deprived circumstances can be legitimately compared to their effects upon well-nourished Western patients with different kinds of tolerance to disease (cf. Shah, 2007; Glickman *et al.*, 2009).

- Withholding or distorting safety information. Big pharma has sailed close to the boundary of the law in consistently withholding information about the risks posed by certain medications. In 2008, after a four-year investigation, the Medicines and Healthcare products Regulatory Agency (MHRA) criticised GlaxoSmithKline for not providing proper safety information over the anti-depressant Seroxat, which has been associated with an increased suicide risk amongst young people. The MHRA decided against legal action (even though there is evidence that a number of young people may have taken their lives after using the drug) on the less than robust grounds that it would be "unlikely to secure a conviction" (Rose, 2008). Similarly, the arthritis drug Vioxx was withdrawn in 2004 after evidence emerged that it was responsible for up to 140,000 deaths due to heart and other complications. Merck, the company responsible for manufacturing it, had not only distorted data in original trials but had intimidated doctors who expressed doubts about its effectiveness (Giles, 2008). Vioxx quickly became Merck's second-largest seller, generating over $10 billion in US sales alone, but, to date, it has paid out less than $5 billion in compensation and no one within Merck has been prosecuted or even disciplined for misleading the public in this way (ibid.).

Engineering the very small: biotechnology, nanotechnology and new horizons for micro-crime

As new varieties of CBNT emerge and their commercial potentials are exploited, new forms of CNBT-enabled offending also seem inevitable. The rapid developments in biotechnology in recent years – in particular the colonisation of agriculture by genetically modified organisms (GMOs) – presents an obvious example of this, one that is already proving to be a fertile area for criminological research (cf. Walters, 2010). Agribusiness corporations have been eager to promote GM food as a panacea for global food production, and a formidable industry of experts committed to "proving" its safety has begun to close ranks around it. Claims by the World Health Organization (WHO) that it has "no effects on human health" (WHO, 2010b) have been challenged by practitioners like the Soil Association. They point instead to "a worrying body of published, peer-reviewed scientific evidence from controlled animal studies ... that demonstrates that GMOs cause a wide range of serious unexpected health impacts" (Azeez and Nunan, 2008).

This flurry of claims and counterclaims around the implications of genetic modification returns us to one of the fundamental questions about technology – what kinds of regulatory limits do we want to place upon our capacity to create enhancements that are not "natural"? The widespread contamination between modified and natural plant species – in spite of the many reassurances that this "could not" happen (cf. FOE, 2006; EUBusiness, 2007) – forces us to engage with this dilemma in new ways. By 2005, 39 countries worldwide had been affected by some form of GM contamination incident, with the UK second to the US in the number of incidents – even though it has no (official) GM crop industry (Genewatch, 2005). Yet contamination is not subject to any legal sanction at present, in spite of the obvious risks it poses. Instead, powerful agribusinesses have been adept at turning the law to their own advantage. For example, companies like Monsanto often use intellectual property law against farmers found to have newly modified plants amongst their own crops, even where this is the result of a contamination (a series of cases brought against a Canadian farmer by Monsanto is one well-known example – cf. Barlett and Steele, 2008). The spread of "bio-hegemony" (cf. Newell, 2009) has even led to rumours that Monsanto was developing a "terminator technology" – genetically engineered plants that produce sterile seeds, so forcing farmers to buy new seed from biotech companies rather than to grow it themselves (cf. Shiva, 1999). This was denied by Monsanto, but "biopiracy" – in which companies attempt to patent variations of important stock products (Shiva, ibid.) – has certainly occurred. There were, for example, attempts by the Texan company Ricetech to patent one of the key cash crops in India, basmati rice (or rather, Ricetech's modified strain of it) (Rai, 2001).

The questionable use of intellectual property law in legitimating this kind of biological imperialism has been further demonstrated in the ongoing struggle to "patent" human genetic structures (Miah, 2003; Andrews, 2009). Around 20 per cent of human genes are now claimed to be "owned" by private interests and the fact that 95 per cent of patent families here bear the stamp of the US Patent Office (compared to just 13 per cent at the European Office) indicates the unmistakable neo-liberal origins of this biological land-grab (Hopkins *et al.*, 2006). Beyond the legal absurdities of claiming to own nature are a host of other, still more significant technological uncertainties around modification itself and the extent to which it should be permissible to "enhance" human genes. The very real prospect of genetically designed humans – the "designer baby" concept (Green, 2007) – has usually been seen in negative or dystopian terms (cf. for example Fukuyama, 2000; Sandel, 2007; Harris, 2007), but at present the ethics around this are unclear and the criminalities inconsistent. Certain concessions are already in place – for example, the UK Human Fertilisation and Embryology Act of 2008 made it legal to engage in tissue typing during pre-implantation genetic diagnosis in order to select "saviour siblings" – offspring who can offer blood or other compatible genetic material to a brother or sister with a serious medical condition (cf. Thorp, 2009). However, specifically altering embryos to this end remains illegal at present. Questions of genetic rights and related criminalities are now amongst the key challenges to our moral order and, as genetic technologies become more widely available, the very real prospect that we could be discriminated against on the basis of our genes emerges – something that the next chapter will explore (Motoc, 2008; see also Murphy, 2009).

However, engineering matter in biological terms is not the only legal challenge likely to arise from our capacity to alter nature at its smallest levels. The latest frontier is the field of "nanotechnology" – which takes its name from the measurement system applied to the very small objects it allows us to manipulate – the nano-metre (roughly one billionth of a metre, or around 1×10^{-9} of a metre) (O'Mathuna, 2009). The implications of being able to manipulate nature at that scale are truly breath taking – whether in new uses for old matter, such as the engineering of tiny "nanomachines" with atoms as the working parts (Drexler, 2001), or the creation of new matter altogether. The commercialisation of nano-technology is already well under way, with global spending in this area rising by 700 per cent between 1997 and 2003 (Roco, 2003). On some estimates, new products utilising nano-scale innovations – like touchscreen mobile phone technology – are now entering the market at a rate of four per week (cf. Bloom, 2008). As a result, global nanotechnology markets could be worth up to anything between 1.5 and 3 trillion dollars by 2012 – especially as countries like China begin to catch up with the USA and Europe in this area (MacKenzie, 2009). The criminogenic potentials of nanotechnology are at this point unclear, though one obvious set of fears centres upon what might happen should this new "frankenstein" matter (or "grey goo") be unleashed into the environment (O'Mathuna, 2009, pp. 53ff). Being able to alter the "signature" of matter also creates obvious new possibilities for fraud. More immediately, the use of nano-particles in beauty products has to led challenges to cosmetics companies over their lack of transparency in safety testing (Which, 2008).

Like all the instances of CBNT-enabled crime we have considered here, misuses of nanotechnology represent categories of technological offending that have scarcely been explored in criminological terms. Given what we have seen, we need to ask why. For not only are chemical, biological or nuclear technologies no less "enabling" than ICTs, they also pose far higher levels of risk. It is true that understanding the science behind these technologies makes analysis of this offending much more complex than that of other varieties, and the prominent role of corporate and state actors complicates liabilities. What cannot be in doubt is that, as problems arising from such technologies continue to grow in scope, conceptualising CBNT-enabled harm in a piecemeal way or regulating it unsystematically is no longer an option.

6   Micro-control

CBNTs and the bio-chemical citizen

> Spray a bug with a toxin and it dies. Spray a man, spray his brain and he
> becomes an insect that clacks and vibrates in a closed circle forever.
> A reflex machine, like an ant.[1]

As with ICTs, the uses of CBNTs to facilitate control are at least as
significant as their role in facilitating crime – if not more so. This chapter
considers the impact of technologies such as DNA profiling, chemical
testing or neural imaging upon policing, detection and other more informal
varieties of social regulation. Central to these impacts has been the role of
CBNTs in engineering a historic shift in the social role of the body – from
a bio-chemical object into a "biometric subject" (Kroker, 2006) – a micro-
resource that can now be used to authenticate identity, predict risk or
secure convictions. Obvious and important legal and ethical questions
arise from this shift – not least whether it fatally undermines the balance
between the potential of CBNTs to make us "safer" and our fundamental
rights.

The body as a control device

When Socrates was sentenced to die by drinking the poison hemlock, he
became one of history's early and more prominent victims of CBNT-enabled
control. Of course the use of poison as a form of state execution within
the Athenian legal system did not form part of any coherent programme
of chemical or biological justice. Punitive uses of chemical processes in the
premodern context were, like criminal uses, largely pragmatic – governed
more by effect than by scientific understanding. It was not until the
seventeenth century onwards that the traditional role of bio-chemical
processes within justice – as resources for pain dispensation – began to be
supplemented with a new function, as sites for the authentications now
essential to contemporary control.

In hindsight it now seems obvious that the birth of the passport and the
creation of bureaucratic identities marked a first stage in this longer-term

process (cf. Torpey, 1999). Even then, however, there was evidence for the impending "biological turn" in control, one seen in Bentham's suggestion that every individual should be tattooed at birth (Torpey, ibid.). The advent of what Agamben has called the "biopolitical tattoo" (Agamben, 2004; see also Aas, 2006) now takes us to a point in history where politics is defined by an "appropriation and registration of the ... biological life of bodies" (Agamben, ibid.) and identity is fixed in purely bio-chemical terms. This involves more than the "bio-power" discussed by Foucault (1998), in which "the true object of the police becomes ... the population" (Martin *et al.*, 1988, s. 160). Rather, there is the formation of the "somatic individual" (Novas and Rose, 2000), moulded by the technical power offered by CBNTs for extending the gaze of power from the exterior of the body towards its deepest structures and processes. It is perhaps a sign of how complete this shift has been that it is now almost impossible to think of security, policing or the legal process without reference to the role of CBNTs in enabling them. But whilst the more focused ways of detecting and determining guilt that they provide have had positive impacts upon justice, a lurch towards generalized bio-chemical justice also entails more questionable trends. As opportunities for work, credit, insurance or even finding a mate become increasingly determined by our physiologies, a new political subject – the "bio-chemical citizen" – emerges, a subject governed by a new and distinctive legal principle that allocates guilt by biological destiny as well as by action and intention.

Bio-chemical justice?: The emergence of forensic science

The power of biological and chemical technologies in helping us to isolate and authenticate micro-physical evidence has been central to their transformation into essential tools of criminal justice. The origins of policing and contemporary detection provided one kind of skill set necessary for this shift, but this new expertise also required a further enhancement – those who could "interpret" as well as gather such data. The origin of this expertise lay within the more complete understanding of physical processes provided by nineteenth-century science, which laid the basis for the techniques now known collectively as "forensic" science.

The rapid development of forensic techniques from the nineteenth century on was partly stimulated by trends in bio-chemical deviance – in particular an (apparent) increase in arsenic poisoning in the eighteenth and nineteenth centuries (cf. Whorton, 2010). This prompted not just new legislative structures like the 1851 Arsenic Act, but a pressing need for more sophisticated ways of testing for toxins. What was to become "forensic chemistry" was initially driven by European researchers such as Marsh and Riensch, who (independently) introduced methods of detecting arsenic in 1836 and 1841 (Coley, 1999). But equally significant as the new chemical tests themselves was the philosophical shift behind them – one that all but defines forensic practice: Locard's principle that "every contact leaves a trace" (see his 1920). This new philosophy fixed the body's emerging role as an active dispenser of bio-chemical "trails" and created the basis for a justice system centred upon the verdict of material authentication. At first, trace evidence was largely limited to what could be detected by the naked eye, but as more powerful technologies of the very small – like microscopes or chemical-testing procedures – became available, invisible traces increasingly complemented the visible ones (cf. Bertomeu-Sánchez and Nieto-Galan, 2006). A significant step in fixing culpability in terms of micro-structure came with Landsteiner's Nobel prize-winning discovery of the four blood groups, A, B, AB and O (Tilstone *et al.*, 2006), which promised to offer evidence with greater authority than visible data like semen or hairs. By around 1900 it had become possible to determine whether blood found at a crime scene was of human or animal origin and, more importantly still, to identify an individual on the basis of their blood structure (ibid.).

Attempts to use specific bodily features or traces as predictors of criminality were less successful. Lombroso's notorious biological reductionist stance represents perhaps the paradigmatic failure of this kind, though few of the (many) other predictive technologies of this early era have stood the test of time. For example, hopes that the galvanometer might provide an "electric confession of our skins" (cf. Dror, 1998, p. 183) or that anthropometry – a metric of identification based on bodily proportions – might offer a literal *portrait parlé* of the criminal (cf. Gloor, 1980) have become emblematic warnings of the dangers in attempting to use CBNTs predictively. Overall, it was the retroductive search for physical traces which proved to be a more successful strategy, with new techniques such as fingerprinting – to which I will return shortly – enabling courts to determine guilt in terms of what the body "had done" or where it had been.

Popular literary fictions about detectives who used science – like Poe's Auguste Dupin, or Sherlock Holmes and his prototypical "crime laboratory" filled with "test-tubes, and little Bunsen lamps",[2] helped to legitimate this new order of justice in the public mind. But the image of quick-witted amateur detectives solving every crime they encountered could never be more than a literary conceit in the face of this technologisation of control, for this now depended upon extensive resources and organised teams of professionals. In 1910 the first dedicated forensic laboratory opened in Lyons, France, followed by the creation of a specialised "crime lab" by the Los Angeles Police Department in 1924 and the UK Metropolitan Police Laboratory in 1935 (Dutelle, 2011).

Contemporary forensic science and its problems

Forensic science now encompasses a sophisticated range of techniques and tests that depend upon the use of CBNTs. With resources like chromatography, spectroscopy or chemical testing, forensics can now turn even the smallest microscopic data – like plant spores or cellular traces – into visible forms of evidence (cf. Jackson and Jackson, 2007). By manifesting the invisible, forensics has acquired a level of trust that has turned the term into a kind of "catch all" phrase applicable to any kind of trace evidence – as the fields of "computer forensics" (where digital data forms the evidential base) or "nuclear forensics" (where the focus is upon nuclear materials) both suggest (Sammes and Jenkinson, 2000; IAEA, 2002). Of course policing and security agencies continue to draw upon macro-scale physical data such as footprints, or discarded cigarette ends, but the authority of such evidence is now usually subordinate to anything that can be gathered from the micro level and will often be dependent upon analysis using some kind of CBNT (cf. Jackson and Jackson, 2007).

It has become common to attribute public faith in the seemingly "magical" reliability of forensic science to the neat fictions of "CSI" style TV crime series or to the uncritical way in which the media invariably reports its successes, rather than its failures (cf. Cole and Dioso-Villa, 2009; Durnal, 2010). But we should not overlook how forensic science also gains authority from the use of CBNTs and their veneer of scientific respectability. All this has made it difficult to evaluate its effectiveness or value for money very objectively. Worse, it has fed into an order of technological regulation that no one has ever formally agreed to. For whilst no one can doubt the broad successes of forensic science, this should not obscure the many serious miscarriages of justice with which its technologies have also been associated (for some examples see Walker and Starmer, 1999; Huff and Killias, 2008; Roach, 2009).

Trust in forensic science to deliver evidential certainty can therefore be associated with at least two ancillary assumptions. First, that the role of CBNTs in shaping its practices guarantees scientific authenticity, and second, that science is a suitable determinant of justice in the first place. The latter assumption will be examined in more detail in Chapter 8, but it should already be clear that the use of technology – even those as powerful as CBNTs – clearly does not entail conformity with the scientific method. Indeed there are times when dependence upon a technology appears to do almost the opposite (Neufeld and Scheck, 2010). As we saw in the case of data-mining technologies, human judgement remains such an ineluctable element of forensic evaluation that, for many, "the nature of forensic science lends itself to an artistic and intuitive approach" (Inman and Rudin, 2001).

A number of recent studies have begun to offer a counterbalance to the elevated public perceptions of forensics as "the" technology of justice (cf. Huber, 1999; Pyrek, 2007). In a widely cited report (NRC, 2009), the US National Academy of Science concluded that our trust in forensic science methods needs far more critical scrutiny than has been the case to date and that too many forensic techniques have been accepted as "reliable" when they have simply not been subjected to the kinds of tests required elsewhere within science. For example, the accuracy of shoeprints or tyre-track analysis was judged to be "impossible to assess"; identifying a person on the basis of microscopic hair analysis offered only "limited" success; few scientific studies were found to offer support for the accurate matching of bite marks; and the science of firearms analysis was argued to be, at present, "fairly limited" (NRC, 2009). Of all the methods used in forensic science, only DNA profiling was judged to stand up to strict scrutiny (though even here, as we shall see shortly, significant problems of accuracy can arise). Of 137 convictions subsequently overturned by DNA evidence, 60 per cent were found to have been based on errors or false statements from crime laboratories about forensic evidence based on blood, hair, bite mark, shoeprint, soil, fibre and fingerprint analyses (Moore, 2009; NRC, 2009). Such conclusions have, inevitably, been challenged by the forensic science establishment, with claims that there is an average of only around 11 per cent of cases where forensic evidence leads to false conclusions or unsafe convictions (Collins and Jarvis, 2009). Of course even if this lower failure rate were to be definitively established (and the verdict on this has not, as yet, been returned), the 11 per cent of individuals who were falsely convicted might justifiably wonder whether the levels of trust placed in forensic science are still too high.

Failures in the scientific method are worrying enough, but there has also been evidence of distortions to forensic evidence by almost every agency involved in the process – from the police to the forensic labs themselves (see Kelly and Wearne, 2002; Luek, 2007; Pyrek, 2007, p. 11; Laville, 2007). Certainly "double-blind" principles of the kind that characterise good science cannot be expected where the agencies responsible for managing forensic resources often have such a clear stake in the outcome, or where forensic science labs are under constant pressure to provide the "right" answers. The use of forensic evidence during trial situations also creates a necessity for "expert witnesses" to interpret it – a significant indication of the way legal process has become subordinate to science and technology norms (cf. Jones, 1994). It is now almost impossible for judges or lawyers to seriously challenge forensic evidence sanctioned by an expert – unless they further the cycle of dependence by calling upon further "expert" advice. These problems become more acute when it comes to the role of the jury, which often accepts the authority of a scientific expert so uncritically (cf. Durnal, 2010) that some have argued that it becomes "irrelevant" in cases where forensic evidence figures centrally (Wrennall, 2010). This inflated respect for technical authority has led the UK's Law Commission to highlight the danger of wrongful convictions created by "charlatan" or biased expert witnesses and to call for far more robust controls (Gibb, 2009).

An obvious danger in too much deference to technical experts arises where their neutrality as witnesses may be compromised. In the adversarial approach that characterises Anglo-Saxon justice systems, competing legal advocates will inevitably choose experts who "best reflect" their legal arguments, rather than experts who offer the most accurate scientific interpretation of what has occurred (cf. Gross, 1991). A "bell curve" effect has often been noted in the selection of expert witnesses (cf. Redmayne, 2001, pp. 201ff), one where defence or prosecution parties tend to choose experts whose opinions lie at the "tails" of the curve of possible evidential interpretations – thereby generating an appearance of scientific support that may not be justified on more accurate weightings (Redmayne, ibid.). Overt bias on the part of the expert witness may further amplify such distortions. For example, institutional biases may influence them to exhibit partisan opinions that favour their employers (albeit unconsciously). In one study of psychologists who had worked as expert witnesses it was found that, of those who had been asked to alter their reports, over 56 per cent had complied (Redmayne, ibid., Slovenko, 2004). And since scientists can never really be "neutral" (theoretically or politically), they may omit consideration of alternative positions or give a disproportionate weight to their own views in interpreting a piece of data.

An example of this was seen in a series of recent miscarriages of justice in the UK, originating from evidence provided by the paediatrician Professor Sir Roy Meadow. Meadow had won his reputation (and knighthood) by publishing a series of scientific papers that identified a psychological condition that he called "Munchausen Syndrome by Proxy" (MSbP), where parents or carers fake symptoms of illness in their children or wards. He led a crusade on behalf of children under threat from parents supposedly affected by this condition and, as a result, was invited to appear as a witness in at least 81 different court cases involving sudden infant death syndrome (SIDS) or "cot death", a number of which ended in convictions for murder. In one case where two cot deaths had occurred in the same family, Meadow told the court that the odds of this occurring were around 73 million to 1 – seemingly irrefutable statistical proof of guilt that the jury was unable to resist. However, the figure was later challenged by the Royal Statistical Society as having "no statistical basis" (RSS, 2001), since the odds of cot death are in fact increased, not decreased, in families where there has been one such incident. This meant that the real figure was a far less damning 75 to 1 chance of a second death occurring. Meadow's stubborn commitment to his scientific prejudices meant that he often failed to put forward evidence that seemed to contradict them – for example, he ignored the fact that it is at least 25 times less likely for babies who die with no obvious reasons to have been murdered than to have died as a result of some perfectly natural cause (cf. Kennedy, 2005). Meadow was eventually struck off the medical register by the General Medical Council on the grounds of serious professional misconduct (a decision subsequently reversed by the High Court) – though not before a number of mothers had served substantial jail sentences and one had later died as an indirect result of the trauma (BBC, 07/11/2007).

The use of probability evaluations in the Meadow case highlights a further problem in the use of forensic evidence – how a "measure" of reliability can be attached to it. Asserting that some datum makes it "85.5 per cent" or "92.7 per cent" likely that a defendant is guilty may appear to confer relative certainty upon a judgment – but on what basis? Attempts to evaluate evidential certainty have been most often seen in the context of "Bayesian" methods of reasoning.[3] The supposed advantages of grounding hypothesis formation within science have led to suggestions that Bayesianism should also be used to enhance legal argumentation and the use of evidence (cf. Robertson and Vigneaux, 1995; Allen and Redmayne, 1997). But the idea that Bayesian inference plus forensic evidence provides us with some kind of legal panacea has been challenged on both methodological and legal grounds (see for example Nissan, 2001). The role of human interpretation remains unavoidable in a legal context, since the prior probabilities necessary for the calculus to function must be assigned subjectively, and on a "one-off" basis (cf. Allen, R. 2008). In 2010 a UK Court of Appeal ruling ("R v T") underlined these suspicions, stating that Bayes' theorem or similar "likelihood ratios" should not be used in evaluating forensic evidence, except where "there is a firm statistical base" (cf. Fenton and Neil, 2011). However, the ruling seems unlikely to end the hopes of those whose believe that a logic of culpability based on forensic science will characterise the technological justice of the future (Fenton and Neil, ibid.).

Beyond questions of subjectivity, scientific validity and a disproportionate dependence upon expert testimony, concerns have also begun to emerge about the mounting costs of forensic technologies (cf. Cohen, 2005). Striking the right balance between a forensics that offers "value for money" and one that has justice as its sole focus is likely to prove increasingly difficult as costs rise and financial restraints hit harder. In the UK, the demise of the FSS (Forensic Science Service) has offered one version of this wider story. Originally part of the Home Office, the FSS was eventually partly privatised (as a government-owned company), which meant not only that state criminal justice agencies were then compelled to "buy" its services, but also that the FSS began to adopt the ethos of other private sector organisations and ignore its public service remit – for example, by refusing to disclose details of the costs of its operations. The decision to close down the FSS altogether (Cookson, 2010b) threatens to create a privatised forensics "market" in the UK, a prospect criticised by the House of Commons Science and Technology Select Committee as "highly undesirable" and which would "pose significant and unacceptable risks to criminal justice" (HCSTC, 2011, p. 3). There are concerns that companies such as LGC Forensics or Orchid Cellmark which now control the UK forensics market may, like any business, increasingly cut corners to keep costs down or to be competitive (for some reflections on privatisation see Lawless, 2010; Lakhani, 2011). This may also produce risks of bias arising through "selectivity" (HCSTC, ibid., p. 79) – i.e. a selective examination of evidence based on cost savings or the needs of a client. Worse still, it may create a class of "high profile", "high priority" cases which have more forensic resources directed towards them than lower-profile ones.

Fingerprinting and the question of infallibility

Of all forensic techniques to have emerged in the last 150 years, perhaps none has seemed so scientifically reliable, to so many, as fingerprinting (cf. Barnes, 2010). And whilst fingerprints are not, strictly speaking, micro-phenomenal traces, many techniques of fingerprint analysis are now dependent upon CBNTs – for example, in the use of chemical testing to facilitate visualisation and verification of print residues (see for example Ricci *et al.*, 2007). But fingerprinting has turned out to be a far less certain technology of justice than was once imagined; indeed, the gradual unravelling of its supposed infallibilities offers a useful warning about the levels of faith placed in more recent authentication technologies – most obviously, evidence based upon DNA. And the increasing regulatory role that finger-printing now plays in contexts outside the criminal justice system anticipates the wider control that CBNT-mediated bodily traces are also beginning to facilitate.

The assumption of infallibility means that fingerprinting has been one of the most frequently used forensic traces, but whilst public faith in it is understandable enough, a little more scepticism within the criminal justice system might have been expected, given what we now know. Instead, senior supervisors in the FBI fingerprint-examination crime laboratory continue to insist that they have "never heard of a single instance of an erroneous identification made in court by an FBI examiner" (Meagher, 2002), whilst of 40 judges who considered whether fingerprint evidence meets current standards of scientific admissibility, "every single judge … determined that fingerprinting passes the test" (Mnookin, 2003). According to the most well-known test of this kind – the so-called "Daubert ruling" (about which there will be a great deal to say in later chapters) – a key requirement for admissibility is a known error rate. But since this has never been defined for fingerprinting, the scientific validity of many matches cannot be definitively evaluated (Coghlan and Randerson, 2005). One consequence of this is the lack of any definitive test for ruling out the possibility that two individuals might share the same fingerprints. Certainly, as a number of studies have now shown, there may be enough cross-overs between fingerprint types for their chief virtue – uniqueness – to be questionable at times (cf. Pankanti *et al.*, 2002). But the obvious conclusion here – that matching is not infallible and false associations are empirically possible (ibid.) – has never been fully accepted.

Without definitive error rates, subjectivity again threatens – with one recent study (Dror *et al.*, 2006) demonstrating how context can significantly modify expert opinion. For example, having been shown sets of prints and told that there was a positive match, the selected experts largely concurred with this, but when the same prints were subsequently shown to the same experts (now with the suggestion that there was no positive match), almost all amended their opinions, often directly contradicting their previous statements (ibid.). Problems of basic competence can exacerbate those around subjectivity. In one recent test over half of a sample group of experts failed to correctly associate a set of prints taken from crime scenes with sample cards containing originals (see Zabell, 2005, p. 167).

Estimations of the extent to which false matches can occur vary from the almost non-existent 1 in 10^{97} chance of error (Coghlan and Randerson, 2005) to anything between 0.8 per cent and 4.4 per cent on average (Cole, 2005). Even if the lower figure here were the more accurate one, this would still result in many unsafe convictions – the 1,900 mistaken fingerprint matches in the US in 2002 alone representing major potential for miscarriages of justice (Cole, ibid.). Error rates in matching should hardly be surprising, given that latent prints (i.e. the visible or invisible print traces left on surfaces) are often of poor quality when compared to "patent" varieties – fingerprints taken under controlled conditions. Improved chemical or light testing has certainly improved the levels of certainty at which judgements can be made – by enabling forensic scientists to see beyond smearing or smudging on the surface to where the print is deposited (Champod and Chamberlain, 2009). But no matter what level of technology is used to improve print visualisation, non-scientific assumptions in judging matches have not been totally eradicated. For example, a latent print and an original print have often been judged as identical simply because they are assumed to come from an identical source (see Cole, 2005, p. 992).

The number of high-profile cases of fingerprint misidentification in recent years indicates why far greater caution in assuming a positive match is required. One of the most widely cited examples involved the FBI's mistaken arrest of a lawyer from Oregon called Brandon Mayfield following the Madrid train bombings of 2004 (Stacey, 2004). The FBI's assertion that it had found an "absolutely incontrovertible" match between Mayfield's prints and latent residues gathered from one of the trains ought to have been immediately implausible, given that Mayfield did not possess a passport and claimed never to have left the USA for over 10 years. When Spanish police eventually produced a more likely fingerprint match with an Algerian resident, the FBI was forced into a humiliating climb-down and the US government paid the lawyer around $2 million in compensation following his lawsuit against it (Eggen, 2006). But such errors are far from exceptional. Cole (2005) has highlighted a number of cases where the use of latent prints has resulted in misidentification and miscarriages of justice – some stretching back to the early 1920s (many of which were not brought to light until the accused had served a considerable amount of time in prison). And these of course are just cases where we happen to now know that there were errors – there have presumably been many more, as yet undetected, misidentifications. Some of these may even have been deliberate. In 1992, for example, it emerged that staff at the New York State Crime Laboratory had routinely been forging fingerprint evidence (Cole, ibid., p. 274) which figured in (at least) 40 cases over the course of eight years – some of them involving serious homicides. The temptations to commit the forgeries were, as the suspects later admitted, strongly influenced by the fact that they knew that it would be easy to get away with, given the levels of faith in the technology (ibid., 279–80).

It is not so much therefore that fingerprinting "doesn't work" – clearly there are many cases when it works very well. The real problem is that the relatively well-supported assumption that "it works most of the time" has been too easily translated into the unquestioning belief that "it works all of the time", or that definitive probability values for the reliability of matches can be assigned. The implications of this for fingerprinting as a tool of justice are bad enough. The fact that such assumptions have also begun to legitimise the use of fingerprinting as an informal regulatory tool beyond the traditional criminal justice system should be of even more concern.

Extending fingerprinting into social control

The extension of fingerprinting into informal social control has been an important first step in the construction of the bio-chemical citizen as an extra-legal subject. But the regulative interest in being able to distinguish between "legitimate" and "illegitimate" individuals (in whatever sense "legitimacy" happens to be defined) means that the use of fingerprinting as a retroductive authentication technology has been increasingly supplemented by the far less scientifically justified function of "pre-emptive" or risk management-style interventions. For example, a key aim of the UK's Project Midas is to issue hand-held fingerprint scanners to UK police – a technology that will enable them to make various pre-emptive moves such as recording fingerprints at the roadside, a power previously limited to situations where someone had actually committed an offence (BBC, 22/11/2006; Irvine, 2008). Of course the reliability of fingerprinting as a pre-emptive indicator of legitimacy is even less secure than where actual offending has occurred. For example, the now defunct UK ID card initiative was heavily criticised for failing to take into account rudimentary matching problems – not least the fact that nearly 4 million individuals (largely those aged over 75) might have prints too poorly defined to serve as proof of identity (Hennessey, 2007). Similar questions about reliability have arisen with biometric uses of fingerprints – in particular, their increasing role in determining access across borders, as in the US-VISIT entry scheme or the European biometric passport initiative (cf. Hornung, 2007). There is scant evidence for any significant improvements in security that have resulted – a point conceded by the European Commission in its proposals for a centralised database of fingerprints for all 27 EU countries (cf. PI, 2008).

Reports that passengers have been able to "spoof" fingerprint controls at borders with the use of tape over their fingertips (Toto, 2009) sound a particular cautionary note about any dependence upon fingerprinting as a technical-regulatory mechanism. As will be discussed shortly, the spoofing problem is a serious one for all technologies of authentication, but it has proved especially troublesome in the case of fingerprinting, given the range of low-cost techniques for fooling the system – from placing gelatine over the fingertips or using play-doh to make moulds (Young, 2005) to more extreme options, such as cutting off somebody's finger to use as the spoof (cf. Mullins, 2007).

A predictable justification for the informal extension of fingerprinting into social control has been the claim that it helps to "reduce crime". The fingerprinting of around 150,000 Roma citizens (including children) by Italian authorities in 2008 was justified precisely on the basis that it was necessary to "crack down on crime" – though no evidence for this claim was produced and the act was condemned by the European Parliament as "clearly racist" (BBC, 10/07/2008). The involvement of children in this forced programme of fingerprinting led to protests from UNICEF, but this is only one of many contexts where children are now being co-opted into fingerprinting regimes. On one recent estimate, nearly two million children in the UK have now been fingerprinted by their schools – usually without any permission from their parents (Gray, 2007; Singh, 2009) – an act perfectly legal under UK data protection law (ICO, 2008). The move forms part of the general securitisation of school environments (McCahill and Finn, 2010) – one which now apparently extends even into the nursery (cf. South Manchester Reporter, 2008). Amongst the supposed advantages of fingerprinting children set out by scanning technology companies such as CRB Solutions are: shorter queues; reduced incidence of pupils leaving school premises; increased school meal take-up; easier healthy eating promotions; removal of cash from the playground and even (really) "alleviation of free meal stigma" (CRB Solutions, 2009; Stop Fingerprinting Children, 2009). But companies like CRB Solutions or Vericool have not been quite so forthcoming about their less salubrious involvements with the private security industry. Vericool, for example, is part of the US company Anteon, which trained Guantanamo Bay interrogators, and amongst its alumni were staff found guilty of engaging in the humiliation of Iraqi prisoners at Abu Ghraib (Shaw, 2006).

As if concerns around the rights of children (and, indeed, their parents) raised by such initiatives were not enough, it is ironic that wider finger-printing also raises concerns about security. The digital storage of prints creates obvious data honey-pots of (available) identities, which, given the poor information security at many schools, is a clear enticement to criminals to attempt to access such data for identification-related theft. Claims by schools that fingerprint data is "stored securely" or that it cannot be compared to "police-style prints" have done little to mitigate parents' concerns (Reid, 2007). In the longer term, there must be concerns that fingerprinting in schools and the enhanced security environments being created there will create a set of cultural expectations that reinforce the "normality" of such control, desensitising students to further, even more coercive technologies that they are likely to face once they leave the school environment.

One likely context for this is within the workplace, where employees are often now required to hand over fingerprints, again for less than transparent reasons. Innovations such as the "Biometric Employee Time Clock", which includes a fingerprint reader and software to manage up to 50 employees, is one amongst many fingerprint and biometric technologies now available to employers (see VeriTask, 2010, amongst many others). Requirements for fingerprinting are also increasingly encountered within the leisure environment. Many popular theme parks – in particular Disneyland – now require fingerprints when customers purchase extended tickets, obscuring the rationale for this within corporate speak. Criticisms that visitors to Disneyworld Orlando are compelled to hand over biometric data have been deflected by the claim that this does not involve the recording of fingerprints – merely "fingerprint information" (Harmel, 2006). The commercial rationale for such policies (to prevent the exchange of expensive multi-day passes) appears prima facie reasonable, though Disney's advisory role to the US government on biometrics suggests that its interest (and expertise) extends slightly beyond mere ticketing security issues. And though Disney, like other entertainment organisations that use them, is keen to reassure visitors that such information is always erased after a defined time period, it is also more than happy to pass on this information to third parties to "protect your safety or security" (Harmel, ibid.).

The use of fingerprinting as an informal control device is not a trend that shows any sign of stopping soon, with sources in the USA reporting a 50 per cent jump in sales of fingerprint-sensor technology each month and the market estimated to grow to around $625 million by 2012 (see for example Upek, 2006). It constitutes a cautionary tale for the widening role of CBNTs in shaping public life, one where a nineteenth-century policing tool becomes a twenty-first-century control technology. Yet the fact that fingerprinting in civil contexts remains as prone to error and misuse as it is in criminal contexts has not provided any extra reason to regulate it more closely. Rather, it becomes a justification for investing in further technologies to ensure its proper function.

The body as a control device: biometrics

A key requirement of any bodily marker, or "biometric" – like fingerprinting – is that it be sufficiently universal, distinctive, permanent and "collectable" to provide reliable identification (cf. der Ploeg, 1999; Delac and Grgic, 2004). By offering a capacity to fix on ever more invisible – and hence (it is assumed) unalterable – bodily features, CBNTs now provide crucial support for this biometric project. Since new biometric markers may always emerge, there is probably no final or definitive list that can be assembled, but one way to simplify how we think about them is to distinguish between two modes of authentication that they provide: static markers, involving fixed information about the body (fingerprints are an obvious example here), or dynamic markers – usually behavioural (see Table 6.1 for some of these and their associated problems).

For a biometric technology to justify an implicit assumption about the bio-chemical citizen – that the "body does not lie" (cf. Aas, 2006), it must demonstrate an acceptable measure of what is called its "crossover error rate" (CER). This is the intersection point between "Type 1" errors – the "FAR" or rate of false acceptances, where an impostor is accepted as a match – and "Type 2" errors – the "FRR" or rate of false rejections, where a legitimate match is denied. Improving a CER faces several problems – not least suppressing background noise – but the reality is that there can never be a perfect match, merely a "score" quantifying the degree of similarity between an input and a template. As with any biometric, the so-called "enrolment" phase – where a "master" template is recorded for use as a later comparator (cf. Woodward *et al.*, 2002) – is crucial, since an inadequately recorded template may generate later matching problems. And once an error gets into a biometric template, a reverse of its intended effect can occur – the authentication of false identities as legitimate.

A further problem is one already seen with fingerprinting – the possibility that a biometric marker may be faked or "spoofed". Researchers have begun to identify a number of examples of this – for example, the use of special contact lenses to spoof iris scanners, or recordings of an original voiceprint to fool voice-recognition systems (cf. Ranger, 2006; Tabula Rasa, 2010). Since spoofing is far easier where stand-alone (i.e. single) forms of biometric are used, the development of multi-modal, or "hybrid" biometrics – where more than one indicator is used to fix identity – is being intensively researched, together with advanced mathematical recognition tools such as Töeplitz matrices (cf. Saeed, 2003). But the possibilities of spoofing add to the growing sense within the security world that biometric technologies are "inherently fallible" (Pato and Millett, 2010). And as awareness of, or expertise in, spoofing techniques becomes more widely disseminated, it is not just that the rationale of these technologies becomes undermined. There must also be concerns that criminal markets specialising in the sale of biometric spoofing techniques will emerge, so generating new varieties and volumes of criminal activity.

Micro-authentication: DNA profiling

Claims that the use of genetic, or DNA, data represents the "the most significant advance in ... the fight against crime since the introduction of

Table 6.1 Commonly used biometrics

Bodily marker	Example
Static	
Face	**Face recognition** – identification by facial features considered to be fixed and unique, such as distances between nose and lip, ear size, or eye-socket depth. **Thermagrams** – infra-red detectors capable of capturing unique facial patterns of heat. *Weaknesses*: <ul><li>small variations may cause errors in automated systems</li><li>individuals *can* easily alter facial features (e.g. by using hoods).</li></ul>
Eyes	**Iris scanning** – identification by characteristic coloured rings around the eyes/pupils. **Retinal scanning** – identification by the unique pattern of blood vessels in the retina. *Weaknesses*: <ul><li>does always work well at a distance. Can be undermined by rapid movements of the head or not looking into the camera</li><li>retinal patterns may be altered by diseases such as glaucoma</li><li>scanning usually needs to take place close up for it to be effective</li><li>equipment may also be prohibitively expensive for general use.</li></ul>
Hand and signature (I)	**Hand recognition** – identification by characteristic hand geometries. **Palmprints** – like fingerprinting, identification by characteristic pattern of markings on palm. Has similar problems to fingerprints. **Fingerprints** – see pp. 144–48. **Signature or handwriting patterns** – these are static forms of recognition that fix upon the distinctive characteristics of the way individuals sign their name. More widely used are the dyanmic varieties (see below). *Weaknesses:* Most suffer from similar problems to fingerprinting – i.e. unknown error rates, subjectivity in matching and so on.
DNA and genetic markers	See below, pp. 152–54.
Other/emerging	<ul><li>Vascular (vein) patterns</li><li>Nails</li><li>Skin patterns</li><li>Knee biometrics</li><li>Odour</li><li>Sweat</li><li>Taste</li><li>Heartbeats.</li></ul> Recognition rates not demonstrably higher than for other metrics. Costs and logistical issues not yet fully tested.

Continued

Table 6.1 Cont'd

Bodily marker	Example
Dynamic	
Voiceprints	**Voice recognition software** – the use of neural nets to 'learn' distinctive speech patterns or sounds associable with an individual's voice. *Weaknesses*: Slight alterations in tone or voice quality (as a result of a cold, a late night, etc.) can fool recognition.
Signature (II)	Actual physical process of writing used as an authenticator. Physical pressure and movement in writing can be harder to mimic than the script itself.
Movement	**Gait/behavioural biometrics** – identification in terms of distinctive patterns of movement. This may also be predictive – for example, in identifying 'suspicious' behaviours such as loitering, or gathering in numbers.
Neural patterns	See pp. 157–59.

Sources: Delac and Grgic, 2004; Pato and Millett, 2010.

fingerprints" (Home Office, 2003) indicate the levels of faith that authorities now place in it. DNA profiling does not involve a mapping of the entire genomic sequence; rather, STR (short tandem repeat) analysis – the most common form of DNA profiling – uses only certain regions within the DNA strand (cf. Li, 2008). These occur repeatedly, and sufficiently uniquely to be referred to as a DNA "fingerprint". This claim to uniqueness is at the heart of the legitimacy of DNA as an authenticator, but from a policing perspective a second strength is its ubiquity. DNA is found in every kind of human cell – be it hair, blood, skin, fingernails or semen – thereby significantly raising the possibility that at least some traces of it will always be deposited – often in ways that fingerprints never could be. Improvements in techniques for extracting DNA have greatly enhanced the possibility of detection (cf. Williams and Johnson, 2008) and this, together with the ease in collecting an original DNA sample (e.g. from mouth swabs), has now ensured that its use has become all but commonplace in most jurisdictions. Its uniqueness also offers other crime control possibilities – for example, its use as a theft-prevention measure has been explored – in the form of invisible synthetic "mist" sprayed over burglars to enable their later identification (cf. Tagliabue, 2010).

As with any authentication technique, DNA profiling stands or falls upon its definitive matching capacity – thereby creating an obvious need to create a fixed "dataset" of samples for later comparison. Problems in using DNA databases were explored in Chapter 4, but beyond these are a range of further issues centring upon collection and the analysis process. As we shall see, such problems must raise serious concerns about the extent to which criminal justice has become so dependent, in such a short space of time, upon a single technology.

DNA profiling: problems of fallibility?

The first great "success" of DNA profiling – its use in 1980 to convict the rapist Colin Pitchfork (Canter, 1995) – may not, on reflection, have been such a resounding triumph for the technology as it once seemed. Rather, it could equally be seen as sounding an early warning note about assumptions of infallibility. For, in the end, pure chance played just as important a role in bringing Pitchfork to justice as the technology of profiling itself. Indeed, without the intervention of chance DNA might actually have produced the opposite of its intended purpose – enabling a suspect to escape, rather than to face justice. It later emerged that Pitchfork had easily subverted the DNA screening of every male in the area (the first time the police had attempted something like this) by arranging for a friend to supply DNA in his place. Fortunately, his accomplice was foolish enough to brag about the switch and this information was passed on to the police. But without this subsequent tip-off it is clear that the false DNA sample would have all but definitively cleared Pitchfork of any connection to the crime (Canter, ibid.).

In effect, Pitchfork had engaged in an early (albeit low-tech) form of biometric "spoofing" – in this case passing off someone else's DNA as his own. Worryingly, evidence has now emerged that far more extensive and sophisticated methods of spoofing DNA than this may already be available. Recent research has indicated how someone armed with basic equipment and adequate knowledge may be able to fake almost unlimited quantities of DNA to fit a desired profile – a fact that raises all kinds of obvious alarm bells (cf. Frumkin *et al.*, 2009). Not only would it undermine the trustworthiness of the technology, but there are other troubling scenarios – not least the prospect of organised criminals acquiring a capacity to generate spoofed DNA to "plant" at crime scenes. Clearly, if significant supplies of spoofed DNA were to begin to circulate, the whole validity of DNA databases and the money invested in them would be seriously compromised. Whilst such capacities are, at present, likely to be "out of reach" for ordinary criminals, as Chapter 4 indicated technical complexity has certainly not prevented criminals from acquiring advanced information technology tools. But spoofing is just one amongst many more potential problems for the use of DNA profiling as a control technology – problems that have tended to be dismissed too easily in the clamour to situate it as an "ultimate" policing panacea. At almost any point in the process of DNA matching – from the "precrime" stage through to the presentation of DNA evidence in the court-room – clear possibilities for error seem to arise, some of which are summarised in the flow chart in Table 6.2.

Recent revelations that UK police had been storing valuable DNA samples in fridges – next to half-eaten take-away meals, ice-cream and blood swabs (Sinclair, 2010) offer a timely reminder that evaluating DNA is not just about technology – but about our relation to it. As with

Table 6.2 Potential problems in the DNA matching process

Possible error	Description
Stage 1: Precrime – subject and records	
Subject anomalies	Genetic abnormalities such as chimerism (where an individual possesses two genetically distinct types of cells) may lead to anomalous profiling results. Non-genetic factors like blood transfusions, prior surgical procedures (such as bone marrow transplants) or illness (for example, leukaemia) may also distort identification (cf. Semikhodskii, 2007, pp. 89ff).
Data bias	Merely being on a DNA database may predispose the possibility of a match. Certain groups in the population who are more likely to be included on the database then become more of a "suspect" population than others.
Stage 2: Crime scene	
Sample degradation	Samples may become suspect because part of a detected sequence has "dropped out" (i.e. become undetectable).
Failures of collection	In 2,500 cases involving murders, rapes and serious assaults between 2001 and 2005, the FSS failed to detect samples of DNA (Laville, 2007).
Use of Low Copy Number (LCN) DNA testing	The use of tiny amounts of DNA data – sometimes no more than a few skin cells – has led to concerns about reliability. The UK is one of the few jurisdictions to use the technique.
"Spoof" DNA (I)	There is evidence that it may now be possible to create and then plant "spoofed" DNA samples at crime scenes (Frumkin *et al.*, 2009).
Stage 3: Processing and matching	
Processing and labelling errors	Up to 100,000 DNA records on the UK database may be erroneous because of clerical errors.
Negligence or incompetence during testing process	Samples may be compromised by errors in handling – for example, mixing up distinct mitochondrial and nucleic DNA sources.
Variations in the number of marker required for a match	Different DNA databases may use different numbers of genetic markers. This has led to miscarriages of justice where crucial markers that established innocence were omitted from the matching process (cf. Rincon, 2011).
Contamination and mixing of samples	Accidental transfer of DNA from one sample to another is not uncommon in laboratories (Thompson, 2008).
External influences	A familiarity with case details or pressure from prosecutors has sometimes influenced crime lab analysts.
"Spoof" DNA (II)	Suspects have evaded or fooled DNA testing by surgical injection of foreign blood and anticoagulants into the bloodstream (cf. CBC, 1999).

Continued

Table 6.2 Cont'd

Possible error	Description
Stage 4: DNA in the court-room	
Failures in legal process	Convictions on the basis of DNA evidence may arise because of inadequacies specific to the legal process. For example: • defence lawyers may not ask for retesting of samples – in spite of possibilities of error • defence lawyers may omit to introduce their own experts to challenge expert testimony • problems of context and bias – judges and jurors may have unreasonable levels of trust in an expert. Guilty verdicts may be influenced by personal prejudice rather than a definitive DNA match (cf. Thompson and Krane, 2003).
Problems of evaluation and interpretation	Legal interpretation and evaluation of supposed DNA matches is subject to a number of common errors. For example: • statistical miscalculations, or errors in reasoning when claiming a match – e.g. "prosecutor's" and "defendant's" fallacies or "ultimate issue errors". For example, to claim there is a 1 in 1 million chance of there being a random link between an accused's DNA and a crime scene sample, cannot be interpreted to mean the same as there is a 1 in 1 million chance of the accused being innocent (cf. Semikhodskii, 2007, pp. 111ff) • failures to consider alternative interpretations of a supposed sample match. For example, "peaks" in the sample DNA which match "peaks" in the suspect's DNA may be only technical artefacts arising from background "noise" or even the DNA testing process itself (cf. Thompson and Krane, 2003).

Note: See MacCartney (2006) for examples of other problems in the DNA matching process.

fingerprinting, this has often been forgotten in the "function creep" that has begun here – especially in the informal regulatory uses of DNA technologies in furthering the emergence of the "bio-chemical" citizen that will be discussed later.

The body as a control device: reading intention

A still deeper use of the body as a control resource now involves its transformation into a device that evidences our attitudes and beliefs. This idea is one that has been envisioned since at least the eighteenth century, when bodily processes like pulses, sweats or blood flow were all proposed as indicators of a subject's mental state (Underwood, 1995). Increasing attention was devoted to the pursuit of technologies that might facilitate this from the late nineteenth century onwards – for example, in devices like Mosso's "plethysomograph", which interpreted changes in the measurement of blood pressure as indicators of fear or tension, or Lombroso's "hydrosphygmograph", which attempted to measure guilt by immersing suspects' hands in water and measuring how changes in blood circulation produced pulses in the water (cf. Matté, 2006).

However quaint or pseudo-scientific such devices now sound, we should not forget that their contemporary counterpart the polygraph or "lie detector" test is based precisely upon the kinds of physiological measure (i.e. blood pressure, pulse and respiration) that motivated these nineteenth-century endeavours (NRC, 2003a). Contemporary polygraph testing begins with a "pre-test stage" where interviews are conducted to obtain "control questions" (or CQs) – comparators against which later responses can be measured. Further comparators intended to enhance the authority of polygraph tests include "directed lie tests" (DLT) – where subjects are instructed to lie and responses are compared to where they are telling the truth; or the "guilty knowledge test" (GKT) – where subjects are given multiple choice-style questions about an incident (say a crime) that contain responses that only a "guilty" person would be aware of (cf. Langleben, 2008). This process of obtaining "templates" has obvious parallels with biometric identification and faces similar problems as to the quality of the subsequent matching process and the degree of interpretation involved in claiming "a match". On what basis, for example, is a control question to be considered relevant? How precisely is a match or mismatch to be determined? And so on. Subjectivity affects every decision here and may be further amplified by the social setting of the test procedure itself, where responses have been shown to be influenced by power imbalances in the interviewer–interviewee relationship or by cultural factors around gender, ethnicity or personality (cf. Granick, 2006). Nor are polygraph tests immune to spoofing, with well-documented examples of ways in which they can be "fooled" – often with minimal training. A standard technique is to suppress the physiological responses upon which testing depends – by meditation or relaxation, biofeedback training or self-hypnosis. Simply squeezing toes, holding the breath or inducing pain can also exaggerate or minimise physiological reactions. If conducted effectively, any of this can make responses between control questions and other questions all but indistinguishable (Gudjonsson, 1988; Bull *et al.*, 2004). In one infamous example a prisoner (falsely) convicted of murder on the basis of a polygraph test was able to tutor 27 fellow inmates (whom he knew to be guilty) in how to fool the polygraph. In less than 20 minutes he had succeeded in helping 23 of the 27 to lie successfully whilst being tested (Ford, 1995; Bull *et al.*, ibid.).

Advocates have been unwilling to accept that polygraph testing can be subverted in this way – and accuracy rates of up to 91 per cent continue to be reported by some (cf. Horvath and Palmatier, 2008). But such certainties quickly become questionable as soon as polygraph tests are subjected to more rigorous scientific scrutiny. In their extensive 2003 report on polygraph/lie detection tests the US National Research Council concluded that the quality of available research was universally low – far below what would gain research funding elsewhere (NRC, 2003a, p. 2). It was judged that the possibility of spoofing "seriously undermine(s) any value of polygraph security screening" (ibid., p. 5), with up to 99 per cent of tests subject to "false positives" on this basis. Such doubts have meant that most jurisdictions do not admit polygraph evidence in court, though they are permitted in Japan and there is a certain level of discretion at state level in the USA, where jurisdictions such as California and Florida permit them if both parties are agreeable. In the USA the also police make extensive use of lie detection; less so in the UK (POST, 2011). An exception to these general rules lies with sex offenders, who are now regularly subjected to polygraph tests in US courts, a policy now being explored in the UK, where offenders can opt for them as part of their probation conditions on release from prison (Ford, 2008; OPSI, 2009).

As with fingerprinting and DNA profiling, questions within the criminal justice system about its reliability have not proved any obstacle to the extension of polygraph testing into informal technological regulation. One key testing ground for these extensions of control has been within the workplace. Though the US Employee Polygraph Protection Act of 1988 (EPPA) was designed to limit the use of lie detection by employers (Department of Labor, 2008), tests can be imposed if someone is "reasonably suspected of involvement in a workplace incident that results in economic loss to the employer" (ibid.) – though "economic loss" is clearly a generously wide concept. In the UK it is legal for prospective employers to use polygraph tests if candidates agree to it (BBC, 11/11/2009) – which rather begs the question of what safeguards exist for candidates who refuse to take a polygraph test. Here, as elsewhere, the lack of any independent checks on test results raises obvious concerns about the validity of conclusions drawn from them or the legitimacy of any actions taken on their basis (cf. TUC, 2007).

Still more insidious has been the gradual imposition of lie detection technologies upon vulnerable groups such as the poor and the sick. Proposals to conduct tests "remotely" – i.e. over the telephone – by using so called "voice risk analysis" (VRA) technologies have raised particular concerns. VRA is claimed to be able to identify liars purely on the basis of vocal patterns and was trialled by the UK government as a way of trapping "benefit cheats" (Sherriff, 2007) and by the insurance industry to "evaluate false claims". Plans by employers to use VRA as a way of deciding when employees "falsely phone in sick" are also under way (Pitcher, 2008). Advocates of VRA claim extraordinary levels of success; for example, during a pilot scheme in the London borough of Harrow the local authority claimed to have saved £300,000 in three months by "rejecting potentially false claims over the phone", whilst the company Highways Insurance argued that it had saved over £11 million in potentially fraudulent motor insurance claims (Arthur, 2009). However, no detailed research has been done to support such claims, and, of course, a "potential" fraud is not the same as an "actual" fraud.

In one of the few independent and scientifically rigorous studies of VRA to be conducted (Eriksson and Lacerda, 2007), it was found to be "at the astrology end of the validity spectrum" (Sample, 2010). Only when users were told that they were being subjected to a test did levels of deception (ostensibly) decline – though this is clearly not the same as detecting a falsehood. The manufacturers of such devices have been far more assiduous in attempting to discredit unfavourable research than in producing convincing evidence for the scientific rigour of their products. In one notorious case, Nemesysco, an Israeli manufacturer of VRA software used in 23 pilot studies conducted by the Department of Work and Pensions, used libel law to force publishers to withdraw online access to Eriksson and Lacerda's critical study (Corbyn, 2010). The Home Office has subsequently dropped plans to use the software after the trials indicated that it was "not good value for money". No comment was made on the £2 million that had been invested in the technology (Sample, 2010).

Reading the brain

Just as fingerprinting anticipated the more pervasive authenticating power of DNA profiles, lie detection technologies could also be viewed as a first step in a more comprehensive project of reading intentions, one that has begun to shift towards brain activity itself. If there really were technologies that made it possible to precisely correlate characteristic brain patterns with criminal behaviours (such as violence) this would not just restore long-standing biological reductionist claims about criminality to the centre of criminological thinking. It would also have obvious and major implications for the process of justice. A range of neural technologies now seem to offer this prospect – for example, Computed Axial Tomography (the CAT scan), which builds up an image by using a combination of X-ray images; functional Magnetic Resonance Imaging (the fMRI scan), which uses magnetic fields and radio waves to image brain structure and brain activity; and positron emission tomography (the PET scan), the most powerful system, which uses small amounts of (short-lived) radioactive material to image brain functioning (Filler, 2009).

The discovery that the prefrontal brain cortices of convicted murderers (areas normally associated with inhibition) exhibited distinctive abnormalities seemed to have offered definitive proof that criminal behaviour might be "read" from brain function (cf. Raine, 2002). But, as Adrian Raine, the psychopathologist who discovered this link, has acknowledged, the use of scanning technology cannot supplant explanations involving the social origins of offending, in that:

> Violent behaviour probably involves disruption of a network of multiply interacting brain mechanisms that predispose to violence in the presence of other social, environmental and psychological predispositions.
>
> (Raine *et al.*, 1997, p. 503)

It is certainly clear that whilst crime rates may change over relatively short periods, genetic brain structure does not (see Rose, 2004 for more on this argument). Such inconvenient facts have not dampened the enthusiasm for placing brain scan evidence at the centre of the judicial process. There are several possible applications, the most obvious of which would be to use neural data as a way of establishing guilt, or as mitigation for an offence (cf. Brown and Murphy, 2010). This remains controversial and has some practical problems that we will return to in a moment, but a second, more limited suggestion has been to use such data in analysing how the cognitive functioning of key legal actors like judges or jurors may affect outcomes, or to assist with more accurate retrieval of memories by witnesses (cf. Mobbs *et al.*, 2007). Beyond these options comes the ultimate control fantasy – to use neural data predictively, as a tool for risk-managing potential criminal activity in advance of any actual offending (cf. Rose, 2010).

The controversies around neural scanning data have not prevented some jurisdictions from using it in the court-room. In 2008 India became the first country to convict an individual of murder on the basis of a brain scan, when data from its BEOS (Brain Electrical Oscillations Signature test) technology was used to determine guilt. Developers of the BEOS technology claimed that it produces characteristic brain patterns when details of a case are read out to a suspect – details that might suggest "memories" of the event. Though BEOS had not been peer reviewed, nor had any scientific papers on it been published in respectable journals, the court accepted that it had proved that the suspect's brain contained "experiential knowledge" that could only be had by the murderer (Giridharadas, 2008) – a decision subsequently revoked by the Indian Supreme Court, which ruled that the use of brain scans was "unconstitutional" (Blakely, 2010). In most other jurisdictions, the uncertain science around brain scan data means that, like polygraph testing, it remains inadmissible as evidence at present. How long the temptations of this permutation of technological justice can be resisted remains to be seen.

In Western jurisdictions neural scans have played a part in influencing the judicial process by supporting defence claims around diminished responsibility – a precedent set during the 1980s trial of the would-be assassin of Ronald Reagan, John Hinckley, whose CAT scans appeared to show brain shrinkage (Taylor, 1982). Images of these were shown in court and, though experts were divided about their significance, they seem to have played at least some part in Hinckley's eventual acquittal on the grounds of insanity (ibid.). Neural evidence suggesting that adolescent brains may be "less developed" than adult brains also contributed to the landmark *Roper* v. *Simmons* judgment,[4] which resulted in the death penalty being struck down for under-18s (cf. Rosen, 2007). But significant problems remain for any more comprehensive use of neural data in mitigating or establishing guilt – not just in relation to defining what should count as a brain abnormality but, more importantly, in determining how far any abnormality can be held causally "responsible" for a criminal act. Though there are well-established defences based on diminished responsibility (in particular, insanity), within UK law the insanity defence was formulated back in 1842 and it is far from clear how this might be made to fit with contemporary neuroscience. A new Law Commission investigation (the first since the Butler Committee report of 1975) aims to clarify issues here (LC, 2008), but until the scientific basis becomes clearer the general conclusion has been that "brain abnormality is not a necessary condition for determining diminished or absent culpability" (cf. Eastman and Campbell, 2006).

Problems in using brain scans to determine guilt retrospectively have not deterred those who argue that such techniques can be used predictively. Certain precedents for interventions of this kind exist, though policies such as "preventative detention" on the basis of the 1983 Mental Health Act – which allows for detention where a risk can be determined on the basis of mental dysfunction – are usually based on expert opinion, not neural data. Elsewhere, the use of neuro-imaging in the workplace, school and elsewhere is now a very real prospect with companies such as the California-based No Lie MRI already offering brain scans to customers who want to demonstrate that they are "telling the truth" (Wise, 2007). Other private sector operators like Preventicum and Scan & Screen now offer full-body MRI "preventative health scans" for around £1,090 – in spite of concerns that these might provide misleading information (Hawkes, 2007). Meanwhile, the advertising industry is eagerly following research in the area, in the hope of finding what would be a kind of consumerist "holy grail" for it – techniques for lighting up those parts of the brain that "make us buy something" (Winnet, 2003). Several companies are now offering expertise in "neuro-marketing" to a number of unnamed major corporations (Wise, ibid.).

Futures: matter control and the bio-chemical citizen

With the advent of nanotechnology – the most recent of our CBNTs discussed in the previous chapter – a new prospect emerges: that bio-chemical control might become so powerful that matter itself can be altered or even created. It is already abundantly clear that nanotechnology at present offers more advantages to control than to criminals. One more obvious application has been within forensics, where the focus upon trace evidence has led to research into the use of nano-tools that read DNA sequences at even smaller levels than is currently possible (cf. McCord, 2008). If successful, this would mean that minute traces – as small as one molecule of DNA – could potentially be "read" and used as evidence. Elsewhere, there is also research into forensic uses of nanotechnology involving the detection and analysis of fingerprints (Pitkethly, 2009), tissue samples, toxic traces and even gun-shot and firearms deposits (Reynolds and Hart, 2004).

It is only a matter of time before nanotechnology finds an application in furthering the new regimes of authentication. Research has already taken place into marking or tagging objects at nano-scales – a prospect that offers new possibilities for security and intellectual copyrighting. Protecting brand and product copyright by watermarking objects with nano-particles or special nano-tags (Wakefield, 2007) also has obvious applications within retail contexts. The use of nanotechnology for identification might even be used in firearms control – gun cartridges coated with tiny nano-tags that then attach themselves to the hands or clothes of crime perpetrators and would prove almost impossible to wash away (Physorg, 2008). Less comfortably, nanotechnologies also have implications for enhancing surveillance capacities, and there have been suggestions that nano-tags might be compulsory when passing through customs, high-security areas or road toll booths. Elsewhere, medical research has been conducted into the use of nano-bots to attack tumours, or, when treated with fluorescent materials, as a way of facilitating internal body imaging (Highfield, 2008). With such developments, even more extensive "somatic" control projects open up, where the entire body becomes a physiological surveillance device, broadcasting everything from neural patterns to temperature changes (cf. Ratner and Ratner, 2004).

The uses of CBNTs in such projects take us further towards the fully fledged bio-chemical citizen. The emergence of this new political subject was presaged when, in 2007, a Boston company announced one of the world's "first DNA dating services" (Wenzel, 2007). For around $1,900 clients would supply DNA samples that would enable the company to match them up with their "genetic mate". The result, claimed the literature, would be genetic mates who would "like each other's natural scents, have more fun in bed and bear healthier children" (ibid.). DNA testing kits are now widely available to purchase – both online and on the high street (Ozimek, 2011) – and can be used for various functions such as paternity testing, testing susceptibility to diseases, tracing ancestry and so on. Such tests face only limited regulation at present – raising concerns about the potentially misleading, or distressing, "diagnoses" they might generate. For example, most tests only partially screen for certain diseases and so may give false impressions of likely susceptibilities. Indeed, detailed research has indicated that many of these tests are about as accurate as flipping a coin (Sample, 2011). Regulation of DNA profiling as an informal control device is only slightly more developed – with the US Genetic Information Non-discrimination Act (GINA) about the only major legislation in this area that is in place at present. GINA was designed to prohibit employers from imposing compulsory testing upon employees or purchasing details of their genetic information. It also aimed to prevent insurers from forcing applicants to take genetic tests as a condition of insurance or using such information to determine eligibility (NIH, 2008). In many regards, however, GINA is already out of date. Other bio-chemical tests such as cholesterol-level measurements are not strictly "genetic", and so stand outside the law – even though these can also be used to determine long-term health risks (Goldgar, 2010). GINA also permits testing during applications for life and disability insurance, excludes businesses with fewer than 15 employees from the regulations, and doesn't prohibit other ways in which employees can gather genetic information – such as from work-sponsored health programmes (ibid.). GINA would also not prevent US plans to store DNA from immigrants, irrespective of whether they had committed any offence (Preston, 2007). Yet, though GINA may be flawed, it does at least offer some protections against genetic discrimination – protections at present conspicuously lacking in the UK and Europe. A working group that has "evaluated options" here (cf. HGC, 2010) is no more reassuring than arguments that European directives on employment or the 2010 Equality Act offer sufficient protections in the short term (cf. Casserly, 2010). Insurers' access to genetic test data is currently limited by a voluntary moratorium, though this is valid only until 2014 and there is no clarity about what will happen subsequently (Genewatch, 2010).

Whilst the potentials of genetics as a regulatory mechanism are only beginning to be explored, what might be called "chemical governance" is already well established. Chemical control can be seen across many contexts – from the (highly partial) control and supply of drugs by the state to new rights of chemical scrutiny assumed by employers. Workplace drug testing is now relatively commonplace in the USA (cf. Tunnell, 2004) but, whilst there may be good reasons for this (it is clearly undesirable for employees in areas such as transport, construction, medicine and so on to be under the influence of drugs), there are also circumstances where such controls seem less acceptable. Employees may have consumed drugs away from the workplace and may have done so many weeks previously. They may also have done this in a perfectly legal setting – during a holiday in a jurisdiction where they are decriminalised, for example. Such choices are surely a private matter, and if there are no negative impacts upon working standards is it really something that employers should have any jurisdiction over? Especially given evidence that employers often abuse the drug testing process by using it as an excuse for sacking workers without having to offer redundancy payments (Taylor, 2009). Between 2008 and 2009, Release reported a huge rise in calls (from 6 per cent of total received to 26 per cent) from employees distressed about the introduction of compulsory drug testing into their workplace. Government guidelines themselves suggest that drug testing in the workplace may have negative effects upon staff–employer relationships (POSTb, 2004).

More sinister has been the increasing use of chemicals as policing or punitive tools. The deaths of 115 hostages at the hands of the Russian military during the Moscow theatre hostage crisis of 2002, almost certainly as a result of the use of the nerve agent BZ, is one of the more extreme examples of the use of chemicals as a control tool (Lancet, 2002), but it is not an isolated one. Interrogation techniques that use chemicals – for example, the practice of "narcoanalysis", or injecting suspects with so-called "truth serums" like sodium pentothal – have also been relatively common. The practice dates back until at least the 1920s in the US, where a depressant and sleeping agent called scopolamine was used in a series of legal cases (Geis, 1959). The later MK Ultra programme operated by the CIA considered a whole palette of narcotic options – not least the use of LSD. And whilst both the US Supreme Court and the European Court of Human Rights have prohibited the use of truth serums and questioned their scientific validity, it is not entirely clear whether this has prevented clandestine uses – there is certainly evidence of this tactic within other jurisdictions. Chemical interrogation was regularly deployed in India as a tool for securing convictions – and was only ruled unconstitutional by the Supreme Court in 2010 (Mahapatra, 2010).

The chemical justice inflicted upon Socrates finds a contemporary parallel in the increasing use of pharmaceuticals as a method of execution. In 1977, Oklahoma became the first US state to use an injection of lethal chemicals to kill convicted criminals, and by 2004 it had disposed of 74 other prisoners in this way – though this was far fewer than Texas's total of 336 by the same year (BOJ, 2004). A global industry now exists to facilitate chemical execution, even drawing in jurisdictions such as the UK that prohibit capital punishment. In 2010 Archimedes Pharma and other British pharmaceutical suppliers were found to be exporting a cocktail of execution chemicals like potassium chloride, pancuronium bromide and sodium thiopental to "clients" such as the California Department of Corrections (cf. Townsend, 2010a). Nor are these isolated cases of chemical governance. From the sedation of prisoners and the mentally ill, through to the suppression of "difficult" children by Prozac, the use of chemicals as a form of social control is well and truly with us.

From the eugenicists of the 1920s and 1930s, through to current advocates of the genetic determination of crime, it is clear how CBNTs and the micro-phenomena to which they allow access have acquired an increasingly powerful regulatory role – one that, as we have seen repeatedly, now extends far beyond the criminal justice system itself. With this has come the emergence of the bio-chemical citizen – characterised not just by the "genetic risks" they pose (cf. Rose, 2000, p. 17) but equally by their chemically, or even atomically, suspect bodies. The implication of this is a technomia that has subverted not just the process of criminal justice, but also our very capacity to understand what it now means to be regulated. For with these "technical instruments ... that appropriate bare life" (Agamben, 2004) we arrive at a new point in the history of justice, one where "mankind has been ... declared the most dangerous of all classes" (ibid.).

7   Of hammers, hairdryers and handguns
Mid- and multi-range technologies

Viciousness in the kitchen …

… and death in the pot.[1]

No study of technological crime and control would be complete without paying at least some attention to our more everyday artefacts – many used so regularly that they are scarcely seen as "technological". But whilst familiar commodities like hammers, hairdryers or lawnmowers may seem trivial in comparison to complex devices like a particle accelerator or a supercomputer, it is not a priori obvious that they are any "less" technological or any less significant in criminological terms. Indeed, given that a defining characteristic of such technologies is their operation within the immediate sphere of bodily action and interaction, the origins of all technology might be said to lie here. And if, as I argue it does, it makes sense to include within this class one of the most significant of all our technologies – the weapon – then any assumption that artefacts here are trivial in comparison to CBNTs or ICTs looks even less plausible.

In this chapter I aim to consider some of the under-considered relations between such artefacts and the processes of crime and justice. These technologies – which, for reasons to be explained shortly, I will henceforth refer to as mid- and multi-range technologies (or MMRTs) – raise some fascinating and in many ways vital questions about technological regulation and offending. Certain of these are familiar enough – the problem of knife crime, for example. Others, like issues around consumer safety, have been far less discussed. Since it has not been common within either criminological or legal discourse to think of MMRTs as "technological", we have fewer theoretical resources for characterising offences involving them as "technologically enabled". On reflection, this may be more of an oversight than it at first seems. For in addition to the useful insights they offer into the character of body–technology interaction, it is in this class of artefacts that perhaps the central question concerning technology and its technomia arises most immediately. Namely, "how technologically enabled" is it desirable (or permissible) to be? For, however, mundane the kinds of enhancements provided by, say, an oven or a pair of socks may be in comparison with genetic modification, the question is in many ways more tangible and therefore far more "human" to us.

Mid- and multi-range technologies

The anthropologist Edward Hall, reflecting upon the varied nature of our everyday technological life, once observed that:

> Man has developed extensions for practically everything he used to do with his body ... Clothes and houses are extensions of man's biological temperature control mechanisms. Furniture takes the place of squatting and sitting on the ground. Power-tools, glasses. ... are examples of material extensions.
>
> (Hall, 1959, p. 79, cited in McLuhan, 1962)

Mumford's distinction between "utensils, apparatus, utilities, tools and machines" (1934, p. 11) – "artefacts to be lived with, used, lived within, operated or set in motion" (ibid.) – has been one of the rare attempts to categorise these more mundane technologies alluded to by Hall. Though never widely adopted, it has influenced later categorisations – as, for example, the inclusion of clothes, spoons and thermostatically controlled boilers in Mitcham's (1994) schema. Especially lacking has been any very clear governing logic to what is common here, with more general labels like "domestic" technologies or "consumer" technologies either failing to capture what is characteristic or excluding key artefacts altogether.

In order to locate these technologies within the "spectrum of artefacts" (cf. Mitcham, ibid.) some defining feature therefore seems to be required. It is here that their role in enhancing our immediate bodily needs and functions becomes significant, for it is on this basis that the cooking pots that feed us, the electric heater that warms us or the flushing toilet that enhances our hygiene all display a common function. All "improve" upon very basic things our bodies do for us – strengthening, lengthening or intensifying basic functions like heat insulation, nourishment or even pleasure. It is with such technologies that we first moved from the organic to the inorganic or, as Bataille puts it, that we first "became human". For they help us to recognise that unless we establish "relations of immanence" with the world that sustains us (Bataille, 1992; see also Tomasi, 2008), our autonomy is necessarily incomplete. It is here, then, that we "re-establish intimacy" with nature (Tomasi, ibid.) – by allowing our tools to become so connected with our bodies that they seem to be all but indistinguishable from the organs they extend. The principle of "invisibility in use", at work here with many artefacts (Clark, 2003, p. 38), reflects Ferren's axiom that "technology is stuff which doesn't work yet" (cf. Adams, 1999) and clarifies why artefacts of this kind often seem "less technological" than others. Given the analytic framework here, these facts suggest a more robust way of linking the bodily immediacy of these artefacts to their function as technologies, one that again centres upon the causal range at which they enable us to act. Thus in contrast to ICTs or CBNTs, which allow us to do things "beyond our reach" – i.e. at a distance (whether near or far) – the function of these technologies seems to primarily operate within a kind of "mid range". That is, their function and effects are largely attuned to the immediate sphere of our bodily reach.

These distinctive scalar characteristics also make it clear why including weapons technologies within this class is plausible – for weapons originated in precisely the same set of concerns and needs as the other technologies that feature here. And in enhancing our immediate needs for security, weapons were key to establishing relations of immanence with the external world – by enabling us to gather nourishment through hunting, or to acquire resources by violence and conquest. But since the causal range of weaponry was very quickly extended beyond close-range capacities for protection or attack (facilitated by sticks or clubs), towards more distant varieties (facilitated by spears, or bows and arrows), it also seems to make sense to think of such weapons as operating across multiple ranges. Thus, whilst designating this class of artefacts or processes as "mid- or multi-range technologies" is of course in part a theoretical convenience, it is not entirely artificial, for it reflects the primacy of the body in shaping technological extension and its spatial reach.

The need to take these artefacts more seriously is emphasised by at least two factors. One is the fact that every technology we have explored – no matter how sophisticated nor how far-reaching its causal range – must come back to a "mid range" in at least one sense – the requirement for its interface to "fit" our body. Given the scale and shape of our bodies, there are clearly a fairly limited number of ways in which we can interact with technological forms – for example, via manipulation-based interfaces (like buttons, keyboards or touch screens), visual or graphical (GUI) interfaces (like VDU screens or microscopes) or sound or voice recognition (VUI) interfaces. How to make technology "body compliant" is now a vital aspect of "user interface" or human-centred design – especially within the development of ICTs (see for example Tilley and Dreyfuss Associates, 2001; Norman, 1990). The development of a specific technical criterion of "usability", formalised in international standards such as ISO 20282 (ISO, 2006), shows how such principles are now central to the wider product design field. Standards for usability may be determined by how the function of an artefact (say, a ticket machine) can be better tailored to users. But crucially, usability is not just about function, but about other relevant bodily factors – such as the "joy of use" – ways in which user–artefact functionality is improved by making the interaction more pleasurable (Hassenzahl *et al.*, 2001). Very similar reflections can be applied to most of the "multi-range" technological artefacts within this class. For example, no matter at what distance a weapon's technology enables us to defend or attack, its functionality depends upon immediate orientations towards our body, whether this is the button that enables us to launch a missile or the handle that enables us to hold and guide a knife.

In many ways MMRTs are a perfect manifestation of the "prosthetic" view of technology endorsed by Freud, in that they form our most spatially immediate "carapace of capacity", the technic exoskeleton that we have come to freely inhabit as much as the skin and bones that once delimited our realm of experience. But this process of familiarisation will also eventually transform more complex technologies like ICTs into "everyday" features of our technologically augmented bodies (cf. Silverstone and Hirsch, 1992). A second reason for the significance of these artefacts lies in the effects they produce. As the recent claim that the "washing machine changed the world more than the internet" (Chang, 2010) suggests, their consequences can often be as significant as any of the more spectacular technological forms we have considered. For whilst the harms produced by a humble dishwasher or floor brush may not be as dramatic as those issuing from biological or information technologies in terms of volume, their impacts may be just as far reaching. And when it comes to weapons, we may have one of the most significant technologies for crime and control that exist.

Crimes with mid-range technologies

Defining the extent to which the misuse of an MMRT can be defined as a "technology crime" is no less difficult than with the other technologies considered here – indeed, in many ways it is more complex. After all, being hit on the head by a hammer, exercising negligence with an ironing board or even shooting someone have simply never been seen as "technological crimes". We might well ask why. Just because the complexity of a high-technology object like a computer captures our attention more completely, this is not in itself a basis for its being "more" technological than an MMRT. In which case there seems to be no good reason why offences involving such artefacts should not also be seen as technologically enabled.

In what follows I will therefore ignore issues around high/low, complex/ less complex technologies and simply take this range of artefacts at face value – as "technological" in virtue of the fact that they extend us. Given this, there are many ways in which MMRTs might serve to extend our capacity to offend, or to impose control, that could be identified. To keep the discussion manageable I will restrict my focus to three key areas of harm and regulation.

1   Outcomes involving our "normal" or folk sense of criminality – that is, the extent to which MMRTs are involved in, or facilitate, standard or

"volume" notions of crime, like violence or property-related offences, and the nature of regulation directed at this.

2   Outcomes involving the performance of such artefacts – in particular, the risks and liabilities they generate and the controls designed to safeguard against this.

3   Outcomes involving the level or degree of enhancement such technologies offer. The question here – namely, how "technological" do we want our technological extensions to be – brings the fascinating issue of "performance enhancement" and its control into focus and illustrates why this is not just an issue for sporting regulators, but for the justice system as a whole.

Some issues here are distinctive to this class but there are also many obvious continuities with those seen in our earlier discussion of ICTs and CBNTs, not least those centring around the question of technological risk. But, as we shall now see, the close relationship between MMRTs and the body makes such questions especially pressing.

Everyday mid-range crimes and their control

The use of MMRTs as policing or control tools is just as unlikely to be thought of as "technological" as is their use in offending. But one indication of the importance of close-range enhancement can be seen in the many control goals it facilitates. From the use of flashlights during police operations, to technologies of confinement such as handcuffs, exerting control at the immediate level of the body is as essential to policing as identifying a DNA strand and, as we saw in Chapter 2, often comes with its own, unique kinds of technical shifts and innovations (see Kelley, 1998 for an example).

In terms of criminality, the easy accessibility of many MMRTs might suggest that their use in furthering property crime or violence is more likely than other, more exotic technological forms. Given what has been called the "dual functionality" or "multiple functionality" of artefacts, seemingly innocent objects can often acquire functions that differ radically from what was originally intended for them (see Kroes and Meijers, 2006; Vaesen, 2011). On this basis, ladders, hammers and wire-cutters may present as many possibilities for criminality as they do for innocent uses. In contrast to knives or handguns, which have what might be called primary functions more obviously conducive to offending, few special controls have been felt to be required for the functionally "innocent" artefacts in this class. We will return to the specific issue of weapon-based crime and control later in the chapter but, as we shall now see, this should not lead us to overlook the offending potentials of less obvious technological artefacts.

Violence and personal gain

The duality of artefact function – what Mitcham also referred to as intrinsic or extrinsic uses (1994, p. 164[2]) – implies that intention can trump technological normativity in determining the kinds of uses to which an artefact is put. For, with the right intention, a ladder offers more than a means of replacing a roof-tile – it can also facilitate a burglary. Similar intentional shifts can transform many other everyday artefacts into tools for theft or violence. Intentionality is not, however, all determining in this regard – artefacts clearly require certain properties conducive to such offences, such as sharpness or hardness. But here too conditions may be fairly loose. After all, it is just as possible to murder someone with a feather cushion as it is with a brick. Intentionality also poses certain legal difficulties for defining such offences as "technological". As already suggested, the role of *mens rea* in determining culpability means that the tool used cannot be a deciding factor – a fact that surely holds even more strongly where the primary function of a tool has been adapted to other ends. In the UK, for example, Crown Prosecution Service (CPS) guidelines state that "Although some weapons are more serious than others the nature of the weapon will not be the primary determinant, as this will depend on its intended use" (CPS, 2010). Thus, in *R* v. *Dorado* [2006] and *R* v. *Proctor* [2000][3] a meat cleaver and a bottle of ammonia respectively were both judged to be "offensive weapons" because in each case they had been used with intention to harm. The role of intention in transforming artefacts into criminal tools raises fascinating questions about the status of enablement and its control. It offers, for example, an obvious reason why specific legal regulation of everyday artefacts to prevent crime would be superfluous – whilst raising difficult questions about why this principle becomes less sure where more overtly "technological" objects like the internet enable the offending.

Similar reflections apply in considering associations between mid-range artefacts and "volume" forms of crime like theft or burglary. Just as the primary function of a chair leg ceases to be relevant when it is used as a weapon, appealing to a screwdriver's primary function as a building tool is no defence if it has been used to break and enter into a property. Here, however, there appears to be a greater readiness to specify when the function of an artefact changes sufficiently for it to become judged as an "offending technology". In the UK, for example, the 1968 Theft Act (§25.1) created the offence of "going equipped" where a person has "any article for use in the course of or in connection with any burglary (or) theft". The vagueness of this condition allows almost any kind of artefact to constitute the enabling feature of an offence, given the right circumstances. In *R* v. *Ferry and Wynn* (1997), for example, the defendants' guilty plea to "going equipped" was probably unavoidable, given that they were found in possession of a cordless drill and other tools in the vicinity of a telephone call-box that had been damaged. But other less obvious technological enablers such as a car, a shirt or even a sliced loaf of bread and tomatoes have also sometimes been defined as "articles" used in connection with theft or fraud (cf. Jefferson, 2003, p. 525). US law is similarly generous in the way it conceptualises the transition between an artefact's (innocent) primary function and a potentially criminal secondary function. For example, under the New York penal code an individual can be found guilty of possessing "burglar's tools" if s/he possesses any object considered to enable forcible entry into a premises (McKinney's Penal Law of New York §140.35; see also Brenner, 2004). Obvious ambiguities arise where an artefact has primary functions that directly enable theft – for example, lock-picking devices. To be found carrying such devices without good reason (i.e. not being a professional locksmith) may well constitute the basis for a prosecution.

The fact that crime statistics usually characterise the criminal use of tools in terms of broad artefactual categories such as "cutting instruments", "blunt objects" or actions such as "strangulation" or "burning" (where it is not clear whether a tool has been used or not) makes it difficult to offer any precise analysis of the extent to which MMRTs facilitate crime. However, some very basic inferences can be made. For example, in 2008 around 4 per cent of murders in the USA (614 out of over 14,000) involved a blunt instrument such as a hammer (FBI, 2008). By contrast, nearly 48 per cent of homicides in the UK involved sharp or blunt implements, and 4 per cent other devices such as poison or motor vehicles (Smith and Flatley, 2010). And whilst only around 6 per cent of homicides in the UK involved the use of firearms (ibid.), nearly 65–70 per cent of homicides in representative states of the USA such as California, Texas and New York involved some form of firearm (FBI, 2009). This indicates the importance of the greater availability of MMRTs as potential enablers of crime.

Leaving to one side for the moment the use of weapons in effecting robbery, it will already be clear that there are many kinds of mid-range artefact that can be used to enable theft. In 2005, for example, over 50 per cent of attempted burglaries in the UK were committed by forcing locks on doors or windows, and (presumably) tools such as screwdrivers, wrenches, crowbars and the like played at least some role here (cf. Walker *et al.*, 2006). The potential for ordinary mid-range objects to acquire secondary functions as burglars' tools has been widely recognised by crime-control experts, who issue regular warnings to householders not to leave items such as garden tools in visible locations (cf. BBC, 23/07/2009). Burglars frequently report that available tools of this kind, along with ladders, hammers and other household items do not just facilitate entry, but may often encourage it. Many seemingly mundane artefacts can also be increasingly tempting targets for theft, as the rising trade in stolen cables and textiles or the purloining of garden furniture or plants indicates (see for example Bennett, 2008).

There is then a varied but clear set of ways in which even the most basic form of artefact can be a target or tool of interest to criminals – though few would associate this with "technological crime". Fewer still would regard it as presenting anything like the same level of threat as an ICT or CBNT. Whether the use of a hammer to effect entry to a premises where £500,000 is stolen amounts to any less significant a form of technological enablement than the computer used to steal £100,000 from a bank account is of course a moot point. But it is clear enough that ladders, brick or wire-cutters are unlikely to be used to define categories of crime any time in the near future.

Mid-range technologies and other criminal harms

MMRTs seem to present more distinctive varieties of technological offending where more abstract kinds of harm are involved – for example, certain forms of anti-social behaviour. This fact also provides evidence for the informal maxim that the more sophisticated the technology involved, the greater readiness there is to define crime as technologically enabled. One example of this has been the increasing association between personal music players or home entertainment systems and new offences around noise pollution. Noise has often been seen as a problem distinctive to technological cultures (Bijsterveld, 2008), and the increase in noise nuisance (in particular that created by vehicles) has been estimated to be a problem for up to one in three households in the UK, with deleterious effects on stress levels and on children's health – especially in deprived areas (Evans *et al.*, 1998; RCEP, 2007). Britain is now one of the noisiest places in Europe, with traffic noise levels in many large cities exceeding World Health Organization guidelines by an average of around 20 decibels (RCEP, ibid.). But though regulations around noise may be more "technology specific", the emphasis is still more upon the outcomes of technology use than on the technology itself. This conceptual gap may explain the uneven enforcement of such regulations. For example, in spite of around 17 different pieces of relevant UK law,[4] prosecutions for noise pollution appear to have nearly halved over recent years. In London alone, the 1,582 recorded offences relating to vehicle noise in 1986 had fallen to just 200 by 2001 (ONS, 2001).

The creation of noise abatement zones (NAZ) under UK law (EPUK, 2010) provides a new, spatialised response to controlling excessive vehicle noise, noise from car radios and car alarms, as well as from loudspeakers and other noise-generating technologies (which even include fireworks). This innovation contrasts favourably with the far more lax regulatory environment within the USA, where agencies like the Office of Noise Abatement and Control (ONAC) and legislation like the 1972 Noise Control Act[5] have been regularly underfunded and underpoliced (see NFA, 2010). At the international level, the UN has various working groups seeking to harmonise the regulation of noise-generating technologies (cf. UNECE, 2010), whilst the EU has plans that will require manufacturers of personal music players to include "safe" exposure levels as default settings on such devices.

One suggestion is that volumes of around 80 decibels would be consistent with 40 hours of safe listening (EU, 2009). Such regulation is not intended to operate in a mandatory way, but by "nudging" industry standards towards new technological norms. The use of personal music players within public spaces has created particular frustrations (Rabinowitz, 2010), and certain jurisdictions have been very proactive in imposing controls upon them. For example, France has laws setting maximum iPod volumes at 100 decibels (Richmond, 2009).

The complexities around regulating sound contrast interestingly with the increasingly widespread use of sound technologies as a *form* of regulation. The use of white noise and other sound as an interrogation device was originally pioneered by the British and American military and secret services (Elliston, 1999), together with the "acoustic bombardment" tactics used during the arrest of the Panamanian leader General Noriega in 1989 (Cusick, 2006). Such techniques have now begin to "trickle down" to more informal levels of social regulation – for example, the way that local authorities and even schools now direct sound technologies at young people to "deal with" their perceived disorderliness. Thus, just as it has become a new form of school discipline to "subject" (*sic*) pupils to classical music whilst in detention (*Guardian*, 2010), classical music has also been used to purge the young from public spaces like bus shelters, tube stations or local convenience stores. One local transport authority gleefully cited Rachmaninov's Symphony no. 2 and Shostakovich's Piano Concerto no. 2 as "particularly" effective (Jackson, 2005). Technological regulation of this kind takes on a more sinister character with the development of devices like the Mosquito, designed to generate unpleasant high-frequency sounds audible only to young people. By late 2009, over 3,500 of the 5,000 or so Mosquito units sold in Europe had been installed in public spaces in the UK (Townsend, 2010b) – even though such devices do not distinguish between innocent or criminal behaviours and can cause extreme discomfort in young children – especially babies. As a result, Mosquito-style devices have been condemned as "degrading and discriminatory" by the Council of Europe, which argued that they violate human rights law provisions prohibiting torture (COE, 2010).

Of course, noise pollution is just one amongst many other areas in which the ubiquity of mid-range technology commodities creates potential problems of technological harm and with that, the need for new forms of regulation. Other risks, such as the toxicities of household disinfectants discussed in Chapters 5 and 6, indicate the rich anti-social potentials of many MMRTs that a wider analysis might consider. Whether it is late-night DIY improvements or the "reckless use of a shopping trolley" (cf. Kentish Express, 2010), MMRTs present a formidable set of resources for engaging in wider forms of offending than violence or property crime alone. One such example – their impacts upon risk – is one we now turn to in more detail.

Mid-range technologies: risk, safety and liability

Given the ever-present spectre of the "technological accident", issues of risk and its regulation are essential themes within any criminological analysis of technology, but they are especially immediate in the context of MMRTs. The fact that many MMRTs are consumer commodities such as white goods or home electronic devices means that the role of technological norms plays an important part in shaping the regulatory picture here (cf. Kroes, 1998; Perrow, 1999). In particular, it highlights the role of con- sumer rights in determining both the extent to which any technological commodity must perform in accordance with what is claimed about it, as well as doing this in accordance with adequate safety standards.

The growth in what are sometimes called "safety crimes" (cf. Tombs and Whyte, 2007) reminds us that regulating the risks around consumer commodities cannot be separated from their origins within the industrial process. Though criminological analysis here has tended to focus upon the risks to workers rather than to consumers, the areas of consumer safety and product liability now represent areas of growing legal significance (cf. Huber, 1990). Yet, as we saw in Chapter 2, regulations directed at the adequate functioning of technological processes and artefacts have not been exclusive to consumer societies. For the more obvious the risk posed to the social order by a technical artefact or skill, the more likely that some form of control will exist around it. Thus, as far back as the Babylonian code of Hammurabi, techniques like construction or medicine have generated specific regulations – for example, the law stating that any builder found responsible for killing the occupants of a unstably built house would be liable for financial penalties or even a death sentence (King, 2004, p. 228). The concept of "an inherently safe design" (cf. Hansson, 2006; MacCollum, 2006) has since become a central technological norm, one that in the context of construction alone has produced a bewildering array of rules. UK build- ing regulations run to 14 separate areas and their numerous sub-clauses and sections have been criticised as "complicated and disorganised" (RIBA, 2010). But disjointedness seems to be endemic to the regulation of consumer commodities – with oversight allocated to multiple agencies like the British Standards Institute (BSI) (which alone has over 27,000 different product safety standards), the Health and Safety Executive (HSE) or local authority trading standards officers.

Accordingly, characterising offending here is by no means straight- forward, arising as it does from infringements to a confusing range of consumer standards, tort law and the basic willingness of regulatory bodies to intervene. Many of these regulatory bodies date back to the origins of contemporary consumerism – for example, the UK Trading Standards Institute (TSI), created in 1881, and the US Federal Trade Commission (FTC), created to enforce the 1914 Federal Trade Commission Act. Together with agencies such as the Office of Fair Trading (OFT), the TSI seeks to enforce constraints upon the performance of goods and services imposed by legislation such as the 1979 Sale of Goods Act,[6] or the 1987 Consumer Protection Act. Such laws confer various statutory rights upon consumers, most obviously the expectation that goods produced "are what they say they are", that their quality is of a satisfactory level and that they are "fit for their purpose" (cf. Chuah and Furmston, 2010). In the USA, the FTC presides over an even wider body of consumer law that includes everything from the Fair Packaging and Labeling Act to the Wool Product Labeling Act[7] (cf. FTC, 2007). The founding brief of the FTC – to prevent "unfair and deceptive acts or practices" – is straightforward enough but, as with consumer protection bodies in the UK, the FTC's powers have been subjected to frequent criticisms from commentators on both the left and right. Right-wing critics have attacked such bodies for interfering with the market's role as a "natural" regulator (cf. Posner, 1969 and arguments against such views in Pitofsky, 1977), whilst critics on the left have often seen consumer protection agencies as ineffective – either because they are judged to be overly influenced by lobbying groups or because they are too weak and too slow in enforcing rulings (Dresser, 2004; Sawyer, 2006). The FTC has been especially criticised for tolerating the self-regulation model in areas where even its own data indicates evidence of harm – such as the corporate targeting of young children in the marketing of unhealthy food (Eggerton, 2008). The OFT has also been accused of lacking transparency and letting companies off the hook (NAO, 2008), and legislation like the 1979 Sales of Goods Act is charged with being "anachronistic", full of "redundancies [and] omissions", and lacking "decisiveness" (Bridge, 2004). In 2008 there were around 26.5 million reported problems with goods or services in the UK – at a cost to consumers of an estimated £6.6bn (OFT, 2008). Over three-quarters of those who suffered harm or violations of consumer rights did nothing or were too confused about from where to seek support, and of those who did only around a quarter went to Trading Standards Services (ibid.). The inadequacies of consumer protection were recently highlighted by the deaths of 15 individuals in the UK between 2007 and 2010 caused by fridge-freezer fires and the failure of the manufacturer, Beko, to make these long-standing problems public, in spite of warnings from the fire services (Milligan, 2011).

The less than clear evaluations of the risks posed by consumer technologies can be better highlighted if we focus purely on volume harms. On this metric, many of the relatively innocuous-seeming artefacts that surround us could be argued to pose greater safety and security risks than other, more hazardous technologies – as Table 7.1 suggests. The fact that injuries arising from tin-openers in 2002 were more than three times as high as those associated with violent muggings (Simmons and Dodd, 2003, p. 84), or that ironing boards appear to present more than twice the threat of chainsaws, is a reminder that we ignore MMRTs as a source of technology risk at our peril. But nor should the harms posed by the everyday objects and artefacts

Table 7.1 Injuries caused by common household items in 2002

Source of injury	Number injured
Coffee tables	20,090
Cats	17,159
Ironing boards	2,829
Chainsaws	1,210
Tin-openers	1,169
Wendy houses	820
Tea/coffee makers	820
Bean bags	738
Ice creams	718
Jacuzzis	287
Dust pans	205

Source: RoSPA (2010).

that surround us be overplayed. The widely cited claim that "swimming pools are 100 times more likely to cause the death of a child than firearms" sounds compelling, but depends upon a number of statistically questionable assumptions (cf. Levitt and Dubner, 2006; Di Nardo, 2006 for criticisms of them).

It is also telling that the regulation of safety and risk has proved to be one of the few areas where the force of technological norms has provoked consistent resistance. Health and safety regulations have been especially challenged – often to the point of outright ridicule. Rather than such protections being accepted as any part of an attempt to develop a more coherent technomia around consumer economies, they are more usually constructed as examples of petty bureaucracy and interference. But, given that this construct is one that has been constantly reinforced by negative stories in the (usually right-wing) press, there must be suspicions that it is the vested interests of industry that are being protected, rather than the public. In 2008, around 1.2 million people in the UK alone claimed to be suffering from an illness arising from inadequate health and safety provision at work (HSE, 2009), with around 246,000 new injuries being reported (ibid.). But the increase in technology use and injury in the workplace does not appear to have produced any significant rise in numbers of prosecutions. Between 2004 and 2008 the number of convictions for breaches of health and safety legislation declined by around 20 per cent (down from 1,025 to 846) (ibid., p. 12). In spite of the ideologically driven ridicule directed at such controls, their introduction has brought clear benefits – with research suggesting that workers are 50 per cent less likely to suffer injury in the workplace where adequate regulations or safety representatives are in place (Reilly *et al.*, 1995). There must, then, be concerns around the way industry not only often determines standards here but also sets the agenda for enforcement.

When it comes to property, technological norms are more zealously enforced, for with advanced consumerism has come the sense that consumers have "rights". The most basic of these is the right to assume that what is purchased "does what it says on the tin" – i.e. it functions in accord with its technological norms. The effects of consumerism in generating harms and criminality have been of increasing interest to criminologists (see for example Hayward, 2004; Hall *et al.*, 2008), though such discussions have tended to focus more upon the negative social impacts of this rather than on the technologies that make consumerism possible. The issue of consumer law – especially in connection with technological artefacts – also offers a potentially rich field for analysis, though the law has often failed consumers where more unconventional damage to property is involved. For example, the recent decision by Sony to install anti-copying root kits onto a user's PC (without permission) – was not covered by any existing provisions, even though it meant that the performance of the PC was impaired or that it was exposed to viruses (Halderman and Felten, 2006).

Underlying all these issues is the question of liability and how this is enforced. For some, the recent expansions in liability law have proved to be somewhat of a mixed blessing – with benefits more likely to be accrued by lawyers rather than by consumers who have suffered failure or injury from an artefact they purchased (Huber, 1990). Business has been highly resistant to liability, and tort law and its greater capacity to fund defence cases has often made it difficult to obtain settlements. Similarly, insurance companies have often been less than ready to conform to rulings of this kind (Lewis, 2006). Consumer rights may also be undermined by the principle established in common law that customers should be sure to "know" what to expect when purchasing goods. But "knowing what to expect" may not always be straightforward in the case of a sophisticated technological commodity, or as the traditional *caveat emptor* (buyer beware) principle suggests. The continued relevance of this principle shows how producers maintain their traditional advantages within technological regulation.

Performance enhancement: criminalities and rule breaking

If it is accepted that technologies can be defined in terms of the way they enhance our capacities to perform tasks, then an obvious but important normative question arises – namely, what, if any, limits should be placed upon enhancement? Aspects of this question have already been touched upon in previous chapters – in particular the regulatory issues around CBNTs and modifications to our genetic make-up (cf. Cameron, 2010). Given their everyday role in social life, MMRTs bring this question into a different kind of focus. In the case of many artefacts of this kind, posing such a question might seem absurd – for example, what purpose would be served by limiting the softness of cushions? But there other forms of immediate bodily enhancements – such as cosmetic surgery, where controls have seemed necessary. Indeed, for some, many enhancements of the human organism represent nothing less than a dystopian nightmare (see for example Fukayama, 2000; Harris, 2007). One area where the normative ambiguities around enhancement have been more fully explored is within the context of sport, where a developed body of rules exists for managing how far performance can be extended. It will be useful therefore to begin by considering how enhancement has been managed within this more restricted domain of regulation, before considering its wider control aspects.

In terms of the immediate body, there seem to be at least three basic templates for enhancement.

Enhancement by external devices

Whilst many sports specifically depend upon the use of an external device in order to be playable – such as a cricket bat or a set of golf clubs – the extent to which these tools can be altered to enhance performance has not always been consistent. There are, for example, very detailed regulations around the tennis racket specifying its size and other factors (ITF, 2011) which have lessened its effects upon performance in comparison to other sporting tools such as the pole used in pole vaulting. The pole can be made of any material and can be of any length (Kukureka and Davis, 2010) – with the result that technical improvements have improved jumping heights from 3.5 metres in 1900 to over 5.5 metres by the 1990s (ibid.). Interesting ambiguities arise where alterations are made to tools not previously covered by any rules but that appear to enhance athletes' capacities. A particular example of this was seen in the context of swimming, where the introduction of new polyethylene suits like the Speedo LZR or other, more advanced versions in the early 2000s had a dramatic impact, including the setting of over 100 new world records within about a year. Though the term "technological doping" was used to describe their effects (Nichols, 2009), no violation of the rules had occurred – so forcing FINA, the world swimming body, to make a new ruling (in 2009). Its judgement that this was an "unacceptable" technological innovation resulted in the suits being banned (Shipley, 2009).

Further regulatory confusions about enhancement arise where an athlete uses technology to overcome certain natural disadvantages, such as a disability. Huge uproar followed the controversial US Supreme Court decision to allow disabled golfer Casey Martin to use a golf cart between holes, on the grounds that this was not a fundamental part of the game, and so was not strictly an enhancement (Reaves, 2001). By contrast, the use of specially constructed carbon fibre "blades" by the double amputee runner Oscar Pistorius was argued to be a technological enhancement in that it directly improved his performance. After a scientific study appeared to support the claim that he derived an "unfair" biomechanical advantage, Pistorius was banned from competing in the 2008 Beijing Olympics (Eason, 2008), though this decision was overturned following an appeal to the Court of Arbitration for Sport. Such thinking might be contrasted with contexts where disability has produced an active legal requirement that performance be enhanced. For example, under UK law, individuals who are unable to read a vehicle number plate at a distance of between 20 and 20.5 metres are legally required to wear glasses when driving.[8]

Our confusions around technological extension mean that there are always gaps to be exploited. Take the role of the calculator – originally seen as "too much" of a cognitive enhancer in the classroom, but one which has now become a commonplace – in contrast to the internet or smartphones, which at present remain largely prohibited in assessment situations. There is increasing evidence that technologies such as these may already be outpacing the capacity of rules to manage them. For example, the growth in plagiarism indicates how individual choices about digital enhancements to learning may be overriding official constraints. Between 4 and 7 per cent of the UK student population have admitted to committing plagiarism, and around 40 per cent to knowing someone else who has cheated (cf. Underwood, 2006), and figures in the US are even higher. One survey there suggested that around 74 per cent of students have admitted to serious cheating in exams, and over 60 per cent to having copied sentences from the internet without citing the source (cf. McCabe, 2005). Some institutions have now taken the decision to confront the issue head on by integrating ICTs into the contemporary learning and assessment environment – as, for example, in Denmark's 2009 decision to permit the use of the internet during exams (Johnson, 2009).

Enhancement by chemicals

A second modality of performance enhancement (sporting or otherwise) is, strictly speaking, more within the remit of CBNTs, in that it involves chemical alterations to physiological processes. But, given that the effects are upon the immediate aspects of bodily performance, it also makes sense to consider the issue in terms of MMRTs. The chemical enhancement of sporting performance is hardly a new phenomenon – athletes in ancient Greece were known to have experimented with various potions and chemical preparations in the hope these might enhance their running, throwing or jumping abilities (see Moffat, 2006). But, as our scientific understanding of physiological processes has developed, attitudes have become more negative and opinion in the sporting world is now almost universally opposed to chemical enhancement. The first controls were introduced in 1928 by the International Association of Athletics Federations, followed much later, in 1966, by the International Cycling Union (UCI) and the main footballing body, FIFA (WADA, 2011). But enforcement has been more difficult and, even with the advent of more stringent testing regimes, chemical enhancement in sport has remained fairly widespread (albeit underground).

Five main chemical families are usually prohibited: anabolic steroids, which help athletes to build muscle; peptide hormones, which occur naturally in the body but which produce similar effects to anabolic steroids; strong analgesic painkillers, like morphine; stimulants such as amphetamines and cocaine, which may improve performance by raising the heart rate; and diuretics, which help the body to lose fluids and so may help boxers to meet their fighting weight (Waddington and Smith, 2008). Confusions begin where other chemicals that have been prescribed for legitimate medical purposes may, as a side effect, partly enhance performance – for example, asthma-related medication or certain treatments for colds (Mottram, 2010). Athletes are permitted to take certain supplements – such as vitamins – though here too there have been problems with substances such as creatine, an amino acid found in muscle structure that has been estimated to be used by anything up to 35 per cent of professional athletes on a regular basis (Puerini and Gorey, 2000) and around 28 per cent of college or non-professional athletes (Metzl *et al.*, 2001). The extent to which creatine really improves performance is questionable, and for every supposed gain there are studies associating it with harms such as heart disease or renal dysfunction (Puerini and Gorey, 2000).

Given these and many other kinds of dilemmas around chemical enhancement in sport, some have argued that there may be good reasons for tolerating it (cf. Foddy and Savulescu, 2007). One argument has centred upon the question of "natural" advantages (such as differences in metabolism rates) and whether it any less "fair" to use chemicals to even these out. The assumption that sport is always about pure "biological potentials" becomes questionable if training regimes are interpreted as a form of technological enhancement – since these arguably change bodily processes and physiology, much like chemicals do. Questions also exist around the extent to which "sports science" techniques create a gap between elite and amateur sports, for this also undermines the desired level playing field. And if the argument that performance enhancement by chemicals must be controlled because it ultimately "harms" athletes is credible, why not apply the same reasoning to sports training regimes, since these too may, on occasions, have harmful outcomes (Foddy and Savulescu, ibid.)?

Beyond the sporting world, pharmaceuticals are also increasingly being used as enhancers in ways only loosely related to medicinal needs, though guidelines are far less clear here. Clearly, where chemicals impair, rather than enhance, performance, controls will often be desirable – no one would advocate a use of chemicals whilst driving vehicles or operating complex machinery. On the other hand, performance enhancement by chemicals has sometimes been state-sanctioned policy. For example, in an attempt to enhance combat performance, over 200 million amphetamine tablets were dispensed to US soldiers in the Second World War – a practice that had commenced during the First World War and that lasted until at least the Vietnam War (Menhard, 2006). Even hallucinogens such as LSD, or "love drugs" like MDMA, have been used to enhance therapy; and, of course, the use of narcotics for enhancing spiritual or creative capacities is well recorded (see for example Greer and Tolbert, 1998; Sessa, 2008).

The interests of the pharmaceutical industry, as we saw in Chapter 5, often complicate the regulation of chemical enhancement. A variety of highly profitable antidepressant, mood-enhancing narcotics such as Prozac, are now regarded as such acceptable forms of physiological alteration that it has become FDA-approved policy in the US for children as young as 6 or 7 years to be "treated" with them – a practice now also endorsed by the European Medicines Agency (EMEA) (Frith, 2006). Critics point to evidence of the heightened risk of suicide that such chemicals produce, arguing that this amounts to nothing less than the mass sedation of vulnerable young people on the basis of dubious new medicalisations like "ADHT" or "bi-polarity" (cf. Diller, 2006; Olfman, 2006). Elsewhere, the mass-marketing of drugs like Viagra, which enhances sexual performance, has reversed many of the usual social restrictions upon pleasure enhancement by chemical – though this is more to do with commercial imperatives than any new social consensus about sexual pleasure.

Conflicts between social norms, commerce and chemical enhancement are also seen in the use of cognitive enhancing "smart drugs". These so-called "steroids for the brain" have found increasing uses within the academic and student worlds, where high brain functioning is clearly a pre-requisite for success (cf. BMA, 2007; Talbot, 2009). Though many "neuro-enhancers" such as Adderall and Ritalin are effectively amphetamines, they can be legally obtained by prescription and offer new kinds of revenue streams to the pharmaceutical industry. Evidence of increased levels of dependency and other health problems have inevitably begun to emerge as a result (Talbot, 2009; Sederer, 2009). As with sport, obvious questions arise about the fairness in "non-enhanced" students having to compete with enhanced ones (cf. Rose, 1993), and calls have arisen for students, like athletes, to undergo compulsory "drug testing" (Davies, 2010).

Long-term enhancement or alteration

At the more extreme end of performance enhancement are those varieties of technological intervention that permanently alter the body and its capacities. At least three basic scenarios for how this might take place exist at present. First is the use of certain medical (usually surgical) processes to alter existing bodily appearance or capacity – as, for example, with breast augmentation or laser eye treatments. A second option involves the kind of modifications to genetic structures discussed in Chapter 5. This might involve controversial, quasi-eugenic programmes such as the "designer baby" concept, where parents choose from a tick-list of desirable traits (Green, 2007). As we saw, it is now legal in the UK to select for genetic safeguards against certain diseases. A third, still more outlandish option for long-term enhancement is where technology is directly integrated with the human body – a variation of the "cyborg" body idea (Haraway, 1991; Hayles, 1999; Clark, 2003). The more limited examples of this already with us – heart pacemakers or artificial limbs controlled by brain impulses (cf. Drummond, 2010) – are no more than prototypes for the more sophisticated "cyborg" extensions likely to pose future challenges to regulatory frameworks.

In sporting contexts, long-term enhancements of this kind would appear to be completely ruled out, given that any external modification goes so strongly against the spirit of "natural ability". Yet even here a degree of latitude exists where medical interventions produce a human–technology fusion. Prosthetic augmentation involving the use of bone pins and plates, metal knee caps or animal or synthetic tissue have all become permissible forms of treating injury in sport – even though this (arguably) results in long-term physical enhancement (cf. Kjaer, 2002). This greater tolerance towards such "hardware" based enhancements over "software" (i.e. genetic) equivalents has been just as prevalent outside the sporting world. A familiar but significant example of this has been the widespread acceptance of the permanent physical alterations produced by cosmetic surgery. The rapid growth in this form of physical enhancement has been striking – between 2004 and 2006 alone the number of breast enlargements in the UK rose from just 3,700 operations to over 26,000 (Latham, 2008).[9] Since this is a very under-regulated practice it has often been associated with new varieties of harm and new categories of criminal behaviour. Controls around cosmetic surgery have been especially weak in the UK, given that cosmetic surgery procedures are predominantly carried out at private clinics, where there is little outside scrutiny. Incompetence has been the most common cause of legal action – between the early 1990s and 2003 over £7 million worth of compensation was paid out to dissatisfied customers following botched operations – 24 per cent of which had resulted in scarring (MDU, 2003). The ambiguities around regulating this form of enhancement have allowed many cosmetics technologies to be classified as "medical devices" rather than drugs – thereby permitting individuals with inadequate medical expertise to administer botox injections or the use of silicon gels like Macrolane. Jurisdictional gaps have also been created by the globalisation of cosmetic surgery. It has been estimated, for example, that around 30,000 UK citizens now travel abroad for beauty enhancement purposes (Dyson, 2006).

A series of recommendations from the Healthcare Commission attempted to address such failures (HC, 2004), but these were heavily criticised as a result of their failure to set out any proper professional standards and for their commitment to the self-regulatory approach. This contrasts unfavourably with jurisdictions such as France, where only surgeons who are registered specialists can carry out surgical procedures and "experience" – even the possession of a general medical degree – is not regarded as sufficient qualification (Fogli, 2009). It is interesting that concerns about surgical enhancement have often centred far more upon techniques than its desirability per se. Though cosmetic enhancement is something that both genders are now exploring (cf. Bordo, 2000), feminists have often questioned its part in enforcing stereotypical roles (Heyes and Jones, 2009). In the face of endless media endorsements, free vouchers for cosmetic surgery and the fabled "lunch-time boob job", exploitation of traditional gender vulnerabilities around physical appearance rather than enhancement is often the real story (Mercer, 2009; Graham, 2010).

The absence of substantive debate about the desirability of enhancement within the beauty industry is one amongst many symptoms of a general failure to engage with the implications of technological enhancement as a whole. But, in the face of increasingly science-fiction scenarios, this doesn't seem to be a debate that can be postponed indefinitely. Take, as one possible example, the prospect of our bodies becoming so fused with information technologies that they become functioning interfaces – i.e. the hand "becomes" a mobile phone, or an arm a way of accessing the internet (Ward, 2010). Aside from the potential cancers or tumours that such integrations threaten (Feder, 2007), or even the privacy aspects (cf. Foster and Jaeger, 2008), crucial questions are also raised about what we want our bodies to be, the socio-legal controls over this and whom our enhancements ultimately benefit.

Multi-range technologies: the weapon

Weapons and transport technologies present interesting permutations to the spatial aspects of technological extension, a fact that makes them essential to any analysis not just of MMRTs, but of technology in general. For example, transport technologies offer a fascinating "mixed" instance of enhancement in that, whilst they have obviously extended interaction far beyond the normal sphere of the body (by making it more easy for someone in London to go shopping in New York, for example), the body itself is still required to be directly present throughout. Rooted as they are in bodily presence, transport technologies do not therefore offer the true "action at a distance" provided by ICTs. The many criminal and control issues raised by transport technologies (see for example Clarke, 1996; Newton, 2004; Groombridge, 2008) would merit a chapter in themselves, but I want to conclude this discussion by focusing briefly upon the multi-range enhancements provided by the weapon.

Alongside technologies of food and shelter, those centred upon our capacities for defence or attack have been amongst the most significant extensions of the human body. Whether the aim is to expand territory or to defend ourselves against such aims, human security has always involved the requirement for some form of weapons technology (cf. Keegan, 1994; Parker, 2008). The primordial origins of the weapon lie, of course, in the body itself – in our capacity to clench a fist or tighten a grip – but, even within prehistory, these limited options for defence/attack were quickly augmented by other more destructive close-order fighting technologies such as the club or the axe. It also seems that safer, more long-distance forms of combat technologies, like spears, bows and slings, arrived early in weapons development, with evidence for their use dating back as far as 60,000 years (Backwell *et al.*, 2008). Thus, it was not until the advent of explosive technologies like gunpowder that a really new category of weaponry emerged, one that hugely extended range and power. In their combination with other technologies such as ICTs and CBNTs, weapons now constitute highly complex enhancements to our prehistoric capacity for attack and defence, capable of delivering lethal, targeted force at both very far and very close (i.e. at micro level) ranges.

Given the unambiguous associations between weapons technologies and harm, it is remarkable how unevenly the weapon has been handled as a criminogenic technology, or indeed as a coherent class of technology at all. For example, whilst there has been a lively criminological debate around knives or handguns, these have rarely been seen as "technological" problems. As a result, not only have important continuities with more advanced weaponry been obscured, but the striking inconsistencies in the way these differing classes are regulated, barely discussed. Controls have been similarly uneven – often based more upon the status or class of the weapon's bearer than on the relative harms caused. Given its traditional interest in retaining the monopoly on violence, a central influence upon such legal ambiguities has of course been the state.

Gun and knife crime and control

It is somewhat ironic to observe how we have moved from a situation where the use of cutting or stabbing weapons was a legitimate practice of a ruling elite, to one where it is seen as the province of an unregulated street. Controls over gun and knife use have been shaped by culture as well as status, a fact that has produced some very different approaches across different jurisdictions. Some, like the US, have opted for a mixed or laissez-faire approach whilst others, like the UK, have preferred all-out control.

In the UK, 21 per cent of violent incidents in 2008/9 involved a weapon (Walker *et al.*, 2009), with 7 per cent of incidents involving a knife – nearly six times as many as guns, which constituted around 1 per cent of the total (ibid.). As suggested earlier, so-called "blunt" weapons (like hammers) were used at least as commonly used as knives (ibid.), but overall, violent incidents where no weapon was involved were still far more common (78 per cent, ibid.). If such figures are representative, it seems clear that the threat of "non-technological" means of violence – such as hitting, kicking, strangling or drowning – still far exceeds that of knives or guns in many jurisdictions. Certainly, in spite of often hysterical media coverage, the rate of incidents involving knife woundings has shown a long-term downward trend – from 131 per 10,000 citizens in 1981 to 105 in 2008/9 (ibid.). Nor is the common perception that it is young people who are the main perpetrators or victims of knife violence borne out by the evidence. Whilst it is true that young men aged between 16 and 24 are the highest risk group for violence, young people are (notoriously) far more likely to be killed by adults, with 62 per cent of young people below 16 killed by their parents in 2006/7 (CCJS, 2009). Problems in evaluating the nature and level of threat are compounded by classificatory ambiguities around what "counts" as a knife. The Knives Act 1997 and Section 141 of the Criminal Justice Act 1988 set out certain definitions, but Home Office data usually distinguishes simply between knives, glasses, bottles and stabbing implements like screwdrivers. On this basis it emerges that there were about as many stabbing or cutting incidents involving bottle- or screwdriver-like implements in 2008/9 as there were incidents involving knives (Walker *et al.*, 2009).

Though firearm violence is arguably a "more technological" offence than knife crime (if, as suggested earlier, manufacturing complexity is taken as the relevant indicator), it too has never been seen as a "technological" crime in the way credit card fraud has been. But there are also wildly differing interpretations of the threat posed by guns. We just saw how firearms are certainly not the predominant MMRT used in violent offences; indeed, gun violence in the UK fell by 17 per cent between 2007/8 and 2008/9, with just 38 victims of fatal injuries in that year (Walker *et al.*, 2009). But, like knife violence, gun crime generates major headlines and perceptions that it constitutes one of our more serious risks – especially for young people. In fact nearly 50 per cent of firearm offences were committed by the over-40 age group in 2008 – compared to around 19 per cent committed by 10- to 20-year-olds (ibid.). Similarly, 34 per cent of victims were from the 25–40 age range, as compared to 13 per cent from the 10–17 age group (ibid.). As we might expect, in countries with long-established traditions of gun ownership, like Canada, Switzerland and of course the USA, figures for gun violence tend to be higher. The USA is especially notable here, but it is probably not surprising, in a jurisdiction where the constitution legitimates gun ownership, that the majority of murders are carried out using a firearm, especially handguns. Thus, in the USA in 2005, 11,346 individuals died as a result of gun violence, and there were a further 477,040 individual victims of a crime where a gun was used (NIJ, 2010). This compares to just 46 individuals killed as a result of a shooting in the UK in the same year (Walker *et al.*, 2006) – a rate of around 0.15 gun deaths per 100,000 as compared to 3.98 per 100,000 in the USA (Cukier and Sidel, 2006). Such enormous disparities would appear to offer a decisive argument for more effective gun control, but opponents are vociferous in their resistance, arguing that the lower homicide rates in jurisdictions like Canada or Switzerland – around 0.5 per 100,000 (Cukier and Sidel, ibid.) – indicate that it is not gun ownership per se that is the problem. But even if it could be shown that it was something distinctive to the US social that was responsible for higher gun violence (rather than the easy availability of guns), imposing gun controls still appears to be an easy and immediate way in which gun crime could be dramatically reduced. When it comes to regulating technologies, however, "reducing crime" is not, as we have seen, always the governing rationale.

Another variety of argument in favour of legal gun ownership – that guns are essential for "self-defence" – is also questionable. There is no evidence that the risk from violence is any higher in jurisdictions where guns are prohibited – indeed the risk is usually lower. However, a number of high-profile cases where householders have shot intruders has inevitably raised public sympathies around the self-defence argument and has strengthened the case for what in the USA has been termed the "Castle" doctrine – the "right" to defend self or property, by force if necessary (cf. Levin, 2010). The fact that gun availability may actually increase risk – since there is a greater likelihood that intruders as well as householders will also carry guns – is less discussed (see, amongst many pro arguments here, Lott and Mustard, 1997; Lott, 1998; for sceptical arguments see Black and Nagin, 1998; Ayres and Donohue, 2003).

Particular inconsistencies in regulating weapons technologies are seen where they are used by control agents, most obviously the police. There has been a repeated failure to adequately report levels of police-initiated gun violence, and in many cases there have been overt attempts to conceal it. For example, despite the 1994 Violent Crime Control and Law Enforcement Act, which required the US Attorney General to collect and publish an annual report on police shootings, there is still no sign of any coherent systems for recording the (significant) number of individuals shot by US police every year (Butterfield, 2001; Lendman, 2010). US police departments regularly fail to submit data and since this does not in any case distinguish between "justified" or "unjustified" shootings it has been usually impossible to separate outright murder from shooting during the course of duty. As a result, the little research that the US Department of Justice has conducted (cf. Brown and Langan, 2001) has been widely criticised for characterising police shootings as "felons justifiably killed by police" (ibid.).

Even where clear evidence is produced that police have used guns inappropriately, sanctions usually remain minimal. In the USA there has been a well-established pattern of failure to secure convictions against officers involved in fatal shootings – especially where this involves victims from minority communities (AI, 1999). And though police in the UK famously "do not carry guns" on a day-to-day basis, the resort to firearms has subtly but significantly increased in recent years, with operations involving authorised gun use in the Metropolitan Police rising from 2,447 in 2001 to 5,044 in 2008/9 (Home Office, 2010). An increase in fatal shootings – many under dubious circumstances – has been an inevitable result, though the failure to prosecute has been as common a pattern in the UK as it is the USA. Of 14 fatal police shootings in the UK between 1995 and 2005, verdicts of lawful killing were advanced in all but three cases, and where there were challenges, police were subsequently cleared of criminal behaviour (*Times*, 2005; Squires and Kennison, 2010). Not surprisingly, the failure to adequately punish misuses of weapons technologies, or even to collect adequate data about this, has been even more pronounced within military contexts. During the conflict in Iraq, civilian casualties were (notoriously) never recorded by the military, in spite of widespread evidence of disproportionate shootings (Leigh, 2010) – not least the 300 civilians shot by US soldiers in incidents at checkpoints (IBC, 2010). The massacre at Haditha, where soldiers murdered 24 civilians, was widely documented (ibid.) and, though this constituted a war crime under the Geneva and Hague conventions, the US military eventually dismissed charges or acquitted the soldiers involved (Ferran, 2010). The failure to adequately regulate the many private security armies that have now become a feature of contemporary war resulted in many further illegal shootings and massacres (cf. Uessler, 2008).

Hi-tech weaponry and criminality

Military capacity has now been vastly extended by advanced weapons technologies – from guided missiles and biological weapons to landmines and cluster bombs. In spite of their power, the regulation of such devices remains almost totally voluntary, centring upon conventions or private arrangements between interested states – like the US–Soviet SALT and START agreements discussed earlier. As a result, the use of advanced weapons technologies almost always stands outside the remit of international law – certainly none of the major powers has ever been prosecuted for using them in the contemporary era (cf. Dhanapala, 2002; Joyner, 2009). Their impacts upon military casualties are, for obvious reasons, usually beyond criminal jurisdiction, but even where such technologies harm civilians, defining culpabilities can be a highly complex legal issue (cf. McMahan, 2009). No matter how much we might all agree that killing civilians is morally wrong, it remains legal under both the Geneva Convention and the more recent Statute of Rome if it occurs as a result of "attempting to hit a military target" (Melzer, 2008). Technological advances in weaponry have indirectly exacerbated this legal lacuna – by producing a reluctance to engage in overt inter-state combat amongst major powers. The shift towards what has been called "asymmetric warfare" (Schroefl *et al.*, 2009) – where sophisticated weaponry is deployed against vastly inferior armed forces and/or civilian populations – has been one result. Mounting evidence of civilian suffering in conflicts as varied as Iraq, Gaza, Chechnya or Tibet has also been accompanied by a consistent failure to comply with the spirit of international regulations or to punish states that violate them (McMahan, 2009).

The sheer variety of such technologies exacerbates the problem of inadequate legal frameworks or the monopolies exerted by states. But we should not let the destructive capacities of "exotic" weaponry, such as bio-chemical capabilities, make us overlook the more widespread and regular harms produced by conventional weapons. Landmines alone are associated with at least 5,000 new victims identified yearly – most of them civilians (ICRC, 2009). These are meant to be regulated by the 1983 Convention on Certain Conventional Weapons (CCW) and the 1997 Mine Ban Treaty (which banned the use of anti-personnel mines), but around 37 countries (including the US, Israel, Russia and China), many with significant stockpiles of anti-personnel mines, have not yet ratified it (ICBL, 2011). Equally deadly has been the use of cluster bombs. In just 11 weeks of the 1998/9 Kosovo conflict, between 230,000 and 290,000 of these were dropped and around 30,000 were left unexploded on the ground (Landmine Action, 2007). In theory, cluster bombs are meant to be regulated by the Convention on Cluster Munitions (CCM), ratified by over 100 countries in 2008, which prohibits all use, stockpiling, production and transfer of cluster munitions. But signatory states are not prevented from working with states that have not yet signed up to the convention.

These and similar loopholes enable states to claim a moral high ground whilst evading or ignoring international agreements. A typical example of such moral evasions has been seen in the use of white phosphorus (WP), a form of napalm that ignites and burns on contact with oxygen, reaching temperatures of up to 1,500°F. As a chemical substance, the use of WP as a weapon was proscribed under both the 1925 Geneva Protocol and the 1993 Chemical Weapons Convention (CWC). However, Article II.9(c) of the CWC allows for uses "not connected with the use of chemical weapons and not dependent on the use of the toxic properties of chemicals as a method of warfare" – for example, as a way of creating smokescreens for troops, or for illuminating targets. Exploiting this regulatory gap has enabled many states to remain within the terms of the CWC whilst deploying WP in ways that have produced horrific injuries. During the US assault upon Falluja in the Iraq war, large amounts of WP were deployed, resulting in numerous casualties (cf. Shane, 2005), whilst the Israeli incursion into Gaza in January 2009 represented an even more cynical exploitation of the legal loopholes around the deployment of this substance. In spite of vociferous denials, Israel eventually conceded that it had used WP during its earlier invasion of Lebanon (Rappaport, 2006), but followed the US tactic of claiming that the way that it had been used was not as a weapon and so did not violate the CWC. The many casualties consistent with WP burns (ibid.) suggested that Israeli denials were at best questionable. So too did widespread evidence on the ground in Gaza in 2009 – not least the large numbers of spent shells and canister liners containing white phosphorus found on apartment roofs and residential courtyards. For many, this meant that Israeli actions in Gaza amounted to war crimes (HRW, 2009), though no successful action has been produced against either the US or Israel nor, so far as we know, has any form of internal disciplinary action followed.

"Less-than-lethal" weapons technology and control

Lethality is no longer the only issue shaping the regulation of weapons technologies. As the legitimacy of violence in maintaining order has become increasingly questioned – at least in democratic contexts – pressures to comply with human rights and legal requirements to limit force have stimulated the development of so-called "less-than-lethal" or "soft" weapons technologies (Rappert, 2007). By deploying non-lethal technologies, state and other control agents can maintain control over "criminal" elements whilst appearing to be sensitive to rights to gather or to protest. And by coupling non-lethal weapons technologies with softly coercive forms of crowd control such as kettling and public order surveillance, states have been remarkably successful in effectively stifling protest, whilst appearing to tolerate it. However, the assumption that soft weapons facilitate control without causing serious injury or death has been challenged by mounting evidence to the contrary.

The origins of soft weaponry can be traced to a number of pre-industrial technologies – from protective devices such as shields to early forms of psychological warfare. Whilst helmets and plastic shields have been standard issue for most police forces since the 1980s, more aggressive, though still "non-lethal", tools such as CS gas have been available for longer (Rappert, 2007). The unrest and protests of the 1960s were a major stimulus in the project to develop new weaponry of this kind, though the thin line between civil and military deployments was starkly demonstrated in the way CS gas was used not just against protestors, but also as a chemical weapon on the battlefield in Vietnam, where over 15 million tons of the material was used (Davison, 2006). An impressive array of options are now on offer, including projectiles like rubber bullets and water cannons, optical and acoustic weapons like light-flash grenades and audible sound generators or electrical weapons such as electric cattle prods, "stun batons" and, more recently, the "taser". Policing agents have access to a wide range of these soft weapons, with tasers and chemical sprays like Mace all but standard-issue kit in many forces – especially in the USA (Hummer, 2007). But even in their short life span many of these less-than-lethal weapons – in particular tasers – have turned out to be very lethal, indeed fatal. Between 2001 and 2004 alone, for example, over 70 individuals in the USA are thought to have died as a result of the use of M26 or X26 tasers – though coroners often colluded in obscuring accurate figures by attributing death to other reasons, such as intoxication (AI, 2004). Claims that use of tasers and similar has reduced violence during arrests are difficult to prove, given the lack of good data and the role of manufacturers in sponsoring research (AI, ibid.).

A range of still more "advanced" methods of soft control are now under development – for example, ultra-sonic weapons that cause disorientation; aqueous sticky polymers that inhibit movement; malodorants that create feelings of disgust and nausea; laser and high-intensity light beams that induce temporary blindness; and microwave heat guns that can raise the temperature of the body to nearly 41°C (105.8°F) and so (purportedly) reduce aggression (cf. NRC, 2003b; Hummer, 2007). There are important balances to be struck in the way this branch of weapons technology is evolving. Whilst soft weapons are obviously preferable to live ammunition, the corrosive effects that they produce upon the use of public space may result in other equally undesirable outcomes in the long run – not least, an increasing separation between the state and its citizens that has so often been the result of technologisation. The serious consideration given by the US authorities to using bacteriological incapacitants in the 1970s (Davison, 2006) – just as these were in the process of being banned as weapons of war – is just one indication of how easily crowd control can blur with crimes against humanity wherever a technological "fix" is available. Given that avoiding militarisation was a key objective in the development of civilian policing, deciding how far we want the increasingly blurred line between hard and soft weaponry to regulate public space is one of the central criminological questions of our era.

Conclusion

As a category of technology, MMRTS do not, as we have seen, present the most immediately obvious or homogenous class of artefacts. The boundaries here are far less clear than we saw in the cases of ICTs or CBNTs, partly because of the variety of artefacts that constitute the class, partly because of their multi-range forms of causal enablement. The suspicion that this category of technological artefacts might be no more than shorthand for "the rest" is one not entirely without foundation. Yet it is also plausible to claim that this constitutes a central class of technology, for it is one that all technologies ultimately draw upon, or reduce to. Either way, the relative lack of legal and criminological consideration of such artefacts has been an important oversight in the regulation of technology. For, as technology enables us to enhance our bodies in more dramatic and more subtle ways, it is not just the more sensational effects, like genetic alteration, that ought to be of interest in shaping its control. Equally worthy of attention are the more everyday incremental changes that are the province of this loose collection of artefacts, since these may have just as significant long-term impacts upon social life and justice. Whether it is an electronic toothbrush that enhances our teeth-brushing abilities or an injection to make us more attractive, these technologies demonstrate constant and subtle ways in which bodily capacity is altered, for better or worse. In turn, the ragbag of manufacturers' guidelines, codes of practice, trading standards, liability law, consumer rights and safety and risk protections that characterise their regulation presents us with our most immediate experience of a more pervasive control force at work – the technological regulation that now shapes our world and to which we now turn in more detail.

8   Technology, science and justice

Man frees himself from nature in order to submit himself to the constraints of his own production.[1]

Technology's increasingly central role in shaping the criminal justice process has, as we have seen, been set against an uncertain conceptual and legal backdrop. Not just in terms of what makes a use or a misuse "technological" but, crucially, in terms of what justifies any technical intervention. This question becomes even more pressing when we turn directly to the authority of law in the face of these changes, for, given the seemingly extensive power of technology to shape the legal process, or indeed social regulation as a whole, we might well ask why or on what basis this is tolerated. In this chapter I want to press the questions of why the law does not just serve to enforce the regulation of technology but often appears to endorse a regulation by technology. This has major implications for justice, for if the law becomes secondary to the force of technological imperatives, then we are left with no clear way of preserving our rights.

At the heart of these issues is the question of legitimation – the basis upon which the apparent deference to technology's regulatory authority both in and beyond the criminal justice system is secured. The key legitimation strategies here are now familiar enough – technology, we are told, "improves" criminal justice, technology "works" or, most commonly, technology "increases efficiencies" and saves on costs. In other words, not much has changed here since Weber (1992), Marcuse (1964 and 1982) and others questioned the instrumental rationalities that now shape the operation of many of our key social institutions. The uncertain justifications for this might be seen in terms of the legitimation crisis discussed by Habermas, for he specifically identified part of this in terms of the way technology now "penetrates into the consciousness of the depoliticized mass of the population, [and] take[s] on a legitimating power" (1970, p. 105). In this chapter I will consider a more subtle rationale at work in this legitimation process, one that implies that by "technologising" justice we in some sense "scientise" it – automatically conferring virtues like reliability, objectivity and measurability upon its operations. The absence of any very coherent account of what technology is, or how precisely it "enables" the justice process has allowed this association to be accepted more easily than it ought to have been, given the significant consequences for due process and legal authority that have followed. Are technological solutions really quite as unproblematically "scientific" as they seem? And even if they are, how do we decide when it is appropriate for science to arbitrate upon justice or when it too must defer to legal authority?

Technocentrism in criminal justice: questions and justifications

The claim that "successful policing relies on scientific innovation" (Home Office, 2010) typifies the kinds of attitude towards science and technology that now drive criminal justice policy. Here, as elsewhere, "scientific innovation" is simply equated with a check-list of new technical devices, and the legitimacy of these tools is, in turn, underwritten by the fact that they are the products of "scientific innovation". Circular reasoning of this kind has ensured that developments reckoned "likely to influence policing in the next few years" (USNIJ, 2010) are invariably seen as technological developments – for example, "biometric, electromagnetic imaging, encryption, geo-location, lab-on-a-chip; 3G mobile phones" (ibid.). Similarly, improvements to justice itself are reduced to the task of acquiring "improved information and data systems, automated vehicle locators, smart sensors ..., knowledge management in patrol and response operations, automated forensic analysis ... or improved methods for DNA extraction" (ibid.). The "significant science and technology gap" identified by the 1967 US Crime Commission (cf. Conley, 1994) instigated a sea-change in political attitudes towards technological justice and led to an increase in spending that has now become a flood. In this brave new world, over £8.5 million of the £12 billion UK crime control budget in 1998/99 was invested in CCTV (NACRO, 2002) whilst spending on technology by the US Department of Justice (DOJ) nearly trebled in the post 9/11 period, with a 22 per cent increase between 2009 and 2010[2] alone (USDOJ, 2010). Even in an age of financial austerity, technological justice appears to be a luxury we can always afford. Thus, we see a projected more than doubling of the budget for the European Network and Information Security Agency (ENISA) – from €8 million to around €19 million by 2016 (HOC, 2010) – or a proposed £63 million rise in spending on "cybersecurity" by the UK's Coalition Government (Williams, 2011). And this comes on top of extensive previous investments like the £186.2 million provided for UK police forces as part of the Home Office's DNA Expansion Programme between April 2000 and March 2004 (HC, 2005b) or the estimated £400 million annual investment in forensic provision by the UK police (ibid.). The striking lack of resistance to such spending – and there are many more examples that might be cited – has a lot to do with our sense that to be armed with technology is – almost by definition – to be acting "scientifically", and therefore more effectively and legitimately. Accordingly, with each technological augmentation, policing slowly blurs into "police science", or crime control into "crime science".

The pervasiveness of such views is witnessed in the way they now hold across the political spectrum. New Labour's policies were integral to the contemporary technocentrism of British criminal justice, and the shift to the right that followed the 2010 general election brought little change to this thinking. The Coalition Government's statement of intent to "use innovative science and technology to improve capabilities and safeguard public confidence across the broad range of policing activities" (NPIA, 2010b) parallels the informal ideological harmony between US Democrats and Republicans in making justice technology compliant wherever possible (cf. Wyrick, 2011). Criminological thinking, by contrast, presents a less homogenous set of opinions. Here at least two almost diametrically opposed positions about the validity of technological justice and science's role in legitimating it have evolved. These might be characterised, very loosely, as follows:

(i)   *The Gold Standard view*: There is a close convergence with practitioner views here in the belief that the use of technology represents a kind of "gold standard" in administering justice, one that is unproblematically legitimated by science and scientific evidence. The successes of technology in reducing crime are a scientifically measurable fact, serving to justify why investments in more and "better" technology are continually required to ensure that the police, or criminal justice agents, maintain an edge over criminals.

(ii) *Techno-legal dystopianism*: In stark contrast, techno-legal dystopian views see the technologisation of criminal justice as questionable, specifically because science often delegitimates rather than justifies it. The faith placed in the objectivity of science is not just narrow "scientism" but has distorted effective evaluation of the success or failure of technological interventions. Even more significantly, such interventions have become associated with coercive forms of regulation that enhance control at the expense of justice.

Clearly, each of these positions represents variations upon the earlier, well-established perceptions of science and technology discussed in previous chapters, and so says nothing definitively new. But, in the context of criminal justice, the implications of scientific-technical authority in determining guilt are so fundamental that it will be useful to consider them, and the disagreements over the extent to which science is able to legitimate technological justice, in more detail.

Law, science and technology: science as the gold standard

The idea that science and technology not only further justice, but also do so unproblematically, is one dating back, arguably, to the origins of the contemporary criminal justice system and its theoretical handmaiden, criminology. The aspiration to shift the focus of crime control towards positivist/ scientific approaches was, as Stan Cohen reminded us, both a founding ideal of criminology and the new criminal justice of the nineteenth century (Cohen, 1988; see also Hayward, 2007). Whether it was Quetelet's attempt to represent the "averages" of crime mathematically, or Lombroso's belief that criminality could be detected by scientific means, a form of "physics envy" has always characterised large sections of the criminological project.

The faith in science as a basis for justice has been underlined in the contemporary context by claims that, in applying it to the criminal justice process, there is an all but automatic "increase in liberty" (Sherman, 2009). But in the enthusiasm for proclaiming that crime control must be about "applying established scientific approaches and techniques" (Laycock, 2005, p. 9), the nineteenth-century positivist approaches to crime control often seem forgotten. Instead there has been a perception that this represents a new idea – a radical shift that sets the "Johnny upstarts" whose mission is to challenge the prevailing "non-scientific" orthodoxies within the field (Smith and Tilley, 2005, p. xv) against a criminology, or a criminal justice, that is "poor in evidence" (Sherman, 2009). This striking failure of historical understanding has not always augured well for the wider credibility of the gold-standard position. In place of critical approaches to technology are evangelical calls for experimental criminology to "invade" "policing and prosecution. … guided by scientific principles" (ibid., p. 23). And, instead of nuanced analyses of technological offending, orders are issued to the scientific–engineering community to act as scouts in a never-ending search for "STIs" (scientific–technological innovations) that offer "swifter, fairer, more efficient justice" (Ekblom, 2005, p. 33). Throughout, science is invariably granted a kind of "magisterial, legitimacy granting aura" (Marx, G., 2007, p. 366), one where "technological controls, presumably being science based, are justified as valid, objective, neutral, universal, consensual and fair" (ibid.). The outcomes are familiar enough – claims of efficiency, the use of arcane scientific language and statistical data, quantitative measures and "targets", and the extensive use of technology as a criminal justice "fix".

So entrenched is the belief that by invoking science an intellectual high ground is secured, that the scientific–technical management of crime is seen as spelling the end for "traditional" criminology (cf. Clarke, 2004). In terms of the argument here, however, there seem to be at least two major gaps in the rationale for such claims. First, whilst a great many prescriptive claims are made about science, and many assertions about how scientific technological solutions are, there is hardly anything of substance said about technology. Second, and more importantly, there is almost no account provided for how or on what basis a technological solution is legitimated by science or scientific methods. One result has been a very thin sense of what technological offending is or what technological offenders might amount to. Instead, technology and technological extension are seen in largely instrumentalist terms as tools waiting to be used by criminals. Similarly "STIs" are invariably limited to the pursuit of standard criminal behaviours, such as property crime, or standard criminal protagonists, such as the "car thief". Less immediate, but equally significant forms of crime enabled by technology – such as corporate fraud, state violations of communications technology, pollution, dumping of chemicals – barely figure as issues, and there has been little or no sense that the regulation of technology might itself be a criminological issue – nor, indeed, even any sense that it *needs* effective regulation. Without far more detailed analysis of technology, or any good arguments for why a continuity between scientific method and technological solutions is assumed to hold, the gold-standard approach does not provide any very critical insights about the legitimacy of technological justice.

Techno-legal dystopianism

As suggested earlier, the "critical turn" in our perceptions of technology was also a product of the nineteenth century, when the impacts of rapid industrialisation raised concerns that could not be easily ignored. At first, however, the new crime control of the period remained largely immune from such doubts. Instead, thinking about criminal justice largely conformed with the new enthusiasm for applying science to social problems – enthusiasms seen variously in the positivism of Comte and St Simon or in the views of "les industriels" – the industrial and technical elite of the nineteenth century (cf. Pickering, 1993). Thus, the advent of professionalised policing, forensic detection or the statistical measurement of crime was lauded as a kind of panacea, offering a new form of justice that could only improve upon previous systems. This consensus began to be challenged in the face of two key shifts.

One was methodological, deriving from increased suspicions about the idea of a "science" of crime and the failures of prediction seen in the misguided reductionism of Lombroso, Ferri and Sheldon (cf. Young, 2003; Davie, 2006). A new focus upon the role of social interaction pioneered by the likes of the Chicago School (cf. Park *et al.*, 1925) and developed in the work of Goffman (1959), Garfinkel (1967) and others also suggested that far more was needed to make sense of the multi-variate, multi-causal basis to crime and its control than could be accounted for by reductive scientific–technical models. The unprecedented role of technology in promoting the interests of the totalitarian regimes of the twentieth century was a second influence. Industrialised war and the abuses of justice that technologised rule produced did not just further scepticism of technology amongst intellectuals (cf. Krakauer, 1998; Bauman, 2001). They helped to create a specifically "techno-dystopian" cultural critique, with works like H. G. Wells' *Time Machine*, George Orwell's *1984*, Aldous Huxley's *Brave New World* or films such as Lang's *Metropolis*. This cultural vision of technology as a coercive tool is one that has perhaps been most completely realised in recent times in Philip K. Dick's dark visions of surveillance and social control. By the 1960s these methodological and cultural influences had begun to impact directly upon criminological attitudes towards technology's influence over the justice system. The widespread social unrest of that period and the increasingly technologised state repression of protest were important influences upon seminal critiques such as Foucault's (1970 and 1975), whilst the emergence of the critical, and left realist criminological traditions (cf. Cohen, 1971; Lea and Young, 1984) was, in part, a direct riposte to the spectacle of a justice system focused more upon technical needs than on social solutions.

As suggested, the critiques of technology developed by Marcuse, Adorno and others within the Frankfurt School had already anticipated these growing misgivings. Marcuse's view that the social order was increasingly determined by the technological a priori implied that any liberating potential that technology possessed had instead been turned into a "fetter of liberation – the instrumentalisation of man" (Marcuse, 1964, p. 159). Marcuse's ideas were not a major influence upon criminological thought, but in time very similar perceptions began to emerge. Perceptions of a technologically driven "hypercontrolled" social order (Bogard, 1996) became more common, as did the sense that "technical means of control saturate modern society, colonizing and documenting ever more areas of life" (Marx, G., 2007). As a result, criminal justice processes have become subject to a managerial, technologised "culture of control" (Garland, 2001), one where there is an "increasing resort to technologies such as audit, fiscal control, market competition and devolved management" (Garland, 1997). At the extreme, this suggests that a "society of control" results (Deleuze, 1992), one driven by specific science–technology shifts like digital computers, so that the move from "simple machines – levers, pulleys, clocks" to "machines involving energy" (ibid.) could be interpreted as the real influence in the move from sovereign to disciplinary forms of power (and beyond).

Techno-legal dystopianism often implies that science has a degree of culpability in legitimising this totalising technological control. For either it serves as the kind of denuded, ideological tool portrayed by Marcuse and Habermas or, as Foucault suggests, its very essence is a form of power – one that constructs subjects and then disciplines them through knowledge–power regimes like medicine, psychiatry, or the prison–panopticon. And whether what emerges is the articulated, everyday form of governmentality directed against individual bodies, or a more general biopower exerted over populations, science is always the spectre behind any technological solution to crime, or social policy. In other words, contemporary programmes of tech-nologised justice – from the revived biological essentialist school (cf. Wilson and Herrnstein, 1985) to statistical, measurement-oriented crime control (cf. Young, 2011) – are specifically delegitimated by an uncritical use of science: a stark contrast with gold-standard perspectives.

The techno-legal dystopian perspective offers a useful reminder that science all too often serves to justify unproven technological interventions. And, given what we have seen in previous chapters, the perception is certainly not without foundation. However, because technology itself is again left untheorised, the critique can itself be criticised. It could, for example, be charged with misrepresenting science or, in an inversion of the previous view, with claiming that because technological justice is suspect, so too must science be. Jacques Ellul was once charged with disseminating such negative views of technology that it directly influenced the anti-industrial terrorism of the Unabomber. This is clearly too extreme a judgement, but techno-legal dystopianism might be charged with rejecting techno-logical justice and any benefit it offers on the basis of emotion, rather than evidence.

Technological descriptivism and evaluating the alternatives

The "majority view" of technology amongst criminal justice practitioners and theorists probably lies somewhere in-between the previous positions – if it can be called a view at all. For there is not really a position here – at least in the sense of a well-defined theoretical approach – rather a set of taxonomic concerns with describing or cataloguing the different uses and roles of technology within the justice system. As a result, this "descriptivist" stance towards technology in the justice system is almost always focused upon various technological functions – that is, with cataloguing how technology is used, whether by criminals or criminal justice agents. Thus, we find distinctions made between "technologies of surveillance", "tech-nologies of restraint" and "technologies of access" (Grabosky, 1998); distinctions between hard and soft criminal justice technologies (Byrne and Rebovich, 2007); or typologies of "probative", "coercive", "surveillant" technological functions (Bowling *et al.*, 2008; Leman-Langlois, 2008), and so on. This emphasis upon description has usually meant that little attention is paid to drawing out any negative impacts of technological justice. Rather, as with gold-standard views, the use of new technologies is usually seen in approving terms – interventions that lead to "greater security for citizens, and reduced hazards for criminal justice professionals" (Grabosky, 1998). Such views also tend to follow the gold-standard approach in viewing technology in instrumentalist terms, as a tool where all that counts is the way it is used. Thus, since neither descriptivism nor the previous positions offer much in the way of insights as to why their rejection or endorsements of science-based justice should also be an endorsement of technology-based justice, it is to this question that I now turn in more detail.

Science, technology and justice: bad science?

An obvious way of testing the suggestion that technological justice is legitimated "because it is scientific" is to evaluate the extent to which it really *is* "scientific". And, given that evidence is one of the driving factors for this association, one way to interrogate it might be to see how far there is evidence for the success of a technology in reducing crime, or in furthering justice. We might look, for example, to the "dozens of studies showing that crime can be immediately and … drastically reduced" (Clarke, 2004, p. 58) – in particular, studies such as those which purport to show how "better lighting reduces crime by 20%" (Farrington and Welsh, 2002) or "using steel barriers and ultraviolet property-marking kits reduces burglary by 53%" (Ekblom, 2002). But the problem with such claims – as even their most strident advocates will sometimes accept (see for example Sherman *et al.*, 2002) – is that scientific conclusions are usually far more provisional than this. Indeed, as philosophers of science have consistently pointed out, to assert that any study, observation or evidence can "prove" statements or theories to be correct is to risk the charge of "verificationism". Verificationism has now either been rejected outright or significantly modified so as to accommodate the partial certainties that observations provide (cf. Quine, 1951; van Fraasen, 1980; Misak, 1995). So if there are reasons to question verificationism within natural science, asserting that the worth of technological justice could be established by a study of street lighting, or car alarms – no matter how detailed – looks fairly dubious (cf. Hope, 2004 for more on this point). Even if such studies produced unambiguous findings (which of course they can never do), a positive evaluation of one, two or even 500 technological interventions would never prove the superiority, let alone the legitimacy, of technological justice as a whole.

The reality is that any attempt to definitively establish the desirability of a technological intervention on the basis of a scientific study is doomed to failure. There are no "crucial experiments" or "instances of the fingerpost", as Bacon put this (1994, II, XXXVI), in the social context, and seemingly very few in the natural science context. In fact many have questioned whether even natural science itself offers tests or trials that could decisively arbitrate between two competing scientific explanations (cf. Lakatos, 1974; Weber, 2009). Indeed as Nancy Cartwright has convincingly shown, attempts to measure nature or to generate scientific laws within the artificial environment of the science experiment are often so enclosed from external reality that many scientific laws could, strictly speaking, be viewed as "lies" (Cartwright, 1983). Thus, attempts to find law-like relations in the social world – whether this is between a technological intervention into justice and science or something else altogether, face two related problems. First, the difficulty in creating an experimental context which successfully isolates desired variables from external (undesirable) variables, and second, the difficulty in establishing whether any variables that can be isolated demonstrate real causes or mere correlations.

The most clearly "scientific" form of social science experiment that might be used for such ends is the "randomised control trial" (RCT) that has now become a central methodological strategy for lending a scientific veneer to evaluations of policy measures. Very roughly, an RCT involves a random distribution of trial subjects to two or more groups to test the causal efficacy of a particular social/technical intervention, with randomisation functioning to ensure that other factors have not affected the outcome (cf. Torgerson and Torgerson, 2008). For many, RCTs have appeared to be just the kind of "experiment" that allows social scientists to claim that they are behaving as respectably as their natural science counterparts. As such, they would seem to offer an ideal way of supporting technological justice in more substantive terms. The problem is that, rather than demonstrating scientific legitimacy, the fetishisation of the RCT has often been little more than a demonstration of Poincaré's reputed observation that "natural scientists discuss their results and social scientists their methods".[3] For one thing, the perception that RCTs now occupy a kind of intellectual high ground over more familiar observational methods does not always seem very accurate. In a 2009 study of 50 completed reviews listed in the Campbell Library of Systematic Reviews (Campbell Library, 2009), 54 per cent included non-randomised as well as randomised studies – a fact that suggests that "there is little empirical evidence in the current Campbell reviews to back a dismissal of observational studies when held up against the gold standard of RCT" (Konnerup and Kongsted, 2009, p. 22). Worse, the very fact upon which the legitimating power of the RCT is meant to rest – their superior experimental standards – has often been found wanting. Crime control-oriented RCTs have been especially bad in this regard – often failing to provide adequate information about the randomisation method, details of the analysis or outcome measures (Perry *et al.*, 2010). As a result, many of the RCTs that purport to test technological interventions into the justice process have been undermined by basic methodological problems like the failure to engage in multiple-stage randomisation, or the use of (often highly) selective samples (Sampson, 2010). For example, in one study of the use of the DNA database sponsored by the Home Office and conducted by crime scientists from the Jill Dando Centre, sampling was subsequently found to have been carried out haphazardly, with too-small numbers, no clear conceptual basis and inadequate statistical measures applied to the results (Goldacre, 2009). But the greater reality is that even if an RCT appears to show a "35 per cent regularity" in CCTV's preventing crime this cannot permit analysts to claim that CCTV "works" – certainly not in anything like the same way that a collision between two billiard balls causes a specific and mathematically determinable set of resulting motions.

There may always be unsuspected or intervening variables that have causal significance in the complex variable field of the social world – whether this involves social factors like displacement (Hakim and Rengert, 1981; Conrad, 2005) or technical factors like a flawed experimental method. Thus, as Hough (2010) pointed out, even where RCTs have strong internal validity, they often have very weak external validity.

A sure sign of the uncertain ground upon which claims to scientific legitimacy often rest here is a resort to analogy that is sometimes found. For example, claims that criminal justice is like science, because, like science, it involves "rational thought" (Laycock, 2005, p. 9) are hardly very convincing. After all, so does playing poker or baking bread. Similarly, assertions that criminal justice practice or criminology would be scientific if only they adopted evidence-based approaches like the UK National Institute for Clinical Excellent (NICE) (Sherman, 2009), or that crime science is scientific because it is "like medical science" (cf. Laycock, 2005, p. 6), are acts of wishful thinking that ignore the enormous difference in standards of testing across these domains. Medical science may well be "multi-disciplinary", drawing upon chemistry, biology and other physical sciences, but it is going much too far to claim that crime control is also "scientific" because it too aspires to draw upon such disciplines (cf. Laycock, 2005; Pease, 2005). Thus, whilst scientific knowledge may clearly be used in criminal justice contexts, this does not offer any magic wand for turning criminal justice into a science or for making a technological intervention a scientific one. That DNA is a basis for genetic inheritance is a well-established biological fact that does not alter from case to case. That DNA traces establish the guilt of a suspect is not because, as we saw earlier, any correlations between such traces and demonstrations of guilt are highly context sensitive to the facts of particular situations or the opinions of differing experts. Finally, even if definitive proof could be produced that technological justice was scientific, or was more successful than other approaches, this would still not constitute proof of its desirability. For, no matter how much technological justice might be shown to "work", what could never be shown is that this is what is best for our justice system, or that it is something socially desirable or acceptable. After all there are, no doubt, many scientific tests that would decisively demonstrate how successful technologies for exterminating persistent offenders would be in reducing crime. But this does not constitute any viable argument for adopting them.

If there really were fixed and measurable correlations between technologically driven crime-control approaches and their effect upon the crime rate, one mark of this would presumably be scientifically robust and transparently measurable evidence of continued and corresponding reductions in crime where they are applied. But the inconvenient truth is that overall crime rates appear to have remained stubbornly independent of technological interventions for about as long as crime rates have been measured and technological interventions have been available. Thus, just as the rise in certain types of fraud associated with the advent of printing eventually levelled out, so, presumably, will crimes associated with modern ICTs find their own kind of equilibrium or Quetelet-style "average" – at least until something new emerges. Conversely, just as the advent of fingerprinting technologies has been important in solving specific offences without having any definitive or long-term effect on the overall crime rate, DNA profiling, car alarms and other contemporary technological interventions may push the carpet down in one area of offending but will never eradicate offending as a whole. Of course, one could claim that this long-term downwards trend in crime rates over the last 20 or so years was directly attributable to scientifically based crime-control methods and the "quantity and quality of security" they brought (Farrell *et al.*, 2011). But then one could also claim that it was just because people got nicer. How to design an RCT that would decide this either way would certainly be an interesting methodological challenge.

But if there are serious doubts as to whether science can be validly invoked to legitimate technological interventions, the converse, dystopian idea that science somehow delegitimates such interventions appears no more defensible. Whilst we can all agree that scientific institutions may not be socially neutral, and scientific practice is often striated with the interests of power, there is nothing in the scientific method itself that automatically renders the use of technology as a criminal justice tool "technocratic". It is not enough to claim that science–technology is "anti-human" because it enables manipulations of the natural/social world, or that it is "hegemonic" because it imposes categories upon the world. In both cases the sense that technology is already human has simply been overlooked. Thus, there is a rich relationship between science and technology that is clearly of as much importance in criminal justice as it is elsewhere. It is not one that can be dismissed out of hand or because of prejudices that see technology as irreducibly totalitarian, rather than as extensions of what we already do.

The science–technology connection

At root here is the age-old question of the relation between *techne* and *episteme* – between practical knowledge and theoretical understanding and the extent to which one might support the other. Aristotle's view questioned whether any dependence relation could be established, since he saw *episteme* as concerned with deeper, more unchanging aspects of the world, whilst *techne* is subject to our modifications and therefore is less fixed in its scope (cf. Schummer, 2001). However, he was never very clear about it, and this lack of clarity persists. At the very least, any claim that there "really is" some kind of dependence relation between science and technology – whether this is a legitimising one or something else – requires that the two practices and concepts be distinct in some important way. For if they are not, any purported link collapses into vacuity. That is, where some class of scientific facts or theories S is claimed as a support or a legitimation for some range of technological interventions T, it clearly ought not to be the case that S = T (i.e. S and T ought not to be equivalent in any strong sense). Otherwise this would amount to something legitimating itself. But, on closer inspection, precisely this kind of conceptual contiguity seems to emerge.

Suppose, for example, that we try to claim – as certain theorists of technology have done – that science "precedes" or forms a basis for technological development. This might be taken to mean that technology is a form of what Mario Bunge once called "applied science" (1966) – a kind of materialisation of the rules and processes implicit within the "pure" knowledge base of science. At the same time technology remains distinct from science in virtue of the artefacts and processes that it uses to "put science to work" (cf. Gardner, 1994 and 1995). Priority (but also distinctiveness) might also be claimed in terms of differing intentions – for whilst scientific knowledge aims at knowing the world, technological knowledge could be said to be directed at controlling or manipulating it (Mitcham, 1994, p. 198). In this sense science involves a search for laws of nature, whilst technology involves an application of those laws in order to manipulate nature. In effect, both views manifest Ryle's distinction between "knowing that" and "knowing how" (Ryle, 1949) – where science's methods of knowledge gathering enable us to "know that", which in turn provides guidance for technology's "knowing how" (cf. Polanyi, 1958).

Whilst this seems plausible, the problem is that it also seems possible to argue for precisely the opposite idea – i.e. that technology "precedes" or forms a basis for scientific progress (cf. Ihde, 1983; de Vries, 1996 for more on this view). It is, for example, quite clear that scientific advances are often heavily dependent upon various forms of technical apparatus – indeed the history of science is littered with examples of just this kind of relationship. Take as one instance the discovery of the electric battery, which enabled a programme of research that so decisively advanced our understanding of the forces of electromagnetism that it produced the great theoretical unification culminating in Maxwell's (1861) equations (cf. Shapere, 1998). More recently, it is equally clear that contemporary scientific research into the structure of deep matter would be impossible without the aid of sophisticated technologies such as particle accelerators, neutrino observatories and so on. More simply still, we might point to the role of agricultural technologies in creating the social conditions that made it possible to engage in precisely the kind of abstract thinking that (eventually) led to the development of science itself (for other historical examples see McClellan and Dorn, 2006).

At least three notions of priority/dependency risk being confused in defining this science–technology connection: *conceptual priority*, i.e. where one is in some sense dependent upon the idea of the other; *practical priority*, i.e. where a material advance in one field cannot occur without a material advance in the other; and what we are concerned with here, *normative priority*, i.e. where any application of technology (or science) is justified on the basis of the other. The close proximity between these notions has often impaired our understanding of the basis upon which science is meant to "support" technology. In fact, as Aristotle seemed to conclude, science and technology often appear hopelessly entangled in terms of conceptual and practical priority, so much so that deep interdependence rather than priority appears to hold – what has been referred to as a kind of "symbiosis" between science and technology (Wiens, 1999). One way that this symbiosis might be discerned is in the relation between a scientific law and a technological rule. The scientific law "water boils at 100°C" forms a basis for the technological rule "to boil water, heat it to 100°C", which must be built into any technological artefact, such as a kettle, if it is to successfully boil water. Conversely, there could be no testing of the theoretical claim that water boiled at 100°C without some form of experimental apparatus to test it. If this kind of symbiotic connection is plausible, then it might be interpreted to mean that science and technology cannot ultimately be prised apart sufficiently for one to act as an independent legitimator for the other. Instead, we must accept the existence of a kind of complex – something we might think of as "technoscience" (Agazzi, 1998), one that behaves like a kind of "feedback loop", a mutually reinforcing cycle, where a development in one reinforces a development in another. Such interdependence should come as no surprise, given the idea explored here – that technology extends us or enhances certain capacities. For this seems to be an idea that might equally be applied to science, in that it, too, serves to open up new horizons of action, albeit – as a form of knowledge – in more abstract ways than a purely physical artefact. In other words, science itself might also be viewed as a kind of technology, one that offers new capacities based, in the first instance, upon knowledge of nature, but knowledge that can eventually be transformed into physical tools to control it.

Law, technology and science

Finding interesting philosophical connections in the relationship between science and technology is one thing, but can it offer any guidance on the real question here: whether science serves to legitimate technological interventions into the justice process? If, as we have just suggested, science and technology are deeply conceptually and practically interdependent, then the short answer to this would seem to be "no". This leaves the legal process with a fundamental problem, for if technology, used properly, "is" simply science in all its authority, then why would we need to bother with a trial or with the expense and bother of due process at all? For example, if a DNA test were free of the kinds of qualifications and doubts explored in earlier chapters, guilt could be established without any need for debate, or legal evaluation, simply on the basis of the pristine truth of the science behind it. Thus law would become a "simple transcription device for science, automatically writing into legal decisions whatever facts science has" (Jasanoff, 2005, p. 51). This would clearly be disastrous for the autonomy of the law, but more importantly for any sense of justice as a due process. Instead, "proof of guilt 'beyond reasonable doubt' would have shifted from the court room to the forensic science lab".[4] How, then, do the law and legal process currently seek to manage science–technology in the court-room to preserve themselves from this potential challenge to its autonomy?

The focus has tended to be more upon the validity of scientific evidence (i.e. whether evidence claimed as scientific is admissible) than on the validity of any specific technology intervention, though, as we have seen, this often amounts to very nearly the same thing. Prima facie, it might seem that law should be able to handle the scientific process fairly straightforwardly, given certain obvious continuities between the two practices. Both are (supposed to be) dependent upon evidence; both serve to generate knowledge; both do this through the prism of scepticism, question and argument; and both are key social institutions that command respect and authority. And whilst, for the legal process, knowledge production is meant to culminate in justice and the end of science is centred upon better explanation and understanding, these ends are linked by the common objective of "truth". However, the legal process is also focused on "winning" – and this social goal sometimes comes at the cost of objective truth. On this basis alone, the apparent proximity of law to science is suspect and any assumption that science simply "slots into" the legal process without certain complications must be questionable. Yet, without some clear criteria for determining when it is valid for science–technology to influence the legal process, how could legal argument ever reject the seemingly greater legitimacy of scientific argument?

Until very recently about the only legal criterion for accepting evidence as scientific was the so-called "Frye test", developed within the US justice system. The test, derived from a 1923 case[5] where questions about the admissibility of evidence from a polygraph machine had arisen (cf. Feldman, 1995; Friedman, 1994), set down some very basic, de facto guidelines for admissibility. These stated that the scientific status of a piece of evidence (and its admissibility as such) depended upon whether it was "sufficiently established to have gained general acceptance" within the scientific community. But the guidelines left a lot of questions open. What, for example, is the "scientific community"? How many scientists have to agree for the acceptance to be "general"? What if the science is new or emerging and so hasn't yet been "accepted"? And so on. Worse, Frye delegated responsibility for determining what counted as "scientific" to the scientific community – effectively ceding legal authority to technocrats. But, however unsatisfactory, the Frye test remained – surprisingly – about the only instrument in existence for determining the legal status of scientific evidence until the more detailed 1993 Daubert ruling,[6] which at present constitutes the most definitive statement about the relationship between law, science and technology. For our purposes here, Daubert's most significant contribution was the attempt to reassert legal authority over science in the court-room, something it did by granting a new kind of role to judges – instructing them to act as "gatekeepers" who serve to filter out "good" scientific evidence from the bad in advance of any case coming before a jury. Daubert also went further than Frye by providing more explicit criteria for whether testimony could be accepted as grounded in the "scientific method". This requires it to pass the following tests:

- whether it is empirically testable and subject to falsifiability,
- whether it has been through some process of peer review and publication,
- whether it has a known (or at least potential) error rate, and
- whether it would be sufficiently accepted by a relevant scientific community.

But, however clear these conditions seem at first glance, they begin to unravel when scrutinised more closely. There may, for example, not always be clear empirical testability for a theory (early Darwinian science counts as one obvious instance); peer reviews often deliver no guarantee of validity, since standards often vary so much and, as we saw with fingerprinting, the idea that clear error rates can always be defined is debatable (cf. Jasanoff, 2005). Daubert perpetuates the uncritical assumption that there is broad agreement upon what the scientific method "is" – an assumption that, as we just saw, many scientists or philosophers of science might dispute. But if the nature of the scientific method is contested amongst those who practise or reflect upon it there must be obvious doubts as to how effectively a judge can distinguish between "real" and pseudo-scientific data. Any idea that "science is so obviously science" that judges can unproblematically recognise it as such (Jasanoff, ibid., p. 53) is so implausible that granting the degree of discretion to judges that Daubert licenses must be viewed as questionable. And in any case, Daubert still does not secure the role of judges in making a final call on admissibility. Their continuing dependence upon scientists to make the final call means that that judicial authority remains sufficiently compromised for the charge that Daubert is no more than "Frye in drag" (Rice, 2000) to be a persuasive one.

Of course, it is unreasonable to expect any abstract legal principle to cover every case, so another way of evaluating Daubert is to consider how satisfactorily it has made technological interventions subject to hard science or consistent with the aims of justice. For some there have been positive outcomes – for example, the rise in the number of instances of expert witness evidence being excluded by a judge suggests a kind of reassertion of legal authority over science (Dixon and Gill, 2002). Overall, however, the reception has been critical. One charge has been that Daubert is not used anywhere near as much as it should be, given the frequency in which cases are now decided by scientific data (Neufeld, 2005). More seriously, there is also emerging evidence to suggest that it is having negative impacts upon justice. In particular, the ruling appears to have handed a significant new legal tool to large corporations – and it is significant that those that use or trade in CBNTs (i.e. biotech, pharmaceutical or similar companies) have reaped particular advantages. On the one hand, this might be seen in the tendency of judges to discriminate against "good, but poorly funded science over bigger, more heavily funded varieties" (Smith, 2000). On the other, many corporations themselves have become highly proficient in using Daubert to mount challenges against tort cases (cf. Huber, 1990). And this has meant that, rather than preventing bad technological practice, the ruling may actually be helping to further it. Since cases frequently hang on evidence from opposing experts who differ in their evaluations of whether evidence is "scientific", judges often now dismiss them without any input from a jury – a fact that again advantages corporations over members of the public who may have suffered technological harm. Take, for example, a number of lawsuits brought in the USA against Sandoz Chemicals, manufacturer of the drug Parlodel, a drug that was meant to suppress lactation.[7] The suits alleged that Parlodel resulted in strokes or heart attacks, claims amply supported by evidence derived from an impressive array of sources including animal studies, toxicology studies and the opinions of medical professionals from the Federal Drugs Administration. Yet many judges, citing Daubert, were able to reject whole swathes of this evidence as unreliable – even though Sandoz had already agreed to withdraw the drug (PSKPP, 2003). Since Daubert, the number of summary judgments (judgments made without a full trial – i.e. without a jury) has more than doubled, with 90 per cent of cases being found in favour of the defendant (Dixon and Gill, 2002). Daubert also appears to have encouraged many scientific–technological companies to mount Daubert-style defences outside of the court-room altogether – for example, in the continued challenges to attempts by the Environmental Protection Agency to regulate pesticides (PSKPP, 2003). Finally, in contexts where Daubert might be expected to be particularly useful in resisting technological justice – i.e. in assisting defendants to challenge questionable forensic evidence – it has proved almost unusable, since defendants can rarely afford the costs necessary to mount the requisite defence.

As it stands, if the legitimacy of technological justice is to be decided on the basis of science, then, given the problems faced by law in determining how to make sense of this relationship, we are in trouble. For it is not just that standards for determining the legitimacy of science and technology in the court-room remain inadequate; they also seem to actively skew the process of justice in favour of those with superior access to technological knowledge and resources. The question, then, is what would work, but at present there do not seem to be any very good alternatives to something like a Daubert standard. One might appeal to more informal mechanisms, like some legal reformulation of the "precautionary principle" – the idea that technological interventions should not be accepted until "proven" to be safe or legitimate (cf. UNESCO, 2005). But, as more of a caveat than a clear principle, it is unclear how this could be applied in legal contexts – and much the same might be said of other, more informal regulatory ideas. European jurisdictions are conspicuously lacking even in anything as comprehensive as Daubert, however unsatisfactory this might be. In the UK the inadequate legal standards for scrutinising science were noted by the House of Commons Select Committee on Science and Technology, which remarked how "the absence of an agreed protocol for the validation of scientific techniques prior to their being admitted in court is entirely unsatisfactory" (HC, 2005c, p. 88). A new Law Commission initiative (LC, 2009) has attempted to plug this gap by considering whether the limited criteria for admissibility that are in place could be improved. But its recommendation for a new statutory test that admits only "sufficiently reliable" testimony or evidence (LC, 2011) is hardly very definitive or original about what reliability is or how "sufficiency" might be determined. For example, its requirement that criteria must be "soundly based" or not dependent upon "flawed data" (LC, 2011, 5.17) is, in effect, a reiteration of standard Daubert criteria such as "status within scientific community" or "empirical testability". Such guidelines then inevitably face many of the same problems as Daubert, whilst also being embroiled within a further spiral of testing – this time to decide where data is "flawed" (for comments and criticism see Gilson, 2009; Wilson, 2010). At present, however, nothing else is on offer.

Criminal justice, law and technomia

There seem to be good reasons, then, for seeing Marcuse's observation that "technological rationality has become political activity" (1964, p. xvi) is now as relevant to the subsumption of the contemporary justice system into technical thinking and tools as it was to politics. But if, as it now seems, the status of science alone is not sufficient to legitimate the technologisation of justice, is there anything that could – apart from the circular justifications of the technological a priori itself and its self-fulfilling promises of greater efficiency? Habermas offered one kind of an option with his insistence that technological thinking is a "project of the human species as a whole" (1970, p. 87; cf. also Feenberg, 1996) – something implicit within our rationality and our constitutive interests. Whilst this has seemed to imply an elision between the human and the technological and the charge that Habermas was engaging in "metabiology" (Kavoulakos, 1998, p. 119), his argument seems merely to reflect something like the one advanced in this book. That is, that technological thinking extends human thinking precisely because technology is an extension of us. Unfortunately, as we have seen here, this does not rule out a kind of hierarchy at work within rationality. That is, rationality is not always perceived as homogenous if it can appear to take different forms (cf. Plantinga, 1993) – some of which may be more influential than others – hence the greater hegemonic impact of technical reason at this historical moment.

At this point the value of restricting the focus of analysis to the operations of technical regulation rather than the nature of technical rationality becomes clearer. For it is in the bare facts of the nomos of technology – its technomia – that the concrete impacts of technology upon justice and the social order are seen most clearly, rather than in differing categories of rational thought. In closing this chapter I want therefore to briefly revisit some of the features of the technomia that have been discerned within the preceding pages. This will, hopefully, leave us with a more precise sense of the structures that technomia has assumed in superseding traditional justice, as well as providing a basis for some possible responses to its subtle regulatory power.

Technological regulation

A useful starting-point for establishing the contours of the contemporary nomos of technology is by way of an earlier distinction between a regulation *of* and regulation *by* technology. For one immediate context where the influence of technical imperatives can be seen is in the influence that it exerts over the institutions meant to control technology. There are at least two primary sites of this kind – one, of course, being the law and the legislative process itself. A second is the informal patchwork of provisions and codes directed at technology that lie outside or beyond law.

1   *Technological regulation within the law.* The proper and obvious site for technological regulation is surely within the law, but on the evidence of this and previous chapters, law is not always in the driving seat here. Aside from the failure to be able to arbitrate over science that has just been seen, there also seem to be as many contexts where the creation of new law is now driven more on the basis of protecting or managing technical norms than of protecting us from the injustices that the pursuit of technological norms may create. The hugely increased flow of technology-specific law has brought us to the stage where certain technologies are the subject of all but autonomous bodies of regulation within the law – arguably constituting kinds of new legal orders altogether – as, for example, in the kind of Lex Informatica defined by Reidenberg (1998). Within this new legal domain, ICTs have sufficed to demonstrably shift legal priorities, generating a dizzying range of new offences, from hacking to online bullying and beyond. This warns us how legal process can become increasingly bogged down with a lesser task of formulating details of appropriate technical standards or in preserving the autonomies of digital technology – at the expense of offering us realistic or integrated

protections from digital harms. And, of course, ICTs are just one kind of techno-legal subject amongst many others, however much they have tended to preoccupy the contemporary legal imaginary. As new and more complex technologies continue to emerge, this distinctively "intra-legal" force of technomia is only likely to expand and to require law to focus upon ever more technical requirements and to interweave them with further new, specialised branches of legal provision – especially around higher-risk technologies such as genetic engineering. And just as law becomes diverted away from its primary focus, so in turn has the authority of law become compromised by the need to cede oversight of these specialised regulations away from the hands of legal experts and into the hands of technical experts. The new deference of judges and other legal custodians to a technical elite whose first duty is toward technical rather than social imperatives is unlike anything we have previously seen and is only likely to increase as technology becomes more complex and detached from human understanding and control.

2   *Technological regulation beyond the law*. The fragility of legal power in the face of technical power is further emphasised in the way that technological regulation so often now operates beyond the law, by way of informal, extra-legal varieties of technical regulation. Technological progress has often been felt to outpace the capacity of the legislative process to "keep up" and the result has been a steady increase in self-regulation and self-governing codes by technical organisations and professions. But this has not resulted in a widening of participation in the governance of technology – rather, it has produced complex rules and systems that are as opaque to legal practitioners as they are to the public. Though self-regulation of this kind is not new, the power of neo-liberal corporatism at the end of the twentieth century and in the early twenty-first has created new and highly favourable conditions for the self-regulation of technology to flourish. With the vast profits to be made from high-technology (or indeed low-technology) artefacts and processes, and the interests of the private sector in maintaining freedom from public scrutiny, independent technical regulation has in fact become its predominant regulatory mode. In this way, regulatory subordination to scientific–technical standards extends far beyond the power of experts in the court-room, or even those – like doctors, engineers, biologists, or chemists – with privileged access to technical knowledge. Rather, it rests equally in the hands of a technical–commercial elite who pursue the rewards that technical norms bring, unaccountably and irrespective of any cost to public justice.

There are, of course, perfectly sensible and prudent aspects to self-regulation in the technical context – if operated wisely. Too much top-down regulation and control can be a negative influence upon technical innovation and its capacity to help us address crucial social problems. Similarly, given the rapid expansion in very high-risk technologies, maintaining public safety will always require expert oversight. If deference to a "technocratic priesthood" were all this entailed, this would be bad, but something that could, eventually, be managed in more transparent ways. However, with it comes another, more social order of risk – a historic reversal in regulatory power, the switch away from human oversight, towards a situation where technology now regulates us.

Regulation by technology

If a consideration of how we regulate technology suggests that our extensions have acquired a kind of upper hand over us, the contours of technical power become even more pronounced when we consider the power technology has now acquired to directly regulate us. From what we have seen in previous chapters, there seem to be at least three contexts for these more "autonomic" forms of technological control (Hildebrandt, 2008b; Hildebrandt and Rouvroy, 2011). One lies in the influence of technical thinking and orientation within our everyday behaviours and attitudes, whilst another lies in our external environment and the way this is constantly striated by the force of technical directives and imperatives. A third lies in a more direct distinctively autonomic power that many technologies have begun to exert over us.

Normative, attitudinal and behavioural shaping

Perhaps the pervasive yet also most subtle way in which technology now regulates us comes from the gradual penetration of *Zweckrationalität* or instrumental–technical thinking into our everyday norms and attitudes. Not only does this incline opinion towards a governing ethos of "narrow utility" (Winner, 1978, p. 327), where concerns with technical norms like efficiency or function have usurped earlier values like the sacred or the aesthetic (cf. Bataille, 1992). At the extreme, this is nothing less than a normative variation on the technological a priori, one that generates its own "independent technical morality" (Ellul, 1964, p. 97) and that no longer "observes the distinction between moral and immoral use" (ibid.). The force of this can be witnessed in a myriad of small, everyday shifts in behaviour and opinion. The way in which we no longer expect universities to deliver learning for learning's sake, but "vocational" technical training; the new social expectations around digital connectedness or the increasing preference for online, rather than face-to-face communication; the transformation of public spaces away from places to gather or in which to interact and into hi-technology, securitised zones of risk management. Taken separately, each of these shifts, and many similar ones, might be harmless enough, but taken together they present a shift in authority and social ordering that suggests what Habermas described as a shift away from "the realization of practical goals" and towards a society geared "toward the solution of technical problems" (1970, p. 103). For criminal justice, such attitudes explain much about why technical solutions have acquired the legitimacy they have, in spite of the lack of any decisive evidence to suggest that they make any definitive improvements to justice.

Environmental control: soft shaping of behaviour

In Don DeLillo's *White Noise*, a character talks of his life being "blessed" by an ATM and "feeling its approval" when it allows him to have money. This nicely describes how the environments and social spaces through which we move and interact are now replete with technical requirements to which we must respond – whether in the emotional way that DeLillo describes or more functionally, as a means to our next end. This surrender might be identified at two levels – the small, everyday "nudging" of technical necessitation and a deeper, more profound range of effects upon our bodies. Of course it would be wrong to see technical necessitation as something entirely new, however pervasive it has now become. As discussed earlier, our tendency to define historical epochs in terms of technology has always implied a recognition that, as McLuhan suggested, our tools may turn out to have a power to shape us. Whether we see this in the introduction of the stirrup and its transformation of warfare (White, 1962), or Mumford's recognition of the clock (rather than the steam-engine) as the "the key-machine of the modern industrial age" (Mumford, 1934, p. 14), one that changed our experience of time and reorganised social life (Giddens, 1990), the technisation of our environments has always profoundly shaped the limits of what we can do, or what we think we can do. But it is the sheer scale and quantity of the way technological imperatives now exert their force that distinguishes our technomia from its earlier manifestations. The requirement to read and obey traffic lights; the restrictions of centrally operated seat belts; the regulative function of a heating thermostat; the demands of an online payment system; the limitations upon accessing our music or video collections imposed by media players; the "approval" of an ATM; or the bleak indifference of an automated supermarket payment till to our lack of change – all suggest pervasive new layers of technological regulation. The attractions of situational crime prevention to policy makers emphasise how easily technical modifications to our environment have been accepted as valid forms of regulation. Such rules pervade every aspect of the social world, but remain forces that, for the most part, are all but invisible to us.

Still deeper and more profound shapings of our world come with the penetration of our bodies or the structure of nature itself by the technologies of matter discussed earlier. It is also striking and somewhat disturbing to see how easily the normative power that these provide has been adapted to the justice process. The authority of a genetic profile, the behavioural modification of a chemical intervention or the damning witness of a neuro-scan are now such familiar components of our justice systems that, taken together, they suggest a far more pervasive landscape of technological control. In this landscape, which stretches from the smallest fragments of matter to the widest spheres of social interaction and out beyond the planet itself, distinguishing human from technological governance has become increasingly harder to do.

Autonomic shaping

On 6 May 2010, the Dow Jones index plunged by 900 points for a few minutes, only for it to suddenly, and just as mysteriously, recover again. The so-called "Flash Crash", as it became known (cf. Mackenzie and van Duyn, 2010), was a direct result of the automated system of algorithms and supercomputers that now manages global trade. A single sale of stock had set in motion an avalanche of automated trading that temporarily wiped around $1,000 billion off stock values (IOSCO, 2011) – evidence that the increasing practice of "high frequency trading", where vast flows of wealth are exchanged within milliseconds, is posing new problems of governance. For the speed of computer algorithms or so-called "trading robots" in buying and selling oversight of these wealth flows is now so fast and complex that their governance has passed far beyond any individual human oversight. Yet, in the wake of the devastating social consequences brought by the banking crisis of 2008, deferring to the autonomic powers of technology to manage the engine of the global economy may not seem like the best idea there has ever been.

But allowing our economic life to be regulated by machines is just one example of this most extreme form of technological regulation. Within the architecture or code identified by Reidenberg, Lessig and others, our capacity to make choices about what to do is a feature of the way "technological capabilities and system design choices impose rules on participants" (ibid., p. 554). That is, such rules were an indirect output of the autonomic constraints imposed by formal architectures. But, as the Flash Crash and other examples have begun to suggest, autonomic controls increasingly operate outside of "purely" technological environments. An automated payment system, an electric fence or the effects of a power cut may, again, be no great matters in themselves – but their cumulative impacts exert far more corrosive effects upon social order.

These successively more determining impacts of technomia upon regulation might be summarised thus (Figure 8.1):

- Intra-legal – the influence of technical regulations within law formation.
- Extra-legal – the influence of technical regulations outside the law, in technical codes, or self-regulation.

- Behavioural and attitudinal modification – the operation of technical regulation as a direct modifier of environments and behaviours.
- Autonomic regulation – the operation of technical regulation as an autonomic and quasi-independent force.

But of course, it is one thing to attribute a structure to this regulatory order, another to explain it. We might therefore justifiably ask how this could have emerged. The interests of power here – commercial or political – have of course been key determinants in destabilising the due process of traditional regulation, especially in a world where technical artefacts have acquired such vital commercial and political significance. But something extra is needed to explain the current ascendancy of technomia. After all, though the relevant elites reap certain material rewards for their role in maintaining and developing this structure, they too are ultimately subject to its demands and dependent upon its support. Thus, in the shift from a Marxist to a Marcusean view of technical power, the ruling class is no longer "the origin of the system of social domination, but must be located in a pre-existing field of instrumentalities it exploits" (Feenberg, 2002, p. 70).

At this point it is worth standing back and asking what the law, or indeed any publicly accountable system of regulation, is meant to be for. And it is not very controversial to respond that the origins of any criminal justice system arise from our concerns to be protected from various harms. In the first instance such concerns involve our bodies or the bodies of those we hold dear, and in the second they involve certain rights that we hold these bodies to possess – in particular, our right to property (in whatever form this takes). But a broader reading of the point of such protections might also see them as seeking to preserve what our bodies or our property enable us to *do* – that is, the range of capacities they offer us. If this broader reading makes sense, it should alert us to the fact that the real direction of legal structure might be better construed as something other than harm prevention *simpliciter*. Rather, it has always been about the preservation of the possibilities that our capacities offer – what Sen has spoken of as the "capabilities" that are open to us (see for example his 1993). Part of the failure of law and legislators, then, has been their failure not just to conceptualise technology effectively, but to see how technology connects to these concerns. For, if technology is something that augments our capacities and capabilities by extending us, then surely law's remit ought equally to be centred on these extensions – where this includes every kind of enhancement, not just obvious ones such as an electronic bank account, or a botox injection. Yet, just as the process of technologisation has increased in pace and the world of the "post-human" becomes our new normal, law remains fossilised around the concerns of a proto-technological era, where extension was limited to simpler tools, like language or property. It might therefore be argued that it is in this failure of law and legal thinking to acknowledge its wider remit that we have been left with the far less

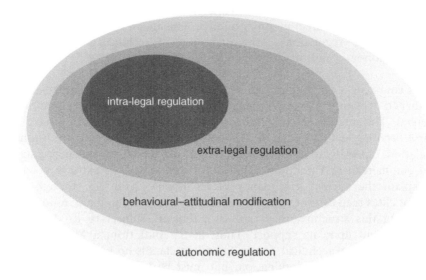

Figure 8.1 A model of contemporary technomia and its regulatory levels

transparent and unaccountable nomos of a technomia. At present we seem
as far away from recognising this as we ever have been, but until we do
recognise it, justice will be only one of the many casualties of a technological
world that originates within us, but that we allow to regulate us as if it
did not.

9   The question concerning technomia

Things are in the saddle and ride mankind.[1]
You can't make it deputy-proof.[2]

Technology changes everything – sort of. Unfortunately, the tendency
to make sweeping generalisations about technology has been almost as
prevalent as the tendency to underestimate its real nature and impacts – a
tendency that seems to have been especially prevalent within the criminal
justice process. In this context – depending upon one's perspective –
technology now offers endless new universes of possibility for the offender,
a panacea for crime control or relentless subordination to a governing
technical elite. As we have seen, the story is less dramatic, yet also more
profound than that. In these closing comments I want to review and
summarise some of the more obvious findings of the previous chapters
and what the wider implications of a technical nomos for criminal justice
and justice in general might be.

Technological offending

The striking lack of any category of technological offending until very
recently is a sure sign that it should not be accepted without far more
critical reflection than has so far been the case. For all the contemporary
enthusiasm for identifying instances of technology crime, it is clear that
there have been enormous confusions around defining or characterising
it very effectively. In particular, the proclivity for associating it with
complex or "high" technology forms has – without any clear justification –
undermined the more comprehensive overview that is so urgently required.
Too often "technology crime" has turned out to simply mean only "ICT-
enabled crime" – with the result that other, higher-risk technologies such
as handguns or industrial chemicals have had only intermittent associations with technological offending. Worse, the misuse of less complex artefacts, like bottles or knives, has rarely been seen as technological at all. At
least five key questions around technological offending appear to require a

clearer answer if the concept is to offer us any genuine explanatory power: how precisely technology "enables" offending; what are the (full) range of its harms; who are the offenders; who are the victims; and what precisely are the criminalities involved?

As a form of extension, the technological enablement of crime, like other varieties of enablement, seems to come in a weak and a strong form. Weak enablement is where the technology contributes to but is not necessary for an offence. For example, I can rob you using a botnot, but it is not essential, since I can also do it by breaking into your house. Strong enablement is where the technology is essential to the offence – that is, it could not be performed without it. The "pure" cybercrimes discussed by Wall (2007) may provide one example of this – one could not, for example, mount a denial-of-service attack upon a network without the use of a computer. Similarly, radioactive pollution could not be distributed across a region without some form of nuclear technology. The previous chapters have suggested that weak enablement is the predominant characteristic of most technological offences, implying that technology crime is largely traditional crime "with bells on" – i.e. with additional scale or range. By contrast, though strong enablement appears to offer more overtly technological forms of offending, it is far more rare at present. Whether that will change remains to be seen, but at present traditional crime remains remarkably resilient in the face of technological change.

This fact has implications for the way we think about the victims of technological offending. For the most part, these are no different than in other criminal contexts – individuals who are robbed, murdered, defrauded, psychologically bullied and so on. But there has been another trend to which strong enablement sometimes points: the growing collectivity of the technological victim, as, for example, where a region is devastated by nuclear waste, a city is destroyed by aerial bombardment, or a mass of individuals are collectively harmed by a malware infection. This phenomenon of collectivity also seems to apply to the technological offender on many occasions. Indeed, there seems almost to be a kind of a maxim here – the greater the complexity of the technological resource, the greater the likely complexity of the technological offender. For just as there is a division of labour involved in building a chemical processing plant, so too does the enactment of a technological crime often require a degree of collectivity – offenders that are specifically plural in nature – like states, corporations, new political groupings and so on. One would be hard put to see much evidence for this in much of the writing on technology crime – just as the weak legal sanctions against collective technological offenders suggest that the law has not always taken them very seriously, either. But the significance of collectivity does not rule out individual misuses of technology. There is a rich history of ways in which individuals have sought to exploit their extensions illicitly – whether by way of a pointed stick or a vial of poison. Individual offenders have also been more than competent in taking advantage of advanced technologies. There is nothing that prevents a lone stalker from misusing a social networking site, or a terrorist from seeking to distribute harmful bacteria. But in the end, at least some degree of organisation will usually be required to access more advanced means – after all, electronic networks, or the industrial use of biological and chemical phenomena, are the products of complex social organisation and institutions. Thus, their misuse will tend to be a more considered affair than spontaneously reaching for a knife.

But when it comes to the question of defining technological misuse as criminal, several problems tend to arise. Many forms of technology crime have a slightly artificial feel to them, originating as they do in new, technology-specific legislation. Indeed many harms are not obviously criminal at all, being constructed around *mala prohibitae*-style offences, or violations against codes of conduct, breaches of safety regulations or professional standards and so on. We have seen special difficulties created by the role that intention plays in shaping the way an artefact is judged to carry criminal culpability. On the one hand, this was registered in the latent "multiple functionality" of artefacts, where technological function can be changed by the simple expedient of a social actor changing how they use an object. For, given this, an electric lamp, or a skipping rope, may be no less significant potential technologies of murder than a garotte or a fertiliser bomb. But intention also manifests itself in the way determinations of criminal guilt have centred upon behaviour and its *mens rea* aspects rather than the specific involvement of any tool. That is, in legal terms the determination of *mala in se* or guilty intention is attached to the act, or the intentions behind, rather than to the means by which the act is carried out. As it stands then, both our concept of this offending and the way it is handled legally appear to offer support for the instrumentalist presumption that "technology is neutral".

We might ask why certain misuses of technology have been more readily perceived as criminogenic, or have been subjected to more stringent punitive sanctions than others. However, one rationale just suggested – that this is decided by the volume or scale of harm a technology enables – has not always appeared to be applied very consistently. For example, the potential harms enabled by CBNTs far exceed the seriousness of those enabled by ICTs, but have not been policed and legislated against in anything like equivalent terms. Similarly, more frequent harms, arguably, arise from spilt coffee or incomprehensible manufacturers' instructions than from cases of hacking. So, either intention or the volumes of harm caused must be determining in every case, or else *every* technology must be viewed as a potential source of offending – serious or otherwise. There can be no halfway house here.

It might be asked, given these and other complications, whether the notion of technological offending presents us with too many difficulties for it to be worth bothering with. Especially since part of our problems in dealing with this is that there are very few offences that are not "enabled" in at least some way. However, given the destructive, disruptive potentials of so many advanced technologies, it also seems unwise to completely ignore the construct of a "technological offence". It is certainly plausible that our failure to develop a robust notion of technological offending has allowed another kind of agenda to take shape, one where the "crisis" around technological control of the kind we have seen with ICTs creates a sense that the criminal justice system is "inadequate" in the face of technology crime. For with this has come a need for special (often extra-legal) regulation, one that poses serious challenges to justice. In an era of industrialised destructive power, where the very structure of matter can be distorted or smashed and life itself modified (or terminated forever), technological crime clearly ought not to be dismissed out of hand. But the Promethean option – to see technology crime as the product of our wider crimes "against nature" – goes too far. But until we develop a more sophisticated sense of the many ways in which society as well as nature can be harmed by technology, practical regulative responses to this remain unclear.

Technological control

Beyond offending, the second cluster of questions with which this book has been concerned has involved the way in which technology is regulated or, perhaps more significantly, how it regulates us. In terms of more straightforward, human-authored control uses, there seem to be many more examples than with offending, and a clearer set of contexts where we can point to such interventions. But the novelty of technology control should not be overstated – the long-term association between a control of technology – whether as an enabler of force or as a resource for knowledge and sovereign power – has been noted throughout the previous discussions. It was with the emergence of the new criminal justice systems of the nineteenth century that more diverse control functions emerged. These shifted technology away from its predominant role as an enhancer of force and towards other, more subtle modes of governance. Given the scale and character of contemporary technological control solutions, and the willingness to implement them *as* solutions, there seems to be good reason for thinking that we are at the onset of a very different stage in the relationship between technology and control. For, just as we have reached a point of unprecedented extension to bodily capacity, this has inevitably translated into parallel extensions to control.

The extent of the regulatory power that technology now offers to control can be seen in its all-encompassing spatial and "scalar" dimensions – extending the reach of our gaze, or our capacity to intervene, from the smallest, most microscopic entities, throughout social space and even beyond the planet. In temporal terms, options for real-time interventions have also been augmented by technologies that enhance the past and future

gaze of control. On the one hand, this involves a capacity for more comprehensive "past oriented" scrutiny in the form of technologies for detecting,
analysing and interpreting the bio-chemical or informatic traces and
trails we leave behind. On the other hand, the rise in "future oriented" risk
management-style interventions has depended almost entirely upon technological devices – whether these are the software tools that we use to try
to "predict" individual behaviours or outcomes, or the scanning devices that
we imagine can tell us what someone is intending to do. In the context
of justice, this has resulted in a very significant shift: a move away from
guilt determined retrospectively, on the basis of actual deeds, towards the
"precrime" idea, where we may be suspect in advance of any wrongdoing –
sometimes on the strength of our genetic structures alone. The advent of the
inherently suspect, bio-chemical citizen has been very much facilitated by
the fact that such extensions to control have not been matched by parallel
extensions to legal authority – in particular legal structures that properly
address the issue of enhancement and extension, a point to which we shall
return shortly.

A more immediate and pragmatic question has been the extent to which
these new technologies of control really do anything very useful. Such a
question would, of course, seem faintly ridiculous to most criminal justice
practitioners. The idea that technology is essential in order to "outpace" the
criminal, to secure convictions or to enhance justice has become a matter
of such self-evident truth that to question it would merely be perverse.
The many and various legitimations of this mindset – more effective, better-
targeted arrests; continued, measurable reductions in crime; more complete
control over public disorder; or getting rid of "red tape" and "bureaucracy"
– have seemed less self-evident when analysed in closer detail. Whether it is
the poor return on conviction rates from measures like CCTV or DNA, the
spiralling costs of technology solutions or the striking lack of impact on
long-term, overall crime rates, uncomfortable questions arise about the value
of such interventions – especially given the other costs to justice. We also
might wonder whether the standard response to such questions – that technological control offers greater "efficiency" in crime control – is really the
best ideal to aim for in running a criminal justice system. For Rawls, there
was no escaping the "subordinate place of efficiency in justice as fairness"
(1971, p. 272), and we have seen that justice and efficiency are rarely
comfortable bedfellows, given the ways in which the latter can so easily
undermine the former. Thus, whilst efficiency may often be a useful *method*
for attaining justice (i.e. in ensuring a better distribution of "deserts"),
it seems to remain unsatisfactory as an end. A more developed sense
of technology as an extension might illustrate why efficiency is not guaran-
teed to be the result of any extension, and hence cannot be put forward
as one of its a priori virtues. Take, for example, the so-called Chindogu
("useless") approach to technology (see Fackler, 2007 for an interesting
Chindogu approach to situational crime prevention), which involves the

deliberate attempt to design artefacts that operate inefficiently or in unnecessarily complex ways. Or the Bataillean notion of technology, which sees it as nothing more than a generator of waste and surplus (cf. Tomasi, 2008). These may not be the usual ways that technological processes have been seen, but they demonstrate that there is no necessary connection between technology and efficiency. Certainly nature, arguably the most productive of all machines, does not always endorse narrow efficiencies – as the cases of the peacock's tail or the fiddler crab's claw amply demonstrate. And, given what we have seen of the way in which the criminal justice process or other social institutions function, a "Chindogu" interpretation has often seemed to provide a more accurate reading of their operations. Thus, in ceding control to technology we need to be clear that any compromises to justice that result may have far more to do with a fetishisation of the technological norm than a genuine desire to realise efficiency.

Justice, technological justice and technomia

What conclusions can be drawn about the wider question of this book: the relation between increased technologisation within the justice system and justice itself? Whilst our focus here has, of necessity, been primarily upon criminal justice, it is clear enough that many of the trends discussed earlier also relate to justice in its wider sense. And whether justice is seen in terms of fairness, entitlement, the public good or individual rights and capabilities, the implications of the way technology is being used within criminal justice systems are not always very comfortable for these wider notions. Technological interventions are clearly not always associated with fair or equitable outcomes, whether these are the unequal distribution of surveillance power, the steady flow of miscarriages of justice directly attributable to technology, or the ease with which sanctions against high-technology forms of offending have been evaded, as compared to low-technology instances such as knife crime. Nor are entitlements or rights within the justice process always respected in the face of technology – most obviously, in the deference to technological norms and experts over rights to due process, to privacy and so on have indicated. There are also obvious questions about the impacts of technology-driven justice upon the public good – for example, in the bias towards legally protecting commercial needs over public needs, whether this relates to failures to prosecute polluters, incompetent management of personal information, or the over-prescription of painkilling medication.

If we think of justice in terms of Sens' (1993) notion (as capabilities that we lack or possess) it becomes clearer how the failure to appreciate the key aspect of technology – its role in enhancing or extending capacity – has all too often permitted technological regulation to fail us in this regard. The conclusion must be that legal authority, founded as it was in an age of less extended humans or less extended social interaction, has simply not kept up with the variety and power of the new kinds of extended bodies that we use and occupy. And just as the failure to modernise our regulatory institutions has left us vulnerable, so too has our reluctance to jettison some of our primaeval fears about technological change. For the erosion of formal or transparent regulation of technology has also been furthered by the ancient – but false – disjunct made between the "natural" and the artificial, the human and the technic. As the scope and reach of technology have grown, the fears generated by these disjunctions have gradually blended with newer versions that have been at the heart of many of the dystopian reflections of the modern age – in particular, the sense that technology will somehow "take over" from us, or destroy everything in some vast cataclysm. Standing, as we are, on the edge of an age where automated systems are likely to run vast areas of the social world, or a single accident really could spell the end of humanity, the power of such fears, arguably, risks undermining our very sense of what "effective regulation" of technology amounts to.

The result has been to cede authority in determining how technology is judged to be used or misused to less transparent forms of regulation than the law. Yet, as the previous reflections have repeatedly suggested, it is not so much technology itself that has caused the problem, but our readiness to defer to the codes and regulatory practices around technology – its technomia. At present this is too fragmented and too uneven for it to offer the kinds of protections that we have come to expect from traditional law. And too often any balance in the range of social forces that regulate us has become an uneven one. For example, if we look at the regulatory power of the market, in its corporatised form, then, as Lessig argued, "code (i.e. technical architecture) becomes a means by which to transfer decisions from the public realm to the privatized realm", so constituting a way "to convert political rights into market commodities" (Lessig, 1999, 159–63). Similarly, the regulatory role of our social norms seems also to have become subordinate to technological imperatives, for they too act in its image rather than our own. But there is nothing anti-human in these shifts, for in the end, as a feature of our extensions, they are "all too" human.

So what, if anything, might be done to acknowledge the influence of technomia and to reform our legal and regulatory structures in such a way that justice and legal power retain their authority over technical norms and presumptions? To properly address the needs of our post-human age, as is so often the case, small steps seem as likely to offer realisable objectives as the bigger ones. One obvious and easy step of this kind would be to begin to address the utter failures of the self-regulatory approach to technology and its often negative impacts. Whether it is media self-regulation, internet self-regulation, medical self-regulation or self-regulation by the chemical, biological or nuclear industries, time and time again it is the interests of technical–commercial norms that win out over the public interest or the interests of justice. Making the many and various developers of technology more accountable, or ensuring that those who set standards are more open to scrutiny themselves, is of course a huge challenge, but it is not an insurmountable one. In turn, where technology itself occupies a clearly regulatory role, we need a far wider debate over the desirability of this and a more developed sense of appropriate checks and balances. The phenomenon of autonomic technical regulation that we have seen need not, of course, be a problem if it merely functions in the background, as a kind of Parsonian mediator of homeostasis in our social systems rather than as an invisible tool that benefits the interests of the powerful over the weak. Under such constraints, it may even be desirable. After all, I have no free will about my blood circulation – to an extent that it regulates and controls everything I can do – but its function is also essential to me for my survival. The key desideratum for homeostasis, when it works effectively, is when its domain of control is restricted to its specific function. There is, for example, nothing in the operation of our blood circulation that determines our moral behaviour, just as our digestive system does not shape how we punish our children. Technological normativity also needs to work with this more limited focus and with a specific function in place. That it does not, or that we trust it to deliver justice more than we do ourselves, is one of the warning signs that it is we, not technology, that have "gone wrong".

Principles are the foundations of law, as someone might have said – so what does that imply for how we are to reshape our justice system in the face of the pervasiveness of technomia? Certain ideals seem obvious enough. For example, a major source of concern around the use of technology has been the way in which its enhancements have been experienced asymmetrically – by an ability to enact surveillance upon groups who lack the reciprocal power, or to use genetic information that the control agent does not hand over in return. On this basis the principle that "if I can use a technology upon you, you can use it upon me", or perhaps better, "whatever extensions you can have, I can have", seems to be in order. Or it might mean principles requiring greater accountability and openness that show how, or where, any technology is serving as a regulatory mechanism. Developing mechanisms that resemble calls for "open", rather than closed, codes of regulation (cf. Lessig, 2006, pp. 327ff) suggest one way in which technocracy might be challenged, for even though this has been undermined by commercial interests, in the context of the internet, there is no a priori reason why it cannot be made to apply, with sufficient care. There is an obvious practical complication here: the unlikelihood that many would be willing to spend time considering the validity of new regulatory codes around, say, toasters, or would even understand how such codes might work in the case of more complex technologies, like those that function at the nano-level. Perhaps some variations upon the notion of the wiki might be brought to bear here in the creation of more participatory mechanisms for tailoring top-down governance of technology to a more pluralistic civic control, one where technical expertise is both acknowledged and moderated.

It would of course be naive to believe that any such principle could totally circumvent vested interests. Governments will not willingly relinquish their disproportionate control over technology, given the advantages to power that it offers. Similarly, business is unlikely to stop using and designing technology in ways that it thinks best suit its commercial interests. Thus, reforming and adapting technological regulation for an era of mass enhancement cannot be conducted in isolation from wider political change. Whether politics itself is now too submerged within technological imperatives for this to be possible is of course a wider question than can be addressed by this book.

In conclusion, then, it now seems clear that the concerns raised by Heidegger's question about technology were only a starting-point for a wider interrogation of how technology shapes the social order and generates possible harms. If we are to go beyond the sterile dichotomy that tells us that technology is "sometimes harmful, sometimes not", it is essential to see technology as something human – no less part of us than a heart bypass or a contact lens. In which case the question concerning technology is certainly, as Heidegger suggested, a question concerning humanity – but one a with vital additional factor. In the end, it is really a question about human enhancement and how far we are willing, or able, to regulate the extensions that technology offers us and the extent to which such regulations accord with wider principles that we hold to be valuable. When it comes to questions about technology, the question we can no longer ignore concerns its technomia and what this now implies for human culture.

Notes

Introduction

1 Steigler (1998, p. 88).
2 *Industrial Society and its Future (The Unabomber Manifesto)*, Jolly Roger Press, 1995.
3 This abbreviation is a deliberate invocation of the "CBRN" classification (chemical, biological and radioactive weapons) found in security/policy literatures (cf. Cornish, 2007).

1 Technology and its technomia

1 Nietzsche (1982, p. 227).
2 In some versions of the myth Pandora's box (actually a *pithos*, or jar) also contains hope – a striking reflection of the contradictory perceptions technology invokes.
3 Plato also discusses *techne* in dialogues such as Gorgias or the Charmides (Plato, 1997).
4 See the Nicomachean Ethics (IV) for one source here (Aristotle, 1999).
5 Its existence is revealed in correspondence with Engels (cf. Marx and Engels, 1983, pp. 82ff).
6 Taken from a quote originally cited in Bowling *et al.* (2008).
7 These and other examples from Kapp are cited in Mitcham (1994, pp. 23ff).
8 Horkheimer inverted this idea, arguing that "organs are extensions of instruments" (1972, p. 21).

2 Foundations

1 Attributed to Archimedes in Mackay (1991, p. 11).
2 Note that the original version of the Hippocratic oath also contains proscriptions against abortion.
3 Bio-control was also exerted by using women infected with venereal diseases for similar ends.

3 Tele-crime?

1 US Security Operative, *South Park* Episode 12, Series 6.
2 In 2010 the *Daily Mail* was forced to apologise to Facebook after a catalogue of errors and misrepresentations in its reporting of the "dangers" of the site. Another more recent permutation of this kind has been the "Craigslist Killer" (cf. McPhee, 2010).

3 For example, if defined as "the process of limiting risks to children when using technology" (BECTA, 2006, p. 4 – derived from the Children Act 2004), safeguarding need not mean physical intervention.
4 The proposed legislation took its name from the 14-year-old girl who committed suicide following a series of online interactions involving false identities and insults that were characterised in the USA as "cyberbullying". The case was complex and controversial (see Zetter, 2008).
5 Less than three months later Google's "principled stand" was rolled back when it conceded to Chinese government directives to stop redirecting searches to its Hong Kong page (Fiveash, 2010).
6 The estimate was subsequently lowered to £1.2 billion.
7 For example, £372 million relating to telecommunications fraud (as a whole) was included – even though much of it had absolutely nothing to do with identification.

4 Tele-control

1 Peter Arno, American cartoonist.
2 Originally directed at digital telephone networks, CALEA's remit was extended to include broadband/internet communications providers and (some) Voice-over-IP (VoIP) providers in 2005.
3 A number of websites campaigning against Phorm's violations of UK communications law have been set up. See for example dephormation.org.uk.
4 Made by Facebook CEO Mark Zuckenburg (Johnson, B., 2010).

5 Micro-crimes: CBNTs

1 From "The poison squad" – satirical poem about Harvey W. Wiley, MD, first commissioner of the US Bureau of Chemistry, predecessor of the Food and Drug Administration (FDA).
2 A legal framework for commercialised biotechnology began with *Diamond* v. *Chakrabarty* (447 U.S. 303 [1980]) when the US Supreme Court permitted a genetically modified micro-organism to be patented.
3 LIA Annual Meeting, June 5, 1934, Federal Trade Commission, *In the Matter of National Lead Co, et al*, Docket No. 5253, p. 5535.
4 In *U.S.* v. *Johnson* – U.S. 488 221 (1911).

6 Micro-control

1 Phillip K. Dick, *A Scanner Darkly*, c. 15.
2 From the 'Study in Scarlet', in *The Complete Sherlock Holmes*, II, New York: Barnes & Noble, 2003, p. 10.
3 Bayesian inference follows the pattern and provides a way of deciding the likelihood of a hypothesis being true, given a certain piece of evidence. In science this involves a process of refinement depending upon repeated inputs of values – quite unlike the "one-off" set of values seen in a trial.
4 543 U.S. 551 (2005).

7 Of hammers, hairdryers and handguns

1 From Sylvia Plath's poems "Lesbos" and "Temper of time".
2 Mitcham suggests that intrinsic functions might centre upon the Aristotelian idea of "what something does best" (1994, Aristotle NE I.7.1097b24 1098a17).
3 1 Cr App R (S) and 1 Cr App R (S) 295 respectively.

4 For example: the Noise Insulation Regulations (1975–96), the Noise Act (1996) or the Licensing Act (2003).
5 42 USC §4901 et. seq. 40 CFR Parts 204, 211.
6 And amended by the Sale and Supply of Goods Act 1994 and the Sale and Supply of Goods to Consumers Regulations 2002.
7 15 USC §70 & 15 USC §68 (et seq.) respectively.
8 Though there is no legal requirement for drivers who do not use glasses to have an eye test until they are 70 – even though eye-sight begins to decline from around the age of 30.
9 The Healthcare Commission report of 2004 (HC, 2004) cited a figure of 34,646 cosmetic surgery procedures carried out in the UK in 2003–4.

8 Technology, science and justice

1 From Helmut Schelsky's (1961), lecture "Man in Scientific Civilisation", cited in Wiggershaus (1995, p. 587).
2 The DOJ category includes administration and "other".
3 Attributed to Poincaré in Berelson and Steiner (1964, p. 14).
4 John Lea (private correspondence).
5 *Frye* v. *United States*, 293 F. 1013 (D.C. Cir 1923).
6 *Daubert* v. *Merrell Dow Pharmaceuticals* (92–102), 509 U.S. 579.
7 Cf. *Hollander* v. *Sandoz Pharmaceuticals Corp.*, 289 F.3d 1193 (2002).

9 The question concerning technomia

1 Ralph Waldo Emerson.
2 Captain Don Strickland, East Baton Rouge Parish Sheriff's Office.

Bibliography

9/11 Commission 2004 *9/11 Commission Report*, New York: W. W. Norton

Aas, K. 2006 "'The Body Does Not Lie': Identity, Risk and Trust in Technoculture", *Crime Media & Culture* 2(2), 143–58

ACPO 2006 "Good Practice Guide for Computer-Based Electronic Evidence", ACPO Consultation Document

Acton, P., Rogers, M. and Zimmerman, P. 2007 "Beyond the Dirty Bomb: Re-thinking Radiological Terror", *Survival* 49(3), 151–68

Adams, D. 1999 "How to Stop Worrying and Love the Internet", *Sunday Times* 28/08/1999

—— 2005 "Expert Spells it Out: Health Fears Mean Young Should Not Use Mobile Phones", *Guardian* 12/01/2005

Adderley, R. 2003 "Using Data Mining Techniques to Solve Crime", International Conference on Computer, Communication and Control Technologies, Orlando

Agamben, G. 2004 "Bodies without Words: Against the Biopolitical Tattoo", *German Law Journal* 5, 167–69

—— 2005 *State of Exception*, Chicago: University of Chicago Press

Agazzi, E. 1998 "From Technique to Technology: The Role of Modern Science", *Techné* 4(2)

Aglietta, M. 2001 "Whence and Whither Money?", in *The Future of Money*, Paris: OECD, 31–72

Agnew, J. 2001 "The New Global Economy: Time-Space Compression, Geopolitics, and Global Uneven Development", *Journal of world-systems research* 7(2), 133–154

Ahmed, M. 2009 "Teen 'Sexting' Craze Leading to Child Porn Arrests in US", *Times* 14/01/2009

AI 1999 "USA: Race, Rights and Police Brutality", Amnesty International AMR 51/147/1999

—— 2004 "Excessive and Lethal Force? Amnesty International's Concerns about Deaths and Ill- Treatment Involving Police Use of Tasers", Amnesty International AMR 51/139/2004

AJC 2000 "German Firms that Used Slave or Forced Labor During the Nazi Era", American Jewish Committee, see http://www.jewishvirtuallibrary.org/jsource/Holocaust/germancos.html

Albrecht, K. and McIntyre, L. 2005 *Spychips: How Major Corporations and Government Plan to Track your Every Move*, Nashville: Nelson Current

Al-Ghazal, S. 2004 "Medical Ethics in Islamic History at a Glance", *Journal of the International Society for the History of Islamic Medicine* 3(4), 12–14

Allen, N. 2008 "Facebook Killer Jailed for Life", *Daily Telegraph* 17/10/2008

Allen, R. 2008 "Explanationism All the Way Down", *Episteme* 5, 320–28

Allen, R. and Redmayne, M. 1997 "Bayesianism and Juridical Proof", special issue, *The International Journal of Evidence and Proof* 1, 253

Almandras, A 2010 "Sarah's Law: The Child Sex Offender Disclosure Scheme", House of Commons Briefing Note SN/HA/1692

Alperovitz, G. 1995 *The Decision to Use the Atomic Bomb: And the Architecture of an American Myth*, New York: Alfred A. Knopf

Anderson, A. 1995 "Why Prometheus Suffers; Technology and the Ecological Crisis", *Techné* 1, 1–2

Anderson, R., Brown, I., Dowty, T., Heath, W. and Sasse, A. 2009 *Database State*, York: Joseph Roundtree Reform Trust

Andrejevic, M. 2009 "Control over Personal Information in the Database Era", *Surveillance and Society*, 6(3)

Andrews, W. 2009 "Can Corporations Own your DNA?", *CBS* 13/05/2009

Angell, M. 2004 *The Truth about the Drug Companies: How They Deceive Us and What to Do About It*, New York, Random House

Angwin, J. 2010 "The Web's New Gold Mine: Your Secrets", *Wall Street Journal* 30/07/2010

AP 2007 "U.S. Labs Mishandling Deadly Germs", Associated Press, via MSNBC, 02/10/2007

—— 2009 "Pfizer to Pay Record $2.3bn Settlement", Associated Press report, *Guardian* 02/09/2009

—— 2010 "Grocery Manufacturers Spent $1m Lobbying in 1Q", Associated Press/ *Bloomberg Businessweek* 13/05/2010

APACS 2006 "UK Card Fraud Losses in 2005 Fall by £65m", Press Release 06/02/2006

Applebe, G. 2005 "From Arsenic to Thalidomide: A Brief History of Medicine Safety", in Anderson, S. (ed.) *Making Medicines: A Brief History of Pharmacy and Pharmaceuticals*, London: Pharmaceutical Press, 243–60

Appleseed 2009 "Reducing the Unfairness of Videoconferencing", see http://www.appleseeds.net/Portals/0/Documents/Publications/Chapter%206.pdf

Aria 2007 "Grande Paroisse Toulouse", *French Ministry of the Environment* – DPPR /SEI /BARPI, Aria no21329

Aristotle 1999, *Nicomachean Ethics*, 2nd edn, trans. T. Irwin, Indianapolis: Hackett

Arnold, L. 2007 *Windscale 1957: Anatomy of a Nuclear Accident*, New York: Palgrave MacMillan

Arora, V. 2006 "The CAN-SPAM Act: An Inadequate Attempt to Deal with a Growing Problem", *Columbia Journal of Law and Social Problems* 39(3), 300–30

Arthur, C. 2008 "That Cyberwarfare by Russia on Estonia?", *Guardian Technology Blog* 25/01/2008

—— 2009 "The Truth is On the Line", *Guardian* 12/03/2009

—— 2010 "Plan to Store Britons' Phone and Internet Data Revived", *Guardian* 20/10/2010

Ashby, E. and Anderson, M. 1981 *The Politics of Clean Air*, Oxford: Oxford University Press

Asthana, A. 2004 "Sorted: Britain's Postcode People", *Guardian* 30/05/2004

Atomic Archive 2010 "The Atomic Bombings of Hiroshima and Nagasaki", National Science Digital Library http://www.atomicarchive.com/Docs/MED/med_chp10.shtml

Auerbach, J. 1999 *The Great Exhibition of 1851: A Nation on Display*, New Haven, CT: Yale University Press

Axelsen, D. E. 1985 "Women as Victims of Medical Experimentation: J. Marion Sims' Surgery on Slave Women, 1845–1850", *Sage* 2(2), 10–3

Ayres, I. 2007 *Super Crunchers: How Anything Can Be Predicted*, London: John Murray

Ayres, I. and Donohue, J. 2003 "Shooting Down the 'More Guns, Less Crime' Hypothesis", *Stanford Law Review* 55, 1193ff.

Azeez, G. and Nunan, C. 2008 "GM Crops – the Health Effects", Bristol: The Soil Association

Azuonye, C. 1996 *Dogon*, New York: Rosen

Backwell, L., Errico, F. and Wadley, L. 2008 "Middle Stone Age Bone Tools from the Howiesons Poort Layers, Sibudu Cave, South Africa", *Journal of Archaeological Science* 35(6), 1566–80

Bacon, F. 1955 "Of Innovation", in Dick, H. (ed.) *Selected Writings of Francis Bacon*, New York: Modern Library

—— 1994 *Novum Organum*, trans. P. Urbach and J. Gibson, Chicago: Open Court

Baez, F. 2008 *A Universal History of the Destruction of Books*, New York, NY: Atlas & Co

Bailes, K. 1986 "Soviet Science in the Stalin Period: The Case of V. I. Vernadskii and His Scientific School, 1928–1945", *Slavic Review* 45(1), 20–37

Baksi, C. 2009 "'Chaos' Predicted over Virtual Court Pilot", *Law Society Gazette* 16/12/2009

Baldick, R. 1970 *The Duel: A History of Duelling*, New York: Spring Books

Barenblatt, D. 2005 *A Plague upon Humanity: The Hidden History of Japan's Biological Warfare Program*, New York: HarperPerennial

Barlett, D. and Steele, J. 2008 "Monsanto's Harvest of Fear", *Vanity Fair*, May

Barnardo's 2011 *Puppet on a String: The Urgent Need to Cut Children Free from Sexual Exploitation*, Ilford: Barnardo's

Barnes, J. 2010 "History", *The Fingerprint SourceBook*, Washington DC: National Institute of Justice, ch. 1

Bartholomew, R. and Victor, J. 2005 "A Social Psychological Theory of Collective Anxiety Attacks: The 'Mad Gasser' Re-examined", *Sociological Quarterly* 45(2), 229–48

Bartrip, P. 1992 "A 'Pennurth of Arsenic for Rat Poison' The Arsenic Act 1851 and the Prevention of Secret Poisoning", *Medical History* 36, 53–69

Bashford, A. and Levine, P. (eds) 2010 *The Oxford Handbook of the History of Eugenics*, Oxford: Oxford University Press

Bataille, G. 1992 *Theory of Religion*, New York: Zone Books

Bauman, R. 1996 *Crime and Punishment in Ancient Rome*, London and New York: Routledge

Bauman, Z. 2000 *Liquid Modernity*, Cambridge: Polity

—— 2001 *Modernity and the Holocaust*, Ithaca, NY: Cornell University Press

BBB 2005 "Javelin Identity Fraud Survey Report", Better Business Bureau in conjunction with Javelin Strategy and Research

BBC 19/11/1999 "The Growing Threat of Internet Fraud"

BBC 05/06/2006 "7 July Report Highlights Failings"

BBC 19/07/2006 "Bush Uses Veto on Stem Cell Bill"

BBC 22/11/2006 "Motorists to Give Fingerprints"

BBC 05/02/2007 "Google Earth Prompts Indian Fears"

BBC 21/06/2007 "Card Fraud 'Is Not Investigated'"

BBC 07/11/2007 "Alcohol Killed Mother Sally Clark"

BBC 05/06/2008 "Call to prosecute BT for ad trial"

BBC 10/07/2008 "Italy Rebuke on Roma Fingerprints"

BBC 24/07/2008 "Concern over French Nuclear Leaks"

BBC 16/09/2008 "Heart Fears over Common Chemical"

BBC 16/03/2009 "Breakdowns in Police Radio System"

BBC 23/07/2009 "Burglars Become Police 'Advisers'"

BBC 11/11/2009 "Employer Lie Detector Use 'Grows'"

BBC 02/02/2011 "EU Plans Bigger Exchange of Air Passenger Data"

BBC 02/11/2011 "E-criminals 'Target Smartphones and Tablets'"

BCC 2002 "The Food Additives Business", BCC Research Report Code: FOD009D

Beam, C. 2009 "I See You Typing", *Slate* 06/04/2009

Bean, P. 1999 "Technology and Criminal Justice", *International Review of Law, Computers & Technology*, 13(3), 365–71

Beard, M., North, J. and Price, S. 1998 *Religions of Rome, Volume 1: A History*, New York: Cambridge University Press

Beattie, J. M. 1986, *Crime and the Courts in England, 1660–1800*, Princeton, NJ: Princeton University Press

Beaumont, C. 2009 "Augmented Reality: A Technology whose Time Has Come", *Daily Telegraph* 02/09/2009

Beck, A. 1959 "Some Aspects of the History of Anti-Pollution Legislation in England, 1819–1954", *Journal of the History of Medicine* XIV (10), 475ff

Beckwith, M. 1970 *Hawaiian Mythology*, Honolulu: University of Hawaii Press

BECTA 2006 "Safeguarding Children in a Digital World", Coventry: British Educational Communications and Technology Agency, BEC1-15401

Bell, D. 1976 *The Cultural Contradictions of Capitalism*, New York: Basic Books

Benjamin, M. 2005 "Communications Breakdown", *Salon.com* 09/09/2005

Bennett, C.J. 2001 "Cookies, Web Bugs, Webcams and Cue Cats: Patterns of Surveillance on the World Wide Web", *Ethics and Information Technology* 3(3), 195–208

Bennett, L. 2008 "Assets under Attack: Metal Theft, the Built Environment and the Dark Side of the Global Recycling Market", *Environmental Law and Management* 20, 176–83

Bennetto, J. 2007 "Police Struggling to Cope with Rise of Cyber-crime", *Independent* 24/01/2007

Bentley, D. 2010 "Government Axing Websites to Save Millions", *Independent* 25/06/2010

Berelson, B. and Steiner, G. A. 1964 *Human Behavior: An Inventory of Scientific Findings*, New York: Harcourt, Brace and World

Berger, A. 1953 *Encyclopedic Dictionary of Roman Law*, Transactions of the American Philosophical Society, New Series, vol. 43, Pt 2

Berger, P. 1967 *The Sacred Canopy: Elements of a Sociology of Religion*, New York: Anchor Books

Bernard, E. 2007 *Criminal HIV Transmission*, London: NAM

Berry, J. 2010 "Reducing Bureaucracy in Policing, Final Report", Home Office, October

Bertazzi, P., Consonni, D., Bachetti, S., Rubagotti, M., Baccarelli, A., Zocchetti, C., Pesatori, A. C. 2001 "Health Effects of Dioxin Exposure: A 20-Year Mortality Study", *American Journal of Epidemiology* 153(11), 1031–44

Bertomeu-Sánchez, J. and Nieto-Galan, A. 2006 *Chemistry, Medicine and Crime: Mateu J. B. Orfila (1787–1853) and his Times*, Sagamore Beach, MA: Science History Publications

Best, R. and Elea, J. 2011 "Satellite Surveillance: Domestic Issues", Congressional Research Service Report, 7-5700, RL34421

Bhattacharyya, A. 2010 "Stuxnet Hits India the Most", *Hindustan Times* 04/10/2010

Bierne, P. and South, N. 2007 *Issues in Green Criminology: Confronting Harms against Environments, Humanity and Other Animals*, Cullompton: Willan

Bijsterveld, K. 2008 *Technology, Culture, and Public Problems of Noise in the Twentieth Century*, Cambridge, MA: MIT Press

Binfield, K. 2004 *Writings of the Luddites*, Baltimore and London: Johns Hopkins University Press

Binham, C. and Croft, J. 2011 "Twitter Fuels Debate over Super-injunctions", *Financial Times* 09/05/2011

Birkett, P. and Lashmar, P. 2000 "True Cause of Flixborough to Be Revealed after 26 Years", *Independent* 10/04/2000

Bizup, J. 2003 *Manufacturing Culture: Vindications of Early Victorian Industry*, Charlottesville: University of Virginia Press

Black, D. A. and Nagin, D. S. 1998 "Do Right to Carry Laws Deter Violent Crime?", *Journal of Legal Studies (Chicago)* 27, 209–19

Black, E. 2001, *IBM and the Holocaust*, New York: Crown

Blakely, R. 2010 "Indian Police Barred from Using Truth Serums after Court Ruling", *Times* 06/05/2010

Blau, J. 2007 "EU Police Data-sharing Plan Draws Criticism' *Computer Weekly* 19/04/2007

Bloom, J. 2008 "Tiny Particles Hit the Big Time", *Guardian* 04/09/2008

Bloss, W. 2007 "Escalating U.S. Police Surveillance after 9/11: an Examination of Causes and Effects", *Surveillance & Society* 4(3), 208–28

Blumenberg, H. 1957, "'Nachahmung der Natur'. Zur Vorgeschichte der Idee des schöpferischen Menschen", *Studium Generale* 10, 266–83

Blyth, A. and Blyth, M. 1906 *Poisons: Their Effects and Detection*, London: Charles Griffin

BMA 2007 "Boosting your Brainpower: Ethical Aspects of Cognitive Enhancements", Discussion Paper, November

Bodoni, S. 2011 "Facebook, Google Must Obey Stricter EU Data-Protection Rules, Reding Says", *Blomberg* 16/03/2011

Bogard, W. 1996 *The Simulation of Surveillance: Hyper-Control in Telematic Societies*, New York: Cambridge University Press

—— 2006 "Welcome to the Society of Control: The Simulation of Surveillance Revisited", in Haggerty, J. and Ericson, R. (eds) *The New Politics of Surveillance and Visibility*, Toronto: University of Toronto Press

Bonczar, T and Snell, T. 2005 "Capital Punishment, 2004", US Bureau of Justice Capital Punishment Series, NCJ211349

Bonis, J. 2007 "Acute Wiiitis", *New England Journal of Medicine* 356, 2431–32

Booth, C. 2010 *Poverty Maps of London*, LSE Charles Booth Online Archive

Bordo, S. 2000 *The Male Body: A New Look at Men in Public and in Private*, New York: Farrar, Straus and Giroux

Borger, J. 2010 "Nuclear Smuggling: Armenia Arrests Suspected Supplier", *Guardian* 08/11/2010

Borgmann, A. 1984 *Technology and the Character of Contemporary Life*, Chicago: University of Chicago Press

Borkin, J. 1978 *The Crime and Punishment of I. G. Farben*, New York: Free Press

Borland, S. 2008 "MI5 Warns Firms over China's Internet 'Spying'", *Daily Telegraph* 12/04/2008

Bosely, S. 2010 "WikiLeaks Cables: Pfizer 'Used Dirty Tricks to Avoid Clinical Trial Payout'", *Guardian* 09/12/2010

Boswell, J. 1988 *The Kindness of Strangers: The Abandonment of Children in Western Europe from Late Antiquity to the Renaissance*, New York: Pantheon

Bowcott, O. and Evans, R. 2010 "Britain's Secret Biological Weapons: More Monstrous than the Nazis", *Guardian* 16/05/2010

Bowley, G. 2011 "Speed is Money as Cyber Muscle Overruns Markets", *New York Times* 23/01/2011

Bowling, B., Marks, A. and Murphy, C. 2008 "Crime Control Technologies: Towards an Analytical Framework and Research Agenda", in Brownsword, R. and Yeung, K. (eds) *Regulating Technologies*, Oxford: Hart, 51–78

Boyd, C. 2003 "Cyber Threats Risk Net's Future", BBC 16/12/2003

Brack, D. and Hayman, G. 2002 "International Environmental Crime: The Nature and Control of Environmental Black Markets", Workshop Presentation, Royal Institute of International Affairs, May

Brady, B. 2008 "Prisoners 'to Be Chipped Like Dogs'", *Independent* 13/01/2008

Braithwaite, J. 1984 *Corporate Crime in the Pharmaceutical Industry*, London: Routledge & Kegan Paul

Brandeis, L. 1928 "Dissenting Opinion in Olmstead v United States" 477 U.S. 238

Brants, K. and Voltmer, K. (eds) (2011) *Political Communication in Postmodern Democracy: Challenging the Primacy of Politics*, Basingstoke: Palgrave Macmillan

Braslow, J. 1997 *Mental Ills and Bodily Cures: Psychiatric Treatment in the First Half of the Twentieth Century*, Berkeley: University of California Press

Brayshay, M., Harrison, P. and Chalkley, B. 1998 "Knowledge, Nationhood and Governance: The Speed of the Royal Post in Early-modern England", *Journal of Historical Geography* 24(3), 265–88

Brenner, R. 1995 "Agrarian Class Structure and Economic Development in Pre-Industrial Europe", in Aston, T. H. and Philpin, C. H. E. (eds) *The Brenner Debate: Agrarian Class Structure and Economic Development in Pre-Industrial Europe*, Cambridge: Cambridge University Press

Brenner, S. 2004 "Cybercrime Metrics: Old Wine, New Bottles?", *Virginia Journal of Law & Technology* 9, 13

Brey, P. 2004 "Ethical Aspects of Facial Recognition Systems in Public Places", *Journal of Information, Communication and Ethics in Society* 2(2), 97–09

Bridge, M. 2004 "Do We Need a New Sale of Goods Act?", lecture given on 5 May at Queen Mary, University of London

Brignall, M. 2008 "Crime Victim Told He Must Foot the Bill", *Guardian* 29/11/2008

Brown, J. and Langan, P. 2001, "Policing and Homicide, 1976–98: Justifiable Homicide by Police, Police Officers Murdered by Felons", US Department of Justice Report, NCJ 180987

Brown, S. 2006 "The Criminology of Hybrids: Rethinking Crime and Law in Technosocial Networks", *Theoretical Criminology* 10(2), 223–44

Brown, T. and Murphy, E. 2010 "Through a Scanner Darkly: Functional Neuroimaging as Evidence of a Criminal Defendant's Past Mental States", *Stanford Law Review* 62

Brownsword, R. 2008 "So What Does the World Need Now? Reflections on Regulating Technologies", in Brownsword, R. and Yeung, K. (eds) *Regulating Technologies*, Oxford: Hart, 23–48

Bryan, V. 2010 "French Lawmakers Vote to Ban Burqa in Public", *Reuters* 13/07/2010

Buderi, R. 1996 *The Invention that Changed the World: The Story of Radar from War to Peace*, London: Simon & Schuster

Buettner, R. 2008 "Emergency Radio Network Fails Tests", *New York Times* 21/08/2009

Bull, R., Baron, H., Gudjonsson, G., Hampson, S., Rippon, G. and Vrij, A. 2004 "A Review of the Current Scientific Status and Fields of Application of Polygraphic Deception Detection", Final Report of BPS Working Party, Leicester: British Psychological Society

Bunge, M. 1966 "Technology as Applied Science", *Technology and Culture* 7(3), 329–47

—— 1977 "Towards a Technoethics", *Monist* 60(1), 96–107

Bunn, M. 2010 *Securing the Bomb 2010*, Cambridge, MA and Washington DC: Project on Managing the Atom, Harvard University, and Nuclear Threat Initiative

Burleigh, M. 1995 *Death and Deliverance: "Euthanasia" in Germany, c.1900 to 1945*, Cambridge: Cambridge University Press

Butcher, K. and Ponting, M. 2005 "The Roman Denarius under the Julio-Claudian Emperors: Mints, Metallurgy and Technology", *Oxford Journal of Archaeology* 24(2), 163–97

Butterfield, F. 2001 "When the Police Shoot, Who's Counting?", *New York Times* 29/04/2001

Bynum, W. 1994 *Science and the Practice of Medicine in the Nineteenth Century*, Cambridge: Cambridge University Press

Byrne, J. and Rebovich, D. (eds) 2007 *The New Technology of Crime, Law & Social Control*, New York: Criminal Justice Press

Cairncross, F. 1997 *The Death of Distance: How the Communications Revolution Will Change our Lives*, Boston, MA: Harvard Business Press

Cameron, C. 2010 "Regulating Human Enhancement Technologies: The Role of the Law and Human Dignity", *Journal of Law and Medicine* 17(5), 807–15

Campbell, D. and Lee, R. 2004 "The Foot and Mouth Outbreak 2001: Lessons Not Yet Learned", Cardiff: Centre for Business Relationships, Accountability, Sustainability and Society, Cardiff Law School

Campbell Library 2009 *Campbell Collaboration Library of Systematic Reviews*, Campbell Library, see http://www.campbellcollaboration.org/library.php

Campbell, M. 2005 "Cyber Bullying: An Old Problem in a New Guise?", *Australian Journal of Guidance and Counselling* 15(1), 68–76

Canguilhem, G. 1989, *The Normal and the Pathological*, trans. Carolyn R. Fawcett and Robert S. Cohen, New York: Zone Books

Canter, D. 1995 *Criminal Shadows*, London: HarperCollins

Capell, K. 2009 "How Big Pharma Profits from Swine Flu", *Bloomberg Businessweek* 24/11/2009

Cardis, E. and The Interphone Study Group 2010 "Brain Tumour Risk in Relation to Mobile Telephone Use: Results of the INTERPHONE International Case-control Study", *International Journal of Epidemiology* 1–20

Carlin, M. 1998 "Fast Food and Urban Living Standards in Medieval England", in Carlin, M. and Rosenthal, J. (eds) *Food and Eating in Medieval Europe*, London, Rio Grande and Ohio: Hambledon Press, 27–52 (27–28)

Carlson, E. 2001 *The Unfit: A History of a Bad Idea*, Cold Spring Harbor, NY: Cold Spring Harbor Press

Carlyle, T. 1858 *The Collected Works of Thomas Carlyle*, 16 vols, London: Chapman and Hall

—— 2000 *Sartor Resartus*, Oxford: Oxford University Press

Carr, N. 2010 *The Shallows: What the Internet Is Doing to our Brains*, New York: W. W. Norton

Carrick, P. 1991 *Medical Ethics in the Ancient World* Washington DC: Georgetown University Press

Carter, M. 2006 *Living with HIV*, London: NAM Publications

Cartwright, N. 1983 *How the Laws of Physics Lie*, Oxford and New York: Clarendon Press

—— 2007 "Causal Powers", Report 04/07, London: Centre for Philosophy of Natural and Social Science

Casserly, C. 2010 "Is Genetic Discrimination Fear of Disability", *Bionews* 565, 02/07/2010

Castells, M. 1996/2000 *The Rise of the Network Society, The Information Age: Economy, Society and Culture*, vol. I, Cambridge, MA and Oxford: Blackwell

—— 2009 *Communication Power*, Oxford: Oxford University Press

Castronova, E. 2007 *Exodus to the Virtual World: How Online Fun Is Changing Reality*, New York: Palgrave MacMillan

Catalano, S., Smith, E., Snyder, H. and Rand, M. 2009 "Female Victims of Violence", Bureau of Justice Statistics Selected Findings, NCJ 228356

Cate, F. 2008 "Information Security Breaches", Washington DC: Centre for Information Policy Leadership

Cauley, L. 2006 "NSA Has Massive Database of Americans' Phone Calls", *USA Today* 05/10/2006

Cave, R. and Coulson, H. 1965 *A Source Book for Medieval Economic History*, New York: Biblo & Tannen

CBA 2008 "Chemical Business Association Responsible Care Performance", *Chemical Business Association* 07/05/2008

CBC 1999 "Sask. Doctor Sentenced for Rape", *CBC News* 27/11/1999

CCJS 2009 "Young People, and Gun and Knife Crime: A Review of the Evidence", report for 11 Million, London: Centre for Crime and Justice Studies

CDT 2007 "Hiding in Plain Sight: Why Important Government Information Cannot Be Found through Commercial Search Engines", Center for Democracy and Technology & OMB Watch

CEOP 2008 Press Release 1209

—— 2010 *Annual Review 2009–10*

Chamberlain, G. 2009 "No Internet Sex Please, We're Indian. Web Firms Observe New Law", *Guardian* 28/12/2009

Champod, C. and Chamberlain, P. 2009 "Fingerprints", in Fraser, J. and Williams, R. (eds) *Handbook of Forensic Science*, Cullompton: Willan

Chancer, L. and McLaughlin, E. 2007 "Public Criminologies: Diverse Perspectives on Academia and Policy", *Theoretical Criminology* 11, 155

Chang, C. 2007 *The Rise of the Chinese Empire: Nation, State, and Imperialism in Early China, ca. 1600 B.C.–A.D. 8*, Ann Arbor: University of Michigan Press

Chang, H. 2010 *23 Things they Don't Tell you about Capitalism*, London: Allen Lane

Chant, C. (ed.) 1998 *The Pre-Industrial Cities and Technology Reader*, Abingdon: Routledge

Childalert 2011 "Out and About: Death on the Roads", see http://www.childalert.co.uk/article.php?articles_id=196

Childnet 2007 "Cyberbullying", DCSF Publications, PO Box 5050

Chiras, D. 2005 *Environmental Science*, Sudbury, MA: Jones and Bartlett

Choo, R. 2009 "Responding to Online Child Sexual Grooming: An Industry Perspective", *AIC Trends and Issues in Crime and Criminal Justice* 379

Christianson, S. 2010 *The Last Gasp: The Rise and Fall of the American Gas Chamber*, Berkeley: University of California Press

Chuah, J. and Furmston, M. 2010 *Commercial and Consumer Law*, Harlow: Longman

CIA 2003 "The Darker Bioweapons Future", declassified briefing document, see http://www.fas.org/irp/cia/product/bw1103.pdf

CIFAS, Fraud Trends 2006–7 (document no longer accessible)

—— Fraud Trends 2007–8 (document no longer accessible)

—— 2009 "The Anonymous Attacker; A Special Report on Identity Fraud and Account Takeover", London: CIFAS

Clark, A. 2003 *Natural-Born Cyborgs*, Oxford: Oxford University Press

Clark, C. 1997 *Radium Girls: Women and Industrial Health Reform 1910–1935*, Chapel Hill: University of North Carolina Press

Clarke, R. (ed.) 1996 "Preventing Mass Transit Crime", *Crime Prevention Studies*, vol. 6, New York: Criminal Justice Press

—— 2004 "Technology, Criminology and Crime Science", *European Journal on Criminal Policy and Research* 10(1) 55–63

CNN 2001 "S. Africa to appeal on AIDS Ruling" 19/12/2001

—— 2002 "FBI: Cybercrime Rising", *CNN* 08/04/2002

Cockburn, J. S. 1977 "The Nature and Incidence of Crime, 1559–1625", in Cockburn, J. S. (ed.) *Crime in England 1550–1800*, London: Methuen

Coe, L. 1993 *The Telegraph: A History of Morse's Invention and Its Predecessors in the United States*, Jefferson, NC: McFarland & Company, Inc

COE 2010 "Prohibiting the Marketing and Use of the 'Mosquito' Youth Dispersal Device", *Council of Europe*, Doc. 12186, 22/03/2010

Coghlan, A. and Randerson, J. 2005 "How Far Should Fingerprints Be Trusted?", *New Scientist* 2517, 19/09/2005

Cohen, M. 2005 *The Costs of Crime and Justice*, London: Routledge

Cohen, S. (ed.) 1971 *Images of Deviance*, Harmondsworth: Penguin

—— 1988 *Against Criminology*, London: Transaction

Cole, S. 2001 *Suspect Identities: A History of Fingerprinting and Criminal Identification,* Cambridge: Harvard University Press
—— 2005 "More than Zero: Accounting for Error in Latent Fingerprint Identification", *Journal of Criminal Law and Criminology* 95(3)
Cole, S. and Dioso-Villa, R. 2009 "Investigating the 'CSI Effect' Effect: Media and Litigation Crisis in Criminal Law", *Stanford Law Review* 61(6)
Coleman, K. 2005 *A History of Chemical Warfare,* New York: Palgrave MacMillan
Coleman, R. and MacCahill, M. 2010 *Surveillance and Crime,* London: Sage
Coles, J. 2009 "Facebook Killer Jailed for Life", *Sun* 10/09/2009
Coley, N. 1999 "Forensic Chemistry in 19th-century Britain", *Endeavour* 22(4), 143–7
—— 2000 "The British Pharmaceutical Industry", in Russell, C. (ed.) *Chemistry, Society and Environment: A New History of the British Chemical Industry,* print on demand edn, London: Royal Society of Chemistry
Collard, F. 2008 *The Crime of Poison in the Middle Ages,* trans. D. Nelson-Campbell, Westport, CT: Praeger
Collins, J. and Jarvis, J. 2009 *The Wrongful Conviction of Forensic Science,* Crime Lab Report, July
Communications News 2000 "Cyber-crime on the Rise – Industry Trend or Event", 01/06/2000
Computer Economics 2007 "Trends in IT Security Threats: 2007", April
Conley, J. 1994 *The 1967 President's Crime Commission Report: Its Impact 25 Years Later,* Anderson
Conn, K. 2004 "Bullying and Harassment: A Legal Guide for Educators", Alexandria, VA: Association for Supervision & Curriculum Development
Conrad, P. 2005 *The Sociology of Health and Illness: Critical Perspectives,* New York: Worth
Cookson, C. 2010a "Critics Hit at Mobile Phone Cancer Study", *Financial Times,* 17/05/2010
—— 2010b "Forensic Science Service to Close", *Financial Times,* 15/12/2010
Cooper, J. and Sanchez, R. 2011 "Norway Shootings: July 28 as it Happened", *Daily Telegraph* 28/07/2011
Corbyn, Z. 2010 "Research Intelligence: Words of Warning", *Times Higher Education* 25/03/2010
Cordesman, A. 2005 *The Challenge of Biological Terrorism,* Washington DC: Center for Strategic and International Studies
Corley, T. 2003 "The British Pharmaceutical Industry since 1851", in Richmond, L., Stevenson, J. and Turton, A. (eds) *The Pharmaceutical Industry: A Guide to Historical Records,* Aldershot: Ashgate
Cornish, P. 2007 "The CBRN System: Assessing the Threat of Terrorist Use of Chemical, Biological, Radiological and Nuclear Weapons in the UK", London: Royal Institute of International Affairs
Corporate Watch 2010 "Company Files", see http://www.corporatewatch.org.uk/?lid=402
Coughlin, C. 2011 "Stuxnet Virus Attack: Russia Warns of 'Iranian Chernobyl'", *Daily Telegraph* 16/01/2011
CPS 2010 "Sentencing Manual – Possess Offensive Weapon", see http://www.cps.gov.uk/legal/s_to_u/sentencing_manual/possess_offensive_weapon/
—— 2011 "Special Measures", Crown Prosecution Service, Legal Guidance, see http://www.cps.gov.uk/legal/s_to_u/special_measures/

Crace, J. 2007 "Walk on the Wired Side: Jacket that Lets Parents Keep Track of Children", *Guardian* 23/10/07

Crawford, A. 2006 "Networked Governance and the Post-regulatory State?", *Theoretical Criminology* 10(4), 449–79

CRB Solutions 2009 Company website at crbsolutions.co.uk

Crellin, J. 2004 *A Social History of Medicines in the Twentieth Century: To Be Taken Three Times a Day*, London: Haworth Press

Croxson, K. 2007 "Promotional Piracy", *Oxonomics* 2, 1–2, 13–15

CSIS 2008 "Securing Cyberspace for the 44th Presidency", Washington DC: Center for Strategic and International Studies

Cukier, W. and Sidel, V. W. 2006, *The Global Gun Epidemic*, Westport, CT: Praeger Security International

Cullen, W. 2008 *Is Arsenic an Aphrodisiac?: The Sociochemistry of an Element*, London: Royal Society of Chemistry

Cunningham, S. 2005 "Incident, Accident, Catastrophe: Cyanide on the Danube", *Disasters* 29(2), 99–128

Cuomo, S. 2008 "Ancient Written Sources for Engineering and Technology", in Oleson, J. (ed.) *The Oxford Handbook of Engineering and Technology in the Classical World*, Oxford: Oxford University Press

Cusick, S. 2006 "Music as Torture / Music as Weapon", *TRANS-Transcultural Music Review* 10, see http://www.sibetrans.com/trans/trans10/cusick_eng.htm

Daily Mail 2007 "Innocent Man Repeatedly Mistaken for 'Saddam Stooge'", 18/06/2007

—— 2010 "Facebook Killer who Lured Teenager to her Death is Attacked in Prison by Fellow Inmate", 20/04/2010

Davie, N. 2006 *Tracing the Criminal: the Rise of Scientific Criminology in Britain 1860–1918*, Oxford: Bardwell Press

Davies, C. J. 2009 "The Hidden Censors of the Internet", *Wired* 20/05/2009

Davies, C. 2010 "Universities Told to Consider Dope Tests as Student Use of 'Smart Drugs' Soars", *Guardian* 21/02/2010

Davies, G. 2002 *A History of Money from Ancient Times to the Present Day*, 3rd edn, Cardiff: University of Wales Press

Davison, P. 2006 "The Early History of 'Non-Lethal' Weapons", Bradford: Bradford Non-Lethal Weapons Research Project

Deane, A. and Hamilton, D. 2010 "The Price is Wrong: The Cost of CCTV Surveillance in the United Kingdom", London: Big Brother Watch

Deazley, R., Kretschmer, M. and Bently, L. (eds) 2010 *Privilege and Property: Essays on the History of Copyright*, Cambridge: Open Book

Debord, G. 1994 *Society of the Spectacle*, New York: Zone Books

Delac, K. and Grgic, M. 2004 "A Survey of Biometric Recognition Methods", conference presentation, *ELMAR-2004 June*, Croatia

Deleuze, G. 1988 *Foucault*, London: Athlone Press

—— 1992 "Postscript on the Societies of Control", *October* 59, 3–7

Deleuze, G. and Guattari, F. 1983 *Anti-Oedipus: Capitalism and Schizophrenia*, Minneapolis: University of Minnesota Press

Delgado, M. 2007 "Tag Fiasco: Failures in Monitoring Terror Suspects", *Daily Mail* 07/07/2007

Dembner, A. 2001 "Drug Firm to Pay $875M Fine for Fraud", *The Boston Globe*, 04/10/2001, A13

Department of Labor 2008 "Fact Sheet #36: Employee Polygraph Protection Act of 1988", see http://www.dol.gov/whd/regs/compliance/whdfs36.htm

Desai, A. C. 2007 "Wiretapping before the Wires: The Post Office and the Birth of Communications Privacy", *Stanford Law Review* 60, 553ff.

de Vries, M. 1996 "Technology Education: Beyond the 'Technology is Applied Science' Paradigm", *Journal of Technology Education* 8(1)

Dhanapala, V. 2002 "International Law, Security, and Weapons of Mass Destruction", Showcase Program 2002, Spring Meeting of the Section of International Law and Practice, American Bar Association

Die Zeit 2011 "Betrayed by our own Data", *Zeit Online*, 2011

Diffie, W. and Landau, S. 2007 *Privacy on the Line: The Politics of Wiretapping and Encryption*, MIT Press

Dignan, L. 2010 "Virginia's IT Outage Doesn't Pass Management Sniff Test", *Zdnet* 30/08/2010

Diller, L. 2006 *The Last Normal Child: Essays on the Intersection of Kids, Culture, and Psychiatric Drugs*, Westport, CT: Praeger

Dillon, M. and Garland, L. 2005 *Ancient Rome: From the Early Republic to the Assassination of Julius Caesar*, London: Taylor & Francis

Dingle, J. 2005 "Dirty Bombs: Real Threat?", *Security* 42(4) pp.48ff

Di Nardo, J. 2006 "Freakonomics: Scholarship in the Service of Storytelling", *American Law and Economics Review* 8(3), 615–26

Diodorus Siculus 1947 *The Library of History*, Loeb Classical Library, Cambridge, MA: Harvard University Press

Diogenes Laertius 1991 *Lives of Eminent Philosophers*, trans. R. D. Hicks, Loeb Classical Library, Cambridge MA: Harvard University Press

Dixon, C. 2011 "Hate Speech and the Internet: A Vehicle for Violence?", *News One* 14/01/2011

Dixon, L. and Gill, B. 2002 *Changes in the Standards for Admitting Expert Evidence in Federal Civil Cases Since the Daubert Decision*, Pittsburgh, PA: RAND Institute for Civil Justice

Dobb, M. 1973 *Theories of Value and Distribution since Adam Smith*, Cambridge: Cambridge University Press

—— 1998 "Ford and GM Scrutinized for Alleged Nazi Collaboration", *Washington Post* 30/11/1998

Dodd, V. and Lewis, P. 2011 "Kettling of G20 protesters by Police Was Illegal, High Court Rules", *Guardian* 14/04/2011

Dolk, H., Vrijheid, M., Armstrong, B., Abramsky, L., Bianchi, F., Garne, E., Nelen, V., Robert, W., Scott, J. E. S., Stone, D. and Tenconi, R. 1998 "Risk of Congenital Anomalies near Hazardous Waste Landfill Sites in Europe: the EUROHAZCON study", *The Lancet* 352, 423–27

Doria, M. 2007 *Regulation and the Chemical Industry*, London: Royal Commission on Environmental Pollution

Doward, J. and Stevens, J. 2011 "Four Years on, Phone-Hacking Scandal is still Growing", *Observer*, 16/01/2011

Dresser, G. 2004 "Critics Turn on the 'Slow to Act' OFT", *Evening Standard* 28/03/2004

Dretske, F. 1981 *Knowledge and the Flow of Information*, Cambridge: Cambridge University Press

Drexler, K. E. 2001 "Machine-phase Nanotechnology", *Scientific American* 285(3), 74–75

Dror, I., Charlton, D. and Péron, A. 2006 "Contextual Information Renders Experts Vulnerable to Making Erroneous Identifications", *Forensic Science International* 156(1), 74–78

Dror, O. E. 1998 "Creating the Emotional Body: Confusion, Possibilities, and Knowledge", in Stearns, P. and Lewis, J. (eds) *Emotional History of the United States*, New York: New York University Press, 173–94

Drummond, K. 2010 "Human Trials Next for Darpa's Mind-Controlled Artificial Arm", *Wired* 15/07/2010

Dubois, P. 1991 *Torture and Truth*, New York: Routledge

Durnal, E. 2010 "Crime Scene Investigation (as Seen on TV)", *Forensic Science International* 199(1), 1–5

Dutelle, A. 2011 *An Introduction to Crime Scene Investigation*, Sudbury, MA: Jones and Bartlett

Dworkin, R. 1977 "Justice and Rights", in Dworkin, R. (ed.) *Taking Rights Seriously*, Cambridge MA: Harvard University Press, 150–83

Dyson, R. 2006 "Cosmetic Surgery Tourism", *Financial Mail* 13/06/2006

Eason, K. 2008 "Amputee Sprinter Oscar Pistorius Allowed to Compete in Beijing", *Times* 17/10/2008

Eastman, N. and Campbell, C. 2006 "Neuroscience and Legal Determination of Criminal Responsibility, Nature Reviews", *Neuroscience*, 7, 311–18

EC 2003 "Chemical Accidents (Seveso II)", European Commission

—— 2006 "What is Reach?", European Commission

Eckerman, I. 2004 *The Bhopal Saga – Causes and Consequences of the World's Largest Industrial Disaster*, Hyderabad: Universities Press

Economist 2010 "The Data Deluge", 25/02/2010

Edwards, A. 2010 "Evaluation of the Cardiff Night-time Economy Co-ordinator (NTEC) Post", Working Paper 133, Cardiff: Cardiff Centre for Crime, Law and Justice

Edwards, R. 2009 "French Student Murders: Dano Sonnex and Nigel Farmer Jailed for Life", *Daily Telegraph* 04/06/2009

Edwards, S., Edwards, T. and Fields, C. (eds) 1996 *Environmental Crime and Criminality: Theoretical and Practical Issues*, New York: Garland

EFF 2006 "CALEA", San Francisco: Electronic Frontier Foundation

Eggen, D. 2006 "U.S. Settles Suit Filed by Ore. Lawyer", *Washington Post* 30/11/2006

Eggerton, J. 2008 "Kids' Activists, Critics React to FTC Report", *Campaign for Commercial Free Childhood* 29/07/2008

Eisner, M. 2003 "Long-term Historical Trends of Violent Crime", *Crime and Justice: A Review of Research* 30, 83–142

Ekblom, P. 2002 "Stirchley Burglary Reduction Project, Birmingham, UK", Paper presented at the European Crime Prevention Network Conference: Summaries and Project Descriptions, Aalborg, 126–32

—— 2005 "How to Police the Future: Scanning for Scientific and Technological Innovations which Generate Potential Threats and Opportunities in Crime, Policing and Crime Reduction", in Tilley, N. and Smith, M. (eds) *Crime Science*, Cullompton: Willan

El Hai, J. 2005 *The Lobotomist: A Maverick Medical Genius and his Tragic Quest to Rid the World of Mental Illness*, New York: John Wiley

Ellis, K. 1958 *The Post in the Eighteenth Century: A Study in Administrative History*, Oxford: Oxford University Press

Elliston, J. 1999 *InTERRORgation: The CIA's Secret Manual on Coercive Questioning*, 2nd edn, San Francisco: AK Press

Ellul, J. 1964 *The Technological Society*, New York: Vintage Books

—— 1992 "Betrayal by Technology", video cassette, Amsterdam: Stichting ReRun Produkties

Elmer, G. 2004 *Profiling Machines*, Cambridge, MA: MIT Press

Elzinga, H. and Nijboer, J. 2006 "Probation Supervision through GPS", *European Journal of Crime Criminal Law and Criminal Justice* 14, 366–81(16)

Emsley, C. 1979 *Conflict and Stability in Europe*, London: Routledge

—— 1987 *Crime and Society in England, 1750–1900 (Themes in British Social History)*, Harlow: Longman

Emsley, J. 2006 *The Elements of Murder: A History of Poison*, Oxford: Oxford University Press

EPA 2010 "Lead Poisoning: A Historical Perspective", from Lewis, J., *EPA Journal* 1985

EPIC 2010 "Radio Frequency Identification (RFID) Systems", Washington DC: Electronic Privacy Information Center

EPUK 2010 "Noise Pollution", Brighton: Environmental Protection UK

Erdbrink, T. 2010 "Iranian Nuclear Scientist Killed, another Injured in Tehran Bombings", *Washington Post* 29/11/2010

Erdkamp, P. 2005 *The Grain Market in the Roman Empire: A Social, Political and Economic Study*, Cambridge: Cambridge University Press

Eriksson, A. and Lacerda, F. 2007 "Charlatanry in Speech Science: A Problem to Be Taken Seriously", *International Journal of Speech, Language and the Law* 14, 169–93

ESC 2007 "What Does the Law Say about Human Embryonic Stem Cell Research in Europe?", *EuroStemCell.org*

Espiner, T. 2006 "'Police Drowning in CCTV Data': Acpo", *Silicon.com* 18/05/2009

—— 2008 "Ashdown: Internet Is a 'Lawless Space'", *ZDNet* 27/11/2008

—— 2010 "Teenagers Accused of Running Cybercrime Ring", *ZDNet* 06/08/2010

Ess, C. 2009 *Digital Media Ethics*, Cambridge: Polity

Etzioni, A. 2000 *The Limits of Privacy*, New York: Basic Books

EU 2009 "EU Acts to Limit Health Risks from Exposure to Noise from Personal Music Players", Press Release, IP/09/1364

EUBusiness 2007 "US Lets Bayer off the Hook for GM Rice Contamination", Press Release 08/10/2007

Evans, G. W., Bullinger, M. and Hygge, S. 1998 "Chronic Noise Exposure and Physiological Response: A Prospective Study of Children Living under Environmental Stress", *Psychological Science* 9, 75–77

Evelyn, J. 1995 "London Redivivm", in de la Bédoyère, G. (ed.) *The Writings of John Evelyn*, Woodbridge: Boydell Press (sections also in Chant, 1998)

Fackler, M. 2007 "Fearing Crime, Japanese Wear the Hiding Place", *New York Times* 20/10/2007

Fahrenthold, D. 2006 "Statistics Show Drop in U.S. Rape Cases", *Washington Post* 19/06/2006

Faigman, D. 1999 *Legal Alchemy: The Use and Misuse of Science in the Law*, New York: St. Martin's Press

Farrell, G., Tseloni, A., Mailley, J. and Tilley, N. 2011 "The Crime Drop and the Security Hypothesis", *Journal of Research in Crime and Delinquency* 48(2), 147–75

Farrington, D., MacKenzie, D., Sherman, L. and Welsh, B. 2002 *Evidence-based Crime Prevention,* London: Routledge

Farrington, D. and Welsh, B. 2002 "Effects of Improved Street Lighting on Crime: A Systematic Review", Home Office Research Study 25

Faulhaber, G. 2006 "Solving the Interoperability Problem: Are We on the Same Channel?", *Federal Communications Law Journal* 59, 493–515

Fay, J. 2011 "Crime UK Site Gets 400m Hits, Drives Down Property Values", *Register* 07/03/2011

FBI 2008 "Crime in the Unites States 2008, Murder Victims by Weapon, 2004–2008", see http://www.fbi.gov/ucr/cius2008/offenses/expanded_information/data/shrtable_08.html

—— 2009 "National Crime Information Center", see http://www.fas.org/irp/agency/doj/fbi/is/ncic.htm

FDA 2010 "Significant Dates in US Food and Drug Law History", see http://www.fda.gov/aboutfda/whatwedo/history/milestones/ucm128305.htm

Feder, B. 2007 "VeriChip and FDA Ignored or Overlooked Animal Studies", *New York Times* 11/09/2007

Feenberg, A. 1991 *Critical Theory of Technology,* New York: Oxford University Press

—— 1996 "Marcuse or Habermas: Two Critiques of Technology", *Inquiry* 39(1), 45–70

—— 2002 *Transforming Technology: A Critical Theory Revisited,* New York: Oxford University Press

Feldman, H. 1995 "Science and Uncertainty in Mass Exposure Litigation", *Texas Law Review* 74

Felson, M. 1994 *Crime and Everyday Life. Insight and Implications for Society,* Thousand Oaks: Pine Forge Press

Fenn, E. 2000 "Biological Warfare in Eighteenth-Century North America: Beyond Jeffery Amherst", *Journal of American History* 86(4), 1552–80

Fenton, N. and Neil, M. 2011 "On Limiting the Use of Bayes in Presenting Forensic Evidence", Draft paper submitted to *Forensic Science International,* see https://www.eecs.qmul.ac.uk/~norman/papers/likelihood_ratio.pdf

Ferguson, C. 2010 "Sexting Behaviours amongst Young Hispanic Women", presentation, British Society of Criminology, Leicester, 2010

Ferran, L. 2010 "Haditha Killings: Last Marine May Not See Trial", *ABC News* 23/03/2010

Filler, A. 2009 "The History, Development and Impact of Computed Imaging in Neurological Diagnosis and Neurosurgery", *Nature Precedings,* prepublication document CT, MRI, and DTI

Fischer, F. 1989 *Technocracy and the Politics of Expertise,* Newbury Park, CA: Sage

Fitch, C., Hamilton, S., Bassett, P. and Davey, R. 2010 *Debt and Mental Health. What Do We Know? What Should We Do?,* London: Royal College of Psychiatrists and Rethink

Fitzgerald, P. and Leopold, M. 1986 *Stranger on the Line: Secret History of Phone Tapping,* London: The Bodley Head

Fiveash, K. 2010 "China Gives Google Nod of Approval, Renews Licence", *The Register* 12/07/2010

Floridi, L. 2003 "Information", in Floridi, L. (ed.) *The Blackwell Guide to the Philosophy of Computing and Information,* Malden, MA and Oxford: Blackwell, 41–61

Flowers, R. and Flowers, H. 2004 *Murders in the United States: Crimes, Killers and Victims of the Twentieth Century*, Jefferson, NC: McFarland

Foddy, B. and Savulescu, J. 2007 "Ethics of Performance Enhancement in Sport", in Ashcroft, R., Dawson, A., Draper, H. and McMillan, J. (eds) *Principles of Health Care Ethics*, 2nd edn, London: John Wiley & Sons, 511–20

FOE 2006 "Cases of GM Rice Contamination in Europe", FoWW Biotechnology Programme

Fogel, D. 2006, *Evolutionary Computation: Toward a New Philosophy of Machine Intelligence*, 3rd edn, Piscataway, NJ: IEEE Press

Fogli, A. 2009 "France Sets Standards for Practice of Aesthetic Surgery", *Clinical Risk* 15(6), 22–226

Ford, Ch. V 1995 *Lies! Lies!! Lies!!! The Psychology of Deceit*, Washington: American Psychiatric Press

Ford, R. 2008 "Sex Offenders Face Lie-Detector Tests to Assess their Risk to the Public", *Times* 20/09/2008

ForeignTradex 2010 "US–Israel Trade Relations", see http://www.foreign-tradeexchange.com/countries/israel.html

Fortune 2008 "Fortune 500: Top Industries: Fast Growers", *CNN Money* 05/05/2008

Foster, K. and Jaeger, J. 2008 "Ethical Implications of Implantable Radio-frequency Identification (RFID) Tags in Humans", *American Journal of Bioethics* 8(8), 44–48

Foucault, M. 1970 *The Order of Things*, New York: Pantheon

—— 1975 *Discipline and Punish: The Birth of the Prison*, New York: Random House

—— 1988 "Technologies of the Self", in Martin, L. H., Gutman, H. and Hutton, R. H. (eds) *Technologies of the Self: A Seminar with Michel Foucault*, London: Tavistock, 16–49

—— 1998 *History of Sexuality Volume 1: The Will to Knowledge*, London: Penguin

Fox, M. 2010 "U.S. Apologizes for Syphilis Experiment in Guatemala", *Reuters* 01/10/2010

Frank, J. 1976 "Body Snatching: A Grave Medical Problem", *Yale Journal of Biology and Medicine* 49, 399–410

Frank, T. 2009 "Use of Federal Database for ID Checks Hits some Bumps", *USA Today* 06/02/2009

French, M. and Phillips, J. 2009 *Cheated Not Poisoned?: Food Regulation in the United Kingdom, 1875–1938*, Manchester: Manchester University Press

Freud, S. 1962 *Civilization and its Discontents*, trans. J. Strachey, New York: Norton

Friedman, R. 1994, "The Death and Transfiguration of Frye", *Jurimetrics* 34, 133

Frith, M. 2006 "Prozac Cleared for Children Aged Eight Despite Fears of Suicide Risk", *Independent* 08/06/2006

Fronc, J. 2009 *New York Undercover: Private Surveillance in the Progressive Era*, Chicago: University of Chicago Press

Frumkin, W., Wasserstrom, A., Davidson, A. and Grafit, A. 2009 "Authentication of Forensic DNA Samples", *FSI Genetics* 4(2), 95–103

FTC 2007 *FTC Practice and Procedure Manual*, Chicago: American Bar Association

Fukuyama, F. 2000 *Our Posthuman Future: The Consequences of the Biotechnology Revolution*, London: Profile Books

Furter, W. 1982 *A Century of Chemical Engineering*, New York: Plenum Press

Gandy, O. 2006 "Data Mining, Surveillance, and Discrimination in the Post-9/11 Environment", in Haggerty, J. and Ericson, R. (eds) *The New Politics of Surveillance and Visibility*, Toronto: University of Toronto Press

Gardner, P. L. 1994 "The Relationship between Technology and Science: Some Historical and Philosophical Reflections. Part 1", *International Journal of Technology and Design Education* 4(2), 123–54

—— 1995 "The Relationship between Technology and Science: Some Historical and Philosophical Reflections. Part 2", *International Journal of Technology and Design Education* 5(1), 1–33

Garfinkel, H. 1967 *Studies in Ethnomethodology*, Englewood Cliffs, NJ: Prentice Hall

Garfinkel, S. and Holtzman, H. 2005 "Understanding RFID Technology", in Garfinkel, S. and Rosenberg, B. (eds) *RFID: Applications, Security, and Privacy*, Addison-Wesley Professional

Garland, D. 1997 "'Governmentality' and the Problem of Crime: Foucault, Criminology, Sociology", *Theoretical Criminology* 1(2), 173–214

—— 2001 *The Culture of Control: Crime and Social Order in Contemporary Society*, Oxford: Oxford University Press

Garner, R. 2002 "The Forensic Polygraph" in Levinson, D. (ed.) *Encyclopedia of Crime and Punishment*, Thousand Oaks, CA: Sage, 725–27

Gartner 2003 "Gartner Says Identity Theft Is up Nearly 80 percent", Gartner, Inc. Press Release

Garton, S. 2010 "Eugenics in Australia and New Zealand: Laboratories of Racial Science", in Bashford and Levine 2010

Gaskill, M. 2003 *Crime and Mentalities in Early Modern England*, Cambridge Studies in Early Modern British History, Cambridge: Cambridge University Press

Geddes, J. 1990 "Iron", in Blair, J. W. and Ramsay, N. (eds) *English Medieval Industries*, London: Hambledon Press, 168–73

Geers, K. 2011 "Smart Phone Applications Help People Meet", *Pennlive* 13/02/2011

Gehlen, A. 1965 "Anthropologische Ansicht der Technik", in Freyer, H., Papalekas, J. C. and Weippert, G. (eds) *Technik im Technischen Zeitlater*, Dusseldorf: J. Schilling, 101–18

Geis, G. 1959 "In Scopolamine Veritas: The Early History of Drug-Induced Statements", *Journal of Criminal Law, Criminology, and Police Science* 50(4), 347–57

GeneWatch 1999 *Leaking from the Lab? The 'Contained' Use of Genetically Modified Micro-organisms in the UK*, Buxton: GeneWatch 28/06/1999

—— 2005 *GM Contamination Report 2005*, Buxton: GeneWatch

—— 2010 *Genetic Testing in Insurance and Employment*, Buxton: GeneWatch

Gerrard G., Parkins, G., Cunningham, I., Hill, W., Jones, S. and Douglass, S. 2007 "The National CCTV Strategy", Report for the Home Office, October

Gerrie, J. 2003 "Was Foucault a Philosopher of Technology?", *Techné* 7(2)

Gibb, F. 2009 "Why the Law Commission Is Worried about Expert Evidence", *Times* 07/04/2009

Giddens, A. 1981 *A Contemporary Critique of Historical Materialism. Volume 1: Power, Property and the State*, London: Macmillan

—— 1990 *The Consequences of Modernity*, Stanford, CA: Stanford University Press

Giles, J. 2008 "How Merck Made a Killing", *Prospect Magazine*, November

Gill, M. and Spriggs, A. 2005 "Assessing the Impact of CCTV", Home Office Research Study 292

Gilligan A 2005 "Revealed: How Blair is Playing the Fear Card", *London Evening Standard* 20/06/2005

Gilson, C. 2009 "The Admissibility of Expert Evidence in Criminal Proceedings in England and Wales", Discussion Paper

Gimpel, J. 1976 *The Medieval Machine: The Industrial Revolution of the Middle Ages*, London: Penguin

Giridharadas, A. 2008 "India's Use of Brain Scans in Courts Dismays Critics", *New York Times* 15/09/2008

GLA 2006 *Report of the 7 July Review Committee*, London: Greater London Authority

Glickman, S., McHutchison, J., Peterson, E. and Cairns, C. 2009 "Ethical and Scientific Implications of the Globalization of Clinical Research", *New England Journal of Medicine* 360(8), 816–23

Gloor, P. 1980 "Bertillon's Method and Anthropological Research", *Journal of the Forensic Science Society* 20(2), 9–101

GNP 2005 "Criminalisation of HIV Transmission in Europe", GNP Europe and Terrence Higgins Trust

Godwin, B. 2003 "Crimewave Set to Continue, Says FBI", *ComputerWeekly* 09/06/2003

Goffman, H. 1959 *The Presentation of Self in Everyday Life*, New York: Doubleday

Goldacre, B. 2009 "Is this a Joke?, Bad Science", *Guardian* 18/07/2009

Goldberg, A. 2010 "Women Caught in a Bad Romance by Bogus US Soldiers", BBC 26/09/2010

Goldenburg, S. 2010 "Obama's Green Agenda under Attack from Group Linked to Chemical Industry", *Guardian* 21/04/2010

Goldgar, C. 2010 "The Genetic Information Nondiscrimination Act (GINA): How PAs Can Protect Patients and their Families", *Journal of American Physician Assistants*, July

Goldsmith J. and Wu T. 2006 *Who Controls the Internet: Illusions of a Borderless World*, Oxford, Oxford University Press

Goodman, N. 1976 *Languages of Art: An Approach to a Theory of Symbols*, Indianapolis: Hackett

Goold, B. 2004 *CCTV and Policing: Public Area Surveillance and Police Practices in Britain*, Clarendon Studies in Criminology, Oxford: Oxford University Press

Gould, S. J. 1981 *The Mismeasure of Man*, New York: Norton

Grabosky, P. 1998 "Technology and Crime Control", AIC, *Trends & Issues in Crime and Criminal Justice* 78, January

Gradwohl, R. B. H. 1976 *Gradwohl's Legal Medicine*, Bristol: J. Wright and Chicago: Year Book Medical Publications

Graham, N. 2010 "The Hard Sell in Cosmetic Surgery Advertising", *British Medical Journal*, 16 March, 340, c1223

Granick, J. 2006 "The Lie Behind Lie Detectors", *Wired* 15/03/2006

Grant, G. 1991 *Technology and Justice*, Concord, ON: House of Anansi Press

Grant, M. 1967 *Gladiators*, New York: Delacorte Press

Gray, S. 2007 "Should Schools Fingerprint Your Kids?", *Time Magazine* 25/09/2009

Greek, D. 2006 "BT Launches Identity Theft Insurance Policy", *ComputerActive* 23/02/2006

Green, R. 2007 *Babies by Design: The Ethics of Genetic Choice*, New Haven, CT: Yale University Press

Greenberg, A. 2010 "Full-Body Scan Technology Deployed in Street-Roving Vans", *Forbes* 24/08/2010

Greenpeace 2002 "Corporate Crimes: Mining Cases", *Archive*, June

Greenwood, J. 1869 *The Seven Curses of London*, Boston: Field Osgood

Greer, G. and Tolbert, R. 1998 "A Method of Conducting Therapeutic Sessions with MDMA", *Journal of Psychoactive Drugs* 30(4), 371–9

Groombridge, N. 2008 "Victims and Offenders in the Great Car Economy", *Howard Journal of Criminal Justice* 47(3), 313–15

Gross, S. R. 1991 "Expert Evidence", *Wisconsin Law Review* 1113–232

Guardian 2010 "Bach to Basics Regime Deters School Troublemakers", 18/01/2010

Gudjonsson, G. H. 1988 "How to Defeat the Polygraph Tests", in Gale, A. (ed.) *The Polygraph Test. Truth, Lies and Science*, London: Sage, 126–36

Gunaratna, R. and Steven, G. 2004 *Counter-terrorism: A Reference Handbook*, Oxford: ABC-CLIO

Gustin, S. 2010 "FCC Passes Compromise Net Neutrality Rules", *Wired* 21/12/2010

Habermas, J. 1970 "Technology and Science as 'Ideology'", in *Toward a Rational Society; Student Protest, Science, and Politics*, Boston: Beacon Press

—— 1991 *The Structural Transformation of the Public Sphere*, Cambridge, MA: MIT Press

Haggerty, J. and Ericson, R. (eds) 2006 *The New Politics of Surveillance and Visibility*, Toronto: University of Toronto Press

Hakim, S. and Rengert, G. (eds) 1981 *Crime Spillover*, Beverly Hills, CA: Sage

Halderman, J. and Felten, E. 2006 "Lessons from the Sony CD DRM Episode", USENIX-SS'06 Proceedings of the 15th Conference on USENIX Security Symposium, vol. 15

Haley, B. 1978 *The Healthy Body and Victorian Culture*, Cambridge, MA: Harvard University Press

Hall, E. 1959 *The Silent Language*, New York: Doubleday

Hall, S., Winlow, S. and Ancrum, C. 2008 *Criminal Identities and Consumer Culture: Crime Exclusion and the New Culture of Narcissism*, Cullompton: Willan

Halliday, J. 2011 "Police Arrest Five over Anonymous WikiLeaks Attacks", *Guardian* 28/01/2011

Hallsworth, S. 2005 *Street Crime*, Cullompton: Willan

Han, J. and Kamber, M. 2006 *Data Mining: Concepts and Techniques*, San Francisco: Morgan Kaufmann

Hanff, A. 2008 "City of London Police – Too complex to spend public money." No DPI, see: https://nodpi.org/2008/09/22/city-of-london-police-to-complex-to-spend-public-money/

Hankinson, R. J. 2008 *The Cambridge Companion to Galen*, Cambridge: Cambridge University Press

Hansson, S. 2006 "Safe Design", *Techné* 10(1)

Haraway, D. 1991 "A Cyborg Manifesto: Science, Technology, and Socialist-Feminism in the Late Twentieth Century", in *Simians, Cyborgs and Women: The Reinvention of Nature*, New York: Routledge, 149–81

Harman, T. 1566 A Caveat for Common Cursitors, Vulgarly Called Vagabonds, in Kinney, A.K. *Rogues, Vagabonds and Sturdy Beggars*, Amherst, MA: University of Massachusetts Press, 1973

Harmel, K. 2006 "Walt Disney World: The Government's Tomorrowland?", *News21*, 01/09/2006

Harmon, K. 2009 "Biohackers' Brewing New Life-Forms in a Basement Near You", *Scientific American* 12/05/2009

Harries, K. 2007 *Law and Crime in the Roman World*, Cambridge: Cambridge University Press

Harris, J. 2007 *Enhancing Evolution. The Ethical Case for Making Better People*, Oxford: Princeton University Press

Harris, R. and Paxman, J. 1982 A *Higher Form of Killing: The Secret Story of Gas and Germ Warfare*, London: Chatto and Windus

Harris, S. H. 1994 *Factories of Death: Japanese Biological Warfare 1932–45 and the American Cover-Up*, London and New York: Routledge

Hartwell, R. M. 1990 "Was there an Industrial Revolution?", *Social Science History* 14(4), 567–76

Harvey, D. 1989 *The Condition of Postmodernity*, Oxford: Blackwell

Hassan, A. and Hill, D. 1986 *Islamic Technology: An Illustrated History*, Cambridge: Cambridge University Press

Hassenzahl, M., Beu, A. and Burmester, M. 2001 "Engineering Joy", *IEEE Software* January/February

Hattenstone, S. and Taylor, M. 2010 "Inquiry Call after Video Evidence Clears Man Accused of Violence at Protest", *Guardian* 25/03/2010

Hawkes, N. 2007 "Scan or Scandal?" *Times* 14/06/2007

Hayes, R. 2008 "An Emerging Consensus: Human Biotechnology Policies around the World", *Science Progress*, November

Hayles, N. K. 1999 *How We Became Posthuman: Virtual Bodies in Cybernetics, Literature and Informatics*, Chicago: University of Chicago Press

Haynes, R. 2006 "The Alchemist in Fiction: The Master Narrative", *Hyle* 12(I)

Hayward, K. 2004 *City Limits: Crime, Consumer Culture and the Urban Experience*, London: Glasshouse Press

—— 2007 "Situational Crime Prevention and its Discontents: Rational Choice Theory versus the 'Culture of Now'", *Social Policy & Administration* 41(3), 232–50

HC 1914 "Report from the Select Committee on Patent Medicines", Session 1914, HC 414

—— 2004 "Provision of Cosmetic Surgery in England", Healthcare Commission Report

—— 2005a "The Influence of the Pharmaceutical Industry", HC 42-I [Incorporating HC 1030-i-iii]

—— 2005b "Forensic Science on Trial", 7th Report, HC 96-1

—— 2005c "Select Committee on Science and Technology", 7th Report

HCSTC 2011 "The Forensic Science Service", House of Commons Science and Technology Committee Report, HC 855, July

Heaton, P. and Garicano, L. 2007 "Information Technology, Organisation and Productivity in the Public Sector: Evidence from Police Departments", CEP Discussion Paper No. 826

Heidegger, M. 1949/1977 "The Question Concerning Technology", in *The Question Concerning Technology and Other Essays*, ed. and trans. W. Lovitt, New York: Harper & Row, 3–35

Hennessey, P. 2007 "Labour Will Force Everyone to Give Fingerprints at ID Card Interview Centres", *Daily Telegraph* 19/02/2007

Herodotus 2004 *The Histories*, trans. C. Godley, Loeb Classical Library, Cambridge, MA: Harvard University Press

Hesiod 2006 *Theogeny* in Schlegel, C. M. and Weinfield, H. (trans.) *Theogony and Works and Days*, Ann Arbor: University of Michigan Press

Heyes, C. and Jones, M. (eds) 2009 *Cosmetic Surgery: A Feminist Primer*, Aldershot: Ashgate

HGC 2010 "Understanding Genetic Discrimination" Human Genetics Commission working group, see hgc.gov.uk "Our Work: Genetic Discrimination"

Hiatt, A. 2004 *The Making of Medieval Forgeries: False Documents in Fifteenth-Century England*, London: British Library

Hickman, M. 2010 "Bad Chemistry: The Poison in the Plastic that Surrounds Us", *Independent* 31/03/2010

Higginson, J. 2011 "Balaclava Ban for Cuts Protest Yobs", *Metro* 28/03/2011

Higham, C. 1984 *Trading with the Enemy*, New York: Dell

Highfield, R. 2008 "Nanoparticle Method May Be Able to Inject Drugs Deep into the Brain", *Daily Telegraph* 22/09/2008

Hildebrandt, M. 2008a "Legal and Technological Normativity: More (and Less) than Twin Sisters", *Techné* 12(3)

—— 2008b "Ambient Intelligence, Criminal Liability and Democracy", *Criminal Law and Philosophy* 2(2), 163–80

Hildebrandt, M. and Rouvroy, A. 2011 *Law, Human Agency and Autonomic Computing: The Philosophy of Law Meets the Philosophy of Technology*, London: Routledge

Hill, A. 2010 "Judges Are Resigned to Jurors Researching their Trials Online", *Guardian* 04/10/2010

Hillyard, P., Sim, J., Toms, S. and Whyte, D. 2004 "Leaving a 'Stain upon the Silence' Contemporary Criminology and the Politics of Dissent", *British Journal of Criminology* 44(3), 369–90

Hobbs, D. 1994 "Professional and Organized Crime in Britain", in Maguire, M., Morgan, R. and Reiner, R. (eds) *The Oxford Handbook of Criminology*, Oxford: Clarendon Press, 441–68 (457ff.)

—— 2001 "The Firm: Criminal Culture and Organisational Logic on Shifting Terrain", *British Journal of Criminology* 41, 549–60

Hobsbawm, E.J. 1969 *The Pelican Economic History of Britain, Volume 3, Industry and Empire*, Harmondsworth: Penguin

HOC 2010 "European Information and Network Safety Agency", Select Committee Comments

Hoffman, D. 1998 *The Oklahoma City Bombing and the Politics of Terror*, Venice, CA: Feral House

Holder, E., Robinson, L. and Rose, K. 2009 "High Priority Criminal Justice Technology Needs", NCJ 225375, Washington DC: National Institute of Justice

Holt, M. and Andrews, A. 2007 "Nuclear Power Plants: Vulnerability to Terrorist Attack", CRS Report for Congress, RS21131

Home Office 2003 "DNA: 21st Century Crime Fighting Tool", July

—— 2006 "Updated Estimate of the Cost of Identity Fraud to the UK Economy", see http://www.identitytheft.org.uk/cms/assets/Cost_of_Identity_Fraud_to_the_UK_Economy_2006-07.pdf

—— 2010 "Statistics on Police Use of Firearms in England and Wales 2008–09"

Hope, C. 2009 "1,000 CCTV Cameras to Solve Just One Crime, Met Police Admits", *Daily Telegraph* 25/08/2009

Hope, T. 2004, "Pretend it Works: Evidence and Governance in the Evaluation of the Reducing Burglary Initiative", *Criminal Justice* 4(3), 287–308.

—— 2006 "Book Review: Crime Science: New Approaches to Preventing and Detecting Crime", *Theoretical Criminology* 10, 245

Hopkins, M., Mahdi, S., Thomas, S. and Patel, P. 2006 "The Patenting of Human DNA: Global Trends in Public and Private Sector Activity (The PATGEN Project)", Brighton: SPRU, Science and Technology Policy Research, University of Sussex

Horkheimer, M. 1972 "Traditional and Critical Theory", in *Critical Theory: Selected Essays*, New York: Herder and Herder

Hornung, G. 2007 "The European Regulation on Biometric Passports", *SCRIPTed* 4(3), 246

Horvath F. and Palmatier, J. 2008 "Effect of Two Types of Control Questions and Two Question Formats on the Outcomes of Polygraph Examinations", *Journal of Forensic Sciences* 53, 889–99

Hough, A. 2010 "Rehab Clinic for Children Internet and Technology Addicts Founded", *Daily Telegraph* 18/03/2010

Hough, M. 2010 "Gold Standard or Fool's Gold? The Pursuit of Certainty in Experimental Criminology", *Criminology and Criminal Justice* 10(1), 11–22

HRW 2009 "Rain of Fire: Israel's Unlawful Use of White Phosphorus in Gaza", Human Rights Watch

HSE 2008 "Major Accidents Notified to the European Commission for: England, Wales and Scotland 2000–2001", http://www.hse.gov.uk/comah/eureport/car2001a. htm

Hsu, S. 2009a "Local Police Want Right to Jam Wireless Signals", *Washington Post* 01/02/2009

—— 2009b "Administration Kills Bush Program to Give Police Access to Spy Satellite Data", *Washington Post* 24/06/2009

Huber, P. 1990 *Liability: The Legal Revolution and its Consequences*, New York: Basic Books

—— 1999 *Galileo's Revenge: Junk Science in the Courtroom*, New York: Basic Books

Hudson, P. 1992 *The Industrial Revolution*, London: Edward Arnold

Huff, C. and Killias, M. 2008 *Wrongful Conviction: International Perspectives on Miscarriages of Justice*, Philadelphia: Temple University Press

Hugill, P. 1999 *Global Communications since 1844: Geopolitics and Technology*, Maryland: Johns Hopkins University

Hulse, C. and Zernike, K. 2011 "Bloodshed Puts New Focus on Vitriol in Politics", *New York Times* 08/01/2011

Hummer, D. 2007 "Policing and 'Hard' Technology", in Byrne and Rebovich 2007, 133–52

Humphrey, J., Oleson, J. and Sherwood, A. 1997 *Greek and Roman Technology: A Sourcebook – Annotated Translations of Greek and Latin Texts and Documents*, New York: Routledge

Hyslop, J. 1984 *The Inka Road System*, New York: Academic Press: New York

IAEA, 2001 "Board of Governors Report to General Conference", Vienna: International Atomic Energy Agency, 14/08/2001

—— 2002 "Tracing the Source: Nuclear Forensics and Illicit Nuclear Trafficking", Vienna: International Atomic Energy Agency, 18/10/2002

—— 2011 "Fukushima Nuclear Accident Update Log", Vienna: International Atomic Energy Agency

IARC 2011 "IARC Classifies Radiofrequency Magnetic Fields as Possibly Carcinogenic to Humans", Press Release 208, May

IAS 2011 "Law of the 12 Tables", *Internet Ancient History Sourcebook*, see http://www.fordham.edu/halsall/ancient/12tables.html

IBC 2010 "For the Public Record, in the Public Interest", Iraq Body Count – analysis, see http://www.iraqbodycount.org/analysis/qa/aclu-ibc/

ICBL 2011 "States Not Party to Treaty", International Campaign to Ban Landmines, see http://www.icbl.org/

ICO 2008 "The Use of Biometrics in Schools", Statement, August, Wilmslow: Information Commissioner's Office

—— 2009 "ICO Seizes Covert Database of Construction Industry Workers", Press Release, 06/03/2009, Wilmslow: Information Commissioner's Office

—— 2010 "Freedom of Information Act: Decision Notice Ref: S50280571, Ihde, D. 1983 *Existential Technics*", Albany: New York University Press

ICRC 2009 "Mine Ban Convention: Despite Progress Made, Victim Assistance Falls Short", Landmines and International Humanitarian Law, International Committee of the Red Cross

Illustrated London News 1858 "Fetes at New York to Commemorate the Laying of the Atlantic Telegraph Cable", 25/09/1858, see http://atlantic-cable.com/1858NY/

Inman, K. and Rudin, N. 2001 *Principles and Practice of Criminalistics: The Profession of Forensic Science*, Boca Raton, FL: CRC Press

Innes, B. 1998 *The History of Torture*, New York: St. Martin's Press

Inness, J. 1992 *Privacy, Intimacy and Isolation*, Oxford: Oxford University Press

Innis, H. 1950/2007 *Empire and Communications*, Toronto: Dundurn Press

Introna, L. and Nissenbaum, H. 2009 "Facial Recognition Technology, A Survey of Policy and Implementation Issues", Report of the Center for Catastrophe Preparedness and Response, New York: New York University

IOSCO 2011 "Regulatory Issues Raised by the Impact of Technological Changes on Market Integrity and Efficiency", International Organization of Securities Commissions Report, CR02/11 July

Irvine, C. 2008 "Police to Use Handheld Fingerprint Scanners in the Street", *Daily Telegraph* 27/10/2008

Isaac, P. 1953 "Air Pollution and Man's Health", *Public Health Reports (1896–1970)*, 68(9), 868–70

ISIS 2009 "Information Systems Improvement Strategy (ISIS): Implementation and Development Programme for 2009–10", London: National Policing Improvement Agency

ISO, 2006 International Organization for Standardization ISO 20282-1:2006, see http://www.iso.org/iso/catalogue_detail.htm?csnumber=34122

ITF 2011 "Rules: The Racket", London: International Tennis Federation

Jackson, A. and Jackson, J. 2007 *Forensic Science*, Englewood Cliffs, NJ: Prentice Hall

Jackson, N. 2005 "Music to Deter Yobs by", BBC 10/01/2005

Jackson, T. 1996 *Material Concerns: Pollution, Profit and Quality of Life*, London: Routledge

Jasanoff, S. 2005 "Law's Knowledge: Science for Justice in Legal Settings", *American Journal of Public Health*, Supplement 1, 95, 49–58

Jefferson, M. 2003 *Criminal Law*, Harlow: Longman

Jeffries, J. 2005 "The UK Population: Past, Present and Future", in Office for National Statistics, *Focus on People and Migration*, Basingstoke: Palgrave Macmillan, ch. 1

Jenkins, B. M. 2008 *Will Terrorists Go Nuclear?*, Amherst, NY: Prometheus

—— 2010 *Would-Be Warriors: Incidents of Jihadist Terrorist Radicalization in the United States Since September 11, 2001*, RAND Occasional Paper Series

Jerome, F. 2002 *The Einstein File: J. Edgar Hoover's Secret War against the World's Most Famous Scientist*, New York: St. Martin's Press

Johnson, B. 2009 "Danish Schools Ready to Trial Internet Access during Exams", *Guardian* 11/05/09

—— 2009a "GPS Wristwatch Helps Parents Track Children", *Guardian* 12/01/2009

—— 2009b "Danish Schools Ready to Trial Internet Access during Exams", *Guardian* 11/05/2009

—— 2010 "Privacy No Longer a Social Norm, Says Facebook Founder", *Guardian* 11/01/2010

Johnson, E. and Monkkonen, E. (eds) 1996 *The Civilization of Crime: Violence in Town and Country since the Middle Ages*, Champaign, IL: University of Illinois Press

Johnson, W. 2010 "Warning over Twitter Impact on Jury Trials", *Independent* 19/11/2010

Johnston, L. and Shearing, C. 2002 *Governing Security: Explorations in Policing and Justice*, London: Routledge

Jonas, H. 1979 *The Imperative of Responsibility: In Search of Ethics for the Technological Age*, Chicago: University of Chicago Press

Jones, C. 1994 *Expert Witnesses, Science, Medicine and the Practice of Law*, Oxford: Clarendon Press

Jones, J. 1993 "The Tuskegee Syphilis Experiment: 'A Moral Astigmatism'", in Harding, S. (ed.) *The "Racial" Economy of Science: Toward a Democratic Future*, Bloomington: Indiana University Press, 275–86.

Jones, S. E. 2006 *Against Technology: From the Luddites to Neo-Luddism*, London: Routledge

Jones, Y. and Newburn, T. 2006 *Plural Policing: A Comparative Perspective*, London and New York: Routledge

Jordan, M. 2006 "Amateur Videos Are Putting Official Abuse in New Light", *Washington Post* 15/11/2006

Josephus 1987 *The Works of Josephus*, trans. W. Whiston, Peabody, MA: Hendrickson

Joyner, D. 2009 *International Law and the Proliferation of Weapons of Mass Destruction*, Oxford: Oxford University Press

Judson, K. 1997 *Myths and Legends of the Pacific Northwest*, Lincoln: University of Nebraska Press

Juvenal 1992 *The Satires*, trans. N. Rudd, Oxford: Oxford University Press

Kablenet 2008 "DNA Database Costs Soar", *Register* 05/09/2008

Kaczynski, T. 1995 *Industrial Society and its Future (The Unabomber Manifesto)*, Jolly Roger Press

Kaeuper, R. 1988 *War, Justice, and Public Order: England and France in the Later Middle Ages*, Oxford: Clarendon Press

Kali-Nyah, I. 2000 *Italy's War Crimes in Ethiopia, 1935–41: Evidence for the War Crimes Commission*, special year 2000 edn, Chicago: The Ethiopian Holocaust Remembrance Committee

Kalla-Bishop, P. 1977 *The Golden Years of Trains, 1830–1920*, London: Phoebus

Kapp, E. 1877 *Grundlinien einer Philosophie der Technik*, Braunschweig: Verlag George Westermann

Kavoulakos, K. 1998 "Nature, Science and Technology in Habermas", *Democracy & Nature* 1, 112–45

Keegan, J. 1994 *A History of Warfare*, New York: Vintage

Kellaway, J. 2002 *The History of Torture and Execution: From Early Civilization through Medieval Times to the Present*, New York: The Lyons Press

Kelley, T. 1998 "Calling on Technology to Build a Better Handcuff", *New York Times* 03/09/1998

Kellner, D. 1999 "Virilio, War, and Technology: Some Critical Reflections", *Theory, Culture & Society* 16(5–6), 103–25

Kelly, J. 2004 *Gunpowder: Alchemy, Bombards, and Pyrotechnics: The History of the Explosive that Changed the World*, New York: Basic Books

Kelly, J. and Wearne, P. 2002 *Tainting Evidence: Inside the Scandals at the FBI Crime Lab*, New York: Free Press

Kelly, L., Lovett, J. and Regan, L. 2005 "A Gap or a Chasm? Attrition in Reported Rape Cases", Home Office Research Study 293

Kennedy, D. 2005 "Cot-death Expert Gave Murder Trial Jury Misleading Evidence", *Times* 22/06/2005

Kentish Express 2010 "Arrests after Shopping Trolley Thrown off Ashford Car Park", 13/05/2010

Kerr, I., Lucock, C. and Steeves, V. 2009 *Lessons from the Identity Trail: Anonymity, Privacy and Identity in a Networked Society*, Oxford: Oxford University Press

Kerr, O. 2005 "Digital Evidence and the New Criminal Procedure", *Columbia Law Review*, January

Kershaw, C., Nicholas, S. and Walker, A. 2008 "Crime in England and Wales 2007/08", *Home Office Statistical Bulletin*, July

Khor, M. 2009 "Row over Seizure of Low-cost Drugs Exposes Dangers of TRIP-Plus Measures", *South Bulletin* 41, 22/09/2009

Kidshield 2010 "Alarming Statistics", see http://www.kidshield.eu/kidshield_alarming_statistics.htm

King, L. (trans.) 2004 *The Code of Hammurabi*, Kila, MT: Kessinger

Kirilenko, A., Samadi, M., Kyle, A. S. and Tuzun, T. 2011 "The Flash Crash: The Impact of High Frequency Trading on an Electronic Market", Working Paper, see http://ssrn.com/abstract=1686004

Kirsner, S. 1998 "Murder by Internet", *Wired* 06/12/1998

Kitten, T. 2010 "Is U.S. Ready for Chip and PIN?", *Bank Information Security News*, June

Kjaer, M. 2002 *Textbook of Sports Medicine: Basic Science and Clinical Aspects of Sports*, Malden, MA: Wiley-Blackwell

Kleinmuntz, B. and Szucko, J. J. 1984 "Lie Detection in Ancient and Modern Times", *American Psychologist* 39(7), 766–76

Koenig, R. 2007 *The Fourth Horseman: The Tragedy of Anton Dilger and the Birth of Biological Terrorism*, Old Saybrook, CT: Tantor Media

Kohn, M. 2004 *Brave New Neighbourhoods: The Privatization of Public Space*, New York: Routledge

Konnerup, M. and Kongsted, H. 2009 "There Is More to Seeing than Meets the Eye: Observational Studies, Research Synthesis, and the Social Sciences", Technical Report 06/09, London: LSE, Centre for the Philosophy of Natural and Social Science Contingency and Dissent in Science

Kowalski, R., Limber, S. and Agatson, P. 2008 *Cyber Bullying: Bullying in the Digital Age*, Malden, MA: Blackwell

Krakauer, E. 1998 *The Disposition of the Subject: Reading Adorno's Dialectic of Technology,* Evanston, IL: Northwestern University Press

Kramer, C. 1972 *Sumerian Mythology*, Philadelphia: University of Pennsylvania Press

Kravets, D. 2009 "Cyberbullying Bill Gets Chilly Reception", *Wired* 30/09/2009

Krebs, C. 2006 "The New Face of Phishing", *Washington Post* 13/02/2006

Kremmer, C. 2008 "Rogue Scientist Could Be Dr Doom", *Brisbane Times* 03/06/2008

Krimsky, S. 1991 *Biotechnics and Society: The Rise of Industrial Genetics*, New York: Praeger

Kroes, P. 1998 "Technological Explanations: The Relation between Structure and Function of Technological Objects", *Techné* 3(3), 18–34

Kroes, P. and Meijers, A. 2006 "The Dual Nature of Technical Artefacts", *Studies in History and Philosophy of Science* 37(1), 1–4

Kroker, A. 2006 *Born Again Ideology: Religion, Technology, and Terrorism*, Victoria, BC: CTheory Books

Kühl, S. 2002 *The Nazi Connection: Eugenics, American Racism, and German National Socialism*, New York: Oxford University Press

Kukureka, S. and Davis, C. 2010 "The Pole Vault for Engineers", presentation, University of Birmingham

Kunert, P. 2011 "Phishers Switch Focus to Targeted Attacks, Warns Cisco", *Register* 01/07/2011

Lace, S. (ed.) 2005 *The Glass Consumer: Life in a Surveillance Society*, Bristol: Policy Press

Lakatos, I. 1974 "The Role of Crucial Experiments in Science", *Studies in History and Philosophy of Science* 4(4)

Lakhani, N. 2011 "CSI Chief Condemns Forensic Cuts", *Independent* 09/01/2011

Lancet 2002 "Chemical Weapons – Shifting the Goal Posts", *Neurology* 1(8), 459

Landes, D. 2003 *The Unbound Prometheus: Technical Change and Industrial Development in Western Europe from 1750 to the Present*, 2nd edn, New York: Cambridge University Press

Landman, A. and Glatz, A. 2009 "Tobacco Industry Efforts to Undermine Policy-Relevant Research", *American Journal of Public Health* 99(1), 45–58

Landmine Action 2007 *Cluster Munitions in Kosovo: Analysis of Use, Contamination and Casualties*, October

Langleben, D. 2008 "Detection of Deception with fMRI: Are we there yet?", *Legal and Criminological Psychology* 13(1), 1–9

Latham, M. 2008 "The Shape of Things to Come: Feminism, Regulation and Cosmetic Surgery", *Medical Law Review* 16(3), 437–57

Latour, B. 1987 *Science in Action: How to Follow Scientists and Engineers through Society*, Cambridge, MA: Harvard University Press

—— 1994 "On Technical Mediation – Philosophy, Sociology, Genealogy", *Common Knowledge* 3(2), 29–64

—— 1999 *Pandora's Hope: Essays on the Reality of Science Studies*, Cambridge, MA: Harvard University Press

—— 2000 "The Berlin Key or How to Do Things with Words", in Graves-Brown, P. M. (ed.) *Matter, Materiality and Modern Culture*, London: Routledge, 10–21

Laville, S. 2007 "Forensic Lab Errors in Hundreds of Crime Cases", *Guardian* 22/02/2007

Lavoie, D. 2009 "Jury Orders Student to Pay $675,000 for Illegally Downloading Music", *USA Today* 31/07/2009

Lawless, C. 2010 "A Curious Reconstruction? The Shaping of 'Marketized' Forensic Science", CARR Discussion Paper No. 63, May

Laycock, G. 2005 "Defining Crime Science", in Tilley, N. and Smith, M. (eds) *Crime Science*, Cullompton: Willan

Lazer, D. (ed.) 2004 *DNA and the Criminal Justice System: The Technology of Justice*, Cambridge, MA: MIT Press

LC 2008 "10th Programme of Law Reform", Law Commission No. 311

—— 2009 "The Admissibility of Expert Evidence in Criminal Proceedings in England and Wales", Consultation Paper No. 190

—— 2011 "Expert Evidence in Criminal Proceedings in England and Wales", Law Commission No. 325, 21/03/2011

Lea, H. 1973 *The Ordeal*, Philadelphia: University of Pennsylvania Press

Lea, J. and Young, J. 1984 *What Is To Be Done About Law and Order – Crisis in the Eighties*, Harmondsworth: Penguin

Leapman, B. 2006 "Three in Four Young Black Men on the DNA Database", *Daily Telegraph* 05/11/2006

Lee, J. 2002 "Briefing: Electronic Tagging of Criminals", *Times* 08/11/2002

Leeson, P. 2010 "Ordeals", see http://ssrn.com/abstract=1530944

Lehmann, C. 2011 "An Accelerated Grimace: On Cyber-Utopianism", *The Nation* 21/03/2011

Lehrer, J. 2010 "Book Review – Carr, N. The Shallows", *New York Times* 03/06/2010

Leigh, D. 2010 "Iraq War Logs Reveal 15,000 Previously Unlisted Civilian Deaths", *Guardian* 22/10/2010

Leman-Langlois, S. (ed.) 2008 *Technocrime: Technology Crime and Social Control*, Cullompton: Willan

Lemos, R. 2007 "Identity Thieves Likely to Be First-Timers, Strangers", *Security Focus* 22/10/2007

Lendman, S. 2010 "Police Brutality in America", *Baltimore Chronicle* 13/07/2010

Leppard, D. 2011 "Police Maps to Expose Criminals", *Sunday Times* 28/06/2011

Lessig, L. 1999 *Code and other Laws of Cyberspace*, New York: Basic Books

—— 2006 *Code 2.0*, New York: Basic Books

Lettice, J. 2009 "ID Cards not Compulsory after all, Says Home Office", *Register* 24/03/09

Levin, B. 2010 "A Defensible Defense? Reexamining Castle Doctrine Statutes", *Harvard Journal on Legislation* 47, 523–53

Levitt, S. and Dubner, S. 2006 *Freakonomics*, New York: William Morrow

Lewis, E. 1937 "Responsibility for Piracy in the Middle Ages", *Journal of Comparative Legislation and International Law*, 77ff.

Lewis, J. 2009 "Police Chiefs Sell 60p Checks for £70", *Daily Mail* 15/02/2009

Lewis, P. 2009a "Italian Student Tells of Arrest while Filming for Fun", *Guardian* 15/12/2009
—— 2009b "Woman 'Detained' for Filming Police Search Launches High Court Challenge", *Guardian* 21/07/2009
—— 2010 "CCTV in the Sky: Police Plan to Use Military-Style Spy Drones", *Guardian* 23/01/2010
Lewis, P. and Valle, M. 2009 "Revealed: Police Databank on Thousands of Protesters", *Guardian* 6/03/2009
Lewis, R. 2006 "How Important are Insurers in Compensating Claims for Personal Injury in the U.K.?", *The Geneva Papers*, 1–17
Leyden, J. 2010 "'Suspicious' Android Wallpaper App Nabs User Data", *Register* 29/07/2010
—— 2011 "Facebook Suspends Personal Data-sharing Feature", *Register* 18/01/2010
Li, R. 2008 *Forensic Biology*, Boca Raton, FL: CRC Press
Li Shu-hua 1954 "Origine de la Boussole 11. Aimant et Boussole", *Isis* 45(2)
Liberty 2011 *DNA Retention*, see http://www.liberty-human-rights.org.uk/human-rights/privacy/dna-retention/index.php
Lichtblau, E. and Risen, J. 2011 "Hiding Details of Dubious Deal, U.S. Invokes National Security", *New York Times* 19/02/2011
Liebowitz, M. 2010 "Analyst: Cybercrime Is 'Spiraling out of Control'", *Security News Daily* 08/12/2010
Lim, H. 2010 "Virtual World, Virtual Land but Real Property", *Singapore Journal of Legal Studie*s 304–327
Lister, S. 2010 "GlaxoSmithKline to Share Malaria Research in Hope of Finding Cure", *Times* 20/01/2010
Literary Digest 1924 "The Sanitary Value of Bleach", June 7
Livingstone, S. and Bober, M. 2004 "UK Children Go Online: Surveying the Experiences of Young People and their Parents", 2, London: LSE Research Online
Lloyd, R. 2007 "Outsourcing and Offshoring Gain Traction in U.K. Legal Market", *American Lawyer* 19/09/2007
LOC 2009 *Library of Congress classification. T: Technology*, Washington DC: Policy and Standards Division, Library of Congress, Cataloging Distribution Service
Locke, J. 1988 *Two Treatises of Government*, P. Laslett (ed.), Cambridge: Cambridge University Press
Lomas, N. 2008 "Police to Get Thousands More Mobiles", *Silicon.com* 22/07/2008
Lott, J. R. 1998 "The Concealed-Handgun Debate", *Journal of Legal Studies* 27, 221–43
Lott, J. R. and Mustard, D. B. 1997 "Crime, Deterrence, and Right-to-carry Concealed Handguns", *Journal of Legal Studies* 26, 1–68
Loyn, H. R. 1984 *The Governance of Anglo-Saxon England, 500–1087*, Stanford, CA: Stanford University Press
Luckenbill, D. 1926 *Ancient Records of Assyria and Babylonia*, Vol 1 Chicago: University of Chicago Press
Luek, T. 2007 "After Falsified Test Results, Kelly Orders Forensic Shakeup", *New York Times* 20/04/2007
Luomala, K. 1961 "A Dynamic in Oceanic Maui Myths", *Fabula* 4, 155–58
Luppicini, R. and Adell, R. (eds) 2009 *Handbook of Research on Technoethics*, 2 vols, Hershey, PA: IGI Global Information Science

Lyon, D. 2001 *Surveillance Society, Monitoring Everyday Life*, Buckingham: Open University Press

—— 2007 *Surveillance Studies; An Overview*, Cambridge: Polity

Macalister, T. and Edwards, R. 2009 "Revealed: Catalogue of Atomic Leaks", *Observer* 21/06/2009

MacAskill, E. 2010 "US Blocks Access to WikiLeaks for Federal Workers", Guardian 03/12/2010

McCabe, D. L. 2005 "CAI Research", see http://www.academicintegrity.org/cai_research.asp

McCahill, M. and Finn, R. 2010 "The Social Impact of Surveillance in Three UK Schools: 'Angels', 'Devils' and 'Teen Mums'", *Surveillance & Society* 7(3/4), 273–89

McCartney, C. 2006 *Forensic Identification and Criminal Justice: Forensic Science, Justice and Risk*, Cullompton: Willan

McClellan, J. and Dorn, H. 2006 *Science and Technology in World History: An Introduction*, Baltimore: Johns Hopkins University Press

MacCleod, M. 2005 "Spam Tsar Sends out Unwanted Message Admitting Defeat in War on Junk E-mail", *Scotland on Sunday* 11/12/2005

MacCollum, D. 2006 *Construction Safety Engineering Principles*, New York: McGraw Hill

McCord, S. 2008 "Nanotechnology and its Potential in Forensic DNA Analysis", *Promega*, September

McCue, C. 2007 *Datamining and Predictive Analysis: Intelligence Gathering and Crime Analysis*, Amsterdam: Elsevier

McGowan, M. 2010 "The Rise of Computerized High Frequency Trading: Use and Controversy", *Duke Law and Technology Review* 016

McGuire, M. 2007 *Hypercrime; The New Geometry of Harm*, Abingdon: Routledge

—— 2008 "From Hyperspace to Hypercrime: Technologies and the New Geometries of Deviance and Control", Papers from the British Criminology Conference 2008

—— 2010 "Online Surveillance and Personal Liberty", in Jewkes, Y. and Yar, M. *Handbook of Internet Crime*, Cullompton: Willan, 492–520

—— 2011 "Organised Crime in the Digital Age", Report on behalf of The John Grieve Centre for Policing and Detica Information and Intelligence, October

McIntosh, M. 1971 "Changes in the Organization of Thieving", in Cohen 1971, 98–133

MacIntyre, A. 1988, *Whose Justice? Which Rationality?*, Notre Dame: University of Notre Dame Press

Mackay, A. 1991 "Archimedes ca 287–212 BC", in *A Dictionary of Scientific Quotations*, London: Taylor and Francis, 11

McKeegan, A. 2010 "Mum's Outrage over Picture of Naked Son on Google Street View", *Manchester Evening News* 29/06/2010

Mackenzie, M. and van Duyn, A. 2010 "'Flash Crash' Was Sparked by Single Order", *Financial Times* 01/10/2010

MacKenzie, T. 2009 "China's Giant Step into Nanotech", *Guardian* 26/03/2009

McKnight, B. (trans.) 1981 *The Washing Away of Wrongs; Sung Tz'u: Forensic Medicine in Thirteenth-century China*, Science, Medicine and Technology in East Asia, 1, Ann Arbor: University of Michigan Center for Chinese Studies, xv

McLuhan, M. 1962 *The Gutenberg Galaxy: The Making of Typographic Man*, Toronto: University of Toronto Press

McLuhan, M. 1964/1994 *Understanding Media: The Extensions of Man*, New York: McGraw Hill
—— with Quentin Fiore 1967 *The Medium is the Message*, New York: Bantam
—— 1969 *Counter Blast*, Toronto: McClelland and Stewart
McMahan, J. 2009 *Killing in War*, Oxford: Clarendon Press
McNeil, J. and McNeil, W. 2003 *The Human Web: A Birds Eye View of Human History*, New York: W.W. Norton
McPhee, M. 2010 "'Craigslist Killer' Philip Markoff Died Amid his Fiancee's Photos", *ABC News* 17/08/2010
Madden, M., Fox, S., Smith, A. and Vitak, J. 2007 "Digital Footprints", Pew Internet & American Life Project
Maddern, P. 1992 *Violence and Social Order: East Anglia 1422–1442*, Oxford: Oxford University Press
Maga, T. 2001 *Judgement at Tokyo: The Japanese War Crimes Trials*, Lexington, KY: University Press of Kentucky
Magennis, H. 1995 "Treatments of Treachery and Betrayal in Anglo-Saxon Texts", *English Studies* 76(1), 1–19
Magner, L. 1992 *A History of Medicine*, New York: Marcel Dekker
Mahapatra, V. 2010 "No Narcoanalysis Test without Consent, Says SC", *Times of India* 05/05/2010
Mailley, J., Garcia, R., Whitehead S. and Farrell, G. 2008 "Phone Theft Index", *Security Journal* 21, 212–27
Mann, D. and Sutton, M. 1998 "Netcrime: More Change in the Organisation of Thieving", *British Journal of Criminology* 38(2)
Mannan, S. and Lees, F. (eds) 2005 *Lees Loss Prevention in the Process Industries*, Amsterdam: Elsevier
Marcuse, H. 1964 *One Dimensional Man*, Boston: Beacon
—— 1982 "Some Social Implications of Modern Technology", in Arato, A. and Gebhardt, E. (eds) *The Essential Frankfurt School Reader*, New York: Continuum, 138–62
Markham, A. 1994 *A Brief History of Pollution*, New York: St. Martin's Press
Marlow, A. 1954 "Hinduism and Buddhism in Greek Philosophy", *Philosophy East and West* 4(1)
Martin, L. H., Gutman, H. and Hutton, R. H. (eds) 1988 *Technologies of the Self: A Seminar with Michel Foucault*, London: Tavistock
Marx, G. T. 2007 "The Engineering of Social Control", in Byrne and Rebovich 2007
Marx, K. 2007, *Capital: A Critique of Political Economy – Volume I*, New York: Cosimo
Marx, K. and Engels, F. 1983 *Letters on "Capital"*, London: New Park Publications
Matté, J. A. 1996 *Forensic Psychophysiology Using the Polygraph: Scientific Truth Verification, Lie Detection*, Williamsville, NY: J.A.M. Publications
Matthews, A. 2001 "Computer Games Make Children Anti-social", *Daily Telegraph* 20/08/2001
Matthews, J. 2000 *Laying Down the Law: A Study of the Theodosian Code*, New York: Yale University Press
Matyszczyk, C. 2008 "Are Google's Street-View Drivers Humans or Robots?", *CNet* 12/08/2008
Mayor, A. 2003 *Greek Fire, Poison Arrows and Scorpion Bombs: Biological and Chemical Warfare in the Ancient World*, New York: Overlook

MDU 2003 "Review of Claims from Plastic and Reconstructive Surgery", *Medical Defence Union* 06/02/2003

Meagher, S. 2002 Testimony in US v Plaza 188 F Supp 2d E. D. PA, Daubert Hearing

Melzer, N. 2008 *Targeted Killing in International Law*, Oxford: Oxford University Press

Mendelsohn, I. 1932 *Legal Aspects of Slavery in Babylonia, Assyria and Palestine*, Williamsport, PA: Bayard Press

Menhard, F. 2006 *The Facts about Amphetamines*, Tarrytown, NY: Marshall Cavendish

Menn, J. and Nuttall, C. 2010 "Berners-Lee Warns Web Success May 'Fragment' Internet", *Financial Times* 20/11/2010

Mercer, N. 2009 "Clinical Risk in Aesthetic Surgery", *Clinical Risk* 15(6), 215–17

Meselson, M. 1991 "The Myth of Chemical Superweapons", *The Bulletin of the Atomic Scientists*, April, 12–15

Metzl J., Small E., Levine S. and Gershel J. 2001 "Creatine Use among Young Athletes", *Pediatrics* 108(2), 421–25

MHB (Morgan Harris Burrows) 2004 "The Processing of Fingerprint Evidence after the Introduction of the National Automated Fingerprint Identification System (NAFIS)", Home Office Online Report 23/04

Miah, A. 2003 "Patenting Human DNA", in Almond, B. and Parker, M. (eds) *Ethical Issues in the New Genetics: Are Genes Us?* Aldershot: Ashgate

Mill, J. S. 1909 *Principles of Political Economy*, London: Longmans, Green

Milligan, B. 2011 "Beko Fridge-freezer Fires Began Four Years Ago", BBC 09/07/2011

Milmo, C. 2010 "Trafigura Found Guilty of Toxic Waste Offence, *Independent* 24/07/2010

Minsky, M. 1980 "Telepresence", *Omni* June, 45–51

Misak, C. 1995 *Verificationism. Its History and Prospects*, London: Routledge

Mitcham, C. 1994 *Thinking through Technology: The Path between Engineering and Philosophy*, Chicago: University of Chicago Press

―― 2003 "Three Ways of Being with Technology", in Scharff, R. and Dusak, V. (eds) *The Philosophy of Technology*, Malden MA: Blackwell, 490–506

―― 2004 "Philosophy of Information Technology", in Floridi, L. (ed.) *The Blackwell Guide to the Philosophy of Computing and Information*, Malden MA: Blackwell, 327–36

Mnookin, J. 2003 "Fingerprints: Not a Gold Standard", *Issues in Science and Technology* 09/10/2003

Mobbs, D. Lau, H., Jones, O. and Frith, C. 2007 Law Responsibility and the Brain, *PLoS Biol* 5(4): e103

Moffat, A. C. 2006 "History of Doping in Sport", in Kayne, S. B. (ed.) *Sport and Exercise Medicine for Pharmacists*, London: Pharmaceutical Press

Monahan, T. and Wall, T. 2007 "Somatic Surveillance: Corporeal Control through Information Networks", *Surveillance & Society* 4(3), 154–73

Moore, S. 2009 "Science Found Wanting in Nation's Crime Labs", *New York Times* 04/02/2009

Morozov, E. 2009 "Cyber-Scare. The Exaggerated Fears over Digital Warfare", *Boston Review* July/August

―― 2011 *The Net Delusion: The Dark Side of Internet Freedom*, New York: Public Affairs

Morris, P. 2006 "MPs Raise Concerns over Tagging of Prisoners", *Independent* 12/10/2006

Morris, S. 2006 "Murder Case Builder Tortured Academic for Bank Details", *Guardian* 06/12/2006

Morris, W. 1884 "Art and Socialism", *Collected Works of William Morris*, vol. XXIII, London: Longmans, Green

—— 1896 *Signs of Change*, London: Longmans, Green

Moskvitch, K. 2011 "Internet of Things Blurs the Line between Bits and Atoms", BBC 03/06/2011

Motoc, I. 2008 "The International Law of Genetic Discrimination: The Power of 'Never Again'", New York University, Center for Human Rights and Global Justice, Working Paper 18

Mottram, D. 2010 *Drugs in Sport*, 4th edn, New York: Routledge

Mullins, J. 2007 "Digit-saving Biometrics", *New Scientist* Blogs 13/06/2007

Mumford, L. 1934 *Technics and Civilization*, New York: Harcourt, Brace

Mumford, S. 2003 *Dispositions*, Oxford: Oxford University Press

Murphy, K. 2010 "Will DNSSEC Kill your Internet?", *Register* 23/04/2010

Murphy, T. 2009 *New Technologies and Human Rights*, Oxford: Oxford University Press

Murray Associates 2011 "1900 – The Whispering Telephone Mouthpiece", Murray's Eavesdropping History Emporium

Murray, D. 2000 "Changing Technologies, Changing Literary Communities", *Language Learning and Technology* 4(2), 43–58

Musil, R. 2010 "Google to Leave China on April 10", *CNet* 18/03/2010

NACRO 2002 "To CCTV or Not to CCTV: A Review of Current Research into the Effectiveness of CCTV Systems in Reducing Crime", *Community Safety Practice Briefing*, May

NaCTSO 2011 "Secure your Fertiliser", London: National Counter Terrorism Security Office

NAO 2002 "Public Private Partnerships: Airwave", National Audit Office, HC 730 Session 2001–2002, 11 April

—— 2008 "Effective Inspection and Enforcement: Implementing the Hampton Vision in the Office of Fair Trading", National Audit Office, URN: 08/734

Naraine, R. 2006 "Cybercrime More Widespread, Skillful, Dangerous than Ever", *Fox News* 13/04/2006

NAS 2008 *Department of Homeland Security Bioterrorism Risk Assessment: A Call for Change*, US National Academy of Science, Washington DC: National Academies Press

Nasheri, H. 2005 *Economic Espionage and Industrial Spying*, Cambridge: Cambridge University Press

NCS 2011 "GETS Program Information", NCS Priority Services

NCSL 2008a "State Cyberstalking, Cyberharassment and Cyberbullying Laws", National Conference of State Legislatures

—— 2008b "Human Cloning Laws", National Conference of State Legislatures

Needham, J. 1954 *Science and Civilisation in China, Vol. I*, Cambridge: Cambridge University Press

Nellis, M. 2006 "24/7/365 Mobility, Locatability and the Satellite Tracking of Offenders", in Aas, K., Gundhus, H. and Lomell, H. (eds) *Technologies of Insecurity: The Surveillance of Everyday Life*, London: Routledge-Cavendish, 105–24

Nellis, M., Bas, R., Beyens, K. and Kaminski, D. 2010 *Electronically Monitored Punishment: International and Critical Perspectives*, Cullompton: Willan

Nelson, J. 1997 "Crime Wave on the Web", *LA Times* 30/11/1997

Neufeld, P. 2005 "The (Near) Irrelevance of Daubert to Criminal Justice and Some Suggestions for Reform", *American Journal of Public Health* 95, S1, 107–13

Neufeld, P. and Scheck, B. 2010 "Making Forensic Science More Scientific", *Nature* 464ff

Newell, P. 2009 "Bio-Hegemony: The Political Economy of Agricultural Bio-technology in Argentina", *Journal of Latin American Studies* 41, 27–57

New Scientist 2008 "Computer Crime a Growing Threat, Warns FBI", 16/10/2008

Newton, A. 2004 "Crime on Public Transport. Static and Non-static (Moving) Crime Events", *Western Criminology Review* 5(3), 25–42

New Yorker 1938 "Tapping the Wires" 18/06/1938 available at: http://www.spybusters.com/History_1938_Tapping_Wires.html

NFA 2010 "Noise Free America", see http://www.noisefree.org/index.php

Nichols, P. 2009 "'Technological Doping' Doesn't Suit Rebecca Adlington", *Guardian* 19/07/2009

Nickel, J. 2006 *Making Sense of Human Rights*, Oxford: Blackwell

Nickelsburg, G. 1977 "Apocalyptic and Myth in Enoch 6-11", *Journal of Bible Studies* 96(3), 383–405

Nietzsche, F. 1982 *Thus Spoke Zarathustra*, in Kaufmann, W. (ed.) *The Portable Nietzsche*, Harmondsworth: Penguin

NIH 2008 "Genetic Discrimination", Issues in Genetics, US National Institute of Health

NIJ 1998 "The Evolution and Development of Police Technology", Technical Report 01/07/1998, Washington DC: National Institute of Justice

—— 2010 "Gun Violence", Topics, Washington DC: National Institute of Justice

Nissan, E. 2001 "The Bayesianism Debate in Legal Scholarship", *Artificial Intelligence and Law* 9(2–3), September

NOAA 2009 "Oil and Chemical Spills", Washington DC: National Oceanic and Atmospheric Administration

Norman, D. 1990 *The Design of Everyday Things* (originally titled *The Psychology of Everyday Things*, 1988), New York: Doubleday Business

Norris, C. and Armstrong, G. 1999 *The Maximum Surveillance Society: The Rise of CCTV*, Oxford: Berg

Norris, J. 2009 *Pistols at Dawn: A History of Duelling*, Gloucester: History Press

Novas, C. and Rose, N. 2000 "Genetic Risk and the Birth of the Somatic Individual", *Economy and Society* 29(4), 485–513

Nozick, R. 1974 *Anarchy, State, and Utopia*, New York: Basic Books

NPIA 2007 National DNA Database Annual Report, National Policing Improvement Agency

—— 2010a "IT and Radio Systems", National Policing Improvement Agency Report

—— 2010b "Science and Innovation in the Police Service 2010–2013", National Policing Improvement Agency Report

NRC 2003a *The Polygraph and Lie Detection*, Washington DC: National Academies Press

—— 2003b *An Assessment of Non Lethal Weapons Science and Technology*, Washington DC: National Academies Press

—— 2006 *Going the Distance? The Safe Transport of Spent Nuclear Fuel and High-Level Radioactive Waste in the United States*, Committee on Transportation of Radioactive Waste, National Research Council, National Academies Press

—— 2008 "Protecting Individual Privacy in the Struggle Against Terrorists: A Framework for Program Assessment", Washington: National Academies Press

—— 2009 *Strengthening Forensic Science in the United States: A Path Forward*, Washington DC: National Academies Press

NTI 2009 "NIS Nuclear Trafficking Database for 2008", Washington DC: Nuclear Threat Initiative

Nummedal, T. 2007 *Alchemy and Authority in the Holy Roman Empire*, Chicago: University of Chicago Press

Oates, J. 2008a "DNA Convictions Fall as Database Doubles in Size", *Register* 11/11/2008

—— 2008b "CRB Database Wrongly Labels Thousands as Criminals", *Register* 13/11/2008

O'Connell, R. 1989 *Of Arms and Men: A History of War Weapons and Aggression*, Oxford: Oxford University Press

OCTA 2011 *European Organised Crime Threat Assessment*, The Hague: Europol

OECD 2001 "Environmental Outlook for the Chemicals Industry", Paris: Organization for Economic Co-operation and Development

OFT 2008 "Consumer Detriment: Assessing the Frequency and Impact of Consumer Problems with Goods and Services", April, OFT992, London: Office of Fair Trading

OII 2008 "Me, My Spouse and the Internet: Meeting, Dating and Marriage in the Digital Age", Oxford: Oxford Internet Surveys

Okowa, P. 2000 *State Responsibility for Transboundary Air Pollution in International Law*, Oxford: Oxford University Press

Olfman, S. (ed.) 2006 *No Child Left Different*, New York: Praeger

O'Mathuna, D. 2009, *Nanoethics*, London: Continuum

ONS 2001 "Noise Offences Relating to Motor Vehicles", Regional Trends 38, Newport: Office for National Statistics

OPSI 2009 *The Polygraph Rules 2009*, Office of Public Sector Information

Ormerod, T., Wang, L., Debbabi, M., Youssef, A., Binsalleeh, H., Boukhtouta, A. and Sinha, P. 2010 "Defaming Botnet Toolkits: A Bottom-up Approach to Mitigating the Threat", The Fourth International Conference on Emerging Security Information, Systems and Technologies, 195–200

Ostfield, M. 2004 "Bioterrorism as a Foreign Policy Issue", *SAIS Review* 24(1), 131–46

Overbye, D. 2008 "Asking a Judge to Save the World, and Maybe a Whole Lot More", *New York Times* 29/03/2008

Ozimek, J. 2011 "Boots Punts Over-the-counter Paternity Test", *Register* 01/02/2011

PA 2010 "Virtual Court Scheme too Expensive, Says Report", Press Association 20/12/2010

—— 2011 "Twitter 'Undermining Privacy Laws'", Press Association 13/07/2011

Pacey, A. 1991 *Technology in World Civilisation: A Thousand Year History*, Cambridge, MA: MIT Press

Page, L. 2007 "Cops and Home Office Plot Uber-CCTV Network", *Register* 22/10/2007

Paget, C. 2010 "Extreme-range RFID Tracking", Presentation, Blackhat USA 2010, Las Vegas, see http://www.tombom.co.uk/extreme_rfid.pdf

Paget, F. 2007 "Identity Theft", *MacAfee White Paper*, January

Pankanti, S., Prabhakar, S. and Jain, A. K. 2002 "On the Individuality of Fingerprints", *IEEE Transactions on Pattern Analysis and Machine Intelligence* 24(8), 1010–25

Pariser, E. 2011 *The Filter Bubble: What the Internet is Hiding from You*, Harmondsworth: Penguin Press

Park, R., Burgess, E. and MacKenzie, R. 1925 *The City: Suggestions for Investigation of Human Behavior in Urban Environments*, Chicago: University of Chicago Press

Parker, G. (ed.) 2008 *The Cambridge Illustrated History of Warfare*, Cambridge: Cambridge University Press

Parliamentary Papers, *1819 Report from the Select Committee on Steam Engines*, Preface

—— 1843 *Report from the Select Committee on Smoke Prevention*, VII

—— 1845 *Second Report of the Commissioners of Inquiry into the State of Large Towns and Populous Districts*

Pascoe, P. 2009 *What Comes Naturally: Miscegenation Law and the Making of Race in America*, New York: Oxford University Press

Pato, J. and Millett, L. (eds) 2010 *Biometric Recognition: Challenges and Opportunities*, Washington DC: National Academies Press

Pattavina, A. 2005 (ed.) *Information Technology and the Criminal Justice System,* London: Sage

Patterson, C. 1985 "'Not Worth the Rearing': The Causes of Infant Exposure in Ancient Greece", *Transactions of the American Philological Association* 115, 103–23

Pawloski, J. 2010 "Two Lacey Teens Arrested in Sexting Case", *Seattle Times* 29/01/2010

Pearce, F. 2010 "Climate Sceptic Wins Landmark Data Victory 'for Price of a Stamp'", *Guardian* 20/04/2010

Pearce, F. and Tombs, S. 1998 *Toxic Capitalism: Corporate Crime and the Chemical Industry*, Aldershot: Ashgate

Pease, K. 2005 "Science in the Service of Crime Reduction' in Tilley, N. (ed.) *Handbook of Crime Prevention and Community Safety*, Cullompton: Willan, 171–97

Pedersen, S. 2006 "Spies in the Post Office: Sovereignty, Surveillance, and Communication in 18th Century Denmark", Paper presented at XIV International Economic History Congress, Helsinki

Penzer, N. 1980 *Poison Damsels*, Manchester, NH: Ayer

Pepper, S. 1992 "Allinson's Staff of Life – Health without Medicine in the 1890s", *History Today* 42, 10

Perkin, H. 1969 *Origins of the Modern British State 1780–1880*, London: Routledge Kegan and Paul

Pernick, M. S. 1996 *The Black Stork: Eugenics and the Death of "Defective" Babies in American Medicine and Motion Pictures in America Since 1915*, Oxford: Oxford University Press

Perrow, C. 1999 *Normal Accidents, Living with High-Risk Technologies*, Princeton, NJ: Princeton University Press

Perry, A. E., Weisburd, D. and Hewitt, C. 2010 "Are Criminologists Describing Randomized Controlled Trials in Ways that Allow Us to Assess Them? Findings from a Sample of Crime and Justice Trials", *Journal of Experimental Criminology* 6, 245–62

Petersen, J. and Zamir, S. 2001 *Understanding Surveillance Technologies: Spy Devices, Their Origins and Applications*, New York: CRC Press

Petryna, A. 2002 *Life Exposed: Biological Citizens after Chernobyl*, Princeton, NJ: Princeton University Press

Pfohl, S. 1994 *Images of Deviance and Social Control*, New York: McGraw-Hill

Philips, A.M. 2002 "Comments on Home Office Response to Trowers Police Federation Report on TETRA: Health and Safety Issues", *Powerwatch* 04/02/2002

Philips, D. 1993 "Crime, Law and Punishment in the Industrial Revolution", in O'Brien, P. K. and Quinault, R. (eds) *The Industrial Revolution and British Society*, Cambridge: Cambridge University Press

PhysOrg.com 2008 "New Nanotechnology Tagging System to Help Solve Gun Crime", 01/03/2008

PI 2007 "Satellite Surveillance", *Privacy International* PHR2006

—— 2008 "EU to announce fingerprinting for all visitors", *Privacy International* 12/02/2008

—— 2010 "Data Protection and Privacy Laws", *Privacy International*

Pickering, M. 1993 *Auguste Comte: An Intellectual Biography: Auguste Comte and Positivism, 1789–1842*, vol. 1, Cambridge: Cambridge University Press

Pilkington, E. 2011 "Bradley Manning May Face Death Penalty", *Guardian* 03/03/2011

Pitcher, G. 2008 "Lie Detectors to Be Used to Detect Genuine Sickness Absence", *Personnel Today* 12/05/2008

Pitkethly, M. 2009 "Nanotechnology and Forensics", *Materials Today* 12(6), 6ff.

Pitofsky, R. 1977 "Beyond Nader: Consumer Protection and the Regulation of Advertising", *Harvard Law Review* 90, 661

Plantinga, A. 1993 *Warrant: The Current Debate*, Oxford: Oxford University Press

Plato 1997 *Complete Works*, Cooper, J. M. (ed.), Indianapolis: Hackett

Plomer, A. 2005 *The Law and Ethics of Medical Research: International Bioethics and Human Rights*, London: Cavendish

Plutarch 1914 *Lives*, vol. I, trans. Perrin, B. Loeb Classical Library, Cambridge, MA: Harvard University Press

Poe, M. 2011 *A History of Communications: Media and Society from the Evolution of Speech to the Internet*, Cambridge: Cambridge University Press

Poku, N., Whiteside, A. and Sandkjaer, B. (eds) 2007 *AIDS and Governance*, Aldershot: Ashgate

Polanyi, M. 1958 *Personal Knowledge: Towards a Post-Critical Philosophy*, Chicago: University of Chicago Press

Polastron, L. 2007 *Books on Fire: The Destruction of Libraries throughout History*, Rochester, VT: Inner Traditions

Poli, J. 1942 "The Development and Present Trend of Police Radio Communications", *Journal of Criminal Law and Criminology* 33(2), 193–97

Polsky, S. and Beresford, S. 1943 "Some Probative Aspects of the Early Germanic Codes, Carolina and Bambergensis", *Boston University Law Review* 23, 183

Pool, I. 1983 *Forecasting the Telephone: A Retrospective Technology Assessment*, Norwood, NJ: Ablex

POP 2011 "TETRA Hacking Is Coming: OsmocomTETRA", Playhouse of Privacy Blog 23/01/2011

Posner, N. 1969 "The Federal Trade Commission", *University of Chicago Law Review* 37, 47

Posner, N. and Ware, G. 1986 *Mengele: The Complete Story*, New York: McGraw Hill

POST 2004a "Terrorist Attacks on Nuclear Facilities", Parliamentary Office of Science and Technology, July, No. 222

—— 2004b "Drug Tests", Parliamentary Office of Science and Technology, Postnote, 228, September

—— 2011 "Detecting Deception", Parliamentary Office of Science and Technology, Postnote, 375, May

Post, S. 1991 "The Echo of Nuremberg: Nazi Data and Ethics", *Journal of Medical Ethics* 17, 42–44

Poster, M. 2001 *What's the Matter with the Internet?*, Minneapolis: University of Minnesota Press

Postman, N. 1993 *Technopoly: The Surrender of Culture to Technology*, New York: Vintage

PRC 2007, "A Chronology of Data Breaches", Privacy Rights Clearinghouse 01/02/2007

—— 2011 "Chronology of Data Breaches Security Breaches 2005–Present", *Privacy Rights Clearing House*, see http://www.privacyrights.org/data-breach

Pred, A. 2000 *Even in Sweden: Racisms, Racialized Spaces, and the Popular Geographical Imagination*, Berkeley: University of California Press

Preston, J. 2007 "U.S. Set to Begin a Vast Expansion of DNA Sampling", *New York Times* 05/02/2007

Price, J. and Sapci, H. 2007 "Telecourt: The Use of Videoconferencing for Involuntary Commitment Hearings in Academic Health Centers", *Law & Psychiatry* 58(1), 17–18

Proctor, R. 1988 *Racial Hygiene: Medicine Under the Nazis*, Cambridge, MA: Harvard University Press

PSKPP, 2003 "Daubert: The Most Influential Supreme Court Ruling You've Never Heard Of", Project on Scientific Knowledge and Public Policy, June

PT 2009a "More Fire and Rescue Services Go Live with Airwave Digital Radio", *Public Technology* 04/03/2009

—— 2009b "BlackBerrys 'Allowing Police to Police Smarter'", *Public Technology* 19/10/2009

Puerini, A. and Gorey, K. 2000 "Sports and Drugs in Primary Care", *Medical Health* 83, 169–72

Pughe, C. E. 2006 "Road Watch", *Engineering & Technology* 1(4), 36–39

Pyrek, K. 2007 *Forensic Science Under Siege: The Challenges of Forensic Laboratories and the Medico-Legal Investigation System*, Burlington, MA: Academic Press

Quine, W. V. O. 1951 "Two Dogmas of Empiricism", *The Philosophical Review* 60, 20–43, reprinted in Quine 1953 *From a Logical Point of View*, Cambridge, MA: Harvard University Press

Rabin, R. 2006 "The Lead Industry and Child Lead Poisoning", *Synthesis/Regeneration* 41

Rabinowitz, P. 2010 "Hearing Loss and Personal Music Players", *British Medical Journal* 340, c1261

Rai, S. 2001 "India–U.S. Fight on Basmati Rice Is Mostly Settled", *New York Times* 25/08/2001

Raine, A. 2002 "The Biological Basis of Crime", in Wilson, J. Q. and Petersilia, J. (eds) *Crime, Public Policies for Crime Control*, Oakland, CA: ICS Press 43–74

Raine, A., Buchsbaum, M. and LaCasse, L. 1997 "Brain Abnormalities in Murderers Indicated by Positron Emission Tomography", *Biological Psychiatry* 42, 495–508

Randall, A. 1995 "Reinterpreting Luddism: Resistance to New Technology in the British Industrial Revolution", in Bauer, M. (ed.) *Resistance to New Technology*, Cambridge: Cambridge University Press, 57–80

—— 2004 "Foreword", in Binfield, K. *Writings of the Luddites*, Baltimore and London: Johns Hopkins University Press

Ranger, S. 2006 "Crime of the Future – Biometric Spoofing?", *Zdnet* 21/07/2006

Rapex 2009 "Annual RAPEX Report 2008 Shows Rise in Number of Dangerous Products Being Detected", Press Release IP/09/594, 20/04/2009

Rappaport, M. 2006 "Israel Admits Using Phosphorus Bombs during War in Lebanon", *Haaretz* 22/10/2006

Rappert, B. 2007 "Policing and the Use of Force: Less Lethal Weapons", *Policing: a Journal of Policy and Practice* 1(4), 472–84

Ratcliffe, J. 2008 "Knowledge Management Challenges in the Development of Intelligence-Led Policing", in Williamson, T. (ed.) *The Handbook of Knowledge Based Policing: Current Conceptions and Future Directions*, London: John Wiley and Sons

Ratner, D. and Ratner, M. A. 2004 *Nanotechnology and Homeland Security: New Weapons for New Wars*, Upper Saddle River, NJ: Prentice Hall/PTR

Rawls, J. 1971 *A Theory of Justice*, Cambridge, MA: Belknap Press of Harvard University Press

—— 2001 *Justice as Fairness: A Restatement*, Cambridge, MA: Harvard University Press

Ray, B. 2007 "Gov Claims Mobile Phone Theft Waning as Penalty Rises", *Register* 11/04/2007

Rayner, J. and Crook, G. (eds) 1926 *The Complete Newgate Calendar*, 5 vols, London: Navarre Society

RCEP 2007 "Study on Urban Environments, Well-being and Health", Royal Commission on Environmental Pollution

Reaves, J. 2001 "The Casey Martin Case: The Supreme Court Takes Up Golf", *Time* 29/05/2001

Redmayne, M. 2001 *Expert Evidence and Criminal Justice*, Oxford: Oxford University Press

Reed, J. 2009 "Police Warn of Teenage 'Sexting'", BBC 04/08/2009

Reid, S. 2007 "The Sinister Truth about what They Do with our Children's Finger-prints, *Daily Mail* 11/10/2007

Reidenberg, J. 1998 "Lex Informatica: The Formulation of Information Policy Rules Through Technology", *Texas Law Review* 76(3)

Reilly, B., Paci, P. and Hall, P. 1995 "Unions, Safety Committees and Workplace Injuries", *British Journal of Industrial Relations* 33(2)

Reiss, J. and Kitcher, P. 2008 "Neglected Diseases and Well-Ordered Science", CPNSS, Contingency and Dissent in Science, Technical Report 06/08

Reitze, A. W. 1999 "The Legislative History of U.S. Air Pollution Control", *Houston Law Review* 36, 679

Rentezi, M. 2008 "The U.S. Radium Industry: Industrial In-house Research and the Commercialization of Science", *Minerva* 46(4), 437–62

—— 2009 *Trafficking Materials and Gendered Experimental Practices: Radium Research in Early 20th Century Vienna*, New York: Columbia University Press

Reston, James Jr., 1994, *Galileo. A Life*, New York: HarperCollins

Reuters 2009 "Monsanto Sues Germany over GMO Maize Ban", 21/04/2009

Reynolds, J. and Hart, B. 2004 "Nanomaterials and their Application to Defense and Homeland Security", *Journal of Metals* 56, 36–39

RIBA 2010 "RIBA Calls for a More Consumer-focused Approach to Building Regulations", November

Ricci, C., Bleay S. and Kazarian, S. 2007 "Spectroscopic Imaging of Latent Finger-marks Collected with the Aid of a Gelatin Tape", *Analytical Chemistry* 79(15), 5771–76

Rice, P. 2000 "Truth in Test Tubes: Standard for Screening Scientific Evidence Is Still Muddled Years after Daubert", *Legal Times* 16/10/2000

Richardson, C. 1986 "Clearing the Air", *Bradford Antiquary* 2(3), 28–34

Richardson, R. 1987 *Death, Dissection and the Destitute*, London: Routledge Chapman and Hall

Richmond, S. 2009, "EU Calls for Volume Limit on MP3 Players", *Daily Telegraph* 28/09/2009

Rincon, P. 2011 "FBI's DNA Database Upgrade Plans Come under Fire", BBC, 17/10/2011

Roach, K. 2009 "Forensic Science and Miscarriages of Justice: Some Lessons from Comparative Experience", *Jurimetrics* 50

Roberts, S. 2011 "Distant Writing", see http://distantwriting.co.uk/default.aspx

Robertson, B. and Vigneaux, G. A. 1995 *Interpreting Evidence: Evaluating Forensic Science in the Court-room*, New York: John Wiley and Sons

Robinson, B. 2011 "Victorian Medicine – From Fluke to Theory", BBC History, see http://www.bbc.co.uk/history/british/victorians/victorian_medicine_01.shtml

Roco, M. 2003 "Government Nanotechnology Funding: An International Outlook", National Science Foundation, 30/06/2003

Roland, A. 1992, "Secrecy, Technology, and War: Greek Fire and the Defense of Byzantium", *Technology and Culture* 33(4), 655–79

Roochnik, D. 1998 *Of Art and Wisdom: Plato's Understanding of Techne*, Park, PA: Pennsylvania State University Press

Rooksby, E. and Weckert, J. 2006 *Information Technology and Social Justice*, Hershey, PA: IGI Global

Rose, D. 2008 "No Prosecution on Suicide-risk Drug", *Times* 07/03/2008

Rose, N. 2000 "The Biology of Culpability: Pathological Identity and Crime Control in a Biological Culture", *Theoretical Criminology*, 4(1), 5–34

—— 2010 "'Screen and Intervene': Governing Risky Brains", *History of the Human Sciences* 23(1), 79–105

Rose, S. 1993 "No Way to Treat the Mind", *New Scientist* 38(1869), 23–26

—— 2004 "Violence 'Not Detectable' by Brain Imaging", BBC 21/12/2004

Rosen, J. 2007 "The Brain on the Stand", *New York Times* 11/03/2007

ROSPA 2010 "Home and Leisure Accident Surveillance System", see http://www. hassandlass.org.uk/query/MainSelector.aspx

RSF 2011 *Internet Enemies*, Reporters Without Borders, see http://12mars.rsf.org/i/ Internet_Enemies.pdf

RSI 2010 "Repetitive Strain Injury", RSI Information Forum, see http://www. rsi-solutions.co.uk/

RSS 2001 "Royal Statistical Society Concerned by Issues Raised in Sally Clark Case", Royal Statistical Society News Release 23/10/2001

Ruggiero, V. 1996 *Organised and Corporate Crime in Europe: Offers that Can't Be Refused*, Aldershot: Dartmouth

Ruiz, M. 2007 "An Explosion in Cyber Crime Sets off Alarms in Europe", *Internet Law Business News* 04/06/2007

Rummel, R. 1998 *Statistics of Democide: Genocide and Mass Murder since 1900*, Rutgers: Transaction Press

Ruskin, J. 1991 *Collected Works Selected Writings*, Clark, K. (ed.), New York: Penguin Books

—— 2005 *Praeterita*, London: Everyman

Russell, C. (ed.) 2000 *Chemistry, Society and Environment: A New History of the British Chemical Industry*, print on demand edn, London: Royal Society of Chemistry

Ryle, G. 1949 *The Concept of Mind*, London: Hutchinson

Sadovnikova, A., Hoyng, H., Hüetlin, T. and Klussmann, U. 2006 "'Walking Dirty Bomb' Tells of London Meetings", *Spiegel* 12/11/2006

Saeed, K. 2003 "Object Classification and Recognition Using Toeplitz Matrices", *Artificial Intelligence and Security in Computing Systems*, London: Springer, 163–72

Salgado, G. 1992 *The Elizabethan Underworld*, New York: St. Martin's Press

Sammes, T. and Jenkinson, B. 2000 *Forensic Computing: A Practitioner's Guide*, London: Springer

Sample, I. 2010 "Government Abandons Lie Detector Tests for Catching Benefit Cheats", *Guardian* 09/11/2010

—— 2011 "Genetics Tests Flawed and Inaccurate, Say Dutch Scientists", *Guardian* 30/05/2011

Sampson, R. 2010 "Gold Standard Myths: Observations on the Experimental Turn in Quantitative Criminology", *Journal of Quantitative Criminology* 26(4), 489–500

Sandel, M. 2007 *The Case against Perfection: Ethics in the Age of Genetic Engineering*, Cambridge, MA: Harvard University Press

Sandoval, G. 2011 "US 'Kill Switch' Bill Gets Freedom Tweak", *CNet* 21/02/2011

Sapienza, J. 2009 "Threat of Online Child Grooming to Grow: Report", *WA News* 07/07/2009

Sawyer, D. 2006 "Mission Impossible?", *The Lawyer* 01/05/2006

Scherer, M. 2010 "Obama's Terrorism Postmortem: Still Not Connecting the Dots", *Time* 06/01/2010

Schiebinger, L. 2004 "Human Experimentation in the 18th century; Natural Boundaries and Valid Testing", in Daston, L. and Vidal, F. (eds) *The Moral Authority of Nature*, Chicago: University of Chicago Press, 384–407

Schierow, L. 2006 "Chemical Facility Security", CRS Report for Congress, RL31530

Schmoch, U. 2008 "Concept of a Technology Classification for Country Comparisons", Final Report to the World Intellectual Property Organization (WIPO)

Schneier, B. 2005 "Cell Phone Companies and Security", *Schneier on Security* 19/12/2005

—— 2008 "CCTV Doesn't Keep Us Safe, yet the Cameras Are Everywhere", *Guardian* 26/06/2008

—— 2009 "We Shouldn't Poison our Minds with Fear of Bioterrorism", *Guardian* 14/05/2009

Schroefl, J., Cox, S. M. and Pankratz, T. 2009 *Winning the Asymmetric War: Political, Social and Military Responses*, New York: Peter Lang

Schummer, J. 2001 "Aristotle on Technology and Nature", *Philosophia Naturalis* 38, 105–20

Sederer, L. 2009 "Paying the Piper: Brain 'Neuroenhancers'", *Huffington Post* 01/06/2009

Seibert, F. 1952 *Freedom of the Press in England 1476–1776*, Urbana: University of Illinois Press

Selden, K. and Selden, M. (eds) 1990 *The Atomic Bomb: Voices from Hiroshima and Nagasaki (Japan in the Modern World)*, Armonk, NY: M.E. Sharpe

Seldes, G. 1943 *Facts and Fascism*, 8th edn, New York: In Fact

Semikhodskii, A. 2007 *Dealing with DNA Evidence: A Legal Guide*, London: Routledge

Sen, A. 1993 "Capability and Well-being", in Nussbaum, M. and Sen, A. (eds) *The Quality of Life*, Oxford: Clarendon Press, 30–53

—— 2009 *The Idea of Justice*, London: Allen Lane

Sengupta, S. 2011 "For Suspected Hackers, a Sense of Social Protest", *New York Times* 26/07/2011

Sessa, B. 2008 "Is it Time to Revisit the Role of Psychedelic Drugs in Enhancing Human Creativity?", *Journal of Psychopharmacology* 22(8), 821–27

Shachtman, N. 2009 "NYPD Wants to Jam Cell Phones During Terror Attack", *Wired* 08/01/2009

Shah, D. 2010 "UK Cyber Security Plans 'Essential for Strong Defence'", BBC 18/10/2010

Shah, S. 2007 "Body Hunting: The Outsourcing of Drug Trials", *Globalist* 31/01/2007

Shane, S. 2005 "The Reach of War: Weapons; Defense of Phosphorus Use Turns into Damage Control", *New York Times* 21/11/2005

Shapere, D. 1998 "Building on What We Have Learned: The Relations between Science and Technology", *Techné* 4(2)

Shapin, S. and Schaffer, S. 1989 *Leviathan and the Air-Pump*, Princeton, NJ: Princeton University Press

Sharan, Y. 2007 "The Bioterrorism Threat", Risk Assessment and Risk Communication Strategies in Bioterrorism Preparedness, NATO Science for Peace and Security Series A; Chemistry and Biology I, 45–54

Sharpe, J. 1996 "Crime in England, Long Term Trends and the Problem of Modernisation", in Johnson, E. and Monkkonen, E. (eds) *The Civilization of Crime: Violence in Town and Country since the Middle Ages*, Urbana: University of Illinois Press, 17–34

Shaw, M. 2006 "Guantanamo Firm Enters Schools", *Times Educational Supplement* 21/07/2006

Shea, D. and Gotton, F. 2004 *Small-scale Terrorist Attacks Using Chemical and Biological Agents*, CRS Report for Congress, RL32391

Sherman, L. 2009 "Evidence and Liberty: The Promise of Experimental Criminology", *Criminology and Criminal Justice* 9(1), 5–28

Sherman, L., Farrington, D., Welsh, B. and MacKenzie, D. 2002 "Preventing Crime", in Sherman *et al.* (eds) *Evidence Based Crime Protection*, London: Routledge, 1–12

Sherriff, L. 2007 "UK Gov Deploys Lie Detectors on Benefits Claims", *Register* 05/04/2007

Shiels, M. 2008 "Cyber Risk 'Equals 9/11 Impact'", BBC 08/04/2008

—— 2010 "Google Street View Accused of Congress 'Snooping'", BBC 09/07/2010

Shipley, A. 2009 "FINA Opts to Ban All High-tech Swimsuits", *Washington Post* 25/07/2009

Shiva, V. 1999 *Biopiracy: The Plunder of Nature and Knowledge*, Cambridge: South End Press

Shutts, D. 1982 *Lobotomy: Resort to the Knife*, New York: Van Nostrand Reinhold

Siddique, H. 2007 "'Probable' New Foot and Mouth Leak from Laboratory", *Guardian* 22/11/2007

Silverstein, K. 1999 "Millions for Viagra, Pennies for the Poor", *The Nation* 19/07/1999

Silverstone, R. and Hirsch, E. (eds) 1992 *Consuming Technologies: Media and Information in Domestic Spaces*, London: Routledge

Simmel, G. 1978 *The Philosophy of Money,* London: Routledge Kegan & Paul

Simmons, J. and Dodd, T. 2003 "Crime in England and Wales 2002/3", Home Office Statistical Bulletin, 1358-510X, 07/03/2003

—— 2009, Health and Safety Executive: Statistics 2008/9 http://www.hse.gov.uk/statistics/overall/hssh0809.pdf

Simpson, B. 2005 "Identity Manipulation in Cyberspace as Leisure Option, Play and the Exploration of Self", *Information and Communications Technology Law* 14(2), 115–31

Sinclair, L. 2010 "DNA Samples Kept in Police Fridge for a Year", *Sky News* 12/01/2010

Sindall, R. 1990 *Street Violence in the 19th Century: Media Panic or Real Danger?* Leicester: Leicester University Press

Singel, R. 2009a "Newly Declassified Files Detail Massive FBI Data-Mining Project", *Wired* 23/09/2009

—— 2009b "DOJ Pays $4M a Year to Read Public Court Documents", *Wired* 01/12/2009

Singer, C., Holy, E. J., Holmyard, E. J. and Hall, A. R. (eds) 1954 *A History of Technology*, Oxford: Clarendon Press

Singh, H. 2010 "Indian Court Finds Chemical Execs Guilty in Bhopal Disaster", *CNN* 07/10/2010

Singh, Y. 2009 "Why Are We Fingerprinting Children?", *Guardian* 07/03/2009

Singman, J. 2000 *Daily Life in Medieval Europe*, Westport, CT: Greenwood

Sjöberg, A. 1975 "The Old Babylonian Eduba" in S. Liebermann (ed) "Sumerological Studies in Honour of Thorkild Jacobsen", *Assyriological Studies* 20, 123–57

Slack, J. 2010 "Big Brother WILL Snoop on your Calls and Clicks", *Daily Mail* 21/10/2010

Slovenko, R. 2004 "Discrediting the Expert Witness on Account of Bias", *Psychiatric Times* 21, 14

Smith, G. 2005 "Comments on the CRS Report 'Small-Scale Terrorist Attacks Using Chemical and Biological Agents'", see http://www.fas.org/irp/crs/RL32391-smith.html

—— 2007 "Exploring Relations between Watchers and Watched in Control(led) Systems: Strategies and Tactics", *Surveillance & Society* 2, 4(4), 280–313

Smith, K. and Flatley, J. 2010 "Homicides, Firearm Offences and Intimate Violence 2008/09", *Home Office Statistical Bulletin*, January

Smith, M. and Tilley, N. 2005 "Introduction", in Smith and Tilley (eds) *Crime Science: New Approaches to Preventing and Detecting Crime*, Cullompton: Willan, xv–xxii

Smith, R. 2007 "Update to the London Assembly 7 July Review Committee Report", London: London Ambulance Service

Smith, W. 2000 "No Escape from Science", *ABA Journal* August, 60–66

Smithers, R. 2007 "Danger to Children from Food and Drink Additives Is Exposed", *Guardian* 06/09/2007

Sobel, R. 2002 "Public Health and the Placebo: The Legacy of the 1906 Pure Food and Drugs Act", *Cato Journal* 21(3), 463ff.

Söderblom, J. 2004 "The Historical Pedigree and Relevance of Suicide 'Martyr' BioTerrorism", World-ICE, see http://world-icc.com/Articles/Martyr.pdf

South Manchester Reporter 2008 "Nurseries Embrace Fingerprint Scanning", 27/03/2008

Southey, T., 1829 *Sir Thomas More: Or Colloquies on the Progress and Prospects of Civilization*, London: John Murray

Spencer, J. 2009, "Telephone Tap Evidence and Administrative Detention in the United Kingdom", in Wade, M. and Maljevic, A. (eds) *A War on Terror? The European Stance on a New Threat, Changing Laws and Human Rights Implications*, New York: Springer

Spielhofer, T., Bielby, G. and Marson-Smith, H. 2009 "Children's Online Risks and Safety: A Review of the Available Evidence", Slough: National Foundation for Educational Research on behalf of UK Council for Child Internet Safety

Spufford, P. 1989 *Money and its Use in Medieval Europe*, Cambridge: Cambridge University Press

Squires, P. and Kennison, P. 2010 *Shooting to Kill? Policing Firearms and Armed Response*, Chichester: Wiley-Blackwell

Stacey, R. (2004) "A Report on the Erroneous Fingerprint Individualization in the Madrid Train Bombing Case", *Journal of Forensic Identification* 54, 707–18

Stahl, A. 2008 "Coin and Punishment in Medieval Venice", in Karras, R., Kaye, J. and Matter, E. (eds) *Law and the Illicit in Medieval Europe*, Philadelphia: University of Pennsylvania Press, 164–79

Staley, K. 2005 "The Police National DNA Database: Balancing Crime Detection, Human Rights and Privacy", Buxton: GeneWatch

Standage, T. 1998 *The Victorian Internet*, New York: Walker & Co

Stevenson, J. 1979 *Popular Disturbances in England 1700–1800*, London: Longmans

Stewart, R. 1994 "The Police Signal Box: A 100 Year History" http://www.eee.strath.ac.uk/r.w.stewart/boxes.pdf

Stiegler, B. 1998 *Technics and Time: The Fault of Epimetheus*, trans. R. Beardsworth, Stanford, CA: Stanford University Press

Stolberg, S. and Harris, G. 2010 "Stem Cell Ruling Will Be Appealed", *New York Times* 24/08/2010

Stop Fingerprinting Children 2009, Campaign Website, now inactive

Strabo 1932 *Geography*, Loeb Classical Library, Cambridge MA: Harvard University Press

Suler, J. 2004 "The Online Disinhibition Effect", *CyberPsychology & Behavior* 7(3)

Sun Tzu 2009 *The Art of War*, trans. L. Giles, USA: Pax Librorum

Suolahti, J. 1963 *The Roman Censors*, Helsinki: Suomalainen Tiedeakatemia

Susskind, C. 1995 *Heinrich Hertz: A Short Life,* San Francisco CA: San Francisco Press

Sutcliffe, R. 2010 "Gambler 'Tortured Bradford Student for his Bank Details'", *Yorkshire Post* 28/07/2010

Swann, J. 2004 "Pharmaceutical Regulation before and after the Food, Drug and Cosmetic Act", in Berry, I. (ed.) *The Pharmaceutical Regulatory Process*, New York: InformaHealthcare, 1–46

Symantec 2010 *Global Internet Security Threat Report: Trends for 2009*, XV, April

Szabo, L. 2008 "Toys with Phthalates Can Be Sold after U.S. Ban Takes Effect", *USA Today* 19/11/2008

Szilard, L. (co-signatory) 1945 "A Petition to the President of the United States", see http://www.atomicarchive.com/Docs/ManhattanProject/Petition.shtml

Tabachnick, D. 2009 "A Tale of Two Cities: Plato's Kingly Techne and Aristotle's Phronetic Rule", *Canadian Political Science Association*, 2009 Annual Conference Papers

Tabula Rasa 2010 "Trusted Biometrics under Spoofing Attacks" http://www.tabularasa-euproject.org

Tagliabue, J. 2010 "A Spray of DNA to Keep the Robbers Away", *New York Times* 18/10/2010

Talbot, D. 2011 "Are We Ready for the Era of Anything?", *Technology Review*, MIT 28/06/2011

Talbot, M. 2009 "Brain Gain: The Underground World of 'Neuroenhancing' Drugs", *New Yorker* 27/04/2009

Tarde, G. 1903 *The Laws of Imitation*, New York: H. Holt

Tarr, J. A. 1992 "The Municipal Telegraph Network: Origins of the Fire and Police Alarm Systems in American Cities", *FLUX Cahiers scientifiques internationaux Réseaux et Territoires* 8(9), 5–18

Taylor, D. 2009 "Rise in Use of Drug Tests to Sack Staff without Redundancy Pay", *Guardian* 18/05/2009

—— 2010 *Hooligans, Harlots and Hangmen: Crime and Punishment in Victorian Britain*, London: Praeger

Taylor, L. B. and Taylor, C. L. 1992 *Chemical and Biological Warfare*, New York: Franklin Watts

Taylor, S. 1982 "CAT Scans Said to Show Shrunken Hinckley Brain", *New York Times* 02/06/1982

Temkin, O. 2002 "What Does the Hippocratic Oath Say?", in *On Second Thought and Other Essays in the History of Medicine*, Baltimore: Johns Hopkins University Press, 21–28

Tetrawatch 2010 "TETRAWATCH: A Research Based Campaign against TETRA Airwave", see http://www.tetrawatch.net/main/index.php

Than, K. 2009 "Googling Fights Dementia, Study Suggests", *National Geographic* 20/11/2009

Thomas, D. 1969 *A Long Time Burning: The History of Literary Censorship in England*, New York: Praeger

—— 2005 "Spam Costs UK businesses £1.3bn a Year", *Personnel Today* 09/03/2005

Thomas, D. and Loader, B. 2000 *Cybercrime: Law Enforcement, Security and Surveillance in the Information Age*, London: Routledge

Thomas, M. 1974 *Police Communications*, Illinois: CC Thomas

Thomis, M. 1970 *The Luddites: Machine-breaking in Regency England*, Hampton, CT: Archon Books

Thompson, L. 2009 "Police Close Down Fake Websites", *Times* 03/12/2009

Thompson, T. 2010 "Crime Software May Help Police Predict Violent Offences", *Guardian* 25/07/2010

Thompson, W. 2008 "The Potential for Error in Forensic DNA Testing", Paper presented at Council for Responsible Genetics (CRG) National Conference, June

Thompson, W. and Krane, D. 2003 "DNA in the Courtroom", in *Psychological and Scientific Evidence in Criminal Trials*, Eagen, MN: West Group, ch. 11

Thomson, J. 1975, "The Right to Privacy", *Philosophy and Public Affairs* 4, 295–314

Thorp, R. 2009 "Saviour Siblings and the Human Fertilisation and Embryology Acts 1990 and 2008", *Plymouth Law Review* 1, 71–94

Tiles, M. and Oberdiek, H. 1995 *Living in a Technological Culture: Human Tools and Human Values*, New York: Routledge

Tilley, A. and Dreyfuss Associates 2001 *The Measure of Man and Woman: Human Factors in Design*, New York: Wiley

Tilstone, W., Savage, K. and Clark, A. 2006 *Forensic Science: An Encyclopedia of History, Methods, and Techniques*, Oxford: ABC-CLIO

Times 2005 "Focus: Victims of Fatal Police Shootings", 21/08/2005

Tobias, J. 1972 *Crime and Industrial Society in the 19th Century*, London: Penguin

Toksen, M. 2007 "Virtual Confrontation: Is Videoconference Testimony by an Unavailable Witness Constitutional?", *University of Chicago Law Review* 74(4)

Tomasi, A. 2008 "The Role of Intimacy in the Evolution of Technology", *Journal of Evolution and Technology* 17(1), 1–12

Tombs, S. and Whyte, D. 2007 *Safety Crimes*, Cullompton: Willan

Tomlinson, H. and Evans, R. 2005 "Tesco Stocks up on Inside Knowledge of Shoppers' Lives", *Guardian* 20/09/2005

Tooley, M. 1998 "The Moral Status of the Cloning of Humans", in Humber, J. and Almeder, R. (eds) *Human Cloning*, Totowa, NJ: Humana Press, 67–120

Torgerson, D. J. and Torgerson, C. 2008 *Designing Randomised Trials in Health, Education, and the Social Sciences: An Introduction*, New York: Palgrave Macmillan

Torpey, J. 1999 *The Invention of the Passport: Surveillance, Citizenship and the State*, Cambridge: Cambridge University Press

Toto, S. 2009 "Woman Uses Tape to Trick Biometric Airport Fingerprint Scan", *Crunchgear* 02/01/2009

Townsend, M. 2010a "US Execution Drugs Supplied Secretly y British Companies", *Observer* 19/12/2010

—— 2010b "Teenager-repellent 'Mosquito' Must Be Banned, Says Europe", *Guardian* 20/06/2010

Toynbee, J. M. 1996 *Death and Burial in the Roman World*, Baltimore: Johns Hopkins University Press

Travers, M. 1995 "Evaluation Research and Criminal Justice: Beyond a Political Critique", *Australian and New Zealand Journal of Criminology* 38(1), 39–58

Travis, A. 2009a "Huge Growth in DNA Database, but No Gain", *Guardian* 07/05/2009

—— 2009b "Detections Using DNA Database Fall Despite Huge Rise in Profiles", *Guardian* 21/10/2009

—— 2010 "DNA Matches Solve only a Fraction of Crimes, Police Admit", *Guardian* 05/01/2010

Traynor, I. 2007 "Russia Accused of Unleashing Cyberwar to Disable Estonia", *Guardian* 12/05/2007

TUC 2007 "Lies, Damned Lies and Lie Detectors: Introducing Lie Detector Tests for Benefit Claimants", TUC Briefing Document, London: Trades Union Congress

—— 2010 "Repetitive Strain Injury (RSI)", see http://www.tuc.org.uk/h_and_s/index.cfm?mins=397

Tucker, J. 2006 *War of Nerves: Chemical Warfare from WWI to Al Qaeda*, New York: Pantheon

Tunnell, K. D. 2004 *Pissing on Demand: Workplace Drug Testing and the Rise of the Detox Industry*, New York: NYU Press

Turkle, S. 1995 *Life on the Screen: Identity in the Age of the Internet*, New York: Simon & Shuster

Turnidge, J. 2004 "Antibiotic Use in Animals – Prejudices, Perceptions and Realities", *Journal of Antimicrobial Chemotherapy* 53, 26–7

Turow, J. 2006 "Cracking the Consumer Code: Advertisers, Anxiety, and Surveillance in the Digital Age", in Haggerty, J. and Ericson, R. (eds) *The New Politics of Surveillance and Visibility*, Toronto: University of Toronto Press

Tyfield, D. 2008 "Enabling TRIPs: The Pharma-biotech-university Patent Coalition", *Review of International Political Economy* 15(4), 535–66

UCS 2008 "Federal Science and the Public Good", Union of Concerned Scientists, December, Cambridge, MA: USC Publications

Uessler, R. 2008 *Servants of War, Private Military Corporations and the Profit of Conflict*, Berkeley CA: Soft Shell Press

UNAIDS 2008 *Criminalization of HIV Transmission*, UNAIDS Policy Brief: August

Underwood, J. 2006 "Digital Technologies and Dishonesty in Examinations and Tests", Nottingham: Qualifications Correction Agency and Nottingham Trent University

Underwood, R. 1995 "Truth Verifiers: From the Hot Iron to the Lie Detector", *Kentucky Law Journal* 84, 597

UNECE 2010 "Vehicle Regulations and Technological Innovations", see http://www.unece.org/trans/main/welcwp29.htm?expandable=99

UNESCO 2005 "The Precautionary Principle", *United Nations Educational Scientific and Cultural Organisations*, March 2005

UPEK 2006 "FIPS 201" Press Release

Ure, A. 1835 *The Philosophy of Manufactures*, London: Chas. Knight

USA Today 2003 "U.S. Military Employs Israeli Technology in Iraq War", 24/03/2003

USDOJ 2010 "2010 Budget Summary", see http://www.justice.gov/jmd/2010summary/pdf/bud-summary.pdf

US GPO 1949–53 Trials of War Criminals before the Nuremberg Military Tribunals under Control Council Law No. 10, Nuremberg, October 1946–April 1949, Washington DC: US GPO

USNIJ 2010 "High-Priority Technology Needs: Improving the Efficiency of Justice", Washington DC: National Institute of Justice

Vaesen, K. 2006 "How Norms in Technology Ought to Be Interpreted", *Techné* 10(1)

—— 2011 "The Functional Bias of the Dual Nature of Technical Artefacts Program, *Studies in History and Philosophy of Science*, forthcoming

van Creveld, M. 1989 *Technology and War: from 2000 BC to the Present*, New York: Free Press

van Dijk, J. 2006 *The Network Society*, London: Sage

van Fraasen, B. 1980 *The Scientific Image*, Oxford: Oxford University Press

—— 1998 *The Scientific Image*, Oxford: Oxford University Press

van Gulik, R. (ed) 2008 *Crime and Punishment in Ancient China*, Tang-Yin-Pi-Shih, Orchid Press

van Natta, D., Becker, J. and Bowley, G. 2010 "Tabloid Hack Attack on Royals, and Beyond", *New York Times* 01/09/2010

van Well, L. and Royakkers, L. 2004 "Ethical Issues in Web Data Mining", *Ethics and Information Technology* 6(2)

Vega, T. 2010 "New Web Code Draws Concern over Privacy Risks", *New York Times* 10/10/2010

VeriTask 2010 "The Biometric Employee Time Clock", see http://www.veritasksoftware.com/time-clock-software-fingerprint-reader-punch-clock.html

Vickers, P. 2004 "Bhopal 'Faces Risk of Poisoning'", BBC 14/11/2004

Vincent, D. 1998 *The Culture of Secrecy: Britain, 1832–1998*, Oxford: Oxford University Press

—— 1999 *The Culture of Secrecy: Britain, 1832–1998*, Oxford: Oxford University Press

Virilio, P. 1995 *Speed and Information: Cyberspace Alarm!*, see http://www.ctheory.net, 08/27/1995

—— with Oliveira, C. 1996 "The Silence of the Lambs: Paul Virilio in Conversation", *Cultural Theory* 19(1–2), 3

—— 2007 *The Original Accident*, Cambridge: Polity

Volokh, E. 2009 "Cyberbullying Bill Gets a Chilly Reception", The Volokh Conspiracy, Blog 02/10/2009

Wacke, A. 2002 "Protection of the Environment in Roman Law?", *Roman Legal Tradition*, 1, 1–24

WADA 2011 "A Brief History of Anti-Doping", World Anti-Doping Agency, see http://www.wada-ama.org/en/

Waddington, I. and Smith, A. 2008 *An Introduction to Drugs in Sport*, London: Routledge

Wakefield, G. 2007 "Nanotechnology Enabled Solutions for Anti-Counterfeiting and Brand Security", Paper for Nanotechnology for Security and Crime Prevention Conference, 18/01/2007, The Royal Society, London

Walker, A., Kershaw, C. and Nicholas, S. 2006 "Crime in England and Wales 2005/06", Home Office Statistical Bulletin 12/06

—— 2009 *Crime in England and Wales, 2008/09*, vol. 1, Croydon: Home Office

Walker, C. and Starmer, K. 1999 *Miscarriages of Justice: A Review of Justice in Error*, London: Blackstone Press

Walker, S. 2004 *Three Mile Island: A Nuclear Crisis in Historical Perspective*, Berkeley: University of California Press

Wall, D. (ed.) 2001 *Cyberspace Crime*, Aldershot: Ashgate

—— 2007 *Cybercrime: The Transformation of Crime in the Information Age*, Cambridge: Polity

—— 2008 "Cybercrime and the Culture of Fear: Social Science Fiction(s) and the Production of Knowledge about Cybercrime", *Information, Communication & Society* 11(6), 861–84

Wall, D. and Yar, M. 2009 "Intellectual Property Crime and the Internet: Cyberpiracy and 'Stealing' Informational Intangibles", in Jewkes, Y. and Yar, M. (eds) *The Handbook of Internet Crime and Criminal Justice*, Cullompton: Willan

Walters, R. 2007 "Food Crime, Regulation and the Biotech Harvest", *European Journal of Criminology* 4, 217–35

—— 2010 *Eco Crime and Genetically Modified Food*, Abingdon: Routledge-Cavendish

Waples, S., Gill, M. and Fisher, P. 2009 "Does CCTV Displace Crime?", *Criminology and Criminal Justice* 9(2), 207–24

Ward, M. 2001 "Tackling Computer Crime", BBC 19/04/2001

—— 2010 "Sensors Turn Skin into Gadget Control Pad", BBC 26/03/2010

Warren, S. and Brandeis, L. 1890 "The Right to Privacy", *Harvard Law Review* 4, 193–220

Warrick, J. 2010 "FBI Investigation of 2001 Anthrax Attacks Concluded; U.S. Releases Details", *Washington Post* 20/02/2010

Warshauer, M. 2003 *Technology and Social Inclusion: Rethinking the Digital Divide*, Cambridge, MA: MIT Press

Washington, H. 2007 *Medical Apartheid: The Dark History of Medical Experimentation on Black Americans from Colonial Times to the Present*, New York: Doubleday

Waterfield, B. 2010 "US and EU Row over Sharing Bank Details", *Daily Telegraph* 04/02/2010

Watson, A., Cairns, J. and Robinson, O. 2001 *Critical Studies in Ancient Law, Comparative Law and Legal History*, Oxford: Hart

Watson, S. 2007 "Man Faces 7 Year Sentence under 'Wiretapping Law' for Filming Police", *informationliberation* 13/05/2007

Wax, P. 2006 "Historical Principles and Perspectives", in Goldfrank, L., Flomenbaum, N., Lewin, N., Howland, M., Hoffman, R. and Nelson, L. (eds) *Goldfrank's Toxicologic Emergencies*, New York: McGraw Hill

Webb, G., Anderson, R. and Gaffney, M. 2006 "Classification of Events with an Off-site Radiological Impact at the Sellafield Site between 1950 and 2000, Using the International Nuclear Event Scale", *Journal of Radiological Protection* 26, 33

Weber, M. 1992 *The Protestant Ethic and the Spirit of Capitalism*, trans. T. Parsons, intro. A. Giddens, London: Routledge.

—— 1994 "The Profession and Vocation of Polities", in Lassman, P. and Speirs, R. (eds) *Weber: Political Writings*, Cambridge: Cambridge University Press

—— 2009 "The Crux of Crucial Experiments: Duhem's Problems and Inference to the Best Explanation", *British Journal for the Philosophy of Science* 60(1), 19–49

Weber, T. 2009 "Cybercrime Threat Rising Sharply", BBC 31/01/2009

Weinberg, A. 1980 "Technological Optimism", *Society* 17(3), 17–18

Weinberger, S. 2008 "Why is Google Earth Hiding Dick Cheney's House", Wired, 23/07/2008

Weiner, N. 1966 *God and Golem, Inc.: A Comment on Certain Points where Cybernetics Impinges on Religion*, Cambridge, MA: MIT Press

Wellman, B. and Haythornthwaite, C. (eds) 2002 *The Internet in Everyday Life*, Oxford: Blackwell

Wells, H. and Wills, D. 2009 "Individualism and Identity: Resistance to Speed Cameras in the UK", *Surveillance and Society* 6(3), 259–74

Welsh, B. and Farrington, D. 2008 "Effects of CCTV on Crime", *Campbell Systematic Reviews*, 17

Welstead, S. 2007 "Know your Customer", *Growing Business* 01/02/2007

Wenzel, E. 2007 "DNA Dating Site Predicts Chemical Romance", *CNet* 17/12/2007

Wertham, F. 1954 *Seduction of the Innocent*, Toronto: Clarke Urqin

Westermann, W. 1984 *The Slave Systems of Greek and Roman Antiquity*, DIANE

Westveer, A., Jarvis, J. and Jensen, C. J. 2004 "Homicidal Poisoning", *FBI Law Enforcement Bulletin* 73(8)

Wheelis, M., 1999 "Biological Warfare before 1914", in Geissler, E. and van Courtland Moon, J. E. (eds) *Biological and Toxin Weapons: Research, Development and Use from the Middle Ages to 1945*, Oxford: Oxford University Press, 8–34

—— 2002 "Biological Warfare at the 1346 Siege of Caffa", *Emerging Infectious Diseases* 8(9), 971–5

Which 2008, "Small Wonder? Nanotechnology and Cosmetics", *Which Briefing*, November

White, L. 1962 *Medieval Technology and Social Change*, Oxford: Oxford University Press

White, R. 2011 *Transnational Environmental Crime: Toward an Eco-global Criminology*, New York: Routledge

Whitehead, T. 2009 "Less than a Third of 'Innocents' Get DNA Removed", *Daily Telegraph* 31/12/2009

—— 2011 "Millions of Innocent Callers to Police Have Details Stored", *Daily Telegraph* 03/01/2011

WHO 2001 "Globalisation, TRIPS and Access to Pharmaceuticals", World Health Organization Policy Perspectives on Medicines, No. 3, Geneva: World Health Organization

—— 2002, "The Human Consequences of the Chernobyl Nuclear Accident", A Report Commissioned by UNDP and UNICEF with the support of UN-OCHA and WHO, Geneva: World Health Organization

—— 2010a *Tobacco Free Initiative*, Geneva: World Health Organization

—— 2010b "20 Questions on Genetically Modified (GM) foods", *Food Safety*, Geneva: World Health Organization

Whorton, J. 2010 *The Arsenic Century: How Victorian Britain was Poisoned at Home, Work, and Play*, Oxford: Oxford University Press

Wiener, N. 1948 *Cybernetics*, Cambridge, MA: MIT Press

Wiens, A. 1999 "The Symbiotic Relationship of Science and Technology in the 21st Century", *Journal of Technology Studies* 25(2), 9–16

Wiggershaus, R. 1995 *The Frankfurt School: Its History, Theories, and Political Significance*, Cambridge, MA: MIT Press

Williams, C. 2008a "UK.gov 'to Drop' Überdatabase from Snoop Bill", *Register* 25/09/2008
—— 2008b "Human Rights Court Rules UK DNA Grab Illegal", *Register* 04/12/2008
—— 2010a "EU Sues UK.gov over Phorm Trials", *Register* 30/09/2010
—— 2010b "Police to Get Greater Web Censorship Powers", *Register* 25/11/2010
—— 2011 "Cyber Police Get Major Funding Boost", *Daily Telegraph* 22/03/2011
Williams, C. A. 2009 "The development of the Police National Computer, 1958–1975, and the Promises and Limitations of Computerisation", Scarman Seminar, Leicester University Department of Criminology, December
Williams, K. 2005 "On-Line Anonymity, Deindividuation and Freedom of Expression and Privacy", *Penn State Law Review* 110(3), 687–702
Williams, M. 2006 *Virtually Criminal*, London: Routledge
Williams, P. and Wallace, D. 1989 *Unit 731: Japan's Secret Biological Warfare in World War II*, New York: Free Press
Williams, R. 1967 "Paradoxically, if the Book Works It to some Extent Annihilates Itself", in Stearn, G. E. (ed.) *McLuhan Hot and Cool*, New York: Dial Press, 188–91.
Williams, R. and Johnson, P. 2008 *Genetic Policing*, Cullompton: Willan
Wilson, A. 2010 "The Law Commission's Proposal on Expert Opinion Evidence: An Onerous Demand upon Judges", *Web Journal of Current Legal Issues* 26/02/2010
Wilson, A. and Baietto, M. 2009 "Applications and Advances in Electronic-Nose Technologies", *Sensors* 9, 5099–148
Wilson, J.Q. 1968 *Varieties of Police Behaviour*, Cambridge MA, Harvard University Press
Wilson, J. Q. and Herrnstein, R. J. 1985 *Crime and Human Nature*, New York: Simon & Schuster
Winner, L. 1978 *Autonomous Technology: Technics-out-of-control as a Theme in Political Thought*, Cambridge, MA: MIT Press
Winnet, R. 2003 "Admen Seek Buy Button in our Brains", *Sunday Times* 17/08/2003
Wired 1997 "NSA Chief: Attacks on Military Computers Rise", 24/10/2007
Wise, J. 2007 "Thought Police: How Brain Scans Could Invade your Private Life", *Popular Mechanic* 15/10/2007
Wiseman T.P. 1970 "Roman Republican Road Building", *PBSR* 38, 122–52
Woodward, J., Orlans, N. and Higgins, P. 2002 *Biometrics*, New York: McGraw-Hill Professional
Wrennall, [initial?] 2010 "Take Physic Pomp: Assessing the Proposals to Address the Problem of Expert Witnesses", *Journal of Social Criminology* 3(1), 2–39
Wright, D., Gutwirth, S. and Friedewald, M. (eds) 2010 *Safeguards in a World of Ambient Intelligence*, London: Springer
WWF 2000 "Reducing your Risk; A UK Guide to Avoiding Hormone Disruptors", WWF Factsheet, Godalming: WWF
Wyrick, P. 2011 "Technology and Criminal Justice Policy", in Ismaeli, K. (ed.) *U.S. Criminal Justice Policy: A Contemporary Reader*, Burlington, MA: JB Learning
Yadav, B. and Mohan, M. 2010 *Ancient Indian Leaps into Mathematics*, New York: Birkhauser
Yar, M. 2005 "The Novelty of Cybercrime: An Assessment in Light of Routine Activity Theory", *European Journal of Criminology* 2(4), 407–27
—— 2011 "From the Governance of Security to Governance Failure: Redefining the Criminological Agenda", *Internet Journal of Criminology*, see http://www.

internetjournalofcriminology.com/Yar_From_the_Governance_of_Security_to_Governance_Failure_April_2011.pdf

Yeung, K. 2008 "Towards an Understanding of Regulation by Design", in Brownsword, R. and Yeung, K. *Regulating Technologies*, Oxford: Hart, 79–108

Young, J. 1989 *Pure Food: Securing the Federal Food and Drugs Act of 1906*, Princeton, NJ: Princeton University Press

—— 2003 "Thinking Seriously about Crime: Some Models of Criminology", in Fitzgerald, M., McLennan, G. and Pawson, J. (eds) *Crime and Society*, London: Routledge, 206–60

—— 2004 "Voodoo Criminology and the Numbers Game", in Ferrell, J., Hayward, K., Morrison, W. and Presdee, M. (eds) *Cultural Criminology Unleashed*, London: GlassHouse

—— 2011 *The Criminological Imagination*, Cambridge: Polity

Young, K. 2005 "Boffins Use Play-Doh to Fool Biometrics", *VNUnet* 13/12/2005

Zanders, J. P. 2003 "International Norms against Chemical and Biological Warfare: An Ambiguous Legacy", *Journal of Conflict and Security Law* 8(2), 391–410

Zetter, K. 2008 "Lori Drew Not Guilty of Felonies in Landmark Cyberbullying Trial", *Wired* 06/11/2009

Zhang, Q. 2010 "Threats of Censorship Loom with New Internet Copyright Infringement Bill", *OpenNet Initiative* 06/10/2010

Zimmerman, P. and Loeb, C. 2004 "Dirty Bombs: The Threat Revisited", *Defense Horizons* 38, 1–11

Zukin, S. 1991 *Landscapes of Power: From Detroit to Disney World*, Berkeley: University of California Press

Index